SPORT PSYCHOLOGY
From Theory to Practice

SPORT PSYCHOLOGY
From Theory to Practice

Mark H. Anshel
University of Wollongong
New South Wales, Australia

GSP

Gorsuch Scarisbrick, Publishers
Scottsdale, Arizona

Acknowledgments

Photographs on pp. 30, 212, and 397 contributed by The Phillies®. All other photographs contributed by *The Signal*, Trenton State College, Trenton, New Jersey.

Editor: John Gorsuch
Consulting Editor: Robert Pangrazi
Production Manager: Carol Hunter
Manuscript Editor: Charlene Brown
Cover Design: Cynthia Lee Maliwauki
Typesetting: Southern California PrintCorp

Gorsuch Scarisbrick, Publishers
8233 Via Paseo del Norte, F400
Scottsdale, Arizona 85258

10 9 8 7 6 5 4 3 2

ISBN 0-89787-610-5

Contents

10 Team Climate: Is Everybody Happy?   287

11 Coaching Child Athletes: Special Needs   327

12 The Female Athlete   361

Preface

I couldn't believe what I was seeing. The coaches of the team that I was observing during the season were (1) screaming obscenities into the faces of their athletes, (2) making promises to players they couldn't (or wouldn't remember to) keep, (3) punishing team members for even the slightest "infractions," (4) refusing to explain to players the reasons for team decisions, policies, and strategies, (5) teaching skills ineffectively, and (6) generally treating team members in a negative and disrespectful manner. I was not surprised that team morale was low. And so was the season record. For me, these observations signaled the need for a book in applied sport psychology. Despite having expertise in the sport that they were coaching, these coaches obviously had much to learn about the psychological needs of athletes.

My experiences as a consulting sport psychologist for several collegiate teams made a very profound, long-lasting impression on me about the present state of sport leadership. Quite candidly, I was appalled at the lack of sophistication in attempting to meet what was already a very difficult goal — influencing the feelings, attitudes, and behaviors of other human beings (competitive athletes) over a prolonged period of time. What I thought were common-sense techniques in effective leadership were being ignored. In fact, these coaches were using strategies for teaching skills, motivating athletes, and planning for competitive events that were no different than those used decades ago. Apparently, the coaching profession was still in the dark ages of management, especially in light of the emergence of sport psychology over the past ten to fifteen years. I saw leadership strategies that consisted of intimidation, threats, guilt, insults, disrespect, and the virtual absence of effective communication and empathy. The sport experience was not enjoyable to the participants. And they lost many games. The team leaders who could have helped these young men and women to reach their goals and to experience their fantasies didn't have the expertise or the interest to achieve these objectives.

Many fine coaches in sport have the insight, skills, and personality to genuinely care about other people and help each athlete to reach his or her performance potential. The teams of these leaders are typically successful, and their members are often very satisfied. What coaches do and how they do it have a significant impact on the athlete's attitude, feelings, and performance. Helping each competitor to reach his or her potential is what coaching is all about. Some leaders, however, do not have the necessary personal skills to elicit the athletes' best efforts. For them, leadership might consist of the destruction of a player's character or giving most of their attention to the starters while ignoring the substitutes. The effective coach takes the time to help a player learn, improve, and contribute to team success. Poor coaches, on the other hand, are consumed only with the final product. The primary purpose of this book is to take the coaching profession together with the sport participant to a higher, more sophisticated level of expertise so that the sport experience is a more satisfying and successful one.

There is a need for a text in applied sport psychology based on credible, published research. Many sport psychology publications do a fine job of explaining the theoretical framework and social-psychological foundations of this discipline. Others offer a handbook approach to using psychological strategies as a sport participant. This text goes in both directions. A deliberate attempt is made here to avoid scientific and statistical jargon so that persons at various levels of education, past experience, and expertise can feel comfortable with its content. Sport examples from media publications are used frequently to nurture the connection between the professional literature and real-life sport experiences. Often combined briefly with theoretical foundations, each chapter was formulated based on the need to explain "real world" sport phenomena and how to maintain, enhance, or diminish it.

I begin the book (chapter 1) with an explanation of the field of sport psychology and the many tasks performed by sport psychologists. To further familiarize the reader with the sport psychology literature, a brief explanation about reading and interpreting sport research is located in Appendix A, a new feature to sport psychology texts. A wealth of information exists in the research literature about the factors—good and bad—that influence performance and about what coaches and athletes can do to promote the good and reduce or eliminate the bad. Having the skills to read published research studies will help practitioners to access this information. This is an attempt to bridge the gap between research and application.

The following are just a few chapter highlights of this text. Chapter 3 explains the underlying causes of the athletes' emotions just prior to the contest and what to do about them. Anxiety and arousal are common feelings in sport that influence performance both directly and indirectly. Thus, coaches and players should help athletes to control these emotions. And how coaches and athletes interpret and explain the causes of the results of a contest also play an important role in future participation, the focus of chapter 4. For instance, a player will feel far less motivated if he or she feels that a lack of ability caused an error or loss. Instead, however, feeling that further effort will help to determine future success will likely increase the individual's motivation and self-image.

This text also includes three chapters that are rather unique in the sport psychology literature. Chapters 8 and 9 deal with communication and counseling, respectively. These topics do exist abundantly in other publications, especially in counseling and educational psychology texts. But they are not commonly applied in sport psychology contexts. Effective communication is the ability to transfer information. Counseling is the ability to listen and to respond to a person's feelings with the appropriate compassion, empathy, and valid information. In sport, the collective purpose of communicating and counseling is to have a positive effect on the athlete's feelings and behaviors, both in and out of the sport domain. It is much more of a science than most people realize. Chapter 13, "Athletes Speak for Themselves," attempts to go to probably the best source for understanding the needs of participants. The results of my conversations with athletes are surprising. What are believed to be widely held "truths" in the coaching profession in turn become myths in the eyes of the athletes. For example, a common habit of many basketball and football coaches is to present a pregame talk that is meant to motivate and "psych up" the team. But many athletes contend that a loud, assertive message has the opposite effect; they're more apt to get "psyched out" than "psyched up." The interviews provide a valuable source of information for effective coaching — through the athletes' eyes.

One underlying theme of this book is that success in sport is not necessarily spelled W-I-N. Despite the pleasure that comes with competing against and beating an opponent, sometimes athletes can derive far more enjoyment from their sport experiences if the quality of their performance during the contest is as important (and for child athletes, even more important) to sport leaders as the final outcome. Kids drop out of sport because it is not fun. Their team's winning percentage rarely has anything to do with it. Coaches and parents have a wonderful opportunity to make a significant contribution to the lives of many individuals in sport. The message of this book is, "If you're going to make the effort to work with athletes, let's do it right!"

I would like to thank the many coaches who gave me the opportunity to interact with them and their players. Without firsthand experience, this book could not have been written with credibility. And I thank my wife, Sheree, for reading and commenting on the first drafts and for just "being there" during the long writing process.

I dedicate this book in honor of my father, Bernard, and to the memory of my mother, Rochelle, for providing me with the opportunity to learn and achieve — and the desire to care about others. They gave to me what I give to my students — 100 percent.

1

The Science of
Sport Psychology

In January of 1985 and again in 1986, the Chicago Black Hawks hockey team went to Las Vegas, Nevada, for a minivacation right in the middle of the National Hockey League season. Player Al Secord was quoted in the newspaper as saying that the team tended to win after such trips. "It is a move designed to make us relax and forget about the long season," he said. Professional golfer Bill Rogers knew that he was in trouble as an athlete when he kept looking at his watch ("actually counting the minutes . . . until I could get home") during a golf tournament. He had no enthusiasm; golf was not fun anymore. So he decided to take some time off, and he came back with the enthusiasm he needed to win. For Rogers, the game is fun again. Major league baseball pitcher Bob James (formerly of the Chicago White Sox) maintains an intimidating approach to relief pitching: He never talks to an opposing hitter. "If they say hello (before the game), I just nod and walk away. . . . You don't ever want to make a hitter feel comfortable."

These three situations have something in common. They all recognize the importance of a mental factor that is at least partly responsible for success in sport. Feeling relaxed, having fun, and intimidating the opposition — the three objectives reflected in these examples — can be instrumental in achieving another objective: winning. More and more athletes and coaches have come to understand that there is more to sport success than practicing and playing the game.

1

Psychological factors certainly influence, and sometimes even determine, the final score of a contest. Understanding these factors is what sport psychology is all about.

WHAT IS SPORT PSYCHOLOGY?

Sport psychology involves properly selecting and motivating athletes so that each participant competes at his or her capacity, using strategies to "psych out" opponents, reducing or coping with extraordinary levels of stress, preventing drug abuse, developing successful team strategies, and teaching skills. Clearly, psychology is a central component of sport competition. Studying and using psychology in a sport situation gives one the ability to describe behavior ("athletes on teams that win consistently are more friendly toward one another than athletes on teams that consistently lose"), to explain behavior ("the upset may have occurred because the favored team was underaroused; the underdogs were up for the game and ready to prove that they could beat a worthy opponent"), and to predict behavior ("if a coach teaches in an angry manner, the athlete will not retain the information because of anxiety and inability to concentrate on the information").

Sport psychology is a science. It is the study of human behavior in the context of competitive sport and of how behavior (performance) is affected by three primary sources: the athlete, the team leader (i.e., the coach), and the environment in which these individuals interact. (See Figure 1.1.)

The Athlete

Sports fans show a genuine interest in "their" teams through attending, watching, listening to, and reading about contests. And the media devotes considerable time to describing the events and the players who perform them. Reporters and announcers have become more sophisticated in their analyses of the factors that underlie performance. They often venture beyond describing someone as a good "game player" to explain the possible reasons for superior play in game situations. However, most sports fans do not consider important psychological factors when they are observing, or trying to explain, sport performance.

For example, champion tennis player John McEnroe has received considerable criticism for losing his temper on the court. However, McEnroe has admitted that he uses anger as a psychological technique to get "psyched up." To sport scientists, this is no surprise. That all athletes have an optimal level of excitation (arousal), which has a marked effect on the quality of their performance, is well documented. Athletes don't want to become too aroused, just stimulated enough to play their best. Whether or not they are appealing to fans, self-induced arousal

Figure 1.1   Factors that affect sport performance

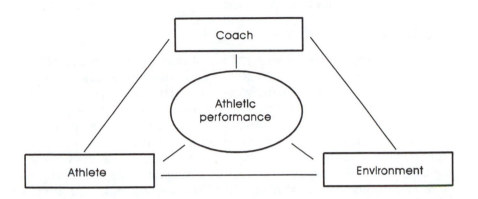

strategies (such as McEnroe's anger on the court) are an integral part of mental preparation for many competitive athletes. The actions of football players on the sideline before the game, "high fives," pregame team cheers, and other warm-up activities performed by the athletes all serve the purpose of establishing the desired emotional effect before the contest. *Mental preparation* is an important factor in sport performance.

Another important factor is *personality*: Is there a "personality type" that is predictive of quality sport performance? Can the coach predict sport success from a paper-and-pencil personality test? Do the personalities differ between athletes and nonathletes, between male and female players, and among athletes in different sports? Sport psychologists have devoted considerable research to the topic of personality in sport. The answers to the above questions might surprise you.

Individual differences is another popular subject of research: Why do athletes differ in their performance even when they have the same skills? Why do some players succeed under pressure in sport while others do not? What psychological factors separate the consistently successful competitor from his or her less successful counterpart? One could write a book on this last question alone.

In the arena of *youth sports*, in which participants typically range in age from 8 to 13 years old, sport psychologists are studying the effects of competitive activities: Should child athletes compete for awards? Do younger athletes have different psychological, emotional, and social needs than older, better-skilled players? If so, how can these needs be met through "healthy" sport involvement?

Another psychological factor to be considered is *motivation*: Why are some athletes more motivated than others, especially when it comes to internal feelings? Why do some play at their best because it's fun or desirable rather than because they are motivated by external factors such as awards, recognition, or money? What are some of the psychological factors that help to motivate athletes, and which ones demotivate them?

The Coach

Playwright Henry Miller once wrote, "The real leader has no need to lead — he is content to point the way." And so it is with effective coaches in sport. Given the resources of player talent and their knowledge of the game, the team leader's primary goal is to develop the physical and mental skills of athletes so that they, individually and as a team, can achieve consistent success. In team sports, how can the coach facilitate the interaction of all team players to promote group identity, player satisfaction, and group cohesion? And, oh yes, does it really matter? Does meeting the players' needs for affiliation and group "togetherness" have much connection to whether or not the team succeeds? Is a player's performance affected by that player's satisfaction in being a team member or by whether he or she has close friends on the team? Playing the "devil's advocate," if winning is the coach's only objective in sport, should anyone care about the athlete's social and emotional needs? Much of the sport psychology literature is devoted to why sport leaders *should* care about issues that go beyond player performance if they want a successful team.

But not all coaches are aware of these important psychological issues. In fact, if we can agree that, in general, coaches learn their trade by observing and listening to other coaches (the modeling effect, or more to the point, "monkey see, monkey do"), perhaps more often than not the athlete's personal needs are not taken into account in preparation for, during, and following the contest or match. For example, psychologist Dr. Daniel Kirschenbaum and his colleagues, in their reviews of the literature dealing with stress and coping in sport (Kirschenbaum et al. 1984a, 1984b), have found that coaches publicly and frequently extol the virtues of criticism in sport. Further, the researchers cited evidence that coaches tend to reject the interventions of others who attempt to modify coaching behavioral patterns.
Observations, interviews, and written reports about coaches in sport confirm that in most instances they virtually ignore sport psychology literature. Researchers have shown that this lack of attention given to sport psychology information may be due to a lack of awareness about it.

For instance, Dr. John Silva's national survey of high school and college coaches indicated that 75 percent were not aware of the *Journal of Sport Psychology* (Silva 1984). However, although 80.1 percent of the coaches surveyed said that they had "never" worked directly with a sport psychologist, 68.2

percent indicated a desire to do so — on a volunteer basis, that is. Would they be willing to pay for such consultation? "Nope," said 64.8 percent. Perhaps they should. Research findings in sport psychology do not support some of the common practices of coaches. Some of these practices may even be harmful. Here are some examples:

The pregame pep talk.   Many coaches, particularly in the sports of basketball and football, give an exciting, emotionally charged talk just before game time. Sport psychologists and some of the more successful coaches argue against a hyped-up pregame talk (see chapter 7). Researchers have found that athletes are already anxious or "pumped-up" for the contest. An arousal-inducing talk before the game tends to excite the players above optimal levels. They become too excited (see chapter 2). A low-key approach in which information is presented may be more effective. Promoting enthusiasm for the contest should begin at practice.

"We gotta win."   Feelings of anxiety and fear of failure already exist in players before the contest. The coach's job is to help the athlete to manage (i.e., to cope with) these feelings (their total elimination is unrealistic and even counterproductive). Pregame messages that express the need to win heighten this anxiety. To review skills and strategies, and then to tell players to go out and have fun is preferable to emphasizing winning.

Criticism.   The effect of criticism on sport performance is clear: Sometimes it is helpful, but at all times its effectiveness is dependent on the manner in which it is communicated. As child psychologist Haim Ginott recommends in his book *Between Parent and Child* (1965), authority figures should criticize behavior ("Jim, you're not keeping your eye on the ball"), not personality or character ("Boy, Sam, that was a dumb play"). The same goes for anger. Ginott claims that anger per se is normal and its free expression should be allowed. But when anger is expressed through abusive and destructive messages that serve no other purpose than to destroy a person's self-image and to promote feelings of guilt, then its potential benefits are void.

Punishment.   How often have you heard a coach yell, "OK, that's two laps around the field or court" because a player committed some infraction or failed in a contest or skill test? Considerable evidence indicates that punishing an individual with exercise reduces that person's desire to be physically active and a well-conditioned sport participant. The association between exercise and punishment is undesirable. A far better tool for punitive purposes is the short-term denial of participation in physical activity or sport, not additional activity.

Many other examples of common coaching practices that have been proven to be incorrect and, when they lead to the emotional destruction of the player, even unethical, are offered throughout this text. This is not to say that coaching is an easy profession. The leader in sport is required to fulfill the demands of many different roles and to deal with numerous psychologically based issues. Some of these issues include:

- motivating individual athletes and the team before, during, and after the season, and before, during, and after the contest;
- positively affecting player attitudes to reduce anxiety and to promote feelings of excitation and loyalty to the coach and team;
- promoting self-confidence and self-esteem in each athlete;
- developing team leadership and morale;
- understanding and meeting the needs of younger athletes;
- identifying the potential and promoting the development of each athlete;
- enhancing performance consistency;
- dealing with, and assisting players to cope with, the stresses, disappointments, and other problems both within and away from the sport arena; and
- conducting practices and preparation for the contest that result in learning skills and strategies.

Each of these issues is of significant importance to the successful participation of sport competitors. And all of these areas are directly tied to meeting the psychological needs and fostering the mental skills of each player. The coach has direct control over, and must take primary responsibility for, helping each athlete to meet these needs. To become successful in sport, athletes depend on the team leader to help them to reach their potential.

The successful management of a team is a complex and sophisticated skill. To make everyone in the group feel that they contribute to team success, and to promote desirable behaviors (e.g., developing quality player leadership, showing team loyalty, and building internal motivation) while inhibiting inappropriate ones (e.g., cheating, exhibiting hostility toward other team members, forgetting skills and strategies, or quitting the team) is a difficult task. Coaches are asked to achieve the most difficult of human objectives: to change the attitudes, feelings, perceptions, and behaviors of others for the good of a team. How? Now *that* is what effective coaching — and the use of sport psychology — is all about. One way to meet these objectives is to create the proper environment for sports participation.

The Environment

In July 1982, this writer had the opportunity to privately interview the late Charlie Lau, then the batting coach (and author of a book on batting) with the Chicago White Sox (Anshel 1986). The purpose of our discussion was to compare conclusions and hypotheses from the professional literature in sport psychology and motor learning with Lau's experiences in playing and coaching

professional baseball for over twenty-five years. Many of his comments are included throughout this book. One area that Lau emphasized was the importance of environmental factors in the successful performance of professional baseball players.

Lau observed that players are almost "paranoid" of making fools of themselves in front of thousands (in the stadium) or millions (on television) of fans. This is one reason why major league players often attribute unsuccessful performances to injuries.

He also found that consistent success and recognition are very important to the player, even at the expense of proper training and practice techniques. Many athletes are not open to new approaches and techniques, and others are extremely sensitive to constructive criticism. Lau pointed out the shortcomings of two common preseason and pregame practices: (1) having pitchers in spring training throw at high velocity before the batters have adequately developed their timing in contacting the thrown ball and (2) during pregame batting practice, allowing batters to swing against pitches that are tossed at half speed as compared to the speed of the pitches during the game. Why do these practices occur? According to Lau, it's a matter of player ego: Pitchers enjoy the success of overpowering hitters during spring training, and hitters relish the chance to demonstrate their batting skills in the presence of their peers during pregame batting practice. Lau's suggestions to slow down the throwing velocity when pitching to teammates during spring training and to speed up the tosses in batting practice are supported by motor-learning researchers.

Another important environmental issue in sport psychology is a concept called *team cohesion*, the "togetherness" of group members. Effective coaches try to foster a team atmosphere in which athletes offer mutual support of one another's efforts, improvement, and performance. Also desirable is that team members feel group satisfaction, the sense of pride in being on the team, representing a school, club, or town, which fosters a willingness to go "all out" to meet the team's needs (e.g., playing second string if necessary) and the demands of success (e.g., staying in proper physical condition).

Some other environmental issues that are the focus of sport psychology include:

- Is there research support for the popular thought of a home-field advantage, or is it a myth?
- How important is it for athletes to experience playing in the specific environmental conditions, such as the time of day, the weather conditions, and the unique characteristics of the area, in which a competitive event will take place?
- Does the cheering or booing of the crowd influence performance? Are quality athletes really affected by crowd reactions?
- Does the effect of environmental conditions on performance depend on the sport? For example, would golfers practicing on a different course experience a significantly greater environmental effect than basketball players playing on a different basketball court?
- Does it matter if teammates do not spend time together away from the sport scene? Is team harmony possible only if the players interact and enjoy one another's company off the field or court?
- Is it a good idea to tell athletes that their parents, a college recruiter or professional scout, or some other evaluator of their performance is observing them play today?
- When is anger and criticism appropriate, and when is it damaging to player development and performance?
- Was columnist Sydney Harris right when he said, "Even the behaviorists concede that praise works twice as well as criticism in providing the incentive to improve — but it is also twice as hard for most people to praise as it is to point out defects"?

These are only some of the many questions concerning how environment can influence the outcome of competitive events in sport. One or more psychological factors is present in each of these examples to a significant degree. It should be obvious to the reader that participating in and coaching competitive athletics is a far more sophisticated endeavor than most spectators, journalists, and even the participants themselves realize.

Over the past twenty years or so, sport psychology has grown to be a legitimate academic discipline (or subdiscipline of physical education) and field of study. As with any academic area, interests among learners, researchers, and practitioners vary, and so do the directions in which interested parties move. Researchers in the area of sport psychology have devoted considerable energy to disseminating scientific findings through journals and have begun to receive appropriate recognition from the academic community. These researchers have examined theories from the behavioral sciences and have published their findings in reputable journals such as the *Journal of Sport Psychology*, the *Journal of Sport Behavior*, the *Research Quarterly for Exercise and Sport*, the *International Journal of Sport Psychology*, the *Canadian Journal of Applied Sport Sciences*, the *Journal of Applied Research in Coaching and Athletics*, and the *Sport Psychologist*. The individuals who have attempted to apply the results of this research (and who, in fact, conduct their own research typically in "real world" sport settings) are a group of scientists/practitioners called *sport psychologists*.

WHAT DO SPORT PSYCHOLOGISTS DO?

For many years, sport psychologists had what is called the "Rodney Dangerfield Syndrome" — they "got no respect." Why? According to Dr. Bruce Ogilvie, a pioneer of applied sport psychology, "The problem has been that we've had too many charlatans, too many cons, and too many people promising too many things." Examples abound. In the 1960s, personality tests were promoted to predict who would become a top athlete. Not surprisingly, these promises were unkept. In the 1970s, such tests were shown to be misleading at best and fraudulent at worst (Morgan 1980). A psychiatrist in San Diego used personality testing to conclude that athletes on the San Diego Chargers football team fit certain personality stereotypes based on their positions on the team. Claims of performance enhancement came from a variety of fields. An optometrist in New York claimed to be able to markedly improve the performance (specifically, the reaction time) of a goaltender on the New York Islanders ice hockey team by repeated trials on a laboratory device. It was a short-lived assertion because subsequent scientific inquiry could not support the claim. The credibility of sport psychology in general, and sport psychologists in particular, was virtually nonexistent.

In recent years, the field of sport psychology has evolved into a respected behavioral science, and the sport psychologist has come to be recognized as a professional. Not only has the profession taken on added status with the publication of reputable scientific journals in which valid and sophisticated research has been published (without which textbooks in sport psychology could not be written), but the formation of professional organizations has allowed sport scientists the opportunity to exchange ideas, to disseminate research findings, and to work together toward the development of new and exciting directions. The acceptance of sport psychology was academically validated with its recognition by the prestigious American Psychological Association in 1984. And in the summer of 1982, the United States Olympic Committee (USOC) invited ten sport psychologists to its headquarters in Colorado Springs, Colorado, "to examine how best this field can become part of USOC's plans for a comprehensive sports medicine program" (Clarke 1984). In the 1984 winter and summer Olympics, a sport psychologist was assigned to virtually every U.S.A. team. Sport psychologists have been working with amateur athletes in Canada (Kidd 1979) and Europe (Vanek and Cratty 1970) for years. But with this evolution of expertise has come an identity crisis raising the questions "Who are we?" and "What is our mission?" (Dishman 1983).

The struggle for identity, recognition, and respect has been a healthy one. Sport scientists and practitioners all have the same objectives: to develop and test theories of behavior in sport, to attempt to explain the psychological factors that underlie sport performance and leadership, and to apply this knowledge to benefit the athlete by conducting field research, consulting with coaches, and working directly with the competitors. The problem has been one of regulation (Nideffer 1981).

Whereas one's status as a doctor or a professor can be clearly established based on earning an academic degree, the identification of a sport psychologist is far less certain. Many professions attempt to maintain quality control over individuals who claim to specialize or to have expertise in a certain area so as to promote the discipline's credibility and to eliminate fraudulent practices. One way to ensure the proper use of techniques is to regulate self-claims of expertise through some sort of licensing or certification. In his preface to *The Ethics and Practice of Applied Sport Psychology*, Nideffer (1981) asserts that "it is important to define the roles a sport psychologist fills, and to identify the educational experiences that should be prerequisites."

Perhaps the dilemma of defining a sport psychologist is not so much due to the lack of regulation (although this remains a serious concern in the field), but rather due to the variety of functions that a sport psychologist performs. As Dishman (1983) suggests, "Sport psychology is defined by what sport psychologists do." We now turn to the various roles of the sport psychologist.

At their meeting in August 1982 in Colorado Springs, Colorado, the USOC's Psychology Advisory Committee divided into three broad areas the services of sport psychologists: clinical services, educational services, and research services.

Clinical services.   This area includes helping athletes who experience severe emotional problems (e.g., depression, anorexia, and panic) and who need treatment over an extended period of time. Although laws vary among states and countries, persons in the United States should not practice clinical sport psychology unless they have full membership in a national psychological, psychiatric, or clinical association and some professional preparation in the sport sciences and a current license to practice counseling.

Educational services.   The teaching component to sport psychology involves helping performers to develop the psychological skills to experience their athletic potential. Relaxation, concentration, imagery and coping with stress are examples of these skills. Sometimes these services are delivered on a group basis and, at other times, individually. The surroundings in which the educational sport psychologist practices usually are in a university/college classroom, as a guest lecturer for local or national sports clubs and organizations, or under contractual agreement to a team or individual athlete for a predetermined period of time. Many university faculty who teach sport psychology tend to lecture and provide counseling services. Because this person is perceived by constituents to possess up-to-date knowledge and expertise in this area, he or she must be reading the most recent professional research literature and have the academic skills to translate this information into applied form. Without the ability to bridge the gap from theory to practice, the educator remains fixed in antiquated, perhaps ineffective, techniques. Imagine being the patient of a physician whose knowledge has been derived from his or her medical education ten or twenty years ago? For this reason, an educational sport psychologist or consultant should have earned at least a master's degree in psychology or have completed a graduate course in sport psychology.

Research services.   A doctorate in psychology or a related field, evidence of scholarly research activity applied to sport behavior, and letters of reference from reputable research institutions that recognize the individual's research attempts and his or her contribution to the field qualifies one to provide research services. The research sport psychologist has two major responsibilities: to publish his or her research findings in a professional journal and to present these results, as well as those of others, to colleagues at professional conferences. A scientist who lacks the skills to communicate about his or her work is mute and, figuratively, nonexistent in the scientific community.

The types of research services that are conducted by sport psychologists include the effects of certain mental techniques on the athletes' psychological state (e.g., arousal or anxiety levels, readiness to perform, or self-confidence) and performance. Sometimes the participant is asked to complete a psychological inventory which may "describe" the current mental status (e.g., state anxiety) or point out certain cognitive strengths and weaknesses of the performer. The effectiveness of certain strategies on altering the subject's mental status and athletic performance may be undertaken. Relationships between certain performance tendencies and the use of cognitive strategies can also be measured. An important key to quality research in applied sport psychology is asking appropriate questions in sport psychology that need further investigation.

In examining the roles of sport psychologists as counselors, educators, and researchers, the question that has often been raised in the literature and at conferences is "Are sport psychologists really psychologists?" Perhaps not. Various national and state organizations around the world mandate certain criteria related to academic training, clinical supervision, and experience before a person can describe and advertise himself or herself as a "psychologist." The purpose for screening members of this profession is to prevent the unqualified, poorly trained, and unethical charlatans from abusing the proper professional standards and training to practice psychology. Although the issue of certification for sport psychologists is still unsettled, many professionals prefer using the terms "sports counselor," "consultant," or "educator" for persons without appropriate qualifications.

These recommendations concerning the roles and qualifications of sport psychologists are not law. They are merely guidelines toward a clearer understanding about the credentials and expertise of individuals who practice sport psychology. They are an attempt to recommend standards for quality control in a relatively new area of practice that unfortunately for years lacked a public image of respect and integrity.

Sport psychologists, then, are not one-dimensional. Based on individual interests and opportunities, the field includes a variety of practices. Perhaps the most recent advances have been in the area of application. In the United States, more and more coaches are recognizing the importance of the mental aspects of physical performance. Many are seeking out specialists — sport psychologists — to help them to enhance their communication and teaching skills and to work directly with their athletes in optimizing physical performance. To date, opportunities to work directly with the athletes have been negligible. Coaches have not been convinced that sport psychologists can add new expertise or can complement the coaches' skills in helping teams to become or to remain successful. This lack of understanding and trust may soon become a thing of the past.

A BRIEF HISTORY OF SPORT PSYCHOLOGY

The late former United States Senator Adlai Stevenson said, "We can chart our future clearly and wisely only when we know the path which has led to the present." Indeed, understanding the foundations and future directions of sport psychology requires information about its history, one that is far older than most students and scholars in the sport sciences realize. As early as 1897, Norman Triplett, a psychologist at Indiana University, published (in the *American Journal of Psychology*) what is believed to be the first experiment directly related to sport psychology. Triplett investigated a phenomenon that we now call *social facilitation*, the favorable effect of observers on one's performance of a motor skill. He noticed that cyclists performed faster when competing against other cyclists, and faster with other cyclists on a tandem bicycle than when alone. And E. W. Scripture, a psychologist at Yale University, concluded in his study (published in *Popular Science Monthly* in 1899) that participating in sport could lead to desirable personality traits. The contemporary view that competitive athletics builds character has its roots in Scripture's research. But like most academic disciplines, sport psychology has a pioneer. Coleman Roberts Griffith, referred to as the "father of sport psychology in America," is acknowledged as the first person to conduct systematic and frequent sport psychology experimentation over a period of several years (Wiggins 1984; and Kroll and Lewis 1970).

Griffith developed the first sport psychology laboratory—the Athletic Research Laboratory at the University of Illinois in 1925, although his research on the psychological factors that affect sport performance began as early as 1918. His primary areas of interest included the learning and performance of motor skills, and personality in sport. He developed equipment for his laboratory that measured awareness of skilled movements; mental alertness; reaction times to sight, sound, and pressure; steadiness; muscular coordination; muscular tension and relaxation; and learning ability (Kroll and Lewis 1970). He was the first scientist to acknowledge, based on an interview with football great Red Grange, that better athletes perform sport skills automatically, in the virtual absence of thinking. He wrote the first sport psychology texts in 1926 (*Psychology of Coaching*) and 1928 (*Psychology of Athletics*) and taught the first sport psychology college course, at the University of Illinois in 1923. In a task that today's sport psychologists would truly envy, Griffith was hired by the Chicago Cubs baseball club to be the team's consulting sport psychologist for the 1938 season. He administered various motor and paper-and-pencil tests to determine each player's current psychological status, ability, and potential as a competitive athlete from spring training to the season's end.

Sport psychology research was at a virtual standstill in the 1940s and 1950s with the exception of the occasional doctoral dissertation. More common during this time was the establishment of motor learning laboratories, including those founded by John Lawther at Pennsylvania State University, Clarence Ragsdale at the University of Wisconsin, C. H. McCloy at the University of Iowa, and perhaps most notably, Franklin Henry at the University of California at Berkeley. This movement provided the field of physical education with a more sophisticated, scientific approach to research in motor behavior.

Subsequently, all sport scientists learned from the improvement in research design, equipment, statistical techniques, and more frequent publication of information pertaining to the psychomotor processes that underlie learning and performing skilled movements. Despite the "striking void...between Griffith's productive years and the work of more contemporary researchers in sport psychology" (Wiggins 1984, p. 14), sport scientists have benefited from these initial attempts in motor research.

It wasn't until the mid-1960s that sport psychology made great strides to become the scientific discipline that it is today. A number of factors contributed to the development of this academic area. Textbooks became more available than ever before. Examples included Bryant Cratty's *Movement Behavior and Motor Learning* (1964), Bruce Ogilvie and Thomas Tutko's *Problem Athletes and How to Handle Them* (1967), and Joseph Oxendine's *Psychology and Motor Behavior* (1967). These books provided an impetus for prolific research and publication in scientific journals, most notably the *Research Quarterly* (now called *Research Quarterly for Exercise and Sport*), the official research publication of physical education in the United States. But even more important to the advancement of sport psychology and motor-behavior scholarship was the proliferation of courses and university programs that led to the emergence of our most prestigious sport scientists.

The final component in the growth of sport psychology was the establishment of four professional associations. The first annual meeting of the North American Society for the Psychology of Sport and Physical Activity (NASPSPA) was held in 1967. Its Canadian counterpart, the Canadian Society for Psychomotor Learning and Sport Psychology (CSPLSP), began in 1969. At first, this organization was affiliated with the Canadian Association for Health, Physical Education, Recreation, and Dance (CAHPERD), but it became an independent society in 1977. In 1975, a subdivision of the American Alliance for Health, Physical Education, Recreation, and Dance (AAHPERD) was created to promote sport psychology within the academic framework of physical education. It was called the Sport Psychology Academy. The purpose of the Academy was to promote theory and research that could be applied in a physical education or sport setting. And more recently (1986), the Association for the Advancement of Applied Sport Psychology (AAASP) came into existence to promote a more "hands-on" approach in sport psychology. The AAASP concerns itself with health psychology (studying the psychological effects of physical activity, for example), intervention (i.e., sport counseling and studying the effectiveness of using psychological and behavioral techniques on sport performance), and social psychology (i.e., examining the influences of environmental factors on emotions and behaviors of athletes and coaches). Finally, sport psychology is recognized around the world through the International Society for Sport Psychology (ISSP).

The purpose of these organizations was and is to provide scholars and practitioners in sport psychology with their own national and international identity as a scientific discipline. It also allows scholars an opportunity to meet annually (1) to exchange ideas, (2) to communicate their research experiences, (3) to hear and interact with established scientists whose work and expertise is well known in areas sometimes peripheral, but applicable, to sport behavior, (4) to debate and perhaps make decisions about controversial issues, and (5) to bring back to their respective departments' programs, and classes new and exciting ideas that are emerging in the field. From these organizations have come new scientific journals (listed in the preceding section) to meet the needs of an expanding field of study. And sport researchers regularly contribute to journals in psychology and social psychology. The recognition of these contributions was reinforced in 1982 when the prestigious American Psychological Association admitted the field of sport psychology as one of its academic disciplines, and the American College of Sports Medicine quickly followed suit. Sport psychology is now recognized by elite members of the academic community as a respected scientific discipline.

SUMMARY

The primary goals of sport psychology are to describe, to explain, and to predict the attitudes, feelings, and behaviors of sport participants — including athletes, coaches, and even crowd members. Persons who are familiar with the psychological factors that underlie sport competition are sport psychologists. Clinical sport psychologists apply research findings by interacting directly with athletes to help them to deal with issues that may impede reaching their performance potentials. Educational sport psychologists, on the other hand, teach psychological skills to inform athletes, coaches, and students about resolving these issues. Research sport psychologists examine the effects of various treatments and environmental situations on the competitor's mental status, ability to execute sport skills, or both.

Currently, numerous professional publications and organizations exist to promote and disseminate new information from the research and practice of sport psychology. Persons who are interested in learning more about this area may wish to become a member of an organization, attend conferences, and read applied literature.

REFERENCES

Anshel, M. H. May/June 1986. Bridging the gap through research and a major league baseball coach. *Coaching Review* 29–32; 34–35.

Clarke, K. S. 1984. The USOC sports psychology registry: A clarification. *Journal of Sport Psychology* 6: 365–66.

Dishman, R. K. 1983. Identity crises in North American sport psychology. *Journal of Sport Psychology* 5: 123–34.

Ginott, H. 1965. *Between Parent and Child*. New York: Avon.

Kidd, B. 1979. Athlete's rights, the coach, and the sport psychologist. In *Coach, athlete, and the sport psychologist*, ed. P. Klavora and J. V. Daniel, pp. 25–39. Champaign, IL.: Human Kinetics.

Kirschenbaum, D. S., and D. A. Withrock. 1984a. Cognitive behavioral interventions in sport: A self-regulatory perspective. In *Psychological foundations of sport*, ed. J. M. Silva and R. S. Weinberg, pp. 81–97. Champaign, IL: Human Kinetics.

Kirschenbaum, D. S., D. A. Withrock, R. J. Smith, and W. Monson. 1987. Criticism inoculation training: Concept in search strategy. *Journal of Sport Psychology*, 6: 77–93.

Kroll, W., and G. Lewis. 1970. America's first sport psychologist. *Quest* 13: 1–4.

Morgan, W. P. 1980. Sport personology: The credulous-skeptical argument in perspective. In *Sport psychology: An analysis of athlete behavior*. 2d ed., ed. W. F. Straub. Ithaca, NY: Mouvement.

Nideffer, R. M. 1981. *The ethics and practice of applied sport psychology*. Ithaca, N.Y.: Mouvement.

Silva, J. M. September 1984. The status of sport psychology: A National Survey of Coaches. *Journal of Physical Education, Recreation, and Dance*, 55: 46–49.

Vanek, M., and B. J. Cratty. 1970. *Psychology and the superior athlete*. London: Macmillan.

Wiggins, D. K. 1984. The history of sport psychology in North America. In *Psychological foundations of sport*, ed. J. M. Silva and R. S. Weinberg, 9–22. Champaign, IL: Human Kinetics.

2

Characteristics of Successful Athletes

How do they do it? How do the best, most consistent sport performers make it to the top and stay there? Is it their total commitment to excellence? An extremely high need to achieve? Is it the incentive to meet more meaningful long-term goals rather than needing the reinforcement of meeting short-term goals like most of us? How do these competitors withstand the physical stress of constant conditioning and practice and the mental stress of performing at optimal levels before thousands, sometimes millions, of spectators?

While spectators observe and appreciate the finesse and skill of elite athletes, researchers study the underlying causes of, and factors that contribute to, their quality performances. This chapter is about identifying and explaining these factors and exploring how the best athletes differ psychologically from less successful competitors. After reading this chapter, you should be able to identify the unique traits, mental processes, and tendencies of elite competitors. Five aspects of successful athletes that will be discussed include their (1) personality characteristics, (2) behavioral tendencies before and during the contest, (3) emotions, feelings, and attitudes, (4) ability to cope with failure and other stressors in sport, and (5) experiences of peak performance.

PERSONALITY TRAITS OF SUCCESSFUL ATHLETES

It would be appealing to delve into the sport personality research and derive a list of ingredients that, when mixed together, form a champion athlete. Early attempts at assessing the personality of athletes resulted in promises of finding such competitors. It was thought that a person's answers on a questionnaire could be used as a measure to predict successful performance. Coaches were at first ecstatic about the possibility of selecting their players based on the ability of a paper-and-pencil test to predict success. As it turned out, the preliminary data from these tests were not used appropriately by coaches or by researchers. In fact, some inventories have been shown to be invalid and unreliable for use with sport competitors (Martens 1975; Fisher 1977).

Personality testing has been limited in recent years. Students of sport psychology and coaches need to take a critical look at the personality issue in sport based on the reviews of sport scientists such as Martens, Fisher, Morgan (1980), and Williams (1980). These individuals have identified a number of weaknesses associated with personality tests and have expressed reservations concerning their use.

Using Personality Tests

Personality can be described in terms of traits possessed by an individual. Traits are considered to be enduring and stable. This means (1) that individuals have a predisposition to act in a certain way under most, but not in all, situations and (2) that their actions are consistent, that is, predictable under various conditions — in sport or otherwise. However, traits derived from personality inventories have not been shown to be consistent from sport to nonsport situations.

One way in which personality testing has been used inappropriately is as a measure of changes in personality (e.g., before versus after the season). This is incompatible with the design of an instrument that tests personality because traits are stable and enduring. Consequently, results cannot be interpreted to measure personality development.

Often personality tests have been used to predict the probability that an individual will achieve sport success. However, researchers have shown that inventories can predict athletic behavior and success only 10 percent of the time (Fisher 1977).

Sometimes the terms and factors used in personality tests are not universally defined. This is what's called comparing apples to oranges. *Athletes* to one researcher might be participants in collegiate intramurals while in another study the term may refer to competitors who represent a school. In addition, sociability, ego strength, shrewdness, dominance, and other traits are defined differently in various tests. Further, different tests are used to measure the same thing, but results differ (Morgan 1980). Thus, the comparison of results from different tests is invalid.

Some personality traits are better predictors of success than others. Personality inventories such as the Sixteen Personality Factors (16 PF) test and the California Personality Inventory (CPI) inherently assume that each of many factors is interpretable to sport situations. But how would a coach interpret a high relationship between dominance and reaction time? Wouldn't traits related to one's anxiety be better predictors of success? Morgan (1980) accurately predicted which athletes would participate on the United States Olympic Wrestling Team in 1972 based on measures of anxiety and a few other traits.

Another concern is that answers to questions on a personality inventory can be faked. Most respected personality tests, especially those used for clinical diagnosis and treatment, have built-in lie scales. Lie scales include questions inserted in the test that are either discarded when the results are computed or used to detect response inconsistencies.

The traditional personality tests by which sport personality has been measured were not created for sport participants. For example, the Minnesota Multiphasic Personality Inventory (MMPI) was originally meant to diagnose mental illness. The California Personality Inventory (CPI) requires a reading comprehension level equal to about the tenth grade. Thus, personality inventories have not typically been constructed for sport participants. Such inventories may not be interpretable and valid as a predictor of sport performance, as they have been used — or misused — in past years.

Despite these reservations, certain personality traits of successful athletes have been identified, albeit not conclusively, in the literature. Evidence does support the existence of a consistent psychological profile of highly successful performers that differs from the profiles of less successful competitors. Whether these traits are inherited, developed, or both is not clear.

A Personality Profile of Elite Athletes

An elite, or champion, athlete has been defined in the literature as a sport participant who competes at the Olympic or professional level or, in some cases, is merely a starter for his or her team (Singer 1972). For the purposes of this text, *elite athletes* will refer to persons involved at the Olympic, collegiate, and professional levels. In some cases, a further analysis of personality traits will focus on the champions (i.e., those who are consistently in the upper echelon of their sport).

Far more studies have been conducted on elite male than on elite female athletes. However, Williams (1980), in her review of research examining the personality characteristics of successful female athletes, concluded that:

- Women on the 1964 U.S. Olympic Team who engaged in individual sports were more dominant, aggressive, adventurous, sensitive, independent, self-sufficient, and introverted than women who engaged in team sports.

- Female competitors in general tended to be assertive, dominant, self-sufficient, reserved, achievement-oriented, and intelligent, and to have average-to-low emotionality.

Read more about female athletes in chapter 12.

Reilly (1979), Paige (1973), and Rasch and Kroll (1964) reviewed the personality research of champion male athletes in soccer, football, and wrestling, respectively. In Reilly's review, the soccer athletes were assessed almost uniformly with the Cattell 16 PF test, and were found to be stable, extroverted, tough-minded, and highly efficient. Researchers using the MMPI across nine European countries found most male soccer players to be aggressive and dominant, especially the Germans and Italians. Brazilian players were higher in intelligence than the other groups. But in general, elite soccer players scored significantly higher on each of these aforementioned traits than less skilled participants and nonathletes.

Football athletes differ from competitors in other sports. Paige (1973) concluded, based on his review, that football athletes "are outstanding for their roughmindedness, extroverted tendencies and self-control. There is some indication that despite the footballer's extroverted traits, he is not as sure of himself as his actions indicate. . . .winners are less sportsmanlike than losers which reflects the 'win at all cost' attitude sometimes found in winning teams" (p. 12). Kroll and Peterson (1964), using the 16 PF inventory, compared personality traits between winning and losing football teams of 176 players (six teams). The most common difference between the teams was the social factor, described in terms of love, kindness, sympathy, and unselfishness. Players on teams with winning records were less sportsmanlike than participants on teams who lost more games than they won. Perhaps these traits are incompatible with success in football.

Not every personality study of football players has revealed unique personality attributes. Rushall (1976), using the 16 PF test, failed to find differences among collegiate players competing in different sports at a Big Ten university. He concluded that personality was not an important factor in football performance. However, in most instances, at least at the elite level, studies indicate that success in football requires extensive tenacity to overcome the skill and effort of opponents, to tolerate injuries, and to maintain a vigorous conditioning program for successful participation. Because of the physical nature of the game, quality players must maintain high self-confidence, even to the point of bravado. (Similarly, boxers tend to brag and to appear very self-confident — even conceited — prior to a fight.) For the football athlete whose commitment to excellence and whose pain threshold are high, but whose tolerance for failure is low, the chance of being successful increases measurably.

Another group of competitors who have received considerable attention are wrestlers. In Rasch and Kroll's (1964) review, the personality profile of wrestlers is less than conclusive. But generally, they tend to score high on sociability, enthusiasm, love of adventure, and group dependency, at least according to the 16 PF test. Gould, Weiss, and Weinberg (1981) compared successful and unsuccessful wrestlers participating in the 1980 Big Ten championship tournament. Highlen and Bennett (1979) studied the top 10 percent of all Canadian wrestlers. In both studies, successful participants scored statistically higher on measures of self-confidence, perceiving their skills as closer to their maximum wrestling potential, and on their ability to focus attention on task-related issues. Finally, Morgan (1979, p. 184) found that wrestlers on the 1972 and 1976 U.S. Olympic Wrestling teams were "uniformly low on tension, depression, fatigue, and confusion, but well above average on vigor."

The traits linked to athletes in soccer, football, and wrestling can be generalized to other sport participants. In general, the quality performers tend to be relatively low in trait anxiety, state anxiety, affiliation, neuroticism, tension, depression, anger, fatigue, and confusion. They score very high in self-confidence, self-concept and self-esteem, vigor, need achievement, dominance, aggression, intelligence, self-sufficiency, mental toughness, independence (autonomy), sociability, creativity, stability, and extroversion (Alderman 1974).

Despite the limitations of personality research, a composite of psychological profiles of elite athletes reveals a person who is mentally healthy, very mature, and committed to excellence. Certainly, these are traits that serve as a model toward which all athletic participants should strive.

BEHAVIORAL TENDENCIES OF ELITE ATHLETES

How are elite athletes different from other athletes in how they approach competitive events? Here is what Ahmad Rashad, former all-pro receiver for the Minnesota Vikings, has to say:

> If you're any good as a receiver, you scout fields. You look for dead spots. I found out long ago that the best footing is often where they paint the lines. I learned to make my cut on the lines. You leave a lot of cornerbacks that way....At the opposite end (of the field), very near the end zone, there was a low, slushy spot, and I could run a post route in there and—literally—give my man the slip. I loved that old place."

Rashad's knowledge of the characteristics of the playing surface serves as an example of the type of intense commitment and dedication that most elite athletes give to game preparation and performance. The hours, weeks, months, and even years of conditioning, practicing, preparing, and struggling to reach their potential is what ultimately separates the elite performers from all others. Sometimes an athlete's pregame preparation can take the form of superstitious behaviors. Three-time American League baseball batting champion Wade Boggs of the Boston Red Sox is noted for his obsession with certain rituals carried out on a specific and detailed schedule.

According to sports columnist Tom Weir, Boggs "always leaves home for the ballpark at 3 P.M., and takes a seat in front of his locker at 4 P.M. . . . Wind sprints have been conducted promptly at 7:17 before each night game, except for the time former Blue Jays' manager Bobby Cox ordered the stadium clock in Toronto to skip from 7:16 to 7:18. Chicken is consumed every day without fail."

Risk-Taking

Another characteristic of highly successful competitors is risk-taking. The term *risk* is defined in most dictionaries as a dangerous element or factor, possibility of loss or injury, hazardous speculation, danger, or peril. In sport, risk has been associated with physical injury during competitive athletics. Sport scientists have studied the tendency of highly skilled athletes to engage in more risk-taking behaviors — actions that can lead to bodily harm or failure — than less skilled competitors.

Sport competition is, of course, inherently risky for all performers. But the elite athlete in particular, more than others, seems to thrive on and to prefer the excitement of engaging in risk-taking behaviors. These behaviors occur most often during situations that require solving problems and making decisions. The quality defensive back in football will guard his opponent (the receiver) more closely than his conservative, less skilled counterpart. Champion divers, skaters, skiers, and gymnasts all tend to "go for it," to attempt very complex coordinated movements, and they usually succeed.

The question becomes, Why do elite athletes take greater and more frequent risks than others? The answer to the question, although still open to further scientific inquiry, might be found in the areas of need achievement, self-confidence, expectations for success, use of cognitive strategies, ability to regulate stress, and need for stimulus-seeking.

Need achievement.   Skilled athletes have high achievement motivation. Need achievement in sport has been associated with winning, the motivation to succeed, and desirable performance outcomes (Malone 1985). (See chapter 5 for more discussion of this topic.)

Self-confidence.   Risk-takers feel confident of two things: that there is a reasonably good chance of success and that they have confidence in their ability. Why do all good competitors have high self-confidence? Primarily because their history of successful sport experiences is extensive. As a result, quality athletes have high self-esteem, and compatible with their past, they expect to have continued success in the future.

Expectations for success. One reason for upsets in sport is that the more successful teams — athletes who are expected to win easily — do not perceive their opponents as threatening to their continued success. Their expectancy of success is too high (Alderman 1974). As Alderman concludes, "the caliber of opposition very definitely affects the strength of an athlete's motive to achieve" (p. 214). How high should the caliber of competition be? Performers are optimally motivated when they feel that they have about a 50 percent chance of success (Atkinson 1957). In many cases, low expectations of success become self-fulfilling prophecies. In an opposite manner, quality athletes have a very high expectancy of success; they expect to win — and they do.

Cognitive strategies. Another reason why elite athletes tend to take more risks is because they use mental techniques that allow them to respond more quickly to opponents and to objects than less successful players do. For instance, they can anticipate stimuli and, thus, respond more rapidly to them than if they had to perceive the stimuli before reacting. Anticipation also allows them to make decisions more rapidly prior to movement execution.

Ability to regulate stress. The ability to remain cool under situations of tension and stress is the true sign of a champion. To take risks in sport when one feels uptight, anxious, or too aroused is very difficult. The key is not to eliminate stress, however, but to regulate it. Coping techniques will be covered extensively later in this chapter.

The ability to cope with failure is another trait of the successful athlete. Coaches should be careful not to overreact to an athlete's mistakes. Especially during competition, the player may concentrate on not making further errors instead of relaxing and concentrating on the proper cues. The participant will be overly cautious in order to avoid further mistakes, and risk-taking will be the last thing on his or her mind. In order to succeed, athletes must have the confidence and skills to take risks. The better players learn from their mistakes, then put them out of their thoughts until after the contest.

Stimulus-seeking. Athletes enjoy the challenge presented in competitive sport. Researchers classify individuals who desire situations that foster tactile and other forms of sensory stimulation as high stimulus-seekers. Stimulus seeking is a motivational factor to participate in sport and to engage in risk-taking behaviors (Malone 1985). Risking is a function of narrowing the margin of safety, both physically in terms of bodily harm and psychologically regarding the probability of success or failure. Malone's (1985) review of literature on risk taking in sport concluded that the athlete's perception of danger creates excitement and a desire to master the environment. Stimulus seeking appears to be based on a chronic level of activation (high excitation) that is easily and quickly rewarded by taking risks in sport. Indeed, the elite athlete thrives on it.

Precompetition and Competition Behaviors

Steve Largent, wide receiver for the National Football League's Seattle Seahawks, holds the league record for receptions in consecutive games. In a discussion of the importance of training for success in sport, Largent serves as a prime example. He makes up for his lack of size (he is only five feet, eleven inches tall and weighs 190 pounds) and lack of speed with diligent game preparation and off-season conditioning. Assistant Seahawk coach Steve Moore says that Largent is "his own motivator, teacher, and preparer. . . . He wins football games through his preparation." He intently watches hours of film and stays after practice to run and rerun patterns with his quarterback, all well after other athletes have gone home.

Rushall (1979) has studied extensively the behavioral patterns of elite athletes before and during the event. He has observed championship-caliber athletes in volleyball, wrestling, swimming, basketball, diving, snow skiing, and rowing. He noted the following pre-event behaviors and tendencies:

- Athletes usually put less effort and intensity into training than they do into the competitive event. Apparently elite athletes do not hold true to the adage "You play as you practice." They seem to produce a level of energy and skill during serious competition that exceeds their achievement in practice, in training, or during less challenging competitions.

- The athlete feels increasingly confident with more detailed competition plans. Therefore, coaches should use competition plans that are specific and detailed. Highly skilled athletes feel comfortable and capable handling a sophisticated approach to contest preparation and implementation.

- Elite athletes have contest contingency plans to implement if things do not go as expected. Athletes feel capable of coping and adapting to unusual situations that arise during the contest. Their confidence about dealing with the unexpected is enhanced by a secondary set of alternatives that they can use during the contest if necessary.

- They prefer to be alone immediately before the contest. Elite athletes tend to use cognitive strategies to relax, review strategies, image successful performance, and use positive self-statements to promote confidence. Rushall contends that this is far more common for individual sport competitors than for team sport participants. Nevertheless, I am aware of several top team sport competitors who share this need.

- Elite athletes prefer to have a coach present during the warm-up period, perhaps as a resource. The athletes feel less precontest anxiety when surrounded by supportive personnel. The coach acts as a source for reassurance and information.

- They don't worry about other competitors before a contest. There is a difference between acknowledging the skills, strengths, weaknesses, and tendencies of an opponent versus being consumed with these thoughts and worrying about them. According to Rushall (1979), elite competitors "do not get preoccupied with contemplating their opponents" (p. 21).

- **They are nervous and tense.** Nervousness and tension translate into high levels of controlled arousal. This is desirable. They use self-statements that reflect a state of readiness and eagerness to compete.
- Top athletes are capable of regaining composure if they become troubled or too excited. The performers know their optimal level of arousal and have trained themselves to control it.
- They can recover lost confidence. Confidence is one of the most salient characteristics of successful athletes in comparison to less successful participants (Bunker and Williams 1986).
- Elite athletes engage in numerous mental rehearsals. Quality performers expect to be successful, and they review images of their successful performance before the contest. This builds confidence and promotes mental practice.
- They can concentrate totally on the upcoming event during preparation. They focus intently on the demands of their upcoming performance instead of observing their opponents during the warm-up period.
- They can accurately assess how well they will do during the competition. Skilled athletes are keenly aware of their physical and mental status before the event and, therefore, are able to predict the quality of their performance in the ensuing event.
- They can deal with unusual circumstances and distractions before and during the event. Top athletes do not allow unpleasant or unexpected circumstances to break their mental preparation. Examples include enduring a delay in the contest, a change in weather conditions, or pre-event harassment; having to wait for transportation to escort them to the event; or lacking appropriate warm-up and locker-room facilities.
- Elite athletes are relatively unaffected by unfamiliar competitive environments. Practicing in an unfamiliar environment before the contest is beneficial to deal with specific features of the area. However, they are able to perform skills competently regardless of the uniqueness of their surroundings.

In addition to differing in their pre-event strategies, highly skilled athletes differ from other performers in their behaviors during the contest:

- They prefer to take the early lead. No matter how much effort is required, "elite athletes attempt to establish superiority as soon as possible without concern for the latter parts of the contest" (Rushall 1979, p. 26).
- Even nonstarters are fully prepared to enter the game. Not every athlete

is ready to participate if he or she is not starting. However, members of elite teams are mentally "into" the game from start to finish.

- They prefer to play their own contest and to regulate their own effort levels. This means that elite performers would like to use certain strategies and skills in the contest without having to react to, or be put on the defensive by, opponents. For example, top runners prefer to regulate the pace of the event.

- They do not tend to "save themselves" for a better finish. Because elite athletes assert themselves early in the event, their goal is to achieve the desired result as soon as possible.

- When fatigue sets in, they concentrate more on technique and effort. This is very good advice. Such concentration serves the purposes of distracting them from sensations of fatigue, reducing the possibility of injuries (which occur more often near the end of contests when fatigue has set in), and helping them to maintain proper form and performance quality. The elite performer will fight fatigue rather than succumb to it.

- They exert maximum effort even when they do not believe that the situation will improve. Quality competitors are well aware of their own performance goals in addition to winning. They maintain an all-out effort throughout every contest.

- Elite athletes are not distracted by physical punishment. The fact that an elite athlete has achieved a certain status in his or her sport reflects an ability to overcome the physical demands that are a part of being a participant. In fact, contact sport athletes actually enjoy the physical aspects of the contest.

- They compete even when they are injured. True, some athletes have a higher tolerance, or threshold, of pain than others, but typically, the elite athlete can focus his or her attention externally on the task and opponents rather than be preoccupied with physical discomfort.

- There is no giving up. Elite competitors are reluctant to give less than their best efforts because they are proud of their ability and past accomplishments.

- They can withstand poor officiating. Poor calls may temporarily upset top performers, but not for long. They express their feelings and then get on with the task at hand.

- They prefer that time-outs be used for productive purposes. Skilled athletes use a pause in the contest (1) to focus their attention on certain aspects of the game or (2) to gather information and energy that can be used to improve their status.

- The skilled athlete handles the pressure of a contest's final stages. According to Rushall (1979, p. 27), "This is an index of confidence that elite athletes have in their own abilities."

- They can concentrate on using aspects of a strategy throughout the whole contest. The best players know what they are supposed to do in great detail and when they are supposed to do it.

- They learn and later use information gained from each contest. This information may come from coaches, teammates, and even from spectators in some cases. They engage in debriefing and self-evaluation to formalize the feedback process, which sometimes changes their strategies in future contests.

A person's performance capacity may be genetically fixed, but what separates the elite athlete from those who are less successful is the willingness to make mental and physical efforts to reach that capacity.

EMOTIONS, FEELINGS, AND ATTITUDES OF ELITE ATHLETES

Numerous attempts have been made by researchers to ascertain the thoughts and feelings of elite, consistently successful athletes before and during the contest in contrast to less successful competitors and nonathletes. What do highly skilled athletes think about, when do they think it, and what effect does this have on their mental preparation and performance?

Mental Approaches to Competition

A mental strategy is a technique a person uses (1) to improve the processing of information to favorably influence learning and remembering or (2) to favorably affect one's emotions such as to reduce anxiety, focus attention, maintain concentration, and cope with stress (Singer 1980).

Consistently successful athletes invoke various mental operations, each serving a different purpose, to benefit performance. For example, one athlete favors a calm, isolated, inactive environment prior to competing, whereas another player prefers noise, the company of teammates, and physical activity for game preparation.

Let's look at some other mental strategies employed by elite athletes.

Self-confidence. Feeling confident is a state of mind, but it is also a strategy when it is used consciously to bolster a performer's motivation, arousal, or aggressiveness. Former tennis champion Jimmy Connors was asked by freelance journalist Craig Modderno, "How important is ego to a professional tennis player?" Connors responded, "At times it's very important, as long as you know when it is and when it's not. Ego on the court is knowing that you're going out there knowing who you are, what you've done, and what you can do. As long as that's where it stops, having a reputation can win you some tennis matches."

Positive self-talk. One of the best ways to maintain self-confidence is to engage in positive self-talk. This is a universal practice among champs. The purposes of self-talk strategies vary. When the technique is used to gain or to maintain self-confidence, focusing inwardly and thinking about one's strengths rather than about one's opponent can generate a sense of being in control and responsible for a contest's outcome.

Another reason to engage in self-talk is to positively analyze the movement. Sue Holloway, 1984 Olympic silver medalist in the kayak pairs competition, engaged in a postrace analysis by asking herself, "Did this work? Did we do this? Or did we forget about it? How are we going to remember this?" For competitors to take the time to self-reflect upon their performances and the possible causes of the outcomes — whether or not they are successful — is important. This self-reflection should be done in a positive manner.

Rushall (1984, p. 57) provides examples of positive self-statements according to four purposes. These are listed in Figure 2.1

Mood words. Does it help one's performance to use certain words during the execution of a movement? Rushall (1984) believes that it does. He contends that thinking or verbalizing certain primal words that have "direct movement counterparts" improves performance. He calls these primal words *performance mood words*. A mood is a movement quality such as speed ("go," "zoom"), strength ("crush," "rip," "push"), balance ("float," "hold"), stability ("easy," "set"), power ("blast," "rip"), and others. He cites research in which the speed of task execution was improved when subjects verbalized or thought "faster, faster" as they performed. Central, then, to the successful use of this strategy is that the words have movement content.

Attentional focus. Quality performers know where and when to focus their attention. This allows them to exclude information that might slow their responses or interfere with their sensations. Orlick (1986) found that championship-caliber competitors do not focus on outcomes while they're performing. Instead, their attention is directed to the task at hand. As Orlick describes it, "The problem with thinking about winning or losing within the event is that you lose focus of what you need to do in order to win. In that sense it is self-defeating" (p. 10).

Arousal regulation. Getting psychologically aroused for the contest is more than a matter of a few "rah-rahs." Superior athletes, more than their less successful counterparts, know two things about the process of getting psyched up: (1) their optimal level of arousal (remember, that's optimal, not necessarily maximal) and (2) when to begin the psyching techniques (see chapter 3).

Figure 2.1   Examples of positive self-statements

Self-Encouragement
"You are doing great"
"Keep achieving those segment goals"
"You are performing according to schedule"
"This is your opportunity to dominate"

Effort Control
"It may hurt but concentrate on flowing movements"
"You have prepared for this, so execute your strategy"
"Others are hurting just as much but they do not have a strategy"

Segment Goal
"The pace was right-on. Now lengthen the stroke"
"You have tackled on every line move that they have made"
"You have forced two turnovers while committing none"

Positive Self-Talk
"Great work"
"This could be even better than anticipated"
"This feels even better than expected"

From Brent S. Rushall (1984). The content of competition thinkings. In W. F. Straub & J. M. Williams (Eds.), *Cognitive Sport Psychology* (pp. 51-62). Lansing, NY: Sport Science Associates.

Making accurate attributions. As discussed in chapter 4, attributions consist of a person's attempts to explain the causes of an event, specifically in response to a performance outcome. Elite athletes more often than not accurately explain the causes of, and tend to feel responsible for, their performance results.

Performance Expectations

In the 1960s and 1970s, heavyweight boxing champion Muhammad Ali shocked a world that was (and is) very uncomfortable with self-centeredness and conceit with his brash proclamation, "I am the greatest." Ali gained notoriety by not only predicting that he would win boxing matches but also announcing before the fight the round in which his opponent would fall. What the world did not realize was that Ali's exercise in apparent vanity was, in fact, a mental strategy that served two purposes: (1) to raise his expectations of success and (2) to lower the expectations of his opponent. No doubt skill had much to do with Ali's success in boxing, but Ali serves as a salient example of the relationship between expecting to do well in competition and doing it. Ali simply said aloud what all quality athletes say to themselves.

The one essential quality that describes the thoughts of a champion is that they are positive. Dr. Denis Waitley, who wrote *The Psychology of Winning* (1978), confirmed the importance of positive expectations when he did extensive interviews with "winners" from various fields of endeavor, including sport. He grouped the characteristics of these individuals into categories of five "attitude qualities."

Positive self-expectancy. Winners have an overall attitude of personal optimism and enthusiasm. They realize that a person usually gets what he or she expects. The self-talk of a winner is, "I was good today; I'll be better tomorrow," while losers lament, "With my luck, I was bound to fail."

Positive self-image. Self-image acts as a subconscious device that governs behavior. Waitley contended that we cannot do what our self-image does not allow us to do. Imagining success begets real-life success. The positive self-talk of winners is, "I can see myself growing, achieving, improving, and winning." Losers say, "They're my hang-ups, faults . . . and I'm stuck with 'em."

Positive self-control. If a winner expects success, he or she is also capable of accepting responsibility for causing the actual outcome. Taking control of the events in one's life is characteristic of winners. Winners take the credit or the blame for their performance. Losers say, "I can't understand why this happened," or "It was someone else's fault, not mine."

Positive self-esteem. Winners are inner-directed. They recognize their uni-

que qualities and develop and maintain their own high standards. They also tend to choose models who exemplify the high goals and achievements to which they aspire. Despite very normal feelings of fear and anxiety, winners do not give in to these emotions. They are secure enough as individuals to respect themselves as well as others. Losers are far less secure and, consequently, need to criticize and undermine others.

Positive self-awareness.   Cratty (1984) reports that "most superior athletes prefer to know all they can about themselves" (p. 6). Waitley agrees; winners know who they are and their potential both as individuals and as athletes. They have learned through experience and through having the security and maturity to ask for and to accept the feedback and judgments of others. Winners say, "I know who I am and where I'm going," whereas losers say, "If I only had the chance."

Effects of Spectators on Performance

Top athletes like an audience. Psychologist Abraham Maslow, in his theory on personality and motivation, contends that one of our greatest needs on our way to self-actualization (fulfilling one's inherent potential) is the need for recognition from others. Athletics provides an important outlet for this need to be met. As Alderman (1974, p. 168) explains, "Athletic success to satisfy the needs for self-esteem also receives massive reinforcement from society via the media and spectators at sports events."

Spectators are, of course, inherent in athletic competition. One could not be a successful athlete while feeling uncomfortable about having others watching. Elite athletes are not only comfortable with being observed by others, they prefer it, as is attested to by the popular concept of the home-court advantage.

Swartz and Barsky (1977) examined the extent to which the home-team advantage — playing in front of one's own fans — is related to game outcome. Based on information obtained from thousands of professional baseball, football, and ice hockey events, and collegiate basketball games, they concluded that the home team won only 53 to 64 percent of the time. They surmised that the home team may have had a slight advantage because audience support generated more offensive production by the home team. Jay Triano, captain of the Canadian men's basketball team in the 1983 World Student Games held in Edmonton, Canada, agrees: "The crowds were great for our games, and the guys were feeling great about themselves because they got a chance to play in their home town against Yugoslavia, and it was really a powerful feeling" (Orlick and Partington 1986, p. 189).

Other possible explanations for better performance at the home arena include higher arousal and aggression levels by the home team and factors related to the visitors' travel, such as a change in time zone, different patterns or arrangements in sleeping and eating, and unfamiliar surroundings. To conclude that the mere

Figure 2.2   Interaction of skill difficulty and type of audience on performance

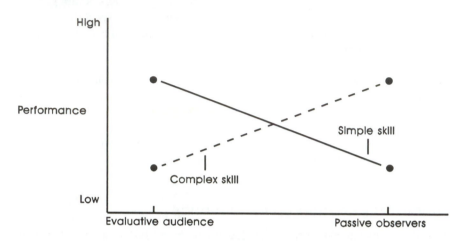

presence of an audience is always sufficient to affect athletic performance would be simplistic and, as discussed later, not supported by research. Other factors partly determine how the competitor is influenced by spectators.

Zajonc (1965) recognized the effect of an audience on sport performance in his model of *social facilitation*. According to Zajonc, the critical factor that decides whether an audience will improve or inhibit performance is whether the performer's dominant response is correct or incorrect (see Figure 2.2). What decides the correctness of a response? At least one, or a combination, of three factors: (1) task difficulty, (2) the person's skill level, and (3) the type of audience. The presence of observers who the athlete believes are qualified to assess performance (an evaluative audience) — judges or scouts, for instance — might inhibit performance if the task is complex for the athlete. Conversely, an evaluative audience may actually improve performance if the individual finds the task relatively simple. But what if a skill is being performed in front of a passive audience or one in front of which the athlete feels nonthreatened? In this case, simple tasks are not performed as well, while responses to complex tasks tend to improve measurably. Take, for example, the influence of the Seattle Seahawks' football fans on their players and, for that matter, on their opponents' performances. The noise volume in an enclosed stadium, the Kingdome, seems to excite the home team. The Seahawks win far more games at home as compared to their road record. Visiting players and coaches complain that the noise makes communicating difficult. Some Seahawk opponents have admitted to feelings of intimidation prior to the contest.

The degree to which an athlete perceives and reacts to the makeup of an audience is referred to as its *evaluative potential*. If this perception hurts performance — perhaps due to heightened anxiety, inappropriate arousal level, poor concentration, and focusing attention improperly, among other possible reasons, then the condition is known as *evaluation apprehension* (Cottrell 1972).

What can athletes and coaches do about this apprehension? First, athletes should focus attention on the task, not on the observers, especially when performing complex tasks. An example of the wrong way to increase player motivation (coaches do it all the time) is to inform the player about the presence of an important audience member. This often backfires; the result is poorer, not better, performance. True, athletes do enjoy, sometimes even need, the presence of spectators to perform at their potential. But the players may not perceive fans — even their own family and friends — with the same evaluative potential as they do scouts for professional teams, college recruiters, or gymnastics judges, for example, who subjectively rate performance.

Second, the athlete who is learning a complex skill should practice until the skill is mastered before performing it in a competitive event. Elite athletes do exactly that. For hours and hours, they practice a new skill or technique so that the presence of judges, the media, opponents, and other spectators will not inhibit their concentration. In fact, highly skilled gymnasts, a champion boxer, and intercollegiate athletes in football, golf, and swimming have indicated to me that they usually ignore members of the crowd. They concentrate on the task at hand. Basketball, volleyball, and wrestling athletes say that the crowd gets them psyched up, but once the event begins (when the ball is in play or when the match begins), they become oblivious to the crowd.

Perhaps the final word — at least for now — on the effects of an audience on performance comes from an analysis of 241 studies involving about 24,000 subjects (athletes and nonathletes) in sport behavior and cognitive tasks (Bond and Titus 1983). The authors — using a statistical technique called meta-analysis in which the results of all topic-related studies, published and unpublished, are combined and then summarized — found that, in general, the effect of an audience could predict performance only 3 percent of the time. Nevertheless, for many athletes, especially nonprofessionals, performance *is* affected by who's watching.

Fears of Failure and Success

Clinical sport psychologist Ronald Smith from the University of Washington in Seattle states, "In my experience, the most common sources of anxiety in athletes are fears of failure and resulting social disapproval or rejection" (1984, p. 160). One of the less fortunate aspects of sport competition is the pressure that athletes feel to meet the expectations of others — especially persons whose opinions the athletes value. The more an athlete succeeds, the more those expectations rise, and the more the pressure increases. In an interview with Canadian sport psychologists Terry Orlick and John Partington (1986, pp. 13–14), Canadian 1984 Olympic double gold medalist swimmer Alex Baumann reported "a tremendous amount of pressure on me . . . because everybody expected me to win, and everybody expected me to break the world record. . . . The pressure came from Canada in general, and then from the whole Canadian team. . . . My heart was pounding because of the pressure and I was unable to sleep between heats and finals. . . . I thought, 'Here goes eleven years of work, and here I come and get a silver medal. . . .' I really wondered if I could ever win feeling that bad."

Another aspect, much less understood among coaches and athletes, is the fear of success or winning. The late Charlie Lau, a well-known major league batting coach, told me in an interview in 1982 that one reason why many hitters with major league skills do not become consistently successful at hitting is due to their fear of performing well. Incredible as this may sound to some people, Lau insisted — and the literature supports him — that some athletes are fearful of living up to the expectations of others after they have demonstrated competent performance. They feel too much pressure to maintain high standards and are not able to deal with criticism from others, notably the media and fans, after performing below previous achievements. So, what happens? They retain, sometimes unconsciously, their mediocrity as athletes. For them, this is a safer, less risky approach. As we will discuss later in this section, the problem of fearing success may be more severe among female athletes.

Fear of failure (FOF).   Most athletes are afraid to fail (Passer 1984). This fear comes not from the fact that the potential for losing a contest is inherent in competitive sport, but from the individual's personal history. For instance, when young children fail or lose in competitive situations, adults may respond in ways that have negative emotional and psychological consequences. Following failure, the child begins to expect a negative evaluation. The individual then associates failure with more intense feelings of shame, guilt, and other unpleasant emotions. Passer concludes that fearing failure is one primary cause of competitive trait anxiety. Even professional and Olympic athletes have this trait to some extent. Most are able to control it. Less effective performers feel, perhaps subconsciously, "If I don't try, I can't fail." This is the worst possible result from FOF. The athlete may decide to withdraw from the competitive situation, either physically by quitting the team or mentally by reducing the effort needed to compete at the level of his or her capability.

The following are some recommendations for coaches and parents to help prevent or reduce FOF in the athlete (Cratty 1983; Passer 1984).

- Regardless of the outcomes, be supportive of the individual's attempts to perform at his or her best. A good example of parental support comes from 1984 Olympic Canadian diving champion Sylvie Bernier, who revealed the following personal story (Orlick and Partington 1986):

  My parents had an important effect. My mother always put a little note in my baggage when I went to competitions. One time I found it in my shoe. The note said, 'You are our champion, no matter what happens.' Then it said, 'Bring me home some chocolates.' I laughed and cried . . . but this helped keep things in perspective.

- **Emphasize better effort**. Athletes need to feel that winning is associated with more practice and other forms of physical and mental preparation. Avoid informing an athlete that losing was due to low ability. Feeling "not good enough" brings on a sense of helplessness and depression. Quitting becomes the best alternative, whether or not it is justified.
- **Define success and failure broadly.** Success in sport is more than winning and losing. Even when an athlete or a team loses a contest, the individual or the entire team may have performed successfully. One's definition of failure should be restricted to specific events or unmet goals, such as missing a particular basketball free throw or failing to break a personal record in track. Every contest comprises numerous successes and failures, and even competitors with poor skills may be complimented on improvement or effort.
- **Have reasonably high expectations** of the athlete's performance. As indicated earlier in this chapter, athletes (and most people, no matter what their field of endeavor) tend to perform in accordance with what others expect of them.
- **Look for signs of FOF.** Examples include chronic complaining (the player is looking for excuses to explain anticipated failure), excessive talking, continued boasting (a cover-up for anxiety), inability to sit still (a display of nervous energy), crying (a stress-release mechanism), frequent absenteeism from practices and games, a quick temper (a sign of considerable insecurity), and the tendency to avoid taking risks during contests.
- **Avoid asking the athlete about his or her emotions**. Questions such as "Are you uptight (scared, anxious)?" tend to invite, not reduce, stress. The athlete thinks that the coach expects these types of thoughts. Or such questions further direct the athlete's attention toward such feelings.

Fear of success (FOS). Do athletes, whose prime objective in sport is to be successful, to meet personal and team goals, to improve performance, and to win contests, actually fear success? In some cases, they might. Cratty (1983, p. 125) reports that clinicians observing this fear in athletes have hypothesized that "the individuals involved simply were afraid of being the best, thus creating a situation in which others would direct their energies toward defeating them. Moreover, the success-phobic athlete may also fear winning, since spectators and fans might not be as solidly behind him or her in the future, preferring to cheer for the underdog rather than the top dog."

Two studies have explored FOS in sport situations. McElroy and Willis (1979) tested female athletes from five different sports and failed to find the FOS dimension. Silva (1982) found that male athletes had less FOS than female athletes.

Although a few elite participants may be uncomfortable with the notion of attaining and maintaining high performance standards, Orlick and Partington's (1986) interviews with sixteen Olympic and World Champion athletes failed to reveal a single incidence of fearing success. Perhaps it's the drive to succeed that truly separates winners — at least those who compete at the national and world levels — from others.

COPING

All those who participate in competitive sports must have the ability to deal with criticism, pain, losing, physical and mental errors, and other sources of stress. Elite athletes have the additional ability to quickly recover from, or ignore, these less pleasant aspects of competitive sports. Instead of maintaining a hostile, frustrated disposition, winners are capable of redirecting their energies in a productive manner. The elite competitor says, "Time to put (the unpleasant experience) behind me and go for it."

Coping with Competitive Situations

How do elite athletes prevent or cope with stress? Unlike the unskilled performer, top competitors (1) plan each aspect of their performance, whether it will occur before or during the event, and (2) have at least one alternative behavior for every planned action (Rushall 1979). An example is the basketball or ice hockey player who, after shooting, approaches the net in anticipation of a rebound. Quality players and teams calmly plan and correctly execute changes in strategy in response to an opponent who is experiencing success. There is no time for anger.

Orlick (1980, p. 187) suggests that the best way to prevent panic situations and anxiety is to begin thinking about and implementing solutions before problems get out of hand. "Ideally, you anticipate and prepare to solve problems before they arise," he says. Thus, in order to institute elaborate alternative techniques rapidly, elite competitors have planned and performed secondary or coping strategies during less demanding events such as practice or under less stressful game situations.

Coping with Pain

One very unpleasant aspect of sport competition is sustaining an injury and enduring the accompanying discomfort. Athletes differ in the degree to which they perceive pain (called *pain threshold*) and tolerate it (referred to as *pain tolerance*). These differences among participants have been studied in clinical

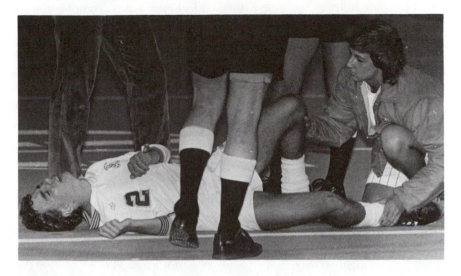

settings in an attempt to understand why some players can cope with sport-related pain better than others.

Ryan (1976) and his colleagues at the University of California at Davis studied pain threshold, the ability to detect the sensation of pain. They found no difference in the pain thresholds of three groups: athletes who engaged in contact sports, noncontact sport participants, and nonathletes. However, differences were noted in pain tolerance, the amount of pain they were willing to tolerate. Contact sport athletes tolerated the most pain, followed by noncontact athletes. Nonathletes tolerated the least amount of discomfort. The authors surmised that one's pain threshold appears to be related to one's physiological makeup, whereas pain tolerance may be more dependent on psychological and environmental factors.

How do elite athletes respond to physical discomfort? According to Rushall (1979, p. 96), "In fatiguing events, better athletes generally know at what stage they become stressed by the pain or discomfort of fatigue." The top performers follow some or all of these four steps in coping with the onset of pain:

1. They use cognitive strategies. Top athletes prepare for pain by developing self-statements and mental imagery that allow them to handle it. Examples include, "I can deal with it because of my plan to handle the pain (fatigue)," "Concentrate on my opponent," and "Focus on technique."

2. They confront and handle the pain. To overpower the feelings of discomfort, athletes use self-statements such as, "You will get through this," "Ignore my body, and concentrate on my opponent (playing assignment)," "Focus on performance efficiency," or "The pain is my cue to get psyched up."

3. Elite athletes cope with pain at critical moments. A competitor may "allow" himself or herself to feel discomfort only at certain times. For instance, players may focus on their injuries only between plays, but they may ignore those injuries when executing movements on the field or when concentrating on their opponents.

4. They use reinforcing self-statements. When the stressful activity ceases, it's time to assess the coping strategy. Questions the athlete might consider asking include: "Was it better to keep it inside?" "Should I communicate my discomfort to the coach or to a friend?" "Am I capable of using a more effective technique, or could I have used this strategy more effectively?"

Coping with Fatigue

That elite athletes are in superb physical condition is not surprising. But then, so are competitors who are not as successful. In other words, although being in top shape may be highly related to the quality of performance, it is not always the primary cause of success. The most physically fit athlete does not always finish ahead of the pack. What appears to be more important is the ability to prevent physical fatigue from significantly impeding performance.

Elite athletes tend to use one of two mental techniques in coping with pain, *association* and *dissociation.* The objective of association is to be "in touch" with one's body and to maintain the necessary effort and motivation to meet challenges and personal goals. This technique demands an internal focus. One Swedish distance runner told me that he was taught to concentrate on planting each foot with every step; this runner was attending internally to performance-induced fatigue. Elite long-distance runners, among others, consciously use an association strategy (Iso-Ahola and Hatfield 1986).

Association can backfire if the athlete is focusing internally on an injury. Sport psychologists have found that one reason why injured athletes do not return to their former performance quality despite an apparent full physical recovery (as determined by a physician) is that their attention is incorrectly aimed toward the injured area rather than on environmental factors such as teammates, opponents, and objects. Monitoring internal bodily functions may be contrary to past habits and not compatible with task demands.

Dissociation entails being mentally preoccupied with external events as opposed to internal feelings and sensations. Exercising in synchronization to music, for example, serves a dissociative function that focuses the performer's attention externally on the musical input and away from the physical responses to vigorous exercise (Anshel and Marisi 1978). This technique can also help injured players to keep discomfort from interfering with the cognitive demands of the contest.

Coping with Sport-Related Stress

Better competitors use techniques to handle stress both during and between contests. Stress in sport can be long term or short term. Chronic stress programs, those that can be implemented between and immediately preceding competitive events, include Gauron's (1986) cognitive self-regulation program. It is based on the athlete's ability to control attitudes, perceptions, thoughts, and "internal dialogue," the potential agents that may interfere with performing at optimal levels. Another program is Meichenbaum's (1985) stress inoculation training, which focuses on strategies to circumvent the unpleasant effects of stress. Describing each program goes beyond the purposes of this chapter. The COPE Model (Anshel 1986; Anshel, Gregory, and Kaczmarek, in press) describes cognitive-behavioral strategies to handle acute (immediate) forms of stress caused mainly by negative input from others, primarily coaches.

COPE is an acronym that describes four cognitive and behavioral strategies that can be used to handle unpleasant input from others. Athletes implement these techniques immediately upon receiving the undesirable input.

C = Control emotions. The immediate reaction of an athlete's mind and body upon exposure to hostile input might be to feel uptight and to be physiologically aroused. This response is known as the "fight-or-flight" reflex in the sympathetic nervous system, and the athlete feels the rush of adrenaline being pumped into the bloodstream.

Skilled competitors use one or both of these techniques to control their emotions: They (1) take a deep breath or (2) take at least partial responsibility for the actions that drew the negative input. They try not to be defensive. When considering whether they deserve such input (i.e., when making causal attributions of performance), they try to remain objective. By controlling emotions at this stage, they can remain aware of, and receptive to, any important information that will contribute to better subsequent performance.

O = Organize input. The objective here is for the athlete to deal rationally with the input. One trait of skilled performers is that they know the difference between important and unimportant or redundant information. A coach who yells, "You fool! How many times do I have to tell you not to attempt a stolen base when we're behind by more than one run?" is providing an important message: "Don't steal a base in certain situations." But the coach is also including a less constructive message when he or she uses name-calling and ridicule as part of the instructions. To maintain the proper mental and physical readiness after exposure to uncomplimentary messages, the athlete must be able to decide what is worthy of attention.

Author John Feinstein, in his best-selling book *A Season on the Brink* (1986) depicts how members of Bobby Knight's basketball team were able to cope with unpleasant input from their well-known coach.

Other Indiana players . . .knew that Knight would say almost anything when he was angry and that the only way to deal with that was to ignore the words of anger and listen to the words of wisdom. . . .When he's calling you an ———, don't listen. But when he starts telling you why you're an ———, listen. That way you'll get better.

Another approach to organizing input is to integrate all of it and then decide what has validity ("I can use this information") and what does not ("The person is angry; the message, if there is one, is inaccurate or based on the person's emotions"). Psychologist Alfred Korzybski (1933) refers to this technique as language discrimination. Although to simply ignore stimuli that serves no purpose to the listener would be nice, a more practical approach is to hear all of it and then develop skills to integrate what is desirable and quickly forget undesirable input.

P = Plan response.   At this point, the coach's hostilities are history. The last thing an athlete should do is to focus on unpleasant feelings. This prevents him or her from maintaining a state of optimal readiness for the next response. Instead, the performer must quickly begin to plan upcoming actions based on recent feedback and experiences. He or she might acknowledge certain strengths, strategies, or tendencies of the opponent or concentrate on correcting his or her own performance. At this stage, the athlete's thoughts must go from integrating information to using it.

E = Execute.   All skilled athletes move with the appropriate precision and speed almost without thinking. This is especially important after receiving negative input. An athlete who has been intimidated or upset by the discouraging remarks of others will hesitate, take fewer risks, be intimidated, and lack self-confidence in subsequent performance. The objective at this stage is to execute purposeful movements with confidence, assertiveness, arousal, and concentration.

PEAK PERFORMANCE

One aspect of competitive sport that clearly separates elite from nonelite athletes is experiencing peak performance, "a state of altered consciousness" (Ravizza 1984, p. 453). The athlete's mental state just prior to and during peak experiences is characterized by complete absorption with the task at hand. This allows for the proper internal attentional focus; that is, the necessary preoccupation with mental and physical readiness and effort. Ravizza claims that the quality of the athlete's experience is heightened in that there is a quicker and clearer focus on movement cues. This results in faster reaction and movement times in a controlled, skillful manner. Sometimes the athlete can actually anticipate the speed, direction, and timing of a stimulus. A person's peak performance does not necessarily exceed that of other persons, but rather surpasses what could be anticipated for that individual in a particular situation. However, such effects are apparently not long term.

Ravizza describes peak sport experiences as being temporary, nonvoluntary, and unique. They are temporary in that the person's altered mental state is short term. They are nonvoluntary, not susceptible to any intervention techniques; neither an athlete, a coach, nor anyone else can "make it happen." And they are certainly unique in that their occurrence is rare. Thus, achieving a championship victory, breaking a performance record, competing on a beautiful day, playing after signing a professional sports contract, and other circumstances or aspects of the sport environment that may have attended a peak experience are not prerequisites of this phenomenon. The only prerequisite to a peak experience is the athlete's mastery of the basic sport skills. There is almost an absence of thinking about executing the skill. And the feelings that accompany peak performance are quite pleasant.

Emotionally, peak performers report an extremely fulfilling and happy psycho-emotional state. Fears, insecurities, and inhibitions dissipate. Evidence has mounted in recent years that such feelings of euphoria during vigorous physical activity have a physiological basis (Morgan 1985). Some athletes refer to their experience of performing in an emotional high as "being in the flow." The concept of *flow* has been interpreted differently in various situations.

Cratty (1984) has classified flow states into four categories:

1. *Anxiety or arousal.* A flow state can be unpleasant or can affect performance negatively. For example, athletes can become so upset that they lose self-control. Getting too psyched up may also overexcite the athlete.

2. *Extremely good feelings.* Cratty refers to this state as a "positive in-performance phenomenon," in which the well-prepared athlete develops very positive feelings during most of the competitive period. The athlete is "into" the event, both mentally and physically, but tends to come out of it when an opponent takes the upper hand.

3. *Mental escaping.* Instead of feeling "in sync" with performance demands, the athlete is mentally escaping from them. This can be favorable, such as the "runner's high," in which performers can dissociate themselves from the physical demands, even pain, of prolonged, arduous physical activity. However, this form of escape can be counterproductive. Cratty argues that the athlete should be attending to the immediate task demands, and perhaps even to the pain of the performance (negative in-performance state), instead of mentally "floating." Injured athletes should not totally ignore their discomfort because they may incur further injuries.

4.   *Postcontest mental break.* Immediately after intense physical competitive activity, athletes need to take a mental break. They are usually —
and normally — unresponsive to questions from the media and tend to
just sit and stare or move very slowly and deliberately. They need to
recuperate from the physical and psychological demands of the contest, from preparation stages to the event's conclusion. Players report
a "buzzing out" or "coming down" period. This is why the immediate
postcompetition period is not the time for coaches to communicate
thought-provoking statements and analyses of the contest.

Figure 2.3 is a list of various feelings that accompany peak performance
(Garfield and Bennett 1984).

So far in this section, we've discussed the psychological components of peak
performance. But certain behaviors and feelings impede experiencing this
phenomenon, even if the athlete possesses all of the important physical characteristics. Garfield and Bennett (1984) assert that the most important factor for
experiencing peak performance is "letting go." Other phrases that describe this
feeling include "going on automatic pilot" or "playing in a trance." But they all
mean performing in the absence of calculating and thinking. Play must be
automatic, natural, and spontaneous. To let go, the athlete must relax his or her
mind and body and use mental pictures to develop concentration "by holding the
mental picture of the desired end result for a few seconds" (p. 181). And, if the
athlete wishes to succeed, the end result imaged must be a successful one.

SUMMARY

Successful athletes differ markedly from their less successful counterparts in
several ways. Despite flaws in personality research, studies have shown that
successful participants tend to be self-confident, have a high need to achieve,
maintain a relatively high self-image, at least in the sport environment, and score
low on personality inventories in trait and state anxiety, tension, depression,
mental fatigue, confusion, and anger. They often score relatively high in mental
toughness, intelligence, sociability, creativity, stability, dominance, aggression,
and extroversion. Still, personality scales should not be used to predict the level
of an athlete's future success, the type of sport for which a person is best suited,
or any other sport-related measure.

Successful athletes have unique habits that they perform before and during
the contest. Before the contest, they use the warm-up as a means to reduce tension
and anxiety; although they prefer to be alone immediately before the contest,
they prefer to have a coach present during the warm-up period; they use mental
imagery to build confidence and rehearse performance strategies; they have

Figure 2.3 Cues of peak-performance feelings

1. *Mentally relaxed.* Inner calm; time slowed; able to focus clearly on details in the present.
2. *Physically relaxed.* Muscles loose throughout body; feelings of warmth; movements fluid; body seems to respond directly and precisely to volition.
3. *Confident/optimistic.* High expectation of success; recognition of challenge and excitement in response to the idea of accepting that challenge; feelings of strength and control.
4. *Focused on the present.* Sense of harmony—that is, of body and mind working together as a unit; no thoughts of past or future; a sense of body performing automatically, without conscious or deliberate mental effort.
5. *Highly energized.* Associated with feelings of joy, ecstasy, intensity, and of feeling "charged" or "hot."
6. *Extraordinary awareness.* An acutely sharp sense of one's whole body and its movements (perceived as physical sensations rather than as thoughts or ideas); acute awareness of other players' movements, size, physical presence, and of how these players think and feel (mental impressions rather than analysis); ability to know what other players are going to do even before they do it; a sensation of being completely in harmony with one's environment.
7. *In control.* Body seems to be automatically doing exactly what you want it to do; mind seems to respond to the environment and to process all information from it in the most efficient and appropriate ways possible; no sense of exerting or imposing control, though everything is happening as you wish it to.
8. *In the cocoon.* Feelings of being in an envelope, with complete access to all of one's powers and skills; feelings of detachment from external environment, even though acutely aware of everything associated with your performance; not reacting to events that detract from the performance; a feeling of euphoric awareness and of containment of one's skills and power; a feeling of invulnerability.

alternative plans to execute during the contest if their original strategy falters; they do not worry about their opponent before the contest and instead concentrate on correct skill and strategy execution; and if their opponent is gaining the upper hand, they are capable of recovering the necessary confidence, composure, and proper skill execution to be successful, either during the same contest or in a subsequent one.

Not surprisingly, elite athletes prefer the presence of big crowds. Research and anecdotal evidence indicates that supportive spectators (e.g., the home crowd) tend to enhance the athletes' arousal and aggression to favorable levels. Performance outcomes are favorable particularly when the person's skill level is relatively high and the task complexity somewhat low. Other factors, however, can inhibit correct skill execution. The spectators' high expectations for team or player success, performing complex skills in the presence of evaluative audience members (e.g. judges or the home crowd), and/or the athlete's perception of a highly skilled opponent may hinder rather than promote sports performance. Still, a perusal of the literature related to audience effects is far from conclusive. The ability to predict performance success based on audience and situational characteristics is quite low.

Elite athletes cope better with competitive events, pain, fatigue, and sport-related stress than nonelite competitors. They understand that stress is an integral part of sport competition. Consequently, they anticipate stress and do not allow it to prevent them from performing optimally. They often invoke the use of mental strategies to cope with these stressors.

Finally, top performers experience a type of short-term mental state called *peak performance* in which the athlete is "absorbed" in the task at hand. The performer is in a state of euphoria, especially during vigorous physical effort, while fear, insecurity, and inhibition dissipate. Also referred to as an emotional high or a state of "flow," athletes in this condition experience improved anticipation, faster reaction and movement time, and a more focused attention to environmental cues.

REVIEW QUESTIONS

1. What are some of the limitations of using personality tests to identify traits of athletes and nonathletes?

2. Despite the limitations you described above, researchers have noticed a few selected personality tendencies in skilled athletes. Describe some of these traits, particularly those that seem to separate athletes from nonathletes. Would you as a coach use personality test scores? Why, or why not?

3. Why are top athletes risk-takers? How would a coach detect risk-taking and promote this trait in an athlete?

4. Elite athletes have certain habits that they conduct before the contest. Describe these habits. What purposes do they serve, both psychologically and physically?

5.   What are some of the unique tendencies of good athletes performed during the event in addition to executing the skills? What psychological and physical purposes do they serve?

6.   Throughout this chapter, reference was made to the use of cognitive (mental) strategies that are initiated in preparation for and during the contest. What general purpose do these techniques serve? Describe five of the strategies, and indicate why and when each should be used.

7.   Various factors in sport influence the behaviors of elite athletes differently than those of nonelite athletes during competition. These include the presence of an audience, the use of aggression, and the fear of failing and succeeding. Describe each of these factors, and indicate how successful athletes handle them to maximize performance either before or during the contest. How can the coach favorably influence the performer for each of these factors?

8.   Why is the ability to cope with sport-related stress important to success? How do elite athletes generally cope with stress in sport? How do they differ from their nonelite counterparts in their ability to handle fatigue, pain, competitive situations, and performance failure?

9.   If you were to describe peak performance, how would you describe it? Can peak performance be planned? Why, or why not?

REFERENCES

Alderman, R. B. 1974. *Psychological behavior in sport.* Philadelphia: Saunders.

Anshel, M. H. 1986. The COPE model: Strategies for stress inoculation in sport. Paper presented at the Association for the Advancement of Applied Sport Psychology conference, October, at Jekyll Island, Georgia.

Anshel, M. H., W. L. Gregory, and M. Kaczmarek. In press. Effectiveness of a technique for coping with criticism in sport. *Journal of Sport Behavior.*

Atkinson, J. W. 1957. Motivational determinants of risk-taking behavior. *Psychological Review* 64: 359–72.

Baumeister, R. F. 1985. Performance under pressure: A self-attention model of choking. Paper presented at the Canadian Society for Psychomotor Learning and Sport Psychology, October, in Montreal, Canada.

Bond, C. F., and L. J. Titus. 1983. Social facilitation: A metaanalysis of 241 studies. *Psychological Bulletin* 94: 265–92.

Bunker, L., and J. Williams. 1986. Building self confidence in sport. In *Applied sport psychology: Personal growth to peak performance,* ed. J. M. Williams. Palo Alto, CA: Mayfield.

Chapman, A. J. 1974. An electromyographic study of social facilitation: A test of the "mere presence" hypothesis. *British Journal of Psychology* 65: 123–28.

Cottrell, N. B. 1972. Social facilitation. In *Experimental social psychology*, ed. C. G. McClintock, pp. 432–58. New York: Holt, Rinehart & Winston.

Cox, R. H. 1985. *Sport psychology: Concepts and applications*. Dubuque, IA: Wm. C. Brown.

Cratty, B. J. 1983. *Psychology in contemporary sport: Guidelines for coaches and athletes*. 2d ed. Englewood Cliffs, NJ: Prentice-Hall.

Cratty, B. J. 1984. *Psychological preparation and athletic excellence*. Ithaca, NY: Mouvement.

Feinstein, J. 1986. *A season on the brink*. New York: Macmillan.

Fisher, A. C. 1977. Sport personality assessment: Facts, fallacies, and perspectives. *Motor Skills: Theory Into Practice* 1: 87–97.

Garfield, C. A., and H. Z. Bennett. 1984. *Peak performance: Mental training techniques of the world's greatest athletes*. Los Angeles: Jeremy P. Tarcher.

Gauron, E. F. 1986. The art of cognitive self-regulation. *Clinics in Sports Medicine* 5: 91–101.

Gould, D., M. Weiss, and R. Weinberg. 1981. Psychological characteristics of successful and nonsuccessful Big Ten wrestlers. *Journal of Sport Psychology* 3: 69–81.

Harris, D. V., and B. L. Harris. 1984. *The athlete's guide to sports psychology: Mental skills for physical people*. Champaign, IL: Human Kinetics.

Highlen, P. S., and B. B. Bennett. 1979. Psychological characteristics of successful and nonsuccessful elite wrestlers: An exploratory study. *Journal of Sport Psychology* 1: 123–37.

Horner, M. S. 1968. Sex differences in achievement motivation and performance in competitive and noncompetitive situations. Ph.D. diss., University of Michigan, Ann Arbor.

Iso-Ahola, S. E., and B. Hatfield. 1986. *Psychology of sports: A social psychological approach*. Dubuque, IA: Wm. C. Brown.

Korzybski, A. 1933. *Science and sanity*. Lancaster, PA: Lancaster Press.

Kroll, W., and K. H. Peterson. 1965. Personality factor profiles of collegiate football teams. *Research Quarterly* 36: 441–47.

Malone, C. 1985. Risk-taking in sport. In *Sport psychology: Psychological considerations in maximizing sport performance*, ed. L. K. Bunker, R. J. Rotella, and A. S. Reilly. Ithaca, NY: Mouvement.

Martens, R. 1975. *Social psychology and physical activity*. New York: Harper & Row.

McElroy, M. A., and J. D. Willis. 1979. Women and the achievement conflict in sport. *Journal of Sport Psychology* 1: 241–47.

Mechikoff, R. A., and B. Kozar. 1983. *Sport psychology: The coach's perspective.* Springfield, IL: Thomas.

Meichenbaum, D. 1985. *Stress inoculation training.* New York: Pergamon Press.

Morgan, W. P. 1979. Prediction of performance in athletics. In *Coach, athlete, and the sport psychologist,* ed. P. Klavora and J. V. Daniel, 173–86. Champaign, IL: Human Kinetics.

Morgan, W. P. 1980. Sport personology: The credulous-skeptical argument in perspective. In *Sport psychology: An analysis of athlete behavior,* ed. W. F. Straub, pp. 330–39. Ithaca, NY: Mouvement.

Morgan, W. P. 1985. Affective beneficence of vigorous physical activity. *Medicine and Science in Sports and Exercise* 17: 94–100.

Nideffer, R. M. 1979. The role of attention in optimal athletic performance. In *Coach, athlete, and the sport psychologist,* ed. P. Klavora and J. V. Daniel, pp. 99–112. Champaign, IL: Human Kinetics.

Orlick, T. 1980. *In pursuit of excellence.* Champaign, IL: Human Kinetics.

Orlick, T. 1986. *Psyching for sport: Mental training for athletes.* Champaign, IL: Human Kinetics.

Orlick, T., and J. Partington. 1986. *Psyched: Inner views of winning.* Ottawa: Coaching Association of Canada.

Paige, R. R. 1973. *What research tells the coach about football.* Reston, VA: AAHPERD Publications.

Passer, M. W. 1984. Competitive trait anxiety in children and adolescents. In *Psychological foundations of sport,* ed. by J. M. Silva and R. S. Weinberg, 130–44. Champaign, IL: Human Kinetics.

Rasch, P. J., and W. Kroll. 1964. *What research tells the coach about wrestling.* Reston, VA: AAHPERD Publications.

Ravizza, K. 1984. Peak performance. In *Psychological foundations of sport,* ed. by J. M. Silva and R. S. Weinberg, pp. 452–461. Champaign, IL: Human Kinetics.

Reilly, T. 1979. *What research tells the coach about soccer.* Reston, VA: AAHPERD Publications.

Rotella, R. J., and S. R. Heyman. 1986. Stress, injury, and the psychological rehabilitation of athletes. In *Applied sport psychology: Personal growth to peak performance,* ed. by J.M. Williams, pp. 343–64. Palo Alto, CA: Mayfield.

Rushall, B. S. 1976. Three studies relating personality variables to football performance. In *Psychology of sport*, ed. A. C. Fisher, pp. 391–99. Palo Alto, CA: Mayfield.

Rushall, B. S. 1979. *Psyching in sport*. London: Pelham.

Rushall, B. S. 1984. The content of competition thinking. In *Cognitive sport psychology*, ed. W. F. Straub and J. M. Williams, pp. 51–62. Lansing, NY: Sport Science Associates.

Rushall, B. S. 1986. On-site intervention techniques for athlete preparation. Paper presented at the Association for the Advancement of Applied Sport Psychology conference, October, at Jekyll Island, Georgia.

Ryan, E. D. 1976. Perceptual characteristics of vigorous people. In *Psychology of sport*, ed. by A. C. Fisher, pp. 432–46. Palo Alto, CA: Mayfield.

Silva, J. M. 1982. An evaluation of fear of success in female and male athletes and nonathletes. *Journal of Sport Psychology* 4: 92–96.

Singer, R. N. 1972. *Coaching, athletics, and psychology*. New York: McGraw-Hill.

Singer, R. N. 1980. *Motor learning and human performance*. 3d ed. New York: Macmillan.

Smith, R. E. 1984. Theoretical and treatment approaches to anxiety reduction. In *Psychological foundations of sport*, ed. by J. M. Silva and R. S. Weinberg, pp. 157–70. Champaign, IL: Human Kinetics.

Swartz, B., and S. F. Barsky. 1977. The home advantage. *Social Forces* 55: 641–61.

Vanek, M., and B. J. Cratty. 1970. *Psychology and the superior athlete*. New York: Macmillan.

Waitley, D. 1978. *The psychology of winning*. Chicago: Human Resources Co.

Williams, J. M. 1980. Personality characteristics of the successful female athlete. In *Sport psychology: An analysis of athlete behavior*, pp. 353–59. Ithaca, NY: Mouvement.

Zajonc, R. B. 1965. Social facilitation. *Science* 149: 269–74.

Zajonc, R. B. 1972. Compresence. Paper presented at the Midwestern Psychological Association Conference, Chicago.

3

Regulating Anxiety and Arousal

Emotions are an integral part of being a competitive athlete. Of constant concern to participants (and to coaches) is reaching and maintaining the proper emotional state that will allow them to perform at their potential. To reach this objective, they must regulate two emotions that play primary roles in performance — anxiety and arousal. After reading this chapter, you should be able to understand state and trait anxiety, how anxiety differs from arousal, the underlying causes of these mental states, and what coaches should and should not do to promote or to reduce the anxiety and arousal of team members.

Given the importance of anxiety and arousal in sport, it is ironic that coaches, athletes, and even sport scientists understand relatively little about them. Perhaps this is why coaches use such a diversity of methods in their attempts to "psych up" without "psyching out" their players. For example, coaches disagree on the effectiveness of a forceful pregame talk, even in sports that demand a high level of energy and aggression. Many leaders foster an exciting atmosphere before the contest, but others use a low-key approach.

For example, veteran National Football League head coach Ron Meyer claims that "there was a lot of emotion at the Alamo, and nobody survived." Walter Alston, the late and very successful manager of the Los Angeles Dodgers baseball team, has suggested that the athlete's "ideal" emotional status and the coach's actions to help the individual reach it are often dependent on the sport.

According to Alston, "A football coach has to fire up his players. Football is that kind of sport. That's why an emotional fellow like Vince Lombardi was such a great coach. Baseball's another kind of sport. You can only play baseball relaxed. You have to stay loose and keep your hands soft. . . .The best way to play this game is low key. If the manager is low key, the players will relax."

Should coaches psych up their teams with excitement and tension? Or should they aim for a more relaxed and subdued mental set? What are the purposes — and validity — of some of the more common pregame techniques that coaches use to mentally prepare their players? Should a pregame talk be given? What should be its purpose, and what type of information should be included? What is the coach's role in fostering an appropriate emotional state for each player, and when should these strategies be implemented? The purpose of this chapter is to examine the two most common and important emotions related to sport success and failure, anxiety and arousal. In particular, we will (1) examine the underlying causes of anxiety and arousal, beginning with the premise that they are not the same thing, and (2) suggest using strategies that will regulate (increase and decrease) and maintain the "proper" level of each of these emotional states.

ANXIETY AND AROUSAL IN SPORT

Understandably, the terms *anxiety* and *arousal* have been used interchangeably by writers, both in the media and the scientific literature. However, in more recent years, sport psychologists and researchers have recognized that anxiety and arousal are not synonymous. They are measured differently and, in fact, require different techniques to regulate them. An example of the problem in understanding these terms is seen in two relatively recent sport psychology textbooks. Iso-Ahola and Hatfield (1986, p. 193–94) take "a multidimensional view of anxiety," asserting that it has "both a physiological and a psychological basis." Although Bird and Cripe (1986) agree that anxiety has a physiological response, they view it as an emotion that is neither defined, determined, nor measured physiologically. Iso-Ahola and Hatfield use the term *anxiety* in virtually the same context that Bird and Cripe use the term *arousal*.

Traditionally, arousal has been interpreted and measured strictly as a physiological process on a continuum ranging from sleep to high excitation (Duffy 1957). Even in current literature, arousal is often determined by changes in heart and respiration rate, extent of sweating, and other physiological measures. However, Oxendine (1970) and Anshel (1985) contend that arousal has an emotional component. Positive feelings (such as excitement, happiness, and anticipation) or negative feelings (such as fear, embarrassment, and depression) form an affective component of arousal. Such emotions may or may not correlate highly with physiological responses. The typical ways of measuring emotional arousal are with paper-and-pencil inventories or interviews.

For the purposes of this book, and compatible with recent literature, *anxiety* is defined as an emotion—in two words, perceived threat. A person who is worried about an upcoming exam and consequently has trouble sleeping is anxious. In sport, anxiety reflects the performer's feelings that something may go wrong, that the outcome may not be successful, or that performance failure may be experienced. Perhaps the performer views an opponent as superior or knows that a member of the audience — a judge, family member, friend, team-mate, or the coach — is evaluating the quality of the individual's performance. This can be threatening, particularly for individuals with relatively low self-confidence, low self-esteem, or a lack of previous success. Such individuals are sometimes referred to as "practice players" or "chokers." They have a tendency to "freeze up" and to perform more poorly during the contest than in practice. They rarely experience their performance potential. This is not to say that anxiety is always undesirable. To succeed in sport, athletes must be aware of potentially threatening situations. Upsets are often caused by an underexcited, less-than-optimally ready team that was favored to win but "forgot" that the opponents wanted to win, too. Anxiety levels must be controlled, not eliminated.

Whereas anxiety is defined as an emotion in this text, arousal, on the other hand, can be either physiologically or psychologically based. The key issues concerning arousal for coaches and athletes are (1) determining the level of arousal that is optimal in a given situation to establish the point of diminishing returns and (2) learning the proper techniques for controlling it. When it comes to feelings of excitation in sport, more is not always better. Let's look at anxiety and arousal more extensively.

Anxiety

Spielberger (1972) was probably the first to categorize anxiety as either a state or a trait. *State anxiety* (A-state) is transitory in that it fluctuates over time. Martens (1977) defines competitive state anxiety as conscious feelings of apprehension and tension due mainly to the individual's perception of the present or upcoming situation as threatening. Often, though not always, anxiety is accompanied by activation of the autonomic nervous system, which is why it is confused with arousal.

Trait anxiety (A-trait), on the other hand, is a relatively stable and acquired behavioral disposition, often depicted as a personality trait. A-trait predisposes an individual to perceive a wide range of nondangerous circumstances as threatening or dangerous. Further, the individual with high A-trait tends to demonstrate A-state reactions beyond what is necessary, given the present sense of danger. Thus, high A-trait athletes will likely become more anxious before a competitive event than low A-trait performers.

It was widely reported in the sports media in the 1960s that Glenn Hall, a standout goalie for the Chicago Blackhawks hockey team, would be sick to his stomach before every game in which he started (so much for the value of a proper pregame meal). Hall's problem is an example of why high A-state is not desirable. In addition to negative emotional and physiological ramifications, anxiety has also been shown to have a deleterious effect on motor performance. Weinberg and Hunt (1976) have shown, through electromyography, that muscular coordination in skilled movements decreases with high A-state.

Figure 3.1   How state and trait anxiety are related

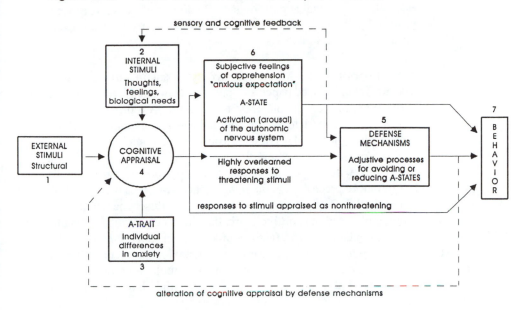

From "Theory and research on anxiety," in *Anxiety and Behavior,* ed. C. D. Spielberger, p. 17.
New York: Academic Press, 1966. Reprinted with permission.

In summary, athletes with high A-state react to a present situation at a given intensity while high A-trait individuals have an underlying tendency to react in a certain way when confronted with sufficiently stressful information. Trait and state anxiety are highly correlated (Hall and Purvis 1980). The A-trait affects an individual's appraisal of the situation, increasing the likelihood that the person will view the situation as threatening and experience an anxiety state. (See Figure 3.1.)

As indicated in Figure 3.1, the individual takes in external stimuli that are perceived as unpleasant or potentially threatening (box 1). This input, along with the person's internal psychological and biological signals (box 2) and his or her personal disposition toward anxiety (box 3), results in an appraisal of the situation on the extent to which it is threatening (box 4). After the appraisal, the individual makes mental and physical adjustments to eliminate, reduce, or prevent the onset of state anxiety (box 5). Relaxation techniques, imagery, positive self-statements, and physical removal from the immediate environment are examples of such adjustments, which are collectively referred to as *defense mechanisms*. Often these techniques are mastered over a long time period. Then they can be initiated very quickly and automatically. These defense mechanisms, combined with the resultant level of A-state (box 6), jointly affect the person's behavior or performance (box 7).

In sport, coaches and athletes want to regulate A-state at manageable levels so that it helps rather than hinders performance. To do this effectively, anxiety has to be measured and monitored. This is done primarily by psychological, physiological, and behavioral methods.

Psychological techniques. Measuring anxiety in this manner is usually accomplished with a standardized paper-and-pencil questionnaire. Several have been published. With one exception, they all measure A-trait, not A-state, anxiety, and few were created for sport populations. For example, Taylor's (1953) Manifest Anxiety Scale (MAS) is used to ascertain chronic (trait) anxiety. However, it does not adequately predict differences between high- and low-anxious persons with respect to learning and performing sports skills (Martens 1971). A more precise measure of A-trait and A-state is the State-Trait Anxiety Inventory (STAI) (Spielberger, Gorsuch, and Luschene 1970). Although still commonly used in sport literature, the STAI's one limitation is that it does not address the thoughts and feelings of athletes in sport situations.

Martens (1977) points out that measures of trait anxiety predict heightened anxiety only in specific types of stress situations (a school classroom versus a sport situation, for example). This means that a person might have a disposition to feel anxious before school exams but not necessarily in sport-related situations — or vice versa. Yet, the person's subjective feelings about how he or she views the competitive situation are the single most important issue in measuring and in experiencing anxiety. The MAS and the STAI do not appear to be valid measures of anxiety as it occurs in sport situations.

To counter these limitations, Martens (1977) published the Sport Competition Anxiety Test (SCAT) as a measure of A-trait, with adult and child versions. SCAT has been used extensively in contemporary sport psychology research. The Competitive State Anxiety Inventory (CSAI) was subsequently created (Martens, Burton, Rivkin, and Simon 1980) to determine a person's A-state. See Anshel (1987) for descriptions and sources for these and other psychological measures of anxiety.

Physiological techniques. Anxiety is not usually measured physiologically because there is no single physiological response to the anxiety state (Sonstroem 1984). For example, the relationship (correlation) between any two measures that are typical physiological measures of anxiety (heart rate and palm sweating, for instance) is quite low, about .10. In addition, the nervous system response to anxiety differs among individuals. While some persons sweat profusely when nervous, others don't at all. The final argument against using physiological measures of anxiety centers, in recent years, on the attempt by scientists to separate emotional from physiological responses to stress. An individual may experience feelings of stress without experiencing the harmful physiological effects often associated with stress. Anxiety, then, is now viewed as a mental state based on feelings about a situation. The person's heart rate, blood pressure, or other physiological measures might not necessarily be affected. Nevertheless, if a coach wanted to help an athlete reduce unwanted heightened anxiety or to determine whether certain techniques were helping, one approach would be to measure changes in one or more physiological signs of emotion such as heart rate, sweating, breathing rate, or others.

Behavioral techniques. We all tend to act somewhat differently in response to a stressful situation. Twitching; pacing; urinating frequently; talking a lot, sometimes in a loud, obnoxious manner; and exhibiting an unfriendly temperament are behavioral examples of anxiety. A coach may suspect that a player is anxious when that athlete's actions are unlike his or her usual behavioral patterns. This measure, however, is subjective and therefore questionable. Martens, Gill, Simon, and Scanlon (1975) have shown that SCAT, a psychological measure of anxiety, is a better predictor of competitive anxiety in athletes than the coaches' observations. More recent research has confirmed this finding.

Still uncertain is the ability of any single means to accurately measure anxiety, particularly in a given situation. Endler (1977) suggests that it may be necessary to isolate the components of each situation that causes an individual to feel anxious. Supporting this recommendation, Deshaires (1980) found that volleyball players who scored similarly on A-state differed significantly in their perceptions of the importance of the sport situation and in the uncertainty of the game's outcome. Another factor that decreases the predictability of anxiety measures is the athlete's ability to adapt to potentially anxiety-producing situations in sport. Identifying anxiety level and predicting performance based on a single measure apparently has its limitations. In fact, some psychologists contend that merely labeling a person's feelings or behaviors as "anxious" might actually provoke and reinforce their occurrence. In sport, this might further erode performance quality.

Arousal

As indicated earlier, whereas anxiety has a psychological basis, arousal has been more often defined physiologically as the intensity of behavior on a continuum from sleep to extensive excitement. *Arousal*, often synonymous in the literature with the terms *drive, activation, readiness,* or *excitation*, is a requisite for optimal sports performance. Reacting, thinking, and moving in sport at efficient speeds can be achieved only if the performer has established an appropriate level of physical and psychological readiness. The intensity of this readiness, or arousal, has been measured by skin conductance (sweating on the palm or fingertips), muscle tension, brain waves, pulse or respiration rate, and blood pressure (Duffy 1957).

Earlier, we discussed briefly that arousal has an emotional component. Oxendine (1970) was perhaps the first to note the importance of positive and negative feelings associated with being physiologically psyched up. Examples of positive affective arousal include joy, elation, ecstasy, interest, happiness, and love. Negative emotions include fear, anger, anxiety, jealousy, embarrassment, disgust, boredom, or rage. Anshel (1985) developed the Children's Arousal Scale in which female gymnasts, aged nine to fourteen years, identified adjectives that described positive and negative feelings of arousal. Positive terms included happy, relaxed, excited, and eager, while negative feelings were scared, worried, sad, upset, nervous, and frightened.

Research on measuring emotional arousal has been scarce. However, Oxendine (1970), based on his observations and interactions with competitors, has intuitively speculated about the level of arousal that is optimal for various sports and sport tasks (see Table 3.1). Evidently, sports tasks that require more relaxed, fine motor skills (such as golf putting or bowling) need markedly less arousal than relatively more powerful, gross motor behaviors (such as football blocking or sprinting).

Table 3.1   Optimal arousal level for some typical sports skills

Level of arousal	Sports skills
#5 (extremely excited)	football blocking and tackling performance on the Rogers PFI test running (220 yards to 440 yards) sit up, push up, or bent arm hang test weight lifting
#4	running long jump running very short and long races shot put swimming races wrestling and judo
#3	basketball skills boxing high jumping most gymnastic skills soccer skills
#2	baseball pitchers and batters fancy dives fencing football quarterback tennis

(continued)

Level of arousal	Sports skills
#1 (slight arousal)	archery and bowling basketball free throw field goal kicking golf putting and short irons skating figure eights
#0 (normal state)	

From J. Oxendine, "Emotional Arousal and Motor Performance," *Quest* 13 (1970): 23–30. Reprinted with permission.

Several theories have been developed over the years to partially explain the relationship between arousal and sport performance.

Drive theory. Hull's (1943) drive theory, later revised by Spence (1956), was the first (see Figure 3.2). According to this theory, performance is dependent on two factors, drive (D) and habit strength (H), illustrated by the formula $P = D \times H$. To Hull, *drive* is a general, nonspecific activation of all behavior. *Habit strength* is the dominance of correct and incorrect responses in motor perfor-

Figure 3.2   Hull's drive theory in which the probability of a dominant response—correct or incorrect—increases with higher arousal level

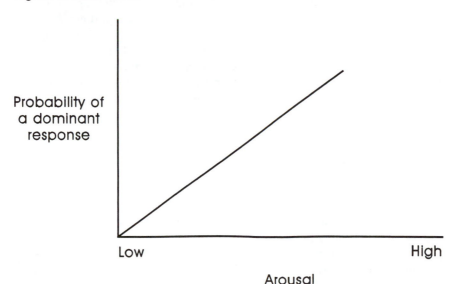

Figure 3.3   Inverted-U hypothesis illustrating optimal arousal level for golf putting and baseball batting

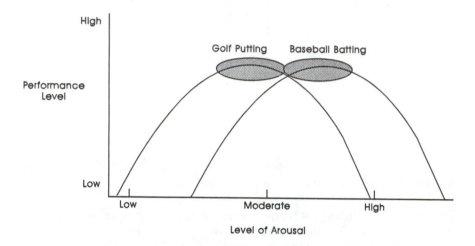

mance. The theory predicts that arousal increases the dominant response, whether or not the dominant response is the correct one. Thus, if the dominant response is correct, as in well-learned or simple skills, then higher arousal will result in better performance. If, however, the proper response has not been mastered or if the performed skill is relatively complex, then more arousal will elicit the incorrect response; quality performance will be inhibited.

This "more is better" approach to explaining the drive/motor performance relationship has been proven neither in research nor in the sport environment. Sport skills are typically very complex. The rapid actions and responses of gymnasts, divers, figure skaters, goaltenders in soccer and hockey, and skiers, to name a few, take hundreds of hours of practice, conditioning, and learning. Sports that demand less arousal (such as golf, archery, and bowling) also require extreme precision for success. The various positions and demands within each of these sports require different levels of arousal. Perhaps the behavior of a defensive lineman in football or of a weight lifter might support the drive theory. But invariably, arousal must be controlled if sport skills are to be performed with optimal efficiency.

Inverted-U hypothesis. In contrast to the direct relationship between arousal and the dominant response as seen in Hull's drive theory, the inverted-U hypothesis, also called the Yerkes-Dodson law (1908), assumes a curvilinear relationship between arousal and performance (see Figure 3.3). Thus, the effect of arousal on performance is based on the optimal level given the particular skill. Remember that "optimal" does not necessarily mean "maximal." For instance, golf putting requires far less arousal than baseball batting, but each has its own arousal requirement for optimal performance. Not only is this optimal level defined differently for each skill, but for each performer's needs and the particular situation as well.

Frank Shorter, 1976 Olympic gold medal winner in the twenty-six-mile marathon, claims that an important key to success in distance running is total relaxation prior to the race. The runner doesn't want to burn up calories needlessly. And an athlete who is relatively unskilled or younger likely needs to feel less excited than his or her more mature counterpart.

The arousal/performance relationship. One cause of poorer performance when arousal is too high is psychological. Individuals with either high arousal or anxiety tend to exclude too much information when performing. An overly excited quarterback or soccer player may not use all of the information available in scanning the field before making a decision about passing the ball. An inaccurate judgment could result. This is referred to as an overnarrowing of attention (Landers 1980). Narrowed attention is often a good strategy, of course, in skills in which the performer initiates the response, such as in golf, archery, or bowling. Here, filtering out extraneous or unimportant input is desirable. But in skills that demand reacting to opponents and making decisions about movement direction, speed, and strategy, narrowed attention tends to hinder performance.

Another factor that interacts with the athlete's arousal is precompetitive trait and state anxiety. Athletes who have high A-trait also have relatively higher A-state (Iso-Ahola and Hatfield 1986). This combination can raise arousal levels beyond desirable limits. From their review of related literature, the authors concluded that (1) both high and low trait-anxious athletes need similarly moderate elevations of A-state prior to competition, but that (2) high A-trait athletes might need higher arousal to perform at their best as compared to low A-trait athletes. This is apparently because high-anxious athletes are usually at a chronically higher level of arousal in all conditions, as illustrated in Figure 3.4. High arousal may not be desirable for child athletes, however. Gould (1984) concluded that child (or relatively low-skilled) athletes are less able to control their anxiety and, consequently, are more apt to be overly aroused. High trait-anxious children do not cope well with high state anxiety and perform less well because of it. Further, youngsters who become easily threatened in evaluative situations — in which someone of "importance" is assessing their performance — or who are high trait-anxious may choose not to participate in the activities (Simon and Martens 1979). One possible reason for the tendency to drop out is the finding that high trait-anxious athletes in general do not often use efficient strategies for coping with stress. Consequently, (1) they are unable to regulate and maintain proper anxiety and arousal levels, and (2) they tend to "choke" in high-pressure sport situations and to perform better in practice — where the pressure is relatively low — and less effectively in games.

Figure 3.4   High trait-anxious athletes tend to perform best at a relatively higher arousal level than low-anxious athletes

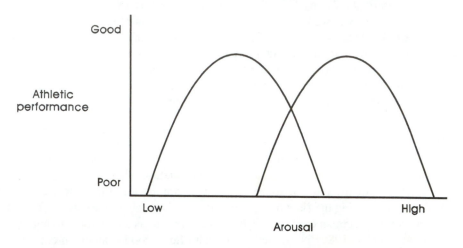

Poorer performance from high arousal is also dependent on muscular tension. Weinberg and Hunt (1976), in a study mentioned earlier, assessed the coordination of neuromuscular activity in high and low trait-anxious subjects when performing an overarm target throw. They created psychological stress in all participants by informing them that their performance was below average based on bogus (fake) information feedback. Using electromyography, they found that the high-anxious group lacked timing and coordination in the muscle groups used for throwing. This is a rare study in that it actually cites lack of neuromuscular coordination as a cause of poorer performance with anxiety or arousal. This explains why muscular relaxation is an effective technique to reduce tension when used prior to performance.

Determining optimal arousal.   What is the "best" arousal level for a particular situation or for a given individual athlete? How can the appropriate or customary level of arousal be ascertained? Generalizations are rarely valid for all participants. To individualize the prescription and treatment for optimal arousal for each competitor would be desirable. According to Klavora (1979), who has studied this problem, an athlete's customary performance quality is associated with his or her customary arousal level.

Klavora suggests that the player's current (state) arousal level immediately prior to and during the contest should be compared with his or her subsequent performance. Then, after the contest, the team leader should determine whether changing the arousal level before or during future contests is desirable.

To test this strategy, Klavora examined senior high school basketball players, comparing their pregame arousal with the quality of their game performance. The participants completed the STAI (Spielberger et al. 1970) just before the game. After the game, the coach evaluated each player's performance on a three-point scale indicating 1 (poor or below performance ability), 2 (average or close to performance ability), or 3 (an outstanding performance). The pairings of pregame arousal and game performance for each athlete were plotted. Examples of two players are illustrated in Figure 3.5.

From these data, Klavora concluded that:

- The two curves conformed to the inverted-U model of the arousal-sport performance relationship. This indicated that the players may have performed poorly or at least below their capability, owing either to a lack of psychological readiness or because of overexcitation.

- The curves are positioned at different levels "indicating that Player 2 is generally a more excitable person than is Player 1" (p. 160).

- Both players have to be psyched up if they are to perform according to the coach's expectations. Marked differences in the arousal levels of the players exist initially. But both need a motivational "boost" prior to the game.

One concern about Klavora's study was the method by which arousal was measured. The State-Trait Anxiety Inventory (STAI), measures anxiety, not arousal. Contemporary scientists now acknowledge that anxiety and arousal are not the same (Anshel 1985). Further, his assessment of arousal was not corroborated with physiological measures such as heart or respiration rate, blood pressure, galvanic skin response (a measure of sweating), or other available measures as suggested by Martens (1977). Since arousal has been traditionally measured as a physiological response (Duffy 1957), it might be argued that the players in Klavora's study felt some other unpleasant emotion such as anxiety (perceived threat) rather than more positive feelings such as excitement or happiness. Nevertheless, Klavora addresses not only an area in need of further research but also an area that has direct application in determining the athlete's optimal arousal level, an issue that has received far more theoretical than applied study.

One possible approach to determining optimal arousal, the difference between feeling "up" as opposed to feeling "uptight," is to pose questions that help the performer to identify certain feelings. Athletes can use these questions (1) to self-monitor feelings and physiological responses prior to and during competition, (2) to accurately identify their feelings, and (3) to remind them to use appropriate physical and mental strategies that can favorably affect mental status. Counseling sport psychologists typically ask athletes to identify the time or game in which they felt they performed at their best and their worst, to describe these performances as accurately as possible, and to describe their feelings and mental attitudes during this time. Specific questions include: "What were you thinking about during this event, if anything?" "Was your concentration easily

Figure 3.5   Raw score profile of two basketball players showing pregame arousal-game performance relationship

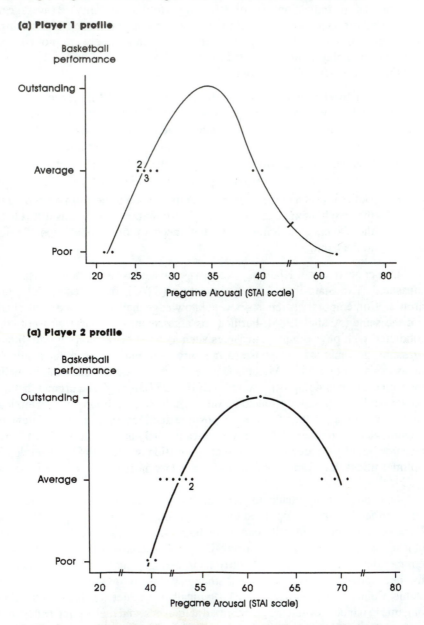

From P. Klavora, "Customary arousal for peak athletic performance," in *Coach, Athlete, and the Sport Psychologist*, ed. P. Klavora and J. V. Daniel, pp. 155–63. Published by the School of Physical and Health Education, University of Toronto, 1979. Reproduced with permission.

attained, or did you have to work hard to concentrate?" "Were you relaxed or tense, and why?" "Describe your focus of awareness; to what were you directing your attention?" Based on an athlete's responses to these questions, coaches or consulting psychologists suggest mental strategies that the performer can use to alter levels of arousal and anxiety to improve his or her mental preparation for competition. The counselor's objectives in asking these questions are to identify the feelings associated with desirable and undesirable performance and to recall the athlete's perceptions of his or her physiological responses at the time of competition.

THE COACH'S ROLE IN GAME PREPARATION

The team leader cannot reach into the heart and mind of each athlete and cause the performer to feel a certain way. Each player has a different mental approach to the contest; and to affect every athlete in the same manner is impossible. This, by the way, is the problem with the so-called "T-E-A-M" approach, which many coaches support. In this strategy, everyone on the team goes through the same mental and physical preparation before the contest. My own experiences with athletes and the sport psychology literature do not support this approach. Athletes, particularly at the more advanced levels, prefer to prepare mentally for the contest in their own way; some players would rather be alone, while others prefer the company of their teammates, for instance. Let's look at some general suggestions that coaches can use in group settings and with individual athletes to help them to manage arousal and anxiety.

Anxiety and Arousal Reducers

Sometimes coaches must help their players to "psych down." Although arousal and anxiety are not identical and often warrant different techniques, several approaches to reducing both mental states can be used.

1.   *Release stress through physical activity.* Precontest emotions are often stressful. Stress is the body's way of preparing for "flight or fight." The athlete is in a physical state that urges him or her to move, yet the athlete remains sedentary. Brisk movement, with accompanying increases in physiological arousal, may relax the athlete because psychological, thought-induced stress is converted to physical stress. This stress-reducing technique is particularly effective with high state-anxious athletes (Morgan 1979). Low-arousal sports such as golf, fencing, or tennis usually require less intense physical activity (walking, for instance) to relax the performer than high-energy activities such as soccer, wrestling, and football.

2.   *Avoid giving the "relax" command.* Coaches commonly tell their

players to relax, especially just before the contest. Sometimes this actually increases tension. "The coach knows I'm uptight," the athlete thinks. Or, athletes may need to feel a degree of tension as preparation for a superior performance, and the coach's request to take it easy may be contradictory to the player's preferred mental state. For the coach to say nothing may be more helpful than using verbal messages that try to alter the player's state of mind.

A warning about this technique seems warranted. Some debate as to the overuse of physical activity during warm-up has occurred. Often, teams seem to exert a game's worth of energy before the contest even begins. There is support in the physiology literature — although more research is needed — that an intensely physical and emotional pregame warm-up might do more harm than good by "zapping" players' energy.

3.   *Promote task familiarity.* Tasks that are familiar to athletes are less anxiety-provoking than novel actions. This is why effective coaches have the players follow a regimented and familiar pregame warm-up routine. On the day of the contest, athletes should engage in activities that are comfortable and in relaxed company. The potential for anxiety is heightened when athletes are less familiar with the schedule, planned activities, and surroundings on the day of a contest. Of course, the activities of game day differ from other days. But coaches can decrease the athletes' nervousness derived from this different schedule by conducting game day rehearsals. Activities and schedules should simulate the anticipated routine, including the times of day that meals are consumed, the same opportunities for practice, and similar weather conditions as the actual contest.

4.   *Simulate games in practice.* Athlete anxiety will be reduced if skills and strategies that will be used in the contest are rehearsed in practice sessions until they are mastered. During the game is not the time to teach new skills.

5.   *Individualize mental strategies.* Athletes differ markedly in the ways that they prepare for competition. Some players prefer a sedate atmosphere that allows for self-reflection, mental imagery, and relaxation. Others desire a more vocal, exciting locker-room atmosphere. The key coaching strategy here is to allow each player to mentally prepare for the contest in the way that he or she finds most comfortable.

6.   *Build self-confidence.* Anxiety is heightened by insecurity, low self-esteem, and the player's perception of the sport situation as threatening. Coaches can increase player confidence not with trite comments ("You'll do fine" or "Go after 'em"), but rather with messages that are based on performance and are informative. Reviewing a player's strengths and areas for further improvement, and articulating the coach's confidence in the player's skill and effort will promote positive thoughts and reduce negative ones.

7.   *Keep errors in perspective.* Physical mistakes are an integral part of the human organism. The coach's response to mistakes directly affects the athlete's stress level. Keeping an error in perspective means: (a) remembering that the error is unlikely to affect the contest's outcome directly, (b) keeping the

player focused on present and future events and, for the moment, forgetful of past mistakes, and (c) helping the athlete to cope with the error so as to avoid negative self-statements, decreased self-confidence, and underexcitement.

8.   *Avoid discussing the team's record.* Thinking about records and outcomes tends to decrease concentration and to increase anxiety. Reviewing the team's losing record or the pressures of maintaining a winning record are counterproductive. The best advice is to concentrate on performance, not outcome, and to let winning take care of itself.

9.   *Respond to an injury.* Coaches should be calm, yet attentive, to the athlete after an injury. In addition to the present pain, injured players must deal with their fear of surgery and with their fear that the injury will end their season or career. The coach's (or athletic trainer's) response to the player's injury will significantly affect the athlete's anxiety level. A supportive, empathetic coach will relax the player, whereas an angry, disappointed coach who ignores the player, even during the rehabilitation period, induces guilt, anxiety, and resentment.

Former successful cross-country and track head coach Dick Abbott, at Western Illinois University, considered it part of his job to "supplement the medical first aid that the training room provided with his own brand of emotional first aid." After the athlete received proper training-room attention, Abbott would step in with concern and reassurance that the injury would heal on schedule. Then he would consult with the athlete on almost a daily basis (Mechikoff and Kozar 1983, p. 82).

10.   *Stop self-focusing.* Carver and Scheier (1981) suggest that persons who feel anxious and have unfavorable expectations about an outcome should not focus internally on these thoughts. Negative thinking tends to exacerbate anxiety and to disrupt future performance. Sometimes such thinking leads to the individual completely disengaging from further activity. Instead, the uptight individual should think about external events — on tasks that need completion. On the other hand, persons who are confident and expect favorable outcomes should focus on their thoughts. These individuals are likely to persist longer on the task.

Precontest Arousal Raisers

Athletes cannot be effective if they're half-asleep or uninterested in competing. Their reactions will be slowed, and their coordination reduced. The nervous system has to be in an optimal state of readiness. Sometimes the coach must bring the team "up" to ensure proper effort and concentration. This is more difficult than most people realize. Here are a few guidelines.

First, the coach must consider each player's skill level, age, psychological needs, playing position, and task. Younger players, for instance, require less psyching up than older, more skilled participants. Less skillful players should focus on form, concentration, and planned maneuvers; high levels of activation, therefore, are more likely to disrupt their performance (Fisher and Motta 1977).

Further, the ability to control emotions improves with age. Hence, younger athletes may become more anxious when they are scolded or exposed to the pressures of winning the contest than their older counterparts, who can keep these pressures and expectations in better perspective.

A second important feature of increasing arousal is acknowledging that some positions and tasks require higher levels of activation than others. As Oxendine (1970) suggests, sports that involve gross motor movement can use higher activation levels than tasks that are highly complex in nature (see Table 3.1 to determine arousal categories for different sport tasks). Defensive linemen in football should be more psyched up than running backs, for instance.

Successful coaches correctly recommend that knowing the needs of individual athletes is a crucial factor for increasing arousal. Many coaches tend to initiate team strategies for mental preparation without realizing that athletes differ as to their psychological needs before the contest. Some athletes need to be psyched up before the contest more than others. The coach's role is to determine each player's optimal arousal level and to help him or her to reach it.

How? Cratty (1983) and Fisher and Motta (1977) recommend that coaches conduct personal interviews with their players to ascertain each person's goals, needs, and expectations of the coaching staff, and also to establish what, specifically, the coach can do to promote the proper precontest arousal level. The coach might decide to assign lockers based on where players can take advantage of the type of atmosphere they desire before the contest. But the most important factor is acknowledging that players differ as to their need for precontest hype.

And timing is everything. For example, it is not a good idea, contrary to popular practice, to get the team excited the night before a game. This would only disturb sleep and concentration. The late Woody Hayes, former football coach at Ohio State University, disagrees with coaches who have their athletes view commercial films that are high in aggression the night before a football game. Visual aids, however, can be effective motivational tools. One visual aid that can be shown at some point before a game, at least in some sports, is the film of last year's contest. Former college football coach and athletic director Dick Tamburo suggests, "If you are going to face a team at the end of the week that humiliated the team the year before, you may want to show the film of last year's humiliating defeat prior to the start of the game." Some coaches would prefer to forget the past, but Tamburo's suggestion might have some merit if the present players are confident and want to prove that they are a better, improved team.

To increase precontest arousal, coaches want to instill a sense of self-confidence in each player. Athletes have a greater need to be reminded of their good qualities than many coaches acknowledge. Feelings of reassurance, reduced anxiety, and expectations for success are essential for positive outcomes. To remind athletes of their past successes is important. Examples include "Based on how I saw you perform in practice this week, I know you're ready" or "This is a better team than our opponents. Think about what you can do well, and be proud of it. Let's prove we're the better team."

Finally, although arousal has an emotional component, certain techniques are used to increase the athlete's physiological arousal level. An aroused athlete experiences an increased rate or intensity of physiological processes such as heart rate, sweating, respiration rate, muscular tension, and brain wave activity. Of course, measuring any of these processes prior to a contest is neither necessary nor desirable. But coaches can institute certain techniques that predictably increase their players' physiological arousal. Examples include (1) increasing voice intensity, (2) using bright indoor lighting, (3) generating loud noises such as clapping, foot-stomping, or fast-paced music, (4) using nonverbal cues such as hand or facial gestures, especially in close proximity to the athlete, (5) contacting the athletes physically, such as holding a player's arm or shoulder (but be careful; abusive physical contact raises anxiety to the detriment of performance), (6) using the players' first names, especially when providing verbal recognition for quality performance, (7) setting immediate performance goals, (8) introducing the players—at least the starting lineup—to the crowd before the contest, and (9) having players engage in physical exercise, which is customary during the precontest warm-up.

If you think that this list of arousal-raisers is too much for one coach to do, you're absolutely right. Often, teams include a leadership role for people called assistant coaches. Less effective head coaches appear to forget that coaching assistants can have a valuable role in regulating the athletes' emotions before and during the contest. Payton Jordan, head coach of the 1968 U.S. Olympic track team, asserts, "If athletes hear you (the head coach) all the time, they will shut you out after a while." My own experience as a sport psychology team consultant supports this view. With time, the content of the head coach's message loses meaning; athletes "tune out" the person who is constantly offering verbal input. And assistant coaches typically establish positive relationships with players. Head coaches would be wise to allow assistants to take over some leadership responsibilities, at least occasionally.

COACHING STRATEGIES FOR HALFTIME AND TIME-OUTS

Halftime is a period during which adjusting, regrouping, reviewing plans and strategies, relaxing, and exchanging information occurs. Athletes should be allowed to remain quiet and "come down" from their first-half efforts and to mentally prepare for the second half (or next period), even in isolation if they so choose. They have special physiological and psychological needs during this time to which coaches must be sensitive. For instance, liquid refreshment is essential to replenish energy and body resources, not only between periods but also during the contest. Sensitivity to their psychological needs will also better prepare them for postrest performance.

For example, as soon as the athletes enter the locker room at halftime or after a period, some coaches tend to shower them with information feedback. Wrong! After vigorous physical activity, fatigue, and heightened arousal, the human system needs to relax for a short time before it can efficiently process and retain additional information. Two suggestions for the coach are warranted: First, hold off offering input to the players for several minutes during a long rest period (halftime, for instance) to allow their information processing systems to focus and concentrate on new input. Second, limit the amount of information that is provided. Coaches may (and often do) have "a thousand things" to tell their players based on their observations. Unfortunately, much of this information will not be remembered and, hence, not used later in the contest due to information overload, fatigue, and their limited ability to incorporate new, perhaps what is for them, very complicated information. Effective teachers of athletes (1) make two or three key points, (2) try to communicate visually (with a chalkboard or physical demonstration) as well as verbally, (3) summarize their points at the end of the session, and (4) include positive comments about their earlier performance as well as reasonably high expectations about the quality of their subsequent performance.

And, speaking of expectations, coaches should use criticism constructively and selectively without losing control (see chapter 8 on techniques for offering critical input). Obviously, critical feedback is essential for learning and altering performance. But too much criticism is like too much of any type of information — it is soon forgotten. Also, critical input should not be communicated in a manner that intimidates or embarrasses the player — criticism in front of teammates, for example. A statement such as "You guys were terrible" has less impact on improving later performance than "We're waiting too long before taking the shot" or "We're playing too loose on defense; stay closer to your opponent."

In addition, coaches who "lose their cool" are communicating ineffectively. Players get caught up in the coach's temper rather than in the message. True, even psychologists contend that anger is a normal emotion of humans. But demonstrating a loss of emotional control and maturity (for example, name-calling, destroying equipment, physically abusing athletes, or making threats) is counterproductive. For successful University of Texas head football coach Darrell Royal, the most effective approach is to accentuate the positive when the team is behind at halftime. His message typically is, "We are better than this; fortunately, we have thirty minutes left." When a coach comes into the locker room and is visibly mad and projects anger and hostility toward the team, he or she is taking a fifty-fifty chance on positive motivational results (Mechikoff and Kozar 1983, p. 53).

INCORRECT COACHING STRATEGIES THAT INCREASE ANXIETY AND AROUSAL

Some anxiety is a good thing. Mature, higher-skilled players need a sense of concern — even urgency — before and during the contest. But coaches do not want their players to be more anxious than necessary. Yet sometimes a coach will use a technique that has the opposite of its intended effect; it unintentionally promotes, rather than reduces, anxiety. Here are some examples of what coaches often do in the mistaken belief that they are helping the athletes:

1.   *Teaching before or during the contest.* Studying minutes before an exam is fruitless because the learner is too tense to retain information. Information cannot be internally rehearsed during moments of high stress, so it is quickly forgotten. The same process occurs in sport. The emotions of high arousal and

anxiety prevent learning to any significant degree, and the absence of physically practicing new skills dooms initial attempts to failure. Coaches must avoid presenting new skills, complicated changes in strategy, and sophisticated explanations. New plays should be saved for the next practice session, and mastered, before being included in competition plans.

2.   *Maintaining that* "We must win this game." Don't the players already know that? Players are usually quite nervous before the contest. Statements that indicate the vital importance of a contest increase the participants' nervousness, not their excitation. Effective coaches focus on reviewing skills and strategies before the contest or between periods — or they say nothing at all. Reminding the players of the importance of winning psychs them out, not up.

3.   *Using criticism as a motivator.* Why do some coaches believe that they can bring a player "up" by putting him or her "down"? Athletes need self-confidence in order to succeed; they need to feel good about their ability to perform at their best and win. Critical or sarcastic remarks tend to have the opposite effect. What about the player who "rises to the occasion" in response to his or her coach's harsh remarks? True, some players may react with vigor, aggression, and determination, and perhaps succeed. Their reaction is "I'll show him!" But the long-term effect is often another story. Criticized players will feel resentment, anger, and less loyalty toward the coach. Poorer performance might result. The recommendation is to base criticism on specific performance and not to use it to play games with a player's mind.

4.   *Saying "Don't do..."* The adage "Never say never" can be translated in this context as "Don't say don't." Coaches who tell their players what not to do are actually reinforcing the wrong behaviors. When a person is told not to do something, the player mentally rehearses and becomes preoccupied with what they should not do instead of with what they should do. In addition, scientists have found that we tend to remember positively stated information better than negative input. Coaches should help athletes to focus on future correct behaviors.

5.   *Setting goals incorrectly.* Sometimes a coach will "require" an athlete to meet what the athlete feels is an unrealistically difficult goal. True, players should find challenging goals motivating. But goals that are too difficult, that are set exclusively by the coach without input from the athlete, and that are based on outcomes (over which the player often has no control) rather than performance, will tend to have a demotivating effect on performance. In fact, many athletes will give up or drop out rather than attempt to meet a goal that they consider to be far beyond realistic expectations. The belief is "If I don't try, I can't fail."

6.   *Inducing guilt.* A common error in coaching is to make athletes feel guilty over their performance. Statements such as "You guys should feel ashamed of yourselves." or "You mean to tell me that the other team is better than you?" do not motivate and enhance player loyalty to the team and coach. According to Kroll (1982, p. 4), "... guilt can contribute to heightened anxiety

and it would appear that guilt is one of the causes of anxiety in the precompetitive situation." Another cause of guilt is asking the athlete to do something that is contrary to the athlete's wishes or character. Examples include instructing a player to purposely injure an opponent or to cheat.

7. *Blaming the referee.* Coaches often become antagonistic to game officials, especially if the team is losing. Essentially, the umpire or referee becomes the scapegoat for the team's loss. Sometimes the coach feels that arguing with the arbiter will motivate the team. The potential problem with this approach is that when athletes feel that the outcome of a contest is not under their control, they feel helpless. Consequently, players do not maintain optimal effort. In extreme cases, they stop trying or quit the team altogether. Coaches have a right and responsibility to communicate with game officials. But when the interaction is negative and persistent, players feel embarrassed ("I expect my coach to behave in a mature manner"), guilty ("I caused the argument"), or helpless ("The ref doesn't like us").

8. *Reminding players who's watching.* Although athletes love a crowd, they seldom respond enthusiastically to being evaluated by persons whose opinions may influence their future success. Judges, scouts, and recruiters are potentially threatening to aspiring players. Consequently, awareness of their presence might cause more harm than good by increasing anxiety (which, as you remember, is defined as "perceived threat"). Coaches would be doing players a favor by not mentioning who is watching.

9. *Maintaining that "I don't have to justify nothing to nobody."* So said an assistant college football coach upon hearing the suggestion that some players would benefit from understanding the reasons behind certain coaching decisions. Let's face it, the coach is in the driver's seat. He or she is the decision maker, and the athletes can either follow or leave the team. But this does not diminish the fact that players often feel more anxious and even less supportive of the decision when asked to do something without an explanation. Why do players have a particular training regimen? Why was a player removed from the game, a certain play called, or a particular strategy used?

Perhaps the term *explain* is more palatable to the coach than *justify,* which may suggest less power, control, and authority. Of course, coaches don't have the time to explain all (or even most) decisions to the participants. But on some issues and in certain situations, to ask for the athletes' thoughts before a decision is made and to explain the decision before any action is carried out makes sense.

10. *Applying the starter/nonstarter double standard.* One way to decrease loyalty to the team and coach is to treat players differently based on their status on the team. Mistreating the players who are less central to the team's success negatively impacts on all team members because athletes need to support one another regardless of their positions. The team leader may necessarily spend more time with starters than with substitutes, especially on larger teams such as in football and baseball. But ignoring substitutes or allowing starting players to

follow one set of rules and policies while the nonstarters follow another increases anxiety and may diminish arousal. Coaches should remember that substitutes are only one injury away from starting.

11.   *Using exercise for punishment*. This practice is one of the great myths in coaching and physical education. Exercise serves the very important purpose of improving one's physical status so that maximal performance can be reached and maintained. For competitors to find conditioning to be meaningful and even pleasant is important. Administering exercise as a form of punishment to athletes is a contradiction in terms. Exercise should be desirable, not something that is a tool to invoke pain or discomfort. Using exercise as punishment turns the athlete away from the very activity that is necessary to promote good performance and health. Coaches want to keep exercise enjoyable.

SUMMARY

Anxiety and arousal are inherent in competitive sport. The proper mental preparation of sport participants to regulate these two emotions, before and during the contest, is among the most complex skills in coaching. The "best" strategies used to accomplish this objective differ from sport to sport. In fact, rarely do two coaches use the same mental approaches in a given contest. When or how to increase or decrease arousal or anxiety is a matter of timing, knowing the needs of each athlete, and understanding the demands of a given sport, task, and position. Ultimately, only the athlete can control his or her own emotions. The coach plays only a supporting role. The purpose of this chapter was to suggest ways in which this role can be carried out more successfully.

Anxiety and *arousal*, although often used interchangeably, are not synonymous. Whereas anxiety is the perceived threat of a situation, arousal can be emotional, caused by positive feelings of excitation and confidence or by negative feelings of fear or sadness, and physiological, as indicated by an increase in the body's level of activation. Sport psychologists use a variety of means to measure anxiety and the emotional and physiological aspects of arousal. Each individual athlete, sport, position on the team, and sport situation has a level of arousal (and, to a lesser degree, anxiety) that will produce optimal performance.

An important role of the coach is to help athletes to determine the level of arousal at which they function best in sport. Before and during the contest, coaches can enact strategies to reduce, maintain, or increase their athletes' arousal so that they reach and maintain an optimal state. And coaches can markedly reduce the usually undesirable state of competitive anxiety. Unfortunately, many coaches ignore the recommendations supported by sport psychologists and often use techniques that are actually counterproductive in establishing the proper pregame and between-period mental set. The recommended do's and don'ts in this chapter are based on the sport psychology literature and anecdotal evidence accumulated by this writer's observations and interviews with athletes of all age groups and skill levels, including professionals.

REVIEW QUESTIONS

1. Define state and trait anxiety. How do they differ? What types of measures would a coach use to determine an athlete's level of trait and state anxiety?
2. How are anxiety and arousal similar and different, both physiologically and psychologically?
3. Is anxiety ever desirable for athletes? If so, under what conditions?
4. What are some causes of state anxiety in sport? Describe five coaching strategies to reduce it.
5. What is the inverted-U hypothesis? How does it vary among athletes, sports, and skills?
6. How can a coach determine whether an athlete is overaroused? Underaroused? Playing at optimal arousal level?
7. Under what conditions would a coach want to increase an athlete's arousal? When is it desirable to lower it?
8. What should the coach do to raise and lower the player's arousal level?
9. Describe three incorrect strategies that coaches use in the mistaken belief that they are raising arousal.

REFERENCES

Anshel, M. H. 1985. Effect of arousal on warm-up decrement. *Research Quarterly for Exercise and Sport* 56: 1–9.

Anshel, M. H. 1987. Psychological inventories used for sport psychology research. *Sport Psychologist* 1: 331–49.

Bird, A. M., and B. K. Cripe. 1986. *Psychology and sport behavior*. St. Louis: Times Mirror/Mosby.

Carver, C. S., and M. F. Scheier. 1981. *Attention and self-regulation: A control-theory approach to human behavior*. New York: Springer-Verlag.

Cratty, B. J. 1983. *Psychology in contemporary sport*. Englewood Cliffs, NJ: Prentice-Hall.

Deshaires, P. 1980. The interactional model of anxiety in a sport competition situation. Paper presented at the North American Society for the Psychology of Sport and Physical Activity, May, in Boulder, Colorado.

Duffy, E. 1957. The psychological significance of the concept of arousal on activation. *Psychological Review* 64: 265–75.

Endler, N. N. 1977. The interaction model of anxiety: Some possible implications. In *Psychology of motor behavior and sport*, ed. D. M. Landers and R. W. Christina, pp. 332–51. Champaign, IL: Human Kinetics.

Fisher, A. C., and M. A. Motta. 1977. Activation and sport performance: Some coaching guidelines. *Motor Skills: Theory Into Practice* 1: 98–103.

Ginott, H. G. 1968. *Between parent and child*. New York: Avon.

Gould, D. 1984. Psychosocial development and children's sport. In *Motor development during childhood and adolescence*, ed. J. R. Thomas, pp. 212–36. Minneapolis: Burgess.

Hall, E. G., and G. Purvis. 1980. The relationship of trait anxiety and state anxiety to competitive bowling. In *Sport psychology: An analysis of athlete behavior*, ed. W. F. Straub, pp. 250–56. Ithaca, NY: Mouvement.

Hull, C. L. 1943. *Principles of behavior*. New York: Appleton.

Iso-Ahola, S. E., and B. Hatfield. 1986. *Psychology of sports: A social psychological approach*. Dubuque, IA: Wm. C. Brown.

Klavora, P. 1978. Customary arousal for peak athletic performance. In *Coach, athlete, and the sport psychologist*, ed. P. Klavora and J. V. Daniel, pp. 155–63. Champaign, IL: Human Kinetics.

Kroll, W. 1982. Competitive athletic stress factors in athletes and coaches. In *Stress management in sport*, ed. L. D. Zaichowsky and W. E. Sime. Reston, VA: AAHPERD Publications.

Landers, D. M. 1980. The arousal-performance relationship revisited. *Research Quarterly for Exercise and Sport* 51: 77–90.

Martens, R. 1971. Anxiety and motor behavior: A review. *Journal of Motor Behavior* 3: 151–79.

Martens, R. 1977. *Sport competition anxiety test*. Champaign, IL: Human Kinetics.

Martens, R., D. Burton, F. Rivkin, and J. Simon. 1980. Reliability and validity of the competitive state anxiety inventory (CSAI). In *Psychology of motor behavior and sport — 1979*, ed. C. H. Nadeau, W. R. Halliwell, K. M. Newell, and G. C. Roberts, pp. 91–99. Champaign, IL: Human Kinetics.

Martens, R., D. Gill, J. Simon, and T. Scanlon. 1975. Competitive anxiety: Theory and research. In *Proceedings of the Seventh Canadian Psycho-Motor Learning and Sport Psychology Symposium*, Quebec City, Quebec, Canada.

Mechikoff, R. A., and B. Kozar. 1983. *Sport psychology: The coach's perspective*. Springfield, IL: Thomas.

Morgan, W. P. 1979. Anxiety reduction following acute exercise. *Psychiatric Annals* 9: 141–47.

Oxendine, J. B. 1970. Emotional arousal and motor performance. *Quest* 13: 23–32.

Simon, J. A., and R. Martens. 1979. Children's anxiety in sport and nonsport evaluative activities. *Journal of Sport Psychology* 1: 163–69.

Sonstroem, R. J. 1984. An overview of anxiety in sport. In *Psychological foundations of sport*, ed. J. M. Silva and R. S. Weinberg, pp. 104–17. Champaign, IL: Human Kinetics.

Spence, K. W. 1956. *Behavior theory and conditioning*. New Haven: Yale University Press.

Spielberger, C. D. 1972. *Anxiety: Current trends in theory and research*. Vol. 1. New York: Academic Press.

Spielberger, C. D., R. L. Gorsuch, and R. E. Luschene. 1970. *Manual for the state-trait anxiety inventory* (self-evaluation questionnaire). Palo Alto, CA: Consulting Psychologists Press.

Taylor, J. A. 1953. A personality scale of manifest anxiety. *Journal of Abnormal and Social Psychology* 48: 285–90.

Weinberg, R. S., and V. V. Hunt. 1976. The interrelationships between anxiety, motor performance, and electromyography. *Journal of Motor Behavior* 8: 219–44.

Yerkes, R. M., and J. D. Dodson. 1908. The relation of strength and stimulus to rapidity of habit formation. *Journal of Comparative and Neurological Psychology* 18: 459–82.

4

Attributions: Postgame Explanations

In chapter 3, we explored the effects of certain emotions, namely anxiety and arousal, that are inherent before and during the contest. This chapter will look at the athlete's feelings after the game is over and the effect of these feelings on future emotions and behaviors in sport. After the contest, athletes collect their thoughts about the preceding event and its outcome. They also reflect on the quality of their performance. Of course, coaches are involved in the same thought processes, but with one difference. They play a more important role than the players in assessing the causes of these contest and performance outcomes. If coaches conclude that winning or losing was the result of high effort and the players' good skills or low effort and poor skills, respectively, the participants will evaluate the contest in one way. If, however, the victory or loss is labeled "a lucky (unlucky) break," the other team is portrayed as the poorer (better) team, or the task is viewed as very difficult, then the players make a different interpretation. It has been said that "To err is human; to blame it on someone else is even more human." And so it seems in sport.

Perhaps the least desirable position in sport is the inevitable and unenviable position of losing. It is not necessarily true, however, that a loss must be interpreted by the participants in a destructive, negative manner. John Robinson, head football coach of the Los Angeles Rams, claims that evaluating why his team lost is of critical importance to coach and players. Coaches are responsible for making an honest and accurate evaluation of good and poor performance so that the causes of the end result can be objectively determined. Only then can the problems be rectified. In this way, instead of blaming one another for unsuccessful attempts, team members can learn from their mistakes and direct their energy toward preparing for the next contest (Mechikoff and Kozar 1983).

The purpose of this chapter is to explain how various explanations affect the player and future performance. By the end of this chapter, you should be able to understand how perceiving events and outcomes in sport as successes or failures affects a person's interpretation of his or her sport performance. Further, the effects of these interpretations on the athlete's subsequent feelings and performances, and the powerful role of the coach in influencing how athletes formulate their causal explanations of performance outcomes should become evident.

THEORETICAL BASIS

The theoretical basis for making causal attributions in sport is that people — coaches, players, parents, spectators, the media, and so on — speculate about the probable causes of winning and losing, or success and failure. Psychologist Bernard Weiner and his colleagues (1971) have suggested that we perceive and explain success and failure in terms of four categories: ability, task difficulty, effort, and luck. Typically, athletes follow the coach's lead in explaining the causes of performance and game outcomes. These explanations are called *causal attributions*. What's important here is that the nature of these explanations often influences the athlete's incentive and the quality of his or her future performances. For instance, researchers have shown that when a player is told that he or she made an error owing to poor ability, they will more likely quit the team than if they interpret the error as due to task difficulty ("that was a tough ground ball"), low effort ("let's work harder in practice to get those"), or even luck ("the ball took an unlucky bounce"). As indicated in Figure 4.1, the four explanations are categorized into two dimensions, stability and locus of control.

Stability

Stability is a function of changes in attributions from situation to situation. Factors that are stable (that is, enduring) are ability and task difficulty. They are relatively consistent; ability is either present for a given task or outcome, or it is not. Task difficulty also does not tend to change very rapidly. True, prolonged practice and skill development will improve performance and reduce task

Figure 4.1   Attribution model based on the four causal explanations for performance outcomes

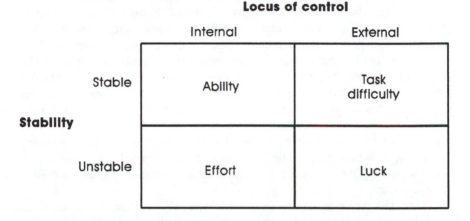

difficulty. But central to the stability dimension is that stable attributes — ability and task difficulty — are more predictable than unstable ones — effort and luck. While a performer can offer high or low effort or be "lucky" or "unlucky" at a given moment, an attribute of high or low ability or perceiving the task at hand as relatively difficult or easy is more long term.

Locus of Control

Locus of control, first popularized by Rotter (1966), explains the extent to which a person (1) feels responsible for his or her performance and (2) is reinforced by performance outcomes. The main issue, then, is the extent to which individuals perceive the results of their performances as under their own control. These feelings seem to persist across different situations and, thus, are viewed as a personality trait. Rotter developed a paper-and-pencil inventory designed to categorize persons into one of two classes: those who have *external* and those who have *internal* dispositions.

Externals (E) perceive (remember that perceptions may or may not be based on reality) relatively little control over events in their lives. Internals (I), on the other hand, tend to believe that their experiences are attributable to their own actions. Hence, the I or E dispositions of athletes predict whether they feel responsible for their own success or failure. Researchers have discovered that males and females often differ on the I-E dimension.

Relatively little research has been completed in examining sex differences in locus of control. Blucker and Hershberger (1983, p. 357) concluded, in their review of related literature, that although differences on causal attribution exist between men and women in general, "there has been very little published research comparing the causal attribution of men athletes with women athletes or women athletes with women nonathletes." Studies generally suggest that females are more external in making causal attributions than males.

Dr. Susan Horner (1968) was among the first to recognize that nonathlete males and females did not react to performance outcomes — nor did they approach tasks — in a similar manner. She identified "fear of success" as a personality trait among women that influenced their success and failure. The results of her research showed that (1) women, much more often than men, felt uncomfortable when they were successful in competitive achievement situations due to its inconsistency with expectations of "feminine" behavior, (2) that the motive to avoid success differed among women, and (3) that the motive to avoid success was more prevalent in competitive achievement situations (competing directly against other people) than when a female competed against an impersonal standard. Thus, the fear-of-success motive was believed to be a feminine characteristic.

Have Horner's conclusions about nonathlete subjects (from 1968) remained valid in more recent years? In a critique of over one hundred studies, Tresemer (1976) found insufficient evidence to support gender differences in fear of success. However, Reis and Jelsma (1978, p. 186) acknowledged that fear of success among females ". . .still remains a valid concept to describe a pattern of taking the blame (lack of ability) and denying credit for success (luck, easy task)."

Do males and females differ as to their sense of mastery over sport-related situations? Researchers have found gender differences in locus of control (Anshel 1979; Blucker and Hershberger 1983; Rejeski 1980). Female internals, in contrast to externals, tend to become more upset in response to negative feedback and are more concerned about performance outcomes. And women in general evaluate their personal ability lower than men, have lower expectations for success, endorse external attributes of task difficulty and luck more than internal attributes of ability and effort, and feel less responsible and satisfied after a positive outcome but also feel less responsibility and dissatisfaction following a negative outcome than men.

The tendency of a person to accept responsibility for success and failure may be more closely related to that person's personality rather than to being male or female. Personality traits such as self-esteem, the need to achieve, and other personality factors that are associated with locus of control are similar among athletes of both sexes. Future research is needed to determine whether gender is a primary factor in predicting I-E disposition. Table 4.1 compares and contrasts the feelings and behaviors of internals and externals (Anshel 1979; Lefcourt 1976; Phares 1976).

Table 4.1   Characteristics that distinguish internals and externals

Internals	Externals
Perceive positive and negative events as a consequence of their own actions	Do not connect the events in their lives with their own actions
Feel they can regulate and be held responsible for most events in their lives	Feel that events are beyond their control
Are markedly affected by environmental factors such as external feedback or performance outcomes	Are not affected physically or emotionally by external feedback or outcomes (which they explain as being caused by luck or chance)
Are easily upset from criticism in skill situations	Are relatively impervious to outside criticism
Prefer situations in which they can employ skill, rather than chance situations	Prefer luck or chance situations
Are very concerned about performance outcome	Are relatively less concerned about outcome
Set relatively high performance goals	Set relatively less challenging goals
Have higher self-confidence and self-esteem	Are lower in self-confidence and self-esteem
Contract for, and earn, higher grades in school	Are less academically successful
Are relatively more common among older people	Are more common in younger age groups

(continued)

Table 4.1   Characteristics that distinguish internals and externals
(continued)

Internals	Externals
Reinforcement and recognition for performance are very important in increasing the chance of recurring success	Reinforcement and recognition for performance are not as important because they do not tend to take responsibility for success or failure
More probable with more frequent successes	Fostered by increasing failure
Persist longer at tasks	Have relatively short persistence
React more adversely to continued failure	Are somewhat less upset by failure
More common in males	More common in females

Sometimes, skilled athletes offer more than one attribute to explain the causes of a performance outcome. Here is professional tennis player Jimmy Connors's interpretation of why he lost a match at Wimbledon in the first round to then newcomer Robert Seguso: "He was serving bomb after bomb (high task difficulty). I was waiting for him to falter just one inch, and I was going to be all over him (Connors's high ability). But he just kept going boom, boom, boom (high task difficulty)." Notice that Connors never suggested that he did not have the ability to win against Seguso. Top athletes almost never say, "I'm not good enough."

Skilled, habitually successful athletes focus on internal causes (ability and effort) to explain their performances (McAuley and Gross 1983). According to Roberts (1984), elite athletes see outcomes as being not necessarily limited to outcomes of events, but also as referring to meeting goals or demonstrating competence. In such cases, skilled athletes do not tend to feel responsible for a team loss. Instead, they will attribute the lack of team success to teammates while viewing their own performance as successful, or at least not contributory to the undesirable outcome. One primary reason for this tendency is the skilled player's history of success.

A high relationship exists between consistent performance outcomes and the causal attributions of athletes, especially children. Roberts (1975), in a study of two hundred Little League baseball players, found that the teams that had consistently won made ability attributions. However, these winning teams did not attribute a lack of ability to explain an occasional loss. Instead, these players thought that low effort or a tougher opponent (task difficulty) was responsible for the team's lack of success but attributed high effort to their own performance. On the other hand, teams that had consistently lost attributed these outcomes to poor personal or team ability. Brawley (1984) also concludes that athletes — at least those below the collegiate level — who consistently fail (or perceive themselves as failures, which is even more important) consider themselves to have low ability. This means that they have little hope for future success and are less likely to respond to failure with increased effort. Even worse, they tend to drop out of the sport or resort to attention-getting (negative) behaviors such as clowning, breaking team rules, and so on. Figure 4.2 gives typical examples of attributions based on the four categories of the Weiner et al. (1971) model.

One area of interest among researchers has been the extent to which locus of control can be shifted, preferably to a more internal state. Researchers disagree about whether a person's locus of control can be changed. Are one's beliefs about self-control over the events in his or her environment a stable personality trait, as some scientists (Phares 1976, among others) contend? Or is one's I-E disposition inferred from momentary feelings that can be assessed on a paper-and-pencil inventory, and are those feelings susceptible to sudden change, as

Figure 4.2   Examples of common causal attributions

Ability attributes
   "We weren't mentally ready."
   "I felt good out there."
   "I really stunk today."
   "I've been kicking (throwing) the ball well lately."

Task difficulty attributes
   "No one could hit that guy today."
   "Her timing was excellent."
   "The other team played better today."
   "We weren't able to stop the big play."
   "Injuries have really hurt us."

Effort attributes
   "I've been working hard in training."
   "We weren't aggressive enough out there."
   "We weren't able to make the big play."
   "Athletes aren't finished when they're defeated; they're defeated
      when they quit."
   "I gave it my best."

Luck attributes
   "We didn't get any breaks."
   "The ref didn't let us play our game."
   "We couldn't find the basket."
   "The weather killed us."

---

proposed by Lefcourt (1976)? In the latter view, a person might feel one way about mastery of his or her environment on one day or in certain situations but feel very differently on another day or in different situations. Attempts to alter one's locus of control, at least after performing a motor task, have not been successful with children (Anshel 1979) and college students (DiFebo 1975).

Based on his review of related literature, Anshel (1979) concluded that one or more of four factors must be present if locus of control is to be altered. First, the person must be exposed to certain environmental conditions over a prolonged period of time. Second, the person must have frequent experiences with the condition. Third, the task being performed in this environment should be perceived as meaningful; the person must be interested in the results from the experience or experiences. And fourth, because locus of control is often based on the information that a person receives about performance, it is important that the source of that information be perceived by the individual as credible and given by, someone whose opinions are respected.

Because our personality traits become more stable with age, to shift I-E disposition in adults, without extensive therapy, is almost impossible. And it is at least very difficult in young children. Nevertheless, coaches in sport have an extreme influence on athletes, sometimes even more so than parents. This influence, along with the length and intensity of involvement with participants, makes a shift in locus of control not only desirable but possible. Based on the four factors listed above, here are a few strategies coaches can implement to help athletes to become more internal.

Environmental conditions. Shifting to an internal locus of control means offering feedback to athletes that is positive; that is based on behaviors ("Good kick, Dan"), not character ("Good thinking, Jill"); and that is consistent (avoiding a "Jekyll and Hyde" change in personality and behaviors toward the players). In addition, the effect of such feedback is long term; it may take weeks, months, or even a few seasons to alter players' feelings about their mastery over performance outcomes or situations in the environment. Athletes need to go from "It's not my fault" to "It's my responsibility." In many cases, this takes a long-term commitment by the coach, as well as by parents and teammates, to get them there.

Frequent experiences. Feelings, particularly if they reflect long-held views about oneself or others, do not change quickly. How we feel about ourselves begins very early in life and becomes reinforced all throughout life. Persons who feel that they can make a difference in their life events likely have been nurtured to feel this way for years. Similarly, if a youngster has never been made to feel responsible for his or her behavior, he or she will maintain this trait for a long time — perhaps always. In order for persons' negative feelings about their influence over the events in their lives to change, they need to experience success based on their own effort and ability on a frequent basis. Only when this mastery is reinforced consistently will their perceptions change about "being in charge" of their destiny.

The coach's role is to provide feedback that reinforces positive performance (even if "positive" means the player's high effort and improvement rather than the final outcome) yet is appropriately critical when necessary. Athletes should not be fed a steady diet of compliments and praise. As Dweck (1975) and others have found, exclusively positive feedback is less productive than exposing a person to instructional input of a critical nature at least occasionally.

Task meaningfulness. Does the athlete find playing this particular sport very important? How does the participant define *success*? Is it defined as merely "getting a chance to play," or is it defined at a more advanced level, such as reaching a particular performance plateau? After all, not all sport participants consider being a successful athlete of significant importance in their lives. Does the performer feel concerned about the performance outcome? Is it of any concern to the person whether he or she succeeds? To alter a person's locus of control, the information feedback should be based on a task that has meaning to the individual, or the person is likely to conclude, "Who cares?"

A credible information source. Coaches cannot influence attitudes, feelings, and actions of athletes if the coaches' messages are not believed. If players receive information that provides them with the incentive to improve and to feel responsible for their performances, the source of the information must be viewed as credible—someone whom the athletes believe, trust, and respect. Only this perception will allow players to feel secure and interested in environmental mastery.

Shifting locus of control to an internalized state takes an extensive, long-term commitment. But given the advantage of feeling in control of and responsible for the events and outcomes in one's life, including athletic performance, the effort is worthwhile. The alternative might be feelings of powerlessness and an inability or unwillingness to reach goals, which would not foster life satisfaction. In extreme cases, a person might feel virtually helpless about influencing the direction of his or her life. This unpleasant condition has been identified in the literature as *learned helplessness*.

Learned Helplessness

In a laboratory study (Anshel and Marisi 1976), subjects were asked to contact a hand-held instrument with a rotating metal disc (about one inch in diameter). For one group, subjects were given an electric shock if their "time on target" did not equal or exceed the best score from the previous four trials. This condition was called *related stress*. Subjects in the unrelated stress group, however, were given electric shock on a random basis, regardless of their performance. A third (control) group performed the same task without electric shock. Results of the study showed that the unrelated stress group, subjects who had no control over their performance outcomes (shock or no shock), performed poorest among the three groups. The related stress group was superior to the others. This study is an example of a common response when a person feels unable to affect the occurrence or elimination of some, often unpleasant, event. An individual's perception that people have no or little control over the effects of their actions leads to a sense of helplessness. Sadly, this condition is responsible for causing significant psychological harm to sport participants, especially less skilled and younger players.

The theory of *learned helplessness* in humans stems from the work of psychologist Carol Dweck (1975), who examined the reasons why children refuse to participate, or make a brief attempt and then quickly give up, in an activity—especially in sport. Such children refuse to stay with, or persist at, an activity because they have little or no control over the outcome, as did the subjects in the unrelated stress group in the Marisi-Anshel study described earlier. These children have learned helplessness.

To understand the condition of learned helplessness, remembering that this is a learned phenomenon is important. This condition is not hereditary, nor is it a viral infection. Feeling inadequate, being "a failure," and feeling unable to alter an unpleasant situation or outcome is based on past experiences. The questions are, What creates learned helplessness? and What is responsible for how a person perceives the cause of his or her success or failure?

Dweck and Reppucci (1973) were interested in determining why children attributed outcomes to high or low ability rather than to high or low effort. As described earlier, ability attributes are relatively fixed. Kids drop out if they feel that failure is due to low ability, especially beginning at about age eleven or twelve years (Roberts 1984). Effort attributes are not fixed and, therefore, can be used to connect successful outcomes with effort or motivation. This is highly desirable in avoiding a helpless mental state. The researchers found that children who persisted longer at the task were more likely to attribute their performance outcomes to effort than were helpless children. The more persistent child also tended to perceive the causes of his or her performance as due to effort ("If I try harder, I'll get better"). Helpless children, those with less persistence, on the other hand, were more likely to attribute failure to their lack of ability rather than to lack of effort. In a sport context, this leads to the viewing of oneself as a consistent failure and to dropping out. Hence, it is advisable that athletes feel that poor performance is due to a lack of effort and can be improved if they try harder — which is under the performer's control. However, feeling in control of an outcome, and the interpretation of that outcome as success or failure, is dependent on the individual's perception.

As Dweck and Reppucci have shown, two children may receive exactly the same number and sequence of success and failure experiences yet react quite differently as a function of whether they interpret the failure to mean that the situation is within or beyond their control. What is responsible for differences in this perception, which, in turn, influences helplessness? Researchers Dweck and Reppucci (1973) and Anshel (1979) describe the presence of at least one of four factors: (1) the person's history of success and failure (greater frequency of success inhibits feelings of helplessness more than failure), (2) the manner in which information feedback is offered ("Nice try, John, but . . ." as opposed to "That was a dumb mistake. Can't you do anything right?"), (3) the frequency with which feedback is offered (perception is more influenced by frequent input), and (4) the source of the information (credible sources — that is, significant others such as coaches, teachers, parents, and friends — have more influence than persons with less credibility).

Reducing Learned Helplessness

The good news about this condition is that it is amendable, especially in childhood. If children can learn to be helpless, they can also be taught to overcome it by changing attributional patterns (i.e., tendencies of explaining the causes of performance outcomes). This is the purpose of Dweck's (1975) attributional retraining program.

Attributional retraining focuses on reinforcing the importance of effort as opposed to less controllable features of the environment such as luck or high task difficulty. And feelings of low ability are extinguished. Directing the attributional patterns of performers toward the unstable variable of effort increases the chance of persisting at a task. Attributional retraining has received research support.

In one study, Dweck (1975) identified children who lacked persistence or tended to be "quitters." These "helpless" children were given one of two treatments: (1) one group was given constant reinforcement for success to develop self-confidence and to overcome a negative reaction to failure and (2) the other group received effort attribution training while experiencing both success and failure. After each trial, subjects were encouraged to attribute their success or failure to their personal effort. Thus, Dweck tried to repattern the children's perception of their performance outcome to a personal factor that could be controlled, an effort attribute. She found that children who received effort attribution training were more persistent, more willing to attribute their performance to effort, experienced less anxiety in an achievement situation, and rated themselves as better performers than did the less persistent children.

Dweck concluded that subjects who were trained to recognize the need for more effort and not the lack of ability as the reason for "failing" responded more productively in subsequent trials; they didn't give up. She surmised, ". . . if a child believes failure to be a result of his lack of motivation, he is likely to escalate his effort in an attempt to obtain the goal" (p. 683).

In summary, then, helpless individuals, including athletes, have some of the following characteristics: They

1. persist less at, withdraw early from, or do not even attempt an activity, especially if it's a new one;
2. attribute failure to a lack of ability, not to a lack of effort;
3. perceive themselves as consistent failures;
4. do not feel that greater effort will result in success;
5. consider luck or low task difficulty to be possible causes for their success;
6. tend to not risk failure, which means that they are less comfortable in learning situations and in attempting new skills;
7. do not feel control over performance outcomes, and interpret failure as beyond their control;

8.   tend to have an external I-E disposition, usually attributing performance to factors not under their control; and

9.   misinterpret or misperceive the actual causes of their poor performance; helpless persons feel that trying to overcome failure is fruitless, whereas nonhelpless performers view failure as a temporary skill deficit.

ATTRIBUTIONS, HELPLESSNESS, AND COACHING

For coaches to know the factors that underlie an athlete's feelings of helplessness and to make the appropriate causal attributions is important. Why, for example, would one player claim that the main reason for his or her failure was an injury (very common in professional sports) and another competitor explain losing as being due to a tough opponent? Why do some coaches claim that their team lost because the opponent was better, while other coaches contend that their own team played poorly? Perhaps most importantly, what effect do these different attributions have on team and player performance?

The Coach's Comments

In sport settings, the coach has tremendous power over the athlete's perception of the situation. The manner in which a player's actions are assessed often dictates how the player explains his or her own playing skills and ability. In fact, comments by parents and others whose opinions are valued has a similar effect (Cratty 1983). The content of the coach's comments before and after performance, either in a game or during practice, not only affects the player's performance but also markedly contributes to whether or not the athlete continues to participate with the team. For example, Roberts (1975, 1984) asserts that child athletes who ascribe the causes of failure to low ability tend to drop out of sport.

How, then, should the coach go about reducing or, better yet, preventing feelings of helplessness in sport? Certainly the coach's objective is to use strategies that will help players to maintain sport participation with the motivation to continue learning and improving. This task should be an easier task if, as Rejeski and Brawley (1983) concluded in their review of related literature, athletes usually evaluate their abilities higher than their coaches do. Specifically, the authors found that each player's self-esteem was directly linked to his or her expectations and perceived ability concerning future performance. Competitors with high self-esteem were more confident in their ability and had higher expectations of future performance than did persons with lower self-esteem. Thus, one very important goal of every coach is to raise and to maintain heightened self-esteem in each team member. And it makes no sense to make statements to athletes that reduce their positive feelings. This is particularly damaging to participants with an external locus of control.

Although skilled athletes, particularly those who are on predominantly winning teams, tend to be internals (Rejeski and Brawley 1983), coaches have two responsibilities regarding the I-E disposition of their athletes. First, they need to know the extent to which each player is willing to take responsibility for performance. Second, they should promote an internal disposition, even if it means using techniques that shift a player's disposition from external to internal. Athletes with an external locus of control do not usually feel responsible for their actions and are less reinforced by the coach's responses to their performance. Neither of these tendencies are desirable for long-term motivation in sport. In Table 4.2, Carron (1984) depicts the influence of each causal attribution on a person's emotional feelings and expectancies.

One approach to fostering an internal locus of control and positively influencing the competitor's motivation before the contest (or during practice) is giving instructions that emphasize effort. A study by Yukelson, Weinberg, West, and Jackson (1981) illustrates the effect of instructional content, referred to by the authors as *attributional instructions*, on performing a sports skill. In their study, college students, all high achievers, engaged in an overhand ball-tossing task. They were told that the scores would be compared to a "standard of excellence" set by other subjects in the study. Thus, the subjects thought that they were competing against others, but in fact, these comparisons were fictitious. The subjects were then told, after a few contrived calculations, that they were either five points ahead of, or five points behind, the norms established by their classmates. Then they were given one of two sets of instructions before continuing the ball-tossing task to induce them to attribute their performance primarily to ability or to effort. The instructions (similar to what a coach might say to a player) were as follows (p. 49):

- *Ability-oriented instructions:* "We've found that the amount of ability an [athlete] has for this [skill] is by far the most important determinant of how well one will perform. This [skill] is pure in the sense that it is relatively unaffected by effort. Your performance is highly dependent upon the ability you possess; some [athletes] just seem to be good at the [skill] while others are not. You will now be given 10 more throws at thet target. Concentrate before each throw for it is the accuracy of your throws that will determine your score."

- *Effort-oriented instructions*: "We've found this (skill) to be heavily influenced by the amount of effort a person puts into the (skill), that is, the motivation one has to do well. There are some slight differences in ability, but they are minor. No one can do well unless they try hard. You will now be given 10 more throws at the target. Remember to concentrate and try to do your best."

Table 4.2   Factors that affect motivation for future participation in sport (Carron 1984, p. 92)

Initial Expectancy	Performance Level	Causal Attribution	Emotional (Affective) Reaction	Expectancy
High[1]	High	Ability, or other stable, internal factors	Maximum pride and satisfaction	Higher
High	Low	Bad luck, difficult task, or lack of effort or other unstable factors	Minimum shame and dissatis-faction	High
Low[2]	High	Good luck, special effort, or the relative ease of the task	Minimum pride and satisfaction	Low
Low	Low	Lack of ability, difficulty of the task, or stable internal factors	Maximum shame and dissatis-faction	Lower

[1]Associated with males
[2]Associated with females

The best performance resulted when subjects attributed their performance to effort rather than ability. As their perception of task difficulty increased, so did intended effort and subsequent performance. The subjects reported that they tried harder when receiving effort instructions. Therefore, informing an athlete that effort is the most important factor in skill development and success will be more motivating and will result in better performance than indicating that ability ("either you have it, or you don't") is most important. Effort attributions are especially important to sport participants with relatively low skills and little past success. In fact, attributing failure to a lack of ability results in the highest incidence of withdrawal from sport compared to other attributes, especially starting at about age ten to twelve years (Roberts 1984).

Using Attributions to Motivate Athletes

The following are some coaching suggestions for preventing, reducing, or eliminating learned helplessness and for using causal attributions to motivate athletes.

1.   *Know when to use internal and external attribution.* Usually, coaches should not use external attributions (task difficulty or luck) to explain the lack of goal achievement or not meeting expectations (Brawley 1980). Better, at least on a consistent basis, is to indicate that future effort must be increased — or maintained if the effort was sufficient — for success rather than blaming the official, bad luck, skill difficulty, or a superior opponent. External attributions for failure might promote learned helplessness, whereby the player feels that he or she can do little to change present or future outcomes. Thus, an athlete who has just struck out against a "hittable" pitcher needs to know that greater effort toward skill development and concentration are needed (internal attributes). Telling the player that the pitcher was very tough or that the umpire's calls were inaccurate (external attributes) may not provide the needed incentive for improvement. Also not helpful are comments that degrade the player's self-esteem or sense of personal ability.

2.   *Teach skills.* Nothing is more important in achieving sport success than learning the skills and performing them proficiently. Skill development improves performance and reduces feelings of helplessness for athletes of all ages. Poor skills promote continued failure. Quality educational attributional statements inform; they give a player the incentive to try harder to improve performance. Such statements also affect players' attitudes about their ability and their role on the team.

3.   *Create sport situations that foster success.* Try to match opponents based on age, skill, and physical maturity. For example, A 120-pound linebacker should not attempt to tackle a 160-pound running back. Athletes should participate after receiving instruction and practice. As discussed in chapter 11, some controversy exists about the rule that all athletes must play in every game, regardless of their skill. Some participants need additional development during practice before they are ready to compete. Athletes can be taught to self-monitor their skill development and to attribute successes to high effort.

4.   *Avoid comparing athletes.* Statements such as "Why can't you dribble the ball like Marge?" or "If you could only run as fast as Bill, Sam" reduce feelings of self-competence. There's nothing wrong with telling a player about the superior skills of an older, more experienced team member, but the emphasis

should be placed on using objective criteria based on standards and reasonable expectations. For instance, explaining to a player the reasons for not starting ahead of another athlete based on performance-based criteria ("Darlene is playing ahead of you, Fran, because she is aggressive in getting rebounds") helps the less skilled performer to understand what he or she must be able to do competently and consistently in order to play. However, players of lesser ability might view the superior skills of a teammate as impossible to overcome, fostering feelings of helplessness. General, subjective statements such as "He's a better player" or "You don't move as quickly as Joan" might promote feelings of inadequacy.

5.   *Offer supportive verbal and nonverbal messages*. This is probably the most important recommendation. Athletes need to feel accepted, even liked, by their coach. Verbal support such as "Good effort, Susan" or " Your dribbling is looking better today, Phil" and nonverbal cues such as a thumbs-up, smile, or pat on the back communicate a sense of acceptance, recognition, warmth, and performance improvement. Avoid messages that attempt to induce guilt ("I'm ashamed of you and the way you played today") or to insult ("You guys can't hit your way out of a paper bag"). Definitely avoid "gallows humor" and sarcasm ("Nice performance, folks. Next time I'll get volunteers from the crowd to take your place"). Chapter 8 on communication techniques offers several specific suggestions on promoting motivation and self-confidence while eliminating learned helplessness, boredom, and unhappiness.

6.   *Be positive when evaluating external factors* such as luck ("We played well today, folks, but the other team had a few good breaks and won. Keep up the good work") and task difficulty ("Don't feel bad. The other team has outstanding talent. It's good to know how good we have to be to win. We learned something today. Stay with it").

7.   *Reflect reality in attributions*. Athletes respect and want honesty from their coaches. Therefore, in addition to avoiding character-destroying comments, coaches (and parents) should "tell it like it is." This means that if a player in fact misjudged a ball (that is, the ball should have been caught), regardless of whether the error affected the score, internal attributions (effort and ability) are appropriate. A statement such as "Oh, that was an unlucky break, Richard" may be perceived as dishonest and might reduce the coach's or parent's credibility in the player's eyes.

A second issue on reflecting reality concerns giving credit when it is due. Some coaches tend to avoid congratulating the athletes after successful performances (as though the players will receive too much praise and get "swelled heads"). Coaches who state, "We got lucky today, guys, but the next team will be much tougher," after their team was successful are missing a great chance to build their players' self-esteem and confidence.

8.   *Avoid effort attributions for failure when the outcome is based on physiological parameters*. For instance, if a distance runner is not successful (in

whatever way "success" is defined by the coach or player), for the coach to say "You didn't try hard enough" is not wise. Athletes whose performance is based on physiological measures (e.g., strength, speed, and cardiovascular endurance) tend to avoid effort attributions for failure because there is no doubt about the effort they expended. According to Rejeski (1980, p. 34), ". . . most sport events provide direct perceptual information regarding effort expenditure. Thus, it may be informationally inappropriate for athletes to perceive that failure was caused by a lack of effort." Not winning the contest or task requiring optimal effort might be correctly attributed to external causes such as the quality of opponents (task difficulty) or, if accurate, some other luck-related causes such as poor weather or illness.

How do elite athletes assess their performance? According to Orlick and Partington (1986, p. 7):

> If the performance was excellent, they will note the mental factors associated with that best performance. In this way, they integrate important lessons into their plan for subsequent competitions. If the performance was off they will try to assess why, paying particular attention to their mental state or focus, before and during the competition. They are extremely good at drawing out the important lessons and then letting the performance go, especially if it was less than their best. Many of the best athletes use their diaries, logs, or some other post-competition evaluation procedure to write down the lessons learned. Some go back to these notes to help direct their focus for subsequent competitions.

Perhaps athletes should be exposed to the words of educator and politician Booker T. Washington, who said, "Success isn't measured by the position you realize in life, but by the obstacles you overcome to reach it."

SUMMARY

How do people explain the causes of events in their lives or, in sport, performance outcomes? Most often, the outcomes of events are attributed to one of four causes. Was their success or failure due to their ability? Their effort? The difficulty of the task they experienced? Or was the outcome interpreted as a matter of luck? The individual's perceptions in using any of these causal explanations is the basis of attribution theory. This area has received much attention from sport psychologists due to its effect on the athlete's motivation and desire to maintain participation in sport. For example, attributions can affect a competitor's interpretation of a contest outcome as success ("Our team lost, but I feel good about my effort") or failure ("I accept the blame for my team's loss today"). Athletes who chronically perceive their performance outcomes as failures and who attribute these failures to their own lack of ability or bad luck tend to drop out of sport sooner and more often than performers who attribute undesirable outcomes to low effort. In other words, the two key issues in helping athletes to make appropriate causal attributions are accuracy and control.

That is, coaches can help players to perceive more of their participation as successful (a superb technique for improving motivation) and can explain the causes of most events as due to high or low effort. Effort can be controlled by the athlete, whereas luck or physical inferiority to opponents is not under the player's control. Feeling that one has little or no control over performance outcomes can lead to learned helplessness (Dweck 1975). Such feelings are typically accompanied by mental and then physical withdrawal from further sport participation. Thus, the coach's comments following an event, either a particular play or the complete contest, strongly influence the athlete's interpretation of that event. This interpretation strongly influence the participant's subsequent emotions, attitudes, and behaviors.

REVIEW QUESTIONS

1. Describe *learned helplessness*. Why is it so potentially harmful, especially in sport? How is it nurtured in sport situations? What can a coach do to reduce or to eliminate it?
2. Based on the Weiner et al. (1971) attribution model, what would be the proper causal explanations for the following situations? (a) A team that consistently wins has just lost a game, (b) A team that tends to lose has just won the game, (c) A player made a physical error on a relatively easy play, (d) The underdog team won, (e) A player failed to catch a pass after slipping on the field, (f) The team, despite making several physical and mental errors, beat a poorly skilled opponent, (g) A batter just struck out against a "poor" pitcher, (h) The referee called a penalty that disallowed your team's goal, and (i) The team just lost to an opponent with inferior skills.
3. What are two advantages of having an internal I-E disposition? Can you think of a way in which being a strong internal could hurt more than help the athlete?
4. In what ways is an external I-E disposition desirable?
5. Describe four ways in which a coach can induce more internality in athletes.

REFERENCES

Anshel, M. H. 1979. Effect of age, sex, and type of feedback on motor performance and locus of control. *Research Quarterly* 50: 305–17.

Bird, A. M., and B. K. Cripe. 1986. *Psychology and sport behavior*. St. Louis, MO: Times Mirror/Mosby.

Blucker, J. A., and E. Hershberger. 1983. Causal attribution theory and the female athlete: What conclusions can we draw? *Journal of Sport Psychology* 5: 353–60.

Brawley, L. R. 1980. Children's causal attributions in a competitive sport: A motivational interpretation. Ph.D. diss., Pennsylvania State University, University Park, PA.

Brawley, L. R. 1984. Attributions as social cognitions: Contemporary perspectives in sport. In *Cognitive sport psychology*, ed. W. F. Straub and J. M. Williams, pp. 212–30. Ithaca, NY: Sport Science Associates.

Carron, A. V. 1984. *Motivation: Implications for coaching and teaching*. London, Ontario, Canada: Sports Dynamics.

Cratty, B. J. 1983. *Psychology in contemporary sport*. Englewood Cliffs, NJ: Prentice-Hall.

DiFebo, J. E. 1975. Modification of general expectancy and sport expectancy within a sport setting. In *Psychology of sport and motor behavior*. Vol. 2, ed. D. M. Landers. University Park, PA: Pennsylvania State University Press.

Dweck, C. S. 1975. The role of expectations and attributions in the alleviation of learned helplessness. *Journal of Personality and Social Psychology* 31: 674–85.

Dweck, C. S. 1980. Learned helplessness in sport. In *Psychology of motor behavior and sport—1979*, ed. C. H. Nadeau, W. R. Halliwell, K. M. Newell, and G. C. Roberts. Champaign, IL: Human Kinetics.

Dweck, C. S., and N. D. Reppucci. 1973. Learned helplessness and reinforcement responsibility in children. *Journal of Personality and Social Psychology* 25: 109–16.

Gill, D. L. 1984. Individual and group performance in sport. In *Psychological foundations of sport*, ed. J. M. Silva and R. S. Weinberg. Champaign, IL: Human Kinetics.

Ginnot, H. G. 1968. *Between parent and child*. New York: Avon.

Gould, D. 1984. Psychosocial development and children's sport. In *Motor development during childhood and adolescence*, ed. J. R. Thomas, pp. 212–36. Minneapolis, MN: Burgess.

Horner, S. 1968. Sex differences in achievement motivation and performance in competitive and noncompetitive situations. Ph.D. diss., University of Michigan, Ann Arbor.

Iso-Ahola, S. E., and B. Hatfield. 1986. *Psychology of sports: A social psychological approach.* Dubuque, IA: Wm. C. Brown.

Lefcourt, H. M. 1976. *Locus of control.* Hillsdale, NJ: Erlbaum.

Marisi, D. Q., and Anshel, M. H. 1976. The effects of related and unrelated stress on motor performance. *New Zealand Journal of Health, Physical Education and Recreation*, 9: 93–96.

McAuley, E., and J. B. Gross. 1983. Perceptions of causality in sport: An application of the causal dimension scale. *Journal of Sport Psychology* 5: 72–76.

McElroy, M. A., and J. D. Willis. 1979. Women and the achievement conflict in sport: A preliminary study. *Journal of Sport Psychology* 1: 241–47.

Mechikoff, R. A., and B. Kozar. 1983. *Sport psychology: The coach's perspective.* Springfield, IL: Thomas.

Orlick, T., and J. Partington. 1986. *Psyched: Inner views of winning.* Ottawa: Coaching Association of Canada.

Phares, E. J. 1976. *Locus of control in personality.* New York: General Learning Press.

Reis, H. T., and B. Jelsma. 1978. A social psychology of sex differences in sport. In *Sport psychology: An analysis of athlete behavior*, ed. W. F. Straub, pp. 276–86. Ithaca, NY: Mouvement.

Rejeski, W. J. 1980. Causal attribution: An aid to understanding and motivating athletes. *Motor Skills: Theory into Practice* 4: 32–36.

Rejeski, W. J., and L. R. Brawley. 1983. Attribution theory in sport: Current status and new perspectives. *Journal of Sport Psychology* 5: 77–99.

Roberts, G. C. 1975. Win-loss causal attributions of Little League players. *Movement* 7: 315–22.

Roberts, G. C. 1984. Children's achievement motivation. In *The development of achievement motivation*, ed. J. Nicholls. Greenwich, CT: JAI Press.

Rotter, G. C. 1966. Generalized expectancies for internal versus external control of reinforcement. *Psychological Monograph* 80 (Whole No. 609).

Tresemer, D. 1976. The cumulative record of research on "fear of success." *Sex Roles* 2: 217–36.

Weiner, B., I. Frieze, A. Kukla, L. Reed, S. Rest, and R. M. Rosenbaum. 1971. *Perceiving the causes of success and failure.* Morristown, NJ: General Learning Press.

Yukelson, D., R. S. Weinberg, S. West, and A. Jackson. 1981. Attributions and performance: An empirical test of Kukla's theory. *Journal of Sport Psychology* 3: 46–57.

5

Motivating Athletes: Do's and Don'ts

How many professions actually require a person to alter another individual's thoughts, feelings, attitudes, and behaviors, sometimes very rapidly, and to maintain the changes over a prolonged time period? No easy task. Yet this is a primary responsibility of coaches in sport. However, unless the athlete is motivated to learn skills and strategies and to perform them with consistent quality, often under stressful situations, the coach's ability to compel these behaviors will be restricted. Ultimately, the athlete's drive to succeed leads to desirable changes in performance quality and outcome. Although motivating athletes may not appear to be a very difficult task, it is far more sophisticated than many individuals believe. After reading this chapter, you should be able to understand the theoretical bases of motivation; to become aware of, and avoid, the many mythical practices used in coaching to motivate competitors (which often have the opposite impact); and to apply effective principles of motivation in a sport context. Consider the following typical examples of "motivation" in sport.

- *Intimidation.* During team tryouts, the coach tells the participants, "Most of you aren't good enough to make this team. You're going to have to go out there and show me you deserve to play for me." Or an athlete makes an error, and the coach threatens, in front of team members, to kick him or her off the team unless they can "get their act together."

- *Threats*. The coach grabs an athlete who has just made an error and, eyeball to eyeball, threatens to knock his block off if he doesn't do it right.

- *Criticism*. "That's the worst performance I've ever seen. If you can't do better than that, then you can leave this team."

- *Criticism and sarcasm*. "Hey, rubber hands, try using a basket to catch the ball," or "My grandmother can pass the ball better than that."

- *Guilt*. "I'm really surprised at you guys. I can't believe what I'm seeing. You guys should be ashamed of yourselves. You call yourselves athletes?"

- *Physical abuse*. The coach requires the athletes to run ten 40-yard sprints in ninety-degree heat after the regular practice session. Or, athletes are awakened at 5 A.M. for a five-mile run as punishment for being late for practice the previous day. Or the coach deprives the athletes of water (for whatever reason), which deteriorates performance at best but which at worst is life threatening.

In these examples, the coach is attempting to induce short-term changes in the behavior of another individual. In doing so, the coach is assuming that the athlete will, in fact, respond favorably to harsh treatment. But what many coaches do not realize is that such forced changes in behavior have only short-term benefits, if any, and that more desirable long-term effects will not be reached. The strategies so commonly used by coaches to motivate athletes can do more harm than good. The purpose of this chapter is to offer a scientific basis for motivation and to recommend strategies that will favorably influence the athlete's feelings and actions.

WHAT IS MOTIVATION?

Because writers and scientists have defined *motivation* in different ways, the use of this concept in a sport-related context needs clarification. The term *motivation* is derived from the Latin word *movere*, meaning "to move." Perhaps sport psychologist Richard Alderman (1974, p. 186) defines motivation most cogently as "the tendency for the direction and selectivity of behavior to be controlled by its connections to consequences, and the tendency of this behavior to persist until a goal is achieved." To give this academic definition some life, let's review a few key words and phrases to determine their implications in sport.

What is the purpose of the activity? What does the coach want the athlete to do? What is the *direction of motivation* (behavior) when the coach tells his or her team, "Come on, play to win!"? And in what direction is the coach motivating a player whom he or she criticizes for asking a "stupid" question or for making "a dumb play"?

Coaches and athletes, sometimes jointly, need to isolate the optimal feelings and behaviors for success, and to determine the best strategies for reaching them. At times, coaches need to solicit input from athletes as to what they find important (*selectivity of behavior*), then provide the individual with the proper direction. Motivation is not automatic.

"You mean if I don't show up to practice on time, I have to get up the next morning at 5 A.M. to go jogging?" "If I don't attend weight-training sessions, I'll be dismissed from the team?" These are examples of behaviors that are controlled by their *connections to consequences*. However, these threatening statements are examples of aversive control of behavior and represent a negative approach to motivation (Smith 1986).

Of what value is motivation in sport unless the athletes continue to perform the desirable behaviors (i.e., unless they *persist*)? The coach's goal in using motivational strategies is to prolong desirable feelings and actions of athletes. Here's an example of how this approach is abused by many coaches. Being in top physical condition (preferably year-round) is an important objective of coaches and players. To use coaching strategies that make physical conditioning fun and enjoyable (such as exercising to music, organizing relay races, and creating an atmosphere free of tension) certainly makes sense. What is the rationale, then, of using physical conditioning as a vehicle for punishment, as so many sport leaders do? Should athletes be asked to run laps or wind sprints as a consequence of inappropriate behavior? The unintended result may be that athletes will be less inclined to exercise and stay in shape on their own, especially after they retire from sport.

Activities are motivating when they are *meaningful* to the person. A task or job has to be perceived as being important toward contributing to successful outcomes, for the team collectively and for the individual.

For persons to feel motivated, they should be involved in an activity in which they can achieve short-term and long-term *goals*. Goals provide direction for effort and the incentive to reach a new level of skill and performance mastery.

How can a coach expect the athlete to be motivated by a goal if the individual is not given the opportunity to learn, practice, improve, and compete? The opportunity to achieve must be *available*, or motivation will fade.

Perhaps one of the most challenging tasks faced by coaches is to motivate every team member by helping each individual to feel that his or her efforts will lead to meeting desirable goals (*expectancy*). Athletes who toil every week during practice, yet are not allowed to appear in any of the contests, or who are given a goal far in excess of their capabilities will not likely be motivated to persist at the activity. Should these athletes feel motivated to meet their goals? In both examples, the athletes will be less likely to go all out.

As indicated earlier, the coach can foster *incentive* in an athlete by pointing out the specific ways in which certain behaviors can lead to goals and outcomes that the performer finds meaningful.

A *motive* is based on the individual's anticipation of the desirability of meeting some goal. It's a function of how important the athlete considers the consequences of certain actions and how strongly the performer desires (*approach motive*) or resists (*avoidance motive*) these ramifications (White 1959). For example, anticipating certain responses from spectators, teammates, or the coach based on one's performance serves as a motive to succeed or to avoid failure.

In summary, the coach's job is to convince each athlete that his or her personal needs and objectives, and those of the team, can be satisfied by (1) pursuing a certain, predetermined course of action, (2) responding to the coach's leadership, and (3) possessing necessary feelings and attitudes associated with performance success.

████████

THEORIES OF MOTIVATION

Theories in psychology help scientists and practitioners to understand the causes of certain actions, which in turn helps them to predict when these behaviors might occur. Ostensibly, particular strategies can then be implemented to favorably affect performance. The theories reviewed in this chapter were chosen based on their application to sport and the extent to which they have received attention in the sport science literature.

Need Achievement

According to most personality studies (see chapter 2 for a brief review), one characteristic of successful athletes is their need to achieve (Cox 1985). This need is commonly referred to as *achievement motivation*. The central focus of this theory is that some individuals derive tremendous satisfaction from success in achievement activities. Persons who are high, as opposed to low, need-achievers (as determined by paper-and-pencil inventories) (1) usually experience more pleasure in success, (2) have fewer and weaker physiological symptoms of state anxiety such as increased heart rate, respiration rate, or sweating, (3) feel responsible for the outcomes of their own actions, (4) prefer to know about their success or failure almost immediately after performance, and (5) prefer situations that contain some risk about the result (McClelland 1961).

Alderman (1974, p. 204) depicts the typical high need-achieving athlete as: ". . . usually fully conscious of the fact that he alone is responsible for how well he performs, he knows immediately (through his own perceptions and the feedback from teammates and spectators) whether he has failed or succeeded in his particular endeavor, and there is always present in sport settings an element of risk as to the outcome of his performance." Alderman warns, however, that some athletes do not consider sports competitions as "pure" achievement settings in that the individual "may be largely motivated by reasons other than achievement."

For example, children may engage in competitive sport to have fun; winning is of relatively minor importance (Gerson 1978). Certainly elite athletes want to win, but many are motivated by the inherent danger of participating in a risky sport such as ski jumping or motorbike racing. Others derive pleasure from physical contact, as is the case with some ice hockey players who compile penalties for fighting and enjoy a "defensive" team role. Still others enjoy being in top physical condition (e.g., distance runners), relish the attention of an admired physique (e.g., weight lifters), or enjoy the peer affiliation available in team sports.

In each of these examples, the individual acts to bring about pleasurable experiences. These are referred to as *approach motives*. But if one's actions serve to prevent something unpleasant from happening, an *avoidance motive* explains behavior (McClelland 1961). An example would be an athlete who participates in sport due to pressure from parents, peers, school coaches, or in some countries, the government (Vanek and Cratty 1970). The importance and the anticipation of success make the approach motive far more common with successful competitors than with their less skilled counterparts.

Alderman (1974) separates the concept of need achievement from motive for achievement. A person can have a high need to achieve but, due to a past history of failure, have a low motive to achieve. He suggests that children with a past history of failure in sport should not be expected to possess a high motive for achievement. In fact, their expectancy for success would probably be quite low. This does not mean, however, that their need to achieve is also low. In fact, unless the high need-achiever with a low approach motive finds a sport in which he or she is successful, the person will tend to stop participating in sport altogether. This is the heart of the fear-of-failure (avoidance motive) phenomenon so common in younger or less successful athletes (see chapters 2 and 11).

Achievement motivation can and should be fostered by coaches and parents. The need to achieve should be reinforced by (1) creating challenging goals ("Let's try to make bat contact more than 50 percent of the time"), (2) teaching skills that lead to performance improvement and success ("In today's practice, we're going to learn a new blocking technique"), (3) giving positive and constructive feedback on performance while avoiding negative and derogatory remarks at all costs ("Janice, I liked how you used your body to block out Martha from getting the rebound"), (4) allowing for risk-taking behaviors and learning from the outcomes — good or bad — rather than responding in a punitive manner ("Jim, give it your best shot to get this guy out; I'd rather not intentionally walk him"), (5) creating situations in which the athlete feels successful, such as emphasizing improvement, skill development, and effort, and (6) ensuring that at the end of a practice or event, the person feels a sense of competence — that they have achieved something or are closer to doing so.

Competence Motivation

White (1959, p. 318) proposed that behavior is directed, selective, and persistent owing to "an intrinsic need to deal (effectively) with the environment." He argues that the need for competence is an inherent part of life starting in childhood. We habitually attempt to master our surroundings, and when we're successful, we feel pleasure. Children in particular are motivated by mastery, curiosity, challenge, and play to satisfy their urge toward competence. Their rewards for achieving competence are feelings of internal pleasure; it's fun, pleasurable, and satisfying. Although the types of tasks and goals change with age, the need for environmental mastery remains a primary motive throughout life.

Competence motivation can be increased by at least two strategies. First, coaches (and parents of child athletes) should try to make competitors feel good about their participation in sport regardless of the outcomes. Effort and improvement should be emphasized rather than — or at least in addition to — winning or losing. Second, sport performers should be taught to formulate accurate perceptions of their ability within "achievement contexts." Does the athlete possess the necessary skill to succeed? What must he or she continue to work on and eventually master? Adults should do everything possible to persuade the athletes to think positive thoughts about their future involvement in sport. This is why learning new skills and having an opportunity to perform them are so important in maintaining motivation. At the same time, to always have an excuse for failing is not productive. If the demands of a sport are too great for an individual, perhaps more time for instruction and practice are needed before the individual is placed in a pressure-filled competitive situation.

Cognitive Evaluation Theory: Intrinsic and Extrinsic Motivation

In recent years, more and more researchers have viewed learners of motor skills as active, not passive, participants in learning. Individuals make conscious decisions about where to focus their attention and use other mental operations to facilitate the processing of information. The cognitive approach to motivation involves making choices about goal-directed behaviors. This is the basis of Deci's (1975) cognitive evaluation theory.

Deci's theory is predicated on two primary drives (*innate needs*) that provide the person with the energy for goal-directed behavior. These are to feel competent and to be self-determining in coping and interacting with one's environment. A

Figure 5.1   The effect of rewards on intrinsic motivation and reasons for sport participation

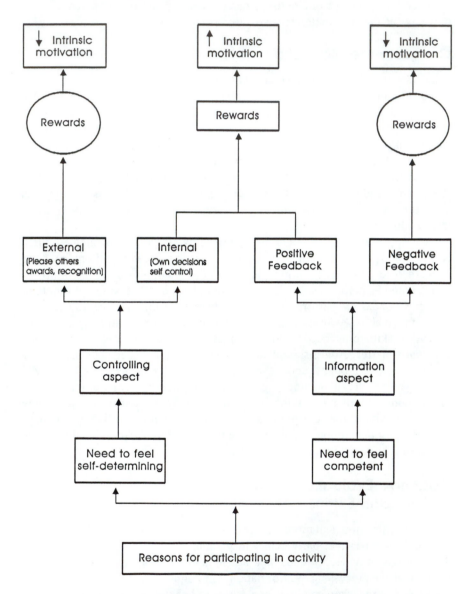

person who experiences success tends to attribute it to high ability. The activity is enjoyable — even fun — and participation continues. A person who participates in activity for its enjoyment and without an external reward is said to be intrinsically (internally) motivated. *Intrinsic motivation* (IM) is highly desirable in sport because it forms the primary basis for a personal decision to participate in sport. The factors that affect IM and the reasons for engaging in sport are illustrated in Figure 5.1.

Actions that are performed voluntarily, without coercion, and are perceived as pleasant are intrinsically motivating. A typical examination of IM includes (1) a measure of each person's initial (baseline) level of motivation for performing a task, (2) the introduction of some treatment, perhaps various types of rewards, offered to one group but not to another (control) group, and (3) a follow-up attempt to assess each person's IM toward the task. The measurement can be conducted with a questionnaire or through a predetermined analysis of the subjects' behaviors. If subjects continue to practice a task to which they were earlier exposed, they would be exhibiting IM. And so are individuals who practice a task or skill without any external demand or reward for doing so.

Extrinsic motivation (EM), on the other hand, is the desire to perform an activity due to the anticipation of some external reward such as money or a trophy (Deci 1975).

Researchers have found, as one might expect, that behaviors that are intrinsically motivated persist longer, are more enjoyable, and enhance the person's self-image more than extrinsically motivated actions. An excellent example of an intrinsically motivated person was the renowned scientist Albert Einstein, who said, "I am happy because I want nothing from anyone. I do not care for money. Decorations, titles, or distinctions mean nothing to me. I do not crave praise. The only thing that gives me pleasure, apart from my work, my violin, and my sailboat, is the appreciation of my fellow workers."

But what happens to a person's IM when he or she is offered extrinsic rewards such as money or a trophy? Why, for instance, do children participate in playground games for the fun of it and then, when placed in a competitive sport situation, care about the score and who wins and loses? Why do kids play sports "to have fun," yet drop out of competitive sport at alarming rates? And why is receiving a trophy so important if having fun is the main reason for participating? Deci's theory proposes two processes by which extrinsic rewards can affect IM: the *controlling aspect* and the *information aspect*. The different ways in which rewards affect motivation are depicted in Figure 5.2.

Controlling aspect. Persons are intrinsically motivated to engage in an activity when they enjoy the activity and want to feel competent. This decision is their own. However, external rewards can shift the person's reason for their participation from internal (e.g., fun, pleasure, or competence) to external means (e.g., trophies, money, or gifts). Extrinsic motivation overrides IM when the source of *control* is no longer within the person. Some common forms of extrinsic motivation include trophies, ribbons, money, parental or peer pressure, and other awards that recognize success. However, without the "reward" of

Figure 5.2   The impact of rewards on intrinsic motivation

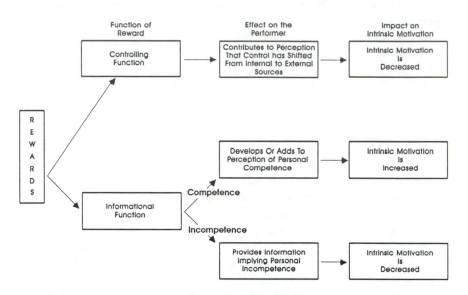

pleasing others or receiving an award, the intrinsic incentive to continue participating may not be strong enough.

The effects of a sports program that relies on a selective reward system whereby some athletes receive tangible rewards and others do not are even more potentially damaging to intrinsic motivation. Does this mean that trophies should never be used? Not necessarily; they may be used in a positive way to convey information about an individual's competence. For example, athletes can receive an award for their effort (e.g., "Most Motivated" or "Best Effort"), improvement (e.g., "Most Improved"), support of other teammates (e.g., "Best Team Player"), leadership (e.g., "Mr. Leadership"), skill ("Strongest Arm"), and so on. In each of these examples, the recipient should feel rewarded for accomplishing a task, meeting a goal, or demonstrating competence. The trophy serves as a reinforcer of this recognition.

Information aspect.   Feelings of competence and self-determination are other factors in the extent to which extrinsic rewards can affect IM. Deci (1975), in support of White (1959), contends that people are attracted to activities in which they feel successful (in which they perceive *competence*). Performers who perceive themselves as competent will likely be intrinsically motivated. Rewards can have the same favorable effect, as long as they increase the person's feelings of competence and self-worth. In this way, rewards can actually foster intrinsic motivation. Therefore, the most effective coaching strategy would be to provide all participants with some recognition for demonstrating success, be it improvement in performance, high effort, or showing competent skill execution.

Self-determination is the second component of the information aspect of promoting IM. *Self-determination* is concerned with the perception of control and responsibility in earning a reward. For instance, a team member who does not feel that he or she contributes to the team's success will feel less self-determination and, therefore, will be less intrinsically motivated in contrast to feelings of high contribution. Coaches can foster the players' feelings of self-determination and personal responsibility for outcomes by consulting players for suggestions about team policies, codes of player behavior, and game strategies and plans. An example would be to ask team members to take turns leading warm-up exercises.

The source and type of evaluations received by the individual seem to dictate whether intrinsic or extrinsic motivation prevails. According to Halliwell (1980, p. 87),

> . . . rewards can either increase or decrease a person's intrinsic motivation. If . . . the controlling aspect is more salient, the rewards will decrease intrinsic motivation. But, if the informational aspect is more salient and provides positive information about one's competence and self-determination, intrinsic motivation will be enhanced. . . . receiving trophies should increase an athlete's intrinsic motivation because they provide him with information about his competence as an athlete. (However) . . . the controlling aspect of these rewards may be more salient than the informational dimension if the reward recipient perceives that his sports involvement is controlled by the pursuit of trophies and other tangible rewards.

Motivation-Hygiene Theory

Based on extensive interviews with people of different professions, Frederick Herzberg and his colleagues at the University of Pittsburgh (1966) found that people have two contrasting sets of needs called motivators and hygiene factors.

Motivators have an uplifting effect and improve a person's performance and attitude toward the task. These feelings, which are long lasting, include achievement, recognition, responsibility, advancement, and personal growth. In sport, athletes feel more motivated if they (1) are recognized by the coach, (2) are given responsibilities that affected the team's success, (3) feel that their skills and performances are improving, and (4) have a sense of self-satisfaction as team members.

Hygiene factors can have a generally depressing effect on performance and attitude toward a task. These factors, not usually long lasting, include policies of the organization, behaviors and experiences with a supervisor, interpersonal relations with colleagues, money, status, working conditions, and feelings of security. Negative factors in any of these areas often result in lower self-esteem, the feeling that one is not deserving of such unpleasant treatment, and general job dissatisfaction. Examples of negative hygiene factors in a sport context include the lack of positive coach-to-athlete or athlete-to-athlete relationships, the performer's feeling of helplessness about improving his or her status on the team, practices that are boring and unrewarding, being treated in a disrespectful manner, and feelings of uncertainty about being wanted as a team member or being allowed to actually participate in contests.

Why use the term *hygiene*? Herzberg claims that this term suggests prevention rather than cure. The coach's (supervisor's) attention to these features will prevent their having a negative impact. Just as good hygiene removes bacteria from the environment, it can also remove the causes of dissatisfaction. Not in themselves motivating (they can prevent unhappiness but do not create happiness), positive hygiene factors are prerequisites for effective motivation. No matter how much a coach uses all of the "right" motivation techniques, lacking a pleasant situation in which to function will prevent, or at least markedly inhibit, the successful motivation of each participant.

For example, critiquing the athlete's performance in the locker room in a hostile, negative, and personal manner, especially in the presence of teammates, is often more stress-inducing than motivating. Teaching and practicing skills is an effort in futility if the player does not believe that skill mastery has a specific purpose and will lead to some desirable outcome. An athlete who has yet to play in any contest usually will not mentally respond to the coach who talks about the importance of learning strategies and assignments for the upcoming contest.

According to Rees (1980), the focus of Herzberg's motivation-hygiene model is to remind us that motivators are effective only if they are given a platform from which to function. This platform is centered on opportunities for self-growth (what Herzberg calls job enrichment) and the feeling that an individual has some control over his or her own behavior — that his or her performance and decisions are at least partly based on self-directed behaviors.

Carron's Motivation Model

Professor Albert Carron (1984) from the University of Western Ontario in Canada recognizes the importance of personal as well as situational factors in his sport motivation model (see Figure 5.3). Some of these factors are alterable and under the person's or coach's control, and others are not. For instance, athletes and coaches have no control over factors such as their personality, the weather, and the actions of opponents and spectators. However, other factors such as the reward system, the structure of practice sessions, and communication techniques can be governed. Carron lists four categories of factors that influence motivation. These include changeable personal factors, nonchangeable personal factors, changeable situational factors, and nonchangeable situational factors.

Changeable personal factors. As discussed earlier, motivation is based on a person's feelings about acting with the proper level of intensity. These thoughts, according to Carron, are under the individual's control. They include

Figure 5.3   A model for motivation in sport and physical

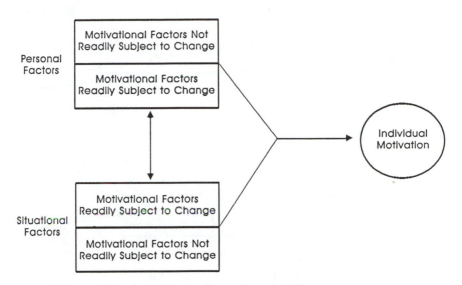

From A. V. Carron, *Motivation: Implications for coaching and teaching*,
London, Ontario, Canada: Sports Dynamics, 1984. Reproduced with permission.

incentive motivation, analysis of performance or event outcomes, intrinsic interest, the expectations of others, and self-confidence.

Incentive motivation refers to the value athletes attach to potential outcomes or experiences that are available to them in sport. If the person finds sport participation desirable and can predict pleasant and rewarding future sport experiences, then he or she will have high incentive to compete. If these positive expectations are actually experienced, motivation will remain high and the performer will persist at the activity.

According to Carron, factors that increase incentive motivation are affiliating with others, developing skills, and feeling excitement, success, status, fitness, and the desire to release energy. To Carron, the most salient reasons for dropping out of sport, or for lacking incentive motivation, are interests in other activities, boredom, injury, and the lack of playing time, success, fun, encouragement from significant others, or skill improvement.

How does the athlete explain the cause or causes of his or her performance results (see chapter 4)? Carron lists six stages in a competitor's explanation, or *analysis*, of the causes of an event's outcome that affect his or her motivation. These are shown in Figure 5.4.

Motivation is enhanced when performers view positive outcomes as a function of their ability, effort, or training rather than as a function of luck or task simplicity. Undesirable outcomes should not be viewed as due to poor

Figure 5.4   The attribution process

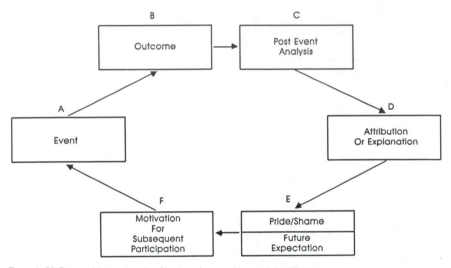

From A. V. Carron, *Motivation: Implications for coaching and teaching*,
London, Ontario, Canada: Sports Dynamics, 1984. Reproduced with permission.

ability (a major cause of quitting sports) but rather as a reflection of task difficulty or, in some cases, low effort. Brawley (1984) contends that athletes who perceive failure as due to a lack of effort can be motivated to change the outcomes of future contests.

Another factor that motivates a person occurs when success is anticipated. Athletes have a higher expectancy for future success than nonathletes if they attribute their performance to being the result of high ability ("I'm good") or low task difficulty ("I can handle this"), both stable (predictable) factors. Athletes will have lower expectations for future success if low ability ("This is tough to do") or high task difficulty ("My opponent is very good") are perceived as the causes of performance failure rather than poor effort or bad luck.

Another changeable personal factor identified by Carron is *intrinsic motivation* (IM). A person who is intrinsically motivated engages in an activity for enjoyment, fun, and other pleasures that are inherent in the activity (see Deci's cognitive evaluation theory in this chapter). The key element in promoting intrinsic motivation in sport, especially with younger athletes, is to help participants to perceive their experiences as rewarding ("I learned something" or "I'm getting better") and pleasant ("This is fun" or "I like my coach").

The fourth personal source of motivation that can be altered is based on the premise that people respond according to the *expectations of others*. If a teacher thinks that his or her student is unintelligent, the student will tend to do poorly in class. The teacher's negative perceptions about the student do not directly cause failure. The problem arises from the teacher's behavior toward the student, based on those (often inaccurate) perceptions. A student viewed by an instructor as intelligent will more likely be successful in class because of positive signals, increased attention, and other motivating influences. This is exactly what Rosenthal and Jacobson (1968) found in a study of inner-city teachers and students. They labeled this phenomenon the self-fulfilling prophecy or the Pygmalion Effect.

Coaches tend to interact with team members differently based on their perceptions of each person's skills. Athletes who are viewed by the coach as important contributors to the team receive far more attention, instruction, feedback on performance, and positive verbal ("Good try, Ralph") and nonverbal cues (thumbs up, smiles, and so forth) than "less important" members. Some athletes get less from their coaches than others, and they respond accordingly. Coaches who observe their team's star player making an error may respond with more expressions of confidence about the athlete's future performance than if the error were made by a substitute player. Further, an athlete who is treated in a disrespectful, negative manner or ignored altogether will have less self-confidence in his or her ability. This will engender a low self-image in the player ("If the coach doesn't think I can do it, I guess I can't"). Whether the expectations that coaches have of each athlete are relatively high or low is likely to influence the athlete's motivation level.

Successful athletes state repeatedly that the single most important component that is responsible for positive outcomes is "knowing you can do it" and having the *self-confidence* (in one's ability and preparation) to meet goals and succeed. The level of self-confidence influences the athlete's effort and persistence at an activity. Highly confident individuals keep going because they anticipate that their hard work will eventually pay off.

Nonchangeable personal factors. Athletes enter the sport arena with an array of learned and established traits. Personality and motor ability are examples. These relatively stable traits are unalterable. Rather than ignoring these factors ("He'll never be as good as 'so and so'"), the coach should consider certain strategies that will best utilize the player's unique talents and that will provide alternatives to help the athlete overcome limitations. For instance, an athlete who is known to get uptight in tense situations should try to avoid such situations, if possible (e.g., in baseball, a high-anxious person should not pinch-hit in tense circumstances). Or even better, the athlete should learn and use mental training techniques that help to manage stress and to reduce negative consequences. Other nonchangeable personal factors include trait anxiety (a person's predisposition to feel threatened by stressful situations) and the need for achievement (discussed earlier).

Changeable situational factors. This category comprises the most commonly used techniques for motivating athletes because situational factors are often under the coach's direct control. For example, a player who is in a slump needs a successful experience to help build his or her self-confidence. This can be structured in practice by creating situations that foster a positive outcome. Strategies such as token rewards, goal setting, variable practice sessions, and social reinforcement are examples.

According to behavioral psychologists, "behavior is strengthened or weakened on the basis of its consequences in the environment, e.g., the events which follow a response" (Rushall and Siedentop 1972, p. 13). The coach who responds to the athlete soon after performance is either positively reinforcing future responses (e.g., with applause, pats on the back, congratulatory statements) or negatively reinforcing future responses (e.g., with scowls, angry statements, stares, or by tossing objects). *Token rewards* reflect positive, not negative, reinforcement. They may be of little worth in themselves, but they have high exchange value (participants can compare their accumulated number of points, for example). Or the items may have inherent value for the recipients. Examples include decals, stars, emblems, or special privileges and treatment. Ostensibly, the selective use of these rewards motivates the individual and team to maintain certain desirable behaviors and to reduce or eliminate others.

In addition to providing the athlete with the incentive to initiate and persist at certain behaviors, *goal setting* also offers a direction or focus for these behaviors. The science of setting goals will be discussed later in this chapter.

Unless *practice sessions* are challenging and exciting, many athletes eventually find them unstimulating and more obligatory than necessary. To have a motivating effect, practice should be novel rather than routine. Attention should be provided to individuals. For example, in recent years the Los Angeles Rams football team has used aerobic dance as an alternative to the more militaristic approach to gaining cardiovascular strength. Other teams use relay races, intrasquad competition, and (confidential) records of the athletes' progress in skill development, and in establishing and meeting goals.

Carron defines *social reinforcement* as "all the positive and negative comments or reactions made by coaches, teachers, parents, and fellow players which serve to convey information of an evaluative nature to the participant" (p. 29). Using social reinforcement intelligently to change behavior often requires planning. When is it appropriate for the coach to threaten a player with punishment, to express anger or disappointment, or to show disapproval nonverbally? When is it time to offer compliments, display affection, and take a less serious, more relaxed posture? Who should receive a certain type of treatment, and who should not? Knowing the individual's personal needs helps the team leader to decide which players need a more sensitive, gentle approach and which ones need a sterner approach.

If social reinforcement is to be effective, the "reinforcer" must be meaningful to the athlete. The coach's use of rewards (positive reinforcers) and punishment or the lack of reward (negative reinforcers) should be understood by the athlete. Neither approach is motivating if the athlete's response is "Big deal."

The timing in offering social reinforcement is also important. A player who is having academic or personal problems or both needs support, not ridicule, from the coach. On the other hand, the athlete who has been given numerous chances to change his or her behavior but has not done so might warrant a stricter approach.

Examples of using social reinforcement include (1) benching and embarrassing an athlete, (2) removing a highly undesirable rule or action (e.g., allowing players to exercise at 3 P.M. instead of at 6 A.M.), and (3) presenting an attractive reward (e.g., verbally praising athletes in public to parents, reporters, or other interested parties).

Perhaps no single factor has a more dynamic effect on the athlete's mental approach to the event — indeed, to being a sport participant — than the coach's *leadership style*. Carron contends that: (1) Athletes want their coaches to care about them, not only as sport participants, but as people, too. Offering positive feedback is one way to show affection. (2) Athletes need and expect to be taught skills by their coach. Only in this way will performance improve. Good coaches are good teachers. (3) The coach's decision style influences motivation. An autocratic coach may be more desirable under certain situations while a humanistic approach is warranted in others (see chapter 7).

Nonchangeable situational factors. Many aspects of sport are inherent in the situation and are not readily changed. Each of these factors can work either in favor of, or against, the athlete's emotions and actions. The crowd, competition itself, and the athlete's group environment (in team sports) are among these nonchangeable factors.

Most participants consider observers to be one of the more pleasant, sometimes very important, aspects of competition. Highly skilled athletes love an audience. Athletes claim that the presence of others arouses and motivates them (Orlick and Partington 1986). However, *spectators* can have a deleterious influence on less skilled and inexperienced competitors. Tasks that are simple, well learned, and often practiced under competitive conditions will benefit from the presence of appreciative spectators. But when the home-team fans respond negatively to their players, the home-crowd advantage disappears and the situation becomes unpleasant for the athletes.

Traits such as the need to achieve and the need to avoid failure influence the desirability and intensity with which a person approaches the competitive situation. *Competition* against an opponent (direct competition) or a standard (indirect competition) may influence performance.

If a player does not get along with his or her teammates, the person's effectiveness may suffer. To perform at optimal levels, participants usually need to feel a sense of camaraderie toward other players. The importance of the *group environment* is often understated in sport.

The frequency with which the team meets individual and team goals is another motivating factor. *Group goals* are usually raised when the team is successful and lowered when it is not. Members of teams that consistently fail to meet team goals (1) express minimal pride in the group, (2) are unwilling to continue setting goals, (3) are less confident in the team's ability to achieve goals, (4) indicate a desire to leave the group, and (5) avoid responsibility for the group's performance, among other factors that hinder motivation.

The Science of Goal Setting

The purpose of setting goals is to motivate and to focus the effort of the performer (Harris and Harris 1984). Not only do most quality competitors tend to set goals, but they use correct guidelines for doing so. Elite athletes correctly set higher, more challenging, yet more realistic goals than their less skilled counterparts (Orlick and Partington 1986). Orlick (1986, p. 6), based on research and his own interviews with highly successful athletes, asserts that when setting goals, athletes should "dream a little. . . . Goals that are unimaginable are unachievable — not because they really are unachievable, but because they were never dreamt of." Elite competitors do not tend to sell themselves short.

According to scientific literature on goal setting, athletes should use the following goal-setting strategies:

1.   *Use performance, not outcome.* Goals should be performance-based rather than dependent on the contest's outcome. Goals that relate to winning, referred to as outcome goals, are not under the athlete's control. This reduces the purposes of goal setting, which is to focus effort and improve motivation. As Orlick (1986) claims, "If you start to assume responsibility for what is beyond your control you are inviting trouble . . . .You should assume responsibility for only that which is within your direct control." (p. 8). *Good examples of performance goals:* (a) "I will relax and feel confident before the meet." (b) "I will make contact with over 50 percent of the pitches thrown." *Poor examples of performance goals*: (a) " We will win the game." (b) "I will be a starter on the team." Neither of these goals is under the player's control and, therefore, undermine motivation and focused effort.

Another advantage of performance-based goals is that they are *observable and measurable*. How would a competitor know if a goal were attained — if performance is successful — unless the executed movements could be seen or measured? In this way, meeting goals becomes motivating to the performer and forms the basis to determine future goals.

2.   *Be realistic.* If one purpose of a goal is to provide incentive, then it has to be within the person's reach. Otherwise the performer will tend to view the goal as unmeaningful and discard it. One way to be sure a goal is realistic is

to base it on past experience. The athlete's recent history of performance will dictate what he or she will be able to do in the near future.

   3.   *Negotiate.* One of my students was a collegiate swimmer who became despondent after her coach told her to swim at a speed that, in her view, was totally unrealistic. She became so depressed and upset about a goal that, for her, was unattainable, that she could not continue to give a 100 percent effort. If her coach would have negotiated the goal based on past performance with input from the performer, the goal-setting strategy would have had its intended benefits.

   Ed Wright, head coach of the ice hockey team at State University of New York at Buffalo, believes that athletes should be involved in the setting of future performance expectations (Mechikoff and Kozar 1983). He sets goals with his athletes individually, and then the athletes set their own personal goals in the presence of Coach Wright. This approach makes sense. If the players refuse to identify with a goal (presumably set by an external agent such as the coach or a parent), then it may not be supported; the player will tend not to feel committed to attain it, and the necessary effort to meet the expectations will not be made.

   4.   *Make them challenging.* Top athletes enjoy — even need — a challenge in order to reach their potential. The suggestion that goals should be realistic and negotiated between player and coach does not mean that they should be easy to attain. On the contrary, goals that are viewed by the performer as too easy do not increase motivation. O'Block and Evans (1984) have developed a formula called interval goal setting (IGS) that allows the competitor to derive goals that are challenging and based on objective criteria — the person's past performance scores. No guesswork should be the basis for setting proper goals. The IGS model is shown in Figure 5.5.

   In an example used by O'Block and Evans, the last five performances for a swimmer performing the fifty-yard freestyle were 26.48, 26.43, 27.12, 27.82, and 26.69.

   A = 26.91 (average of 5 performances)
   B = 26.43 (best time out of 5 performances)
   C = 0.48 (difference between average and best time) (26.91 – 26.43)
   D = B (26.43) (lower boundary of interval or best time out of 5 performan-
      ces)
   E = 25.95 (interval midpoint) (26.43 – 0.48)
   F = 25.47 (upper interval boundary) (25.95 – 0.48)

   The authors contend that the interval midpoint (E) is realistically higher than the performer's best attempt (D). The upper limit (F) of the interval gives the competitor a target for exceptional performance. The result of any attempt that falls within the interval's boundaries can be called successful no matter what the contest's outcome.

   If higher scores are better, as with frequency/accuracy (such as the number

Figure 5.5   The IGS model in which speed of performance is the criterion

Average	Previous best	Midpoint	Upper boundary
A	D	E	F
26.91	26.43	25.95	25.47

Where *speed* is the criterion:

A= Average over the last 5 performances
B = Best time within the last 5 performances
C= Difference between average and best performance
      (A minus B)
D= Lower boundary of interval
E= Interval midpoint (D minus C)
F= Upper interval boundary (E minus C)

___

of contacts or baskets) or length (the shot put or pole vault, for instance) rather than speed, the IGS model is adjusted in these ways:

C = B − A (the difference between the best and average scores)
E = D + C (the interval midpoint)
F = E + C (the upper interval boundary)

5.   *Make them short term and long term*. Elite athletes know at what level they want their performance to be on both a long-term (several weeks or months away) and short-term basis (today or tomorrow's performance). The short-term goal serves the purposes of providing immediate incentive to perform at optimal levels and, predictably, to experience early success. It is important for athletes to feel that their efforts will soon lead to the achievement of some desirable outcome or that success was due to such effort. Short-term goals allow us to meet these needs.

Examples of short-term goals used by top competitors include to run or swim at a particular speed, lift a particular weight in power lifting or weight training, make a given number of tackles, or score a predetermined number of points.

Long-term goals allow a competitor to evaluate the quality of his or her performance when compared to (1) goals that were established or outcomes that occurred before the season and (2) the performance of opponents. Ideally, a series of short-term goals should lead to a realistic, yet challenging, long-term performance goal. Here's an example:

Long-term goal: I will bat .300 at the end of this baseball season. *Series of short-term goals*: (1) I will practice my batting thirty minutes at each practice at least three days a week. (2) I will make solid bat contact with at least 50 percent of the pitched balls. (3) I will be able to hit the pitched baseballs to preselected locations on the field at least 50 percent of the time. (4) In games, I will make ball contact every time at bat. (5) I will average at least two hits in each of the next five games. Other examples of short-term goals based on subcomponents of skilled tasks are listed in Figure 5.6 (Locke and Latham 1985).

Choosing which strategies to use when motivating competitors is often dictated by factors such as the personal needs, age, maturity, and skill development of the individual athlete; the type of sport; and the compatibility between the coach's leadership style and what the player considers to be "appropriate" coaching behaviors. Less-successful coaches might imitate the behaviors of talented, assertive coaches without realizing that behind the scenes, these coaches may have established a very sensitive, caring rapport with each competitor. Many coaches imitate techniques that interfere with the desired result, which is the subject of the next section.

HOW *NOT* TO MOTIVATE ATHLETES

Earlier in this chapter, examples were given of how coaches typically "motivate" athletes, using tactics that make sport psychologists cringe. Many of these techniques do not have their intended effect, especially with younger participants, and many generate only short-term incentives for athletes. In the long run, their influence may actually wane or have the opposite of their intended effect. When I observe coaches interacting with athletes in a negative, unpleasant, berating manner, my thoughts wander to the folly of a husband who demands that his physically abused wife love and cherish him after he injures her. Where's the common sense? Do people tend to respond positively to abusive treatment? Do they give optimal effort on behalf of insensitive, unpleasant leaders? Over the long term, don't people usually respond with more enthusiasm and energy toward others who have earned their respect and trust?

The following is a list of ten of the most common, but erroneous, beliefs and practices used by sport leaders (professionals and volunteers) in their attempts to motivate athletes. They are myths because coaches use these tech-

Figure 5.6   Examples of goals for subcomponents of skilled tasks

Tennis
  10 backhands in a row down the line
  10 volleys in a row alternating left and right corners
  5 first serves in a row in left third of service court; 5 in middle third; 5 in right third
  5 returns of serve in a row deep to the add court

Football
  Wide receiver: 5 over-the-head catches in a row of a 40-yard pass
    5 one-handed catches in a row of a 15-yard pass
  Defensive back: 5 interceptions in a row with receiver using preannounced route
    2 or fewer completions allowed out of 5 tries with receiver running unknown route
  Kicker: 10 field goals in a row from 40-yard line

Baseball
  Infielder: 10 hard grounders in a row fielded without error, 5 to left and 5 to right
  Outfielder: 20 fly balls caught on the run without error (5 to left, 5 to right, 5 in back, 5 in front)
  Hitter: 5 curve balls in a row hit out of infield

Wrestling
  6 takedowns using at least two different techniques against an inferior but motivated opponent in (?) minutes
  6 escapes using at least 3 different techniques in (?) minutes against same opponent

Basketball
  20 foul shots in a row
  30 uncontested lay-ups in a row
  10 jump shots in row from 10 feet
  5 out of 10 jump shots from 40 feet
  Dribbling 2 min. man-on-man against best defensive player without losing ball

Soccer
  10 shots into left corner of goal from 30 feet with goalie not moving from center of goal
  5 goals out of 10 shots from 20 feet with goalie free to move

(continued)

Hockey
    Goalie: stops 10 of 15 shots from 20 feet
    stops 5 of 10 one-on-one situations
    Forward: passes successfully 8 out of 10 times to open man in front of
        net with one defender in between
Lacrosse
    Similar to soccer and hockey
Golf
    6 drives in a row over 200 yards and landing on fairway
    15 puts in a row of 12 feet
    10 9-irons in a row onto green from 75 yards

From *Journal of Sports Psychology*, 1985, No. 3, p. 211. Copyright by Human
Kinetics. Reproduced with permission.

niques and believe in their effectiveness, yet an array of sport literature indicates
that they tend to hinder more than improve motivation.

Myth #1: Exercise for punishment.   "OK, you, that will cost you four
laps for being late to practice." "If you guys would have won on Saturday,
practice would have been over. But you didn't, so we're running an extra ten
laps." Many athletes (and physical education students) are very familiar with
perhaps the most common form of punishment used by coaches and gym
teachers—physical exercise. Whether it's push-ups, sprinting, pull-ups, or jogging, exercise has been used for years as a tool to punish and control the behavior
of students and athletes. Here are three reasons why this approach should be
avoided:

1.   If coaches want their athletes to be in good physical condition (and
      physical educators promote the value of healthy habits), then athletes
      and students should not be taught to associate physical activity with
      punishment. Isn't it more desirable to promote the enjoyment and
      advantages of staying in shape?
2.   The purpose of punishing a person is to prevent the reoccurrence of
      certain undesirable behaviors; therefore, the punishment should be an
      unpleasant experience that is understood to be a direct consequence
      of the inappropriate behavior. Don't athletes in general, especially
      children, actually enjoy being physically active? Perhaps nonpar-
      ticipation in competition would be a more effective form of punish-
      ment for those who have failed to train appropriately.
3.   This technique does not motivate the individual. The person is not
      likely to behave more positively or to have more incentive after
      performing the required activity.

Myth #2: The pregame pep talk.   Age, skill level, the type of sport, and the athlete's personality jointly dictate how an athlete will respond to various pre-event communication styles. Some participants prefer a boisterous, aggressive pregame talk, but others want as little noise and distraction, verbal and nonverbal, as possible. Some coaches use the occasion to review game strategies. The purpose and content of the pregame talk is of less importance than most leaders think, especially at the professional level. Of more importance is the emotional tone and the level of arousal elicited by the message (see chapter 3).

Myth #3: "Cut 'em down to build 'em up."   Most players are uncomfortable hearing derogatory remarks, even about opponents, for several reasons: (1) The remark might not hold true in the upcoming event. Losing to an opponent who has been ridiculed is more humiliating than losing to a respected competitor. Past performance might not be a good predictor of the future for this opponent. (2) It's unrealistic to think that an opponent has weaknesses but no strengths. Every competitor is capable of winning, and every athlete wants to know the strength of that capability. (3) Quality athletes want to think that their success was due to their skills, not because the "other guy" was weak. And (4) athletes have a great deal of empathy and mutual respect toward one another. Some athletes believe that criticizing another sport competitor is stepping on common ground; it's unethical and disloyal. Bob Lilly affirms these thoughts. He contends that "putting down" opponents is ineffective and disruptive to mental preparation, especially when done to build up your own team.

It was halftime in a collegiate football game played in 1982. The home team was losing by two touchdowns. The coach's comments in the locker room consisted of berating every player on the team, calling them "losers," "poor players," "an embarrassment to the university," among other unprintable epithets. Is it surprising that the team went on to lose the game by twenty-three points? And this was a college coach, someone who purportedly had much experience and success earlier in his coaching career.

Myth #4: "Our goal is to win."   In recent years, much has been written in the professional literature about proper goal-setting techniques. One finding that makes most coaches uncomfortable is that winning should not be a competitor's primary goal. All sport participants want to win. But focusing on the individual's performance rather than exclusively on the contest's outcome is more productive. Researchers are convinced that a goal such as "I want to win ten games" will not be as effective as "I will make 60 percent of my free throws."

Myth #5: Treating team players differently.   Athletes become incensed when the coach is not consistent in his or her interactions with all team members. I asked a few successful professional athletes—Jean Beliveau (hockey), Rusty Staub (baseball), and Johnny Robinson (football)—what single trait stands out in their minds about the best coaching they've experienced. They all agreed that the ability to treat everyone with the same respect and maturity was most important. They said that favoritism and inconsistency as coaching behaviors did more to demotivate players than anything else.

Myth #6: "If they don't complain, they're happy." Coaches often assume that a quiet player is contented. Not necessarily! An unhappy player is consumed by his or her own unpleasant thoughts. Instead of focusing on the actions and tendencies of opponents and remembering skills and strategies, dissatisfied players are thinking about issues that interfere with preparing for, and participating in, the contest. It's wrong, therefore, to assume that team members who say nothing to the coach in fact have nothing to say.

Myth #7: "What do athletes know, anyway?" No one can argue with the claim that most coaches have a sound knowledge base about the technical aspects of their sport. By the time a person becomes the head coach of a team, the person tends to feel "in control." But just as good teachers need to stay in touch with learners throughout the skill acquisition period, good coaches monitor and communicate with their athletes during practices and games. Is there a reason why a certain play didn't work? Does the other team have a certain weakness or tendency that we can use to our advantage? Do we have certain weaknesses that we need to work on immediately? Was the official correct in calling that penalty? Ask the players!

Myth #8: The postgame rampage. The contest is over, and the athletes are emotionally and physically drained. At this time, the coach sets the mood in the locker room. What the coach has to say, and how he or she says it, will leave a lasting emotional impression on the athlete. Certainly successful outcomes of competition should be reinforced with verbal recognition and adulation reflecting what went right. But a far more difficult task is to behave in a rational, mature, and professional manner after losing the contest. The ability to interact with players in a mature manner, regardless of the contest's outcome, separates the successful from the mediocre coach. And, as discussed earlier, this is not the time to discuss the details of strategy. The athletes may be too drained to absorb technical information.

Myth #9: The Napoleon Complex. Sometimes the power of directing most, if not all, actions of the players "goes to the coach's head." Some team leaders put a lot of energy into reinforcing the "boss" role with loud, aggressive, and often angry remarks. Coaches who motivate athletes successfully, however, are perceived as secure, knowledgeable, intuitive, and sensitive. They know how to share their power so that all members of the team (including players and assistants) have a sense of ownership and responsibility for team activities and outcomes. Coaches who appear to thrive on, and enjoy, the power of their position are likely to be personally insecure and lacking in self-confidence.

For example, a person was hired to be the head baseball coach after being an assistant with a team for two years. As an assistant, he was particularly well liked by the players because he had a friendly manner and a low-key, sincere style of communication. Soon after becoming head coach, he became aggressive, demanding, and hostile. He threatened to dismiss any player who committed even the slightest infraction. Conditioning exercises were grueling. In fact, he told the team of his intention to "weed out the weak links" on the team. His general communication style went abruptly from humanistic to autocratic. This coach greatly disappointed his players. They became increasingly depressed and began to lose interest in the team's success. The team's low morale was accompanied by a poor win-loss record. A month after the season, the coach resigned to become an assistant coach at another smaller school.

Myth #10: Fear! Some coaches want their athletes to fear them so that they can easily induce their athletes' arousal. Athletes who view their coach as an authoritarian or father figure are particularly susceptible to being afraid of a coach who uses fiery speeches, threats, harsh criticism, and insults to psych them up. Fear is relatively easy to bring about in subordinates. But in fact, threatening coaches invoke anxiety rather than motivation in athletes. And fear breeds resentment and disloyalty toward the coach. As English writer Thomas Fuller once said, "He that fears you present will hate you absent." Thus, fear is likely to diminish the athletes' motivation to persist at the activity.

STRATEGIES FOR MOTIVATING ATHLETES AND TEAMS

Former Oakland Raider football coach John Madden said in an interview, "I only had three rules for my players: Be on time, pay attention, and play like heck when I tell you to." Madden had a profound influence on his team because his demands were realistic, focused on game-related tasks, and sincere. He had tremendous player loyalty. Thus, the challenge for any coach is to find the goals of each athlete — what he or she really wants from participation — and to convince the individual of what he or she must do to reach them.

The ability of a coach to affect the behaviors, feelings, and attitudes of the competitors begins with the coach-athlete relationship. Some of the most important ingredients of this relationship, derived from Hoehn (1983) and Fuoss and Troppmann (1981), include:

- Communicating effectively
- Teaching skills
- Rewarding players with praise and encouragement

- Dwelling on strengths instead of weaknesses
- Appearing organized and in control
- Inserting occasional times for fun and humor
- Developing mutual respect between coach and athlete
- Knowing when to take a break and when to give the athletes a day off
- Developing leadership skills among players
- Supporting the athletes after errors and losses as well as upon making good plays and winning
- Setting limits fairly and consistently on inappropriate behaviors
- Not embarrassing, intimidating, or criticizing the character of an athlete.

Some effective techniques for motivating athletes to reach their potential have been developed by Carron (1984), Jones, Wells, Peters, and Johnson (1982), Cratty (1983), Orlick and Partington (1986), and Mechikoff et al. (1983). These are the "do's" of coaching success.

Get to know each performer. Knowing each team member starts with learning and using each athlete's first name. This promotes trust between coach and athlete. Players who are addessed by their first names become less intimidated by the authority figure. The nonverbal message is "the coach knows and recognizes me. He may even like me." The next step is developing a relationship with the athlete that supersedes the sport arena. This does not include socializing with the players (many of whom are uncomfortable spending their "free time" with their coach) but rather means making an effort to listen to the players' feelings on team-related issues, discussing topics unrelated to the team (e.g., academic experiences, movies, or current events), and showing a genuine concern for the athlete as a person.

Plan it out. Influencing the thoughts and actions of others doesn't usually happen by itself. Effective coaches anticipate using certain techniques that enhance player motivation. Examples include structuring a practice session to improve team morale, using a particular strategy recommended by the players during the contest, interacting with individuals in a manner that will enhance self-confidence, bringing in a guest speaker to address the team, taking a break from the daily grind of practice, and attending to injured athletes to let all team members know that no one is forgotten and that everyone is appreciated for their contribution.

Agree on future directions and actions. American philosopher Eric Hoffer said, "The only way to predict the future is to have power to shape the future." The coach's ability to create and plan for the athletes' future aspirations is dictated by his or her ability to convince players of two things: (1) the worthiness of these aspirations and (2) the athletes' ability to act upon and to achieve them. In order to move in the same direction, the performers must be able to share the coach's vision.

Develop team friendships. Affiliation is a primary need of most sport participants (Alderman 1974). The athlete who does not have at least one friend on the team is rarely a happy member of the group. Group satisfaction often fuels energy to support others. Coaches should help to ensure that each player is interacting on a positive basis with others, at least during practice and games.

Develop skills. There is no greater motivator in sport than success. But success does not happen accidentally. It requires effort and determination. If coaches expect athletes to learn skills, improve their performance, and eventually succeed, they *must* teach skills and strategies.

Everybody needs recognition. The need for prestige, status, dominance, attention, importance, appreciation, and recognition are firmly based in human nature; they underlie human motivation (Fuoss and Troppmann 1981). These needs may even be greater in elite athletes than in nonathletes (Cratty 1983; Vanek and Cratty 1970). An occasional pat on the back, literally and figuratively, gives the athletes a reason for continuing their efforts.

Discipline is not a four-letter word. There's nothing wrong with setting limits on inappropriate behaviors. In fact, many athletes test the coach's ability and willingness to carry out team policies and disciplinary measures. Testing is the individual's way of making sure that the adult guardian (e.g., the parent, coach, or teacher), cares about him or her. According to Ginott (1965, pp. 114–115), "They feel more secure when they know the borders of permissible action." In fact, "When a [person] is allowed behavior that he knows should not be tolerated, his anxiety mounts." The coach who sets limits and responds quickly and appropriately when tested communicates sincerity.

Perceptions are everything. As an old adage says, "An ounce of image is worth a pound of performance." The athlete's perception of his or her role on the team, the interpretation of a coach's actions and statements, and other personally held views are reflections of "the truth" through the athlete's eyes. For example, an athlete may attribute a lack of playing time to a poor relationship with the coach. "The coach just doesn't like me," he or she might complain. If an athlete feels that the coach "does not like me," it's this perception that the coach must react to rather than how the coach really feels. This is especially important if the athlete's perception is wrong. Coaches must deal with reality as their players interpret it.

Make it fun. Undoubtedly, the coach wants to win, but it's dangerous to produce a team climate that is continuously submerged in a sea of hard work, seriousness, and redundant, time-consuming preparation. In human motivation, more is not always better. Having fun and adding some humor promotes intrinsic motivation while it reduces the onset of mental fatigue.

Real coaches eat quiche. Coaches, males and females, should exhibit similar behaviors and attitudes whether interacting with male or female participants. Crying, disclosing personal feelings, and showing aggression should be perceived as normal types of expression for all athletes. Motivation is also an emotion that is virtually blind to gender differences.

Remember that winning is NOT the only thing. At least it shouldn't be. There are so many experiences in sport to feel good about that it's sad to think that the only pleasant experiences are associated with the final outcome. Why dismiss opportunities for satisfaction just because the final outcome was not in the participant's favor? Given the rarity in which most teams win consistently, total reliance on victory as the sole criterion for success in sport will make a lot of athletes — and coaches — feel very unsuccessful. The performer's effort and improvement are examples of other reasons to "celebrate" success.

Beware of the self-fulfilling prophecy. As indicated earlier, it's important to perceive and respond to each athlete in a manner that promotes confidence in his or her capability. To paraphrase Longfellow, athletes should be judged by what they are capable of doing, not based on what they have already done.

When T-E-A-M is a four-letter word. Many coaches seem enamored with the importance of "sticking together," and they promote slogans such as "Teamwork is everything" and "There is no *I* in team." Certainly, something may be said for having camaraderie and good personal relations among team members. Players want very much to have the respect, admiration, and support of their teammates. However, effective coaches understand that the needs, priorities, and personalities of all athletes are not identical. Individual differences that exist among participants are respected — at least to a point — by successful coaches. There is a middle ground regarding when to demand conformity and when to allow players to go their own way. It's the coach's job to find and respect that middle ground.

How to blow your stack for motivation. The late child psychologist Haim Ginott said, "Anger, like a hurricane, is a fact of life to be acknowledged and prepared for" (1965, p. 56). Thus, it's not the absence of anger that should be expected of coaches, but the correct handling of it. The expression of anger can have an arousal-inducing, motivating effect on the athlete. In fact, Ginott contends that "failure to get angry at certain moments would only convey to the [athlete] indifference, not goodness. Those who care cannot altogether shun anger" (p. 57). Ginott's three steps to surviving hostile communication between parent and child have direct implications in sport.

He suggests using three cognitive strategies for the constructive use of anger in sport leadership: accepting (1) that athletes will make the coach angry, (2) that coaches are entitled to feel anger without guilt or shame, and (3) that coaches are entitled to express angry feelings provided they do not attack the athlete's personality or character. An example of proper expression is:

> When I see a lack of effort on the court, I get angry. I feel like you don't really want to play. If that's the case, you have to tell me because I have several players who would love to get in there. If you want to play on this team, Frank, let's see more effort. The choice is yours.

In this example, the coach used no name-calling, no insulting or demeaning statements, and no unrealistic threats. Sometimes an athlete needs, even unconsciously asks for, a verbal "kick in the pants." The important thing is to do it effectively without demotivating the individual.

Motivating the Child Athlete

Children are not miniature adults. They participate in sport for different reasons than older competitors and, therefore, do not have the same needs as those of more mature athletes. Older players have superior skills, are better at coping with sport-related stress, and consider winning to be a primary goal of competition. Children, on the other hand, often do not have adequate skills, are easily upset by and unable to cope with the pressures put upon them by impatient and insensitive adults, and play sports to have fun and to learn new skills (Gould 1984). Chapter 11 includes specific strategies for motivating child athletes.

Motivating the Nonstarter

Making the starters happy and keeping them motivated is easy compared to having the same effect on the substitutes. The psychological problems that beset the "bench-warmer" include frustration, alienation, futility, and a loss of self-confidence (Tutko et al. 1976). Ultimately, the coach's task is to help every substitute to feel that he or she is an important team member. Group identity depends on the coach's ability to define and to communicate each person's role in the group and on the athlete's perception of his or her role as an important contribution to team success. Motivation will be a natural outcome of this process.

How can coaches motivate athletes who have limited playing time? This is where coaching really *is* a science. First (and foremost), avoid labeling anyone a "substitute." Every athlete should feel that he or she is contributing to the team's welfare. This means that starters should not have more privileges than substitutes, even though the coach may put more time into preparing the starting team. A second important suggestion is to provide nonstarters with opportunities to learn and demonstrate skills, particularly under practice conditions that simulate actual competition. No one should feel that they're "wasting their time" practicing for the contest, a frequent complaint of nonstarters. Such opportunities should include a liberal dose of positive verbal and nonverbal cues that indicate admiration, respect, and trust in their ability. Many substitutes erroneously feel that the reason they don't play is because their coach doesn't like them. This is particularly destructive for athletes who want and need a positive relationship with their coach.

In general, strategies for motivating nonstarters should aim toward giving them feelings of importance to the team, indicating that they are contributing in some meaningful way, and providing them with opportunities to learn, improve, and eventually demonstrate their skills in competitive situations. However, the coach should never be dishonest about his or her intentions or in evaluations. For example, promising a date on which an athlete may get into the contest and then reneging on that promise, giving verbal praise of skills without supporting these statements with more playing time, and being less than honest about the reasons why an individual is not playing more often or starting (e.g., "We need a strong bench") will reduce the player's willingness to remain an inactive team member. The coach wants to promote positive future aspirations. Just because the playing time of nonstarters is limited presently doesn't mean that they won't eventually perform at acceptable levels and, perhaps, even start. That may be sooner than coaches think if a starting player is injured. Substitutes should be treated as potential first-string players.

Team Motivation

Clearly, promoting friendship, trust, mutual admiration, respect, and harmony on the team is important. Common sense dictates that athletes who like one another will also tend to support one another. They will be more motivated to be part of a group that meets the goals of its members. Here are some recommendations for the coach:

Compatible group and personal goals. Be sure that the individual's goals are compatible with team goals. The coach should first discuss the team strategy before players develop their goals so that their performance expectations will be realistic. Agreement on team objectives will enhance the individual's incentive to develop and attempt to meet personal goals.

Agreement on team goals. The team should feel a sense of ownership toward group goals. Even when group goals are initially set by the coach, the competitors must identify with them, or they will hardly be motivated to achieve them. Coaches should explain the basis and reasons for group goals and what it will take to reach them.

Dealing with group heterogeneity.   Teams will usually comprise athletes with different needs, different ethnic and racial backgrounds, and different personalities. The coach's role is to ensure that dissimilarity among team members does not distract from the team's purpose and erode group solidarity. Whether team members spend their free time together may be unimportant, but it is quite important that all members get along in preparing for, and participating in, the contest.

Awareness of role.   One way to improve the quality of team interaction is to be sure that every member is aware of his or her role in the group (Carron 1984). Dean Smith, basketball coach at the University of North Carolina (Chapel Hill), is a great proponent of ensuring that each player realizes his or her role on the team and the importance of that role. For instance, a high school baseball coach realized that one of his athletes was not a good hitter but had excellent speed on the base paths. This individual was very proud to be known as the team's leading pinch runner.

Planning interaction.   To prevent cliques and social isolation on the team, Carron (1984) suggests the use of mandatory interaction. The objective of this approach is to ensure personal communication among team members. Examples of preplanned events and situations that require players to interact include the rotation of roommates, preselection of seating arrangements at team meals and on road trips, equal representation in team leadership positions such as cocaptains and committee heads, and the organization of team committees to serve various specifically defined roles. A player without at least one friend on the team is usually not a happy participant.

Allowing for team-coach communication.   Only the naive coach thinks that the absence of a player's complaint automatically signals satisfaction. Not dealing with unpleasant issues is to pretend that they don't exist. Nothing can be farther from the truth. Players who are bothered by certain feelings are less able to concentrate on contest-related tasks, especially in the mental preparation for competition. Providing some vehicle to voice these concerns is healthy because it facilitates confronting issues and dealing with them in a constructive manner to everyone's satisfaction. It's important to "clear the air."

Before the contest.   Pep talks were discussed earlier. The issue here is what to say to the team before competing that will provide incentive regardless of the anticipated outcome. According to Yukelson, an underdog might be addressed this way (1984, p. 234):

> If my team were a decided underdog, I would provide information that we are not as bad as people claim, and that the opposing team has weaknesses and can be beat if we play to our potential. If our team were a decided favorite, I would want to

place the probability of success at the intermediate range of difficulty in order to avoid complacency. I would focus on our opponent's strengths rather than our own strengths. Thus, I would provide proximal short-term goals for the team as an incentive or standard of excellence to shoot for.

After the contest. Motivating athletes does not end after the event. What should the coach say after the contest to affect team motivation? Former all-pro defensive tackle Bob Lilly recommends that a coach just "be himself . . . and speak your heart." He reflects the feelings of professional athletes who are uncomfortable with hostile tirades following a loss. Athletes are also disappointed after losing. At this time, an honest, but sensitive, reflection of the performance should be offered. Lilly suggests that postgame speeches be kept short. The players are tired, sweaty, and generally not mentally receptive to long, drawn-out speeches. There is a tremendous emotional letdown after a contest that inhibits the performer's ability to think clearly and to focus attention for long. Comments should be short, honest, constructive, and, if possible, positive.

SUMMARY

Motivation is both an art and a science. The art of motivating others means having a communication style — verbal and nonverbal — that offers a mixture of credibility, knowledge, and sensitivity. Associated with motivating athletes are numerous myths, practices of coaches that have been handed down over the years with no scientific basis. Often, these techniques do more harm than good. Intimidation, threats, physical abuse, and hostile criticism are examples. Motivation is also a science in that the leader must know when to say something and how to say it.

Different types of motivation have been identified. Achievement motivation, intrinsic and extrinsic motivation, and competence motivation are based on a person's strong desire to achieve and to deal effectively with his or her environment for a prolonged period of time. Carron's (1984) motivation model illustrates the numerous factors that underlie motivation in sport and suggests how team leaders can be sensitive to nonchangeable characteristics about the athletes (e.g., personality) while implementing strategies to enhance motivational factors that are amenable to change. Children, nonstarters, and teams require various motivational techniques of which the coach should become aware.

Finally, one effective method of motivating athletes is to set goals. For best results, goals should be challenging yet realistic and based on previous performance, short term and long term, performance-based rather than outcome-based, and observable and measurable. Coaches and athletes should work jointly to set goals and based on ongoing assessments of performance, should agree to alter them.

REVIEW QUESTIONS

1. The definition of motivation includes key words or phrases that have implications for athletic behavior. For each of the following, explain what the coach should do to promote the athlete's motivation: (a) direction of behavior, (b) selectivity of behavior, (c) persistence, (d) goal achievement.

2. Describe five unique traits of athletes who have a high need to achieve. Given these traits, and others, what approaches should a coach take to motivate athletes with high-need achievement? In contrast, what tactics might be used with low-need achievers?

3. Do you agree with White that the need for competence as a motivator is inherent? Defend your answer. How does Harter expand White's theory? What are the implications for coaches in the use of competence motivation in sport?

4. Deci, in his cognitive evaluation theory, contends that a person's attempt to meet goals is directed by controlling and information aspects. Describe how a coach can increase intrinsic motivation by influencing each of these aspects.

5. How does intrinsic motivation differ from extrinsic motivation? How could a person argue in favor of using awards to increase intrinsic motivation? How could someone argue that the use of awards actually decreases intrinsic motivation and, instead, increases extrinsic motivation?

6. What does the term *hygiene* mean in Herzberg's motivation-hygiene theory? List three hygiene factors. How could a coach prevent or reduce the presence of three of these factors?

7. Carron's model includes four factors that are, or are not, subject to change. Describe and defend the use of 10 techniques a coach could use to motivate athletes using at least two techniques for each of the four factors. For each technique: (a) identify which of the four factors apply, and (b) explain why you feel this technique should facilitate the athlete's motivation level.

8. How do child athletes differ from older, more mature players in primary reasons for participating in sport? What, then, should a coach of youth sports do to motivate younger performers? In what ways would these motivational techniques be *similar to* and *differ from* the motivation of older athletes?

9. What are three advantages of goal setting in sport? Are there any disadvantages? If so, describe at least one situation or condition in which setting a goal is not advisable. Finally, list five examples of goals that incorporate the guidelines listed in this chapter.

10. More sport competitors are substitutes than starters. Sustaining the motivation of these nonstarters is probably one of the more challenging tasks in coaching. Describe (a) why nonstarters are such an important part of the team, and (b) how coaches can keep them motivated.

REFERENCES

Alderman, R. 1974. *Psychological behavior in sport*. Philadelphia, PA: W. B. Saunders.

Atkinson, J. W. 1957. Motivational determinants of risk-taking behavior. *Psychological Review* 64: 359–72.

Baumeister, R. F. October 1985. *Performance under pressure: A self-attention model of choking*. A paper presented at a conference of the Canadian Society for Psychomotor Learning and Sport Psychology, Montreal, Quebec, Canada.

Birch, D., and J. Veroff. 1966. *Motivation: A study of action*. Belmont, CA: Brooks/Cole.

Carron, A. V. 1984. *Motivation: Implications for coaching and teaching*. London, Ontario, Canada: Sports Dynamics.

Cox, R. 1985. *Sport psychology: concepts and applications*. Dubuque, IA: Wm. C. Brown.

Cratty, B. J. 1983. *Psychology in contemporary sport. Guidelines for coaches and athletes*. Englewood Cliffs, NJ: Prentice-Hall.

Crippen, J. J. 1981. *Leadership: Strategies for organizational effectiveness*. New York: Amacom.

Deci, E. L. 1975. *Intrinsic motivation*. New York: Plenum.

Fuoss, D. E., and R. J. Troppmann. 1981. *Effective coaching: A psychological approach*. New York: John Wiley & Sons.

Gerson, R. 1978. Intrinsic motivation: Implications for children's athletics. *Motor Skills: Theory into Practice* 2: 111–19.

Ginott, H. G. 1965. *Between parent and child*. New York: Avon.

Ginott, H. G. 1969. *Between parent and teenager*. New York: Avon.

Gould, D. 1984. Psychosocial development and children's sport. In *Motor development during childhood and adolescence*, ed. J. R. Thomas, pp. 212–36. Minneapolis, MN: Burgess.

Halliwell, W. 1980. Intrinsic motivation in sport. In *Sport psychology: An analysis of athlete behavior*, ed. W. F. Straub, pp. 85–90. Ithaca, NY: Mouvement.

Harris, D. V., and B. L. Harris. 1984. *The athlete's guide to sports psychology: Mental skills for physical people*. Champaign, IL: Human Kinetics.

Harter, S. 1978. Effectance motivation reconsidered: Toward a developmental model. *Human Development* 21: 34–64.

Herzberg, F. 1966. *Work and the nature of man*. New York: Thomas T. Crowell.

Hoehn, R. G. 1983. *Solving coaching problems: Strategies for successful team development*. Boston: Allyn & Bacon.

Jones, B. J., L. J. Wells, R. E. Peters, and D. J. Johnson. 1982. *Guide to effective coaching: Principles and practice*. Boston: Allyn & Bacon.

Locke, E. A., and Latham, G. P. 1985. The application of goal setting to sports. *Journal of Sport Psychology*, 7: 205–222.

McClelland, D. C. 1961. *The achieving society*. Princeton, NJ: Van Nostrand.

Mechikoff, R. A., and B. Kozar. 1983. *Sport psychology: The coach's perspective*. Springfield, IL: Thomas.

Nideffer, R. M. 1981. *The ethics and practice of applied sport psychology*. Ithaca, NY: Mouvement.

O'Block, F. R. and F. H. Evans. 1984. Goal setting as a motivational technique. In *Psychological Foundations of Sport*, ed. J. M. Silva and R. S. Weinberg, pp. 188–196. Champaign, IL: Human Kinetics.

Officer, S. A., and L. B. Rosenfeld. 1985. Self-disclosure to male and female coaches by female high school athletes. *Journal of Sport Psychology* 7: 360–70.

Orlick, T., and C. Botterill. 1975. *Every kid can win*. Chicago: Nelson-Hall.

Orlick, T., and J. Partington. 1986. *Psyched: Inner views of winning*. Ottawa, Ontario, Canada: Coaching Association of Canada.

Rees, C. R. 1980. Motivation-hygiene theory and sport participation— Finding room for the "I" in "team." *Motor Skills: Theory into Practice* 4: 24–31.

Rejeski, W. 1980. Causal attribution: An aid to understanding and motivating athletes. *Motor Skills: Theory into Practice* 4: 32–36.

Roberts, G. C. 1978. Children's assignment of responsibility for winning and losing. In *Psychological perspectives in youth sports*, ed. F. L. Smoll and R. E. Smith, pp. 145–71. Washington, DC: Hemisphere.

Roberts, G. C., D.A. Keiber and J. L. Duda. 1981. An analysis of motivation in children's sport: The role of perceived competence in participation. *Journal of Sport Psychology* 3: 206–16.

Rosenthal, R., and L. Jacobson. 1968. *Pygmalion in the classroom: Teacher expectations and pupils' intellectual development.* New York: Holt, Rinehart & Winston.

Rotella, R. 1983. Motivational concerns of high level gymnasts. In *The mental aspects of gymnastics*, ed. L. E. Uneståhl, pp. 67–85. Orebro, Sweden: VEJE.

Rushall, B. S., and D. Siedentop. 1972. *The development and control of behavior in sport and physical education.* Philadelphia, PA: Lea & Febiger.

Singer, R. N. 1977. Motivation in sport. *International Journal of Sport Psychology* 8: 1–21.

Singer, R. N. 1984. *Sustaining motivation in sport.* Tallahassee, FL: Sport Consultants International, Inc.

Smith, R. 1986. Principles of positive reinforcement and performance feedback. In *Applied sport psychology: Personal growth to peak performance*, ed. J. M. Williams, pp. 35–46. Palo Alto, CA: Mayfield.

Tutko, T., and W. Bruns. 1976. *Winning is everything: And other American myths.* New York: Macmillan.

Vallerand, R. J., and G. Reid. 1984. On the causal effects of perceived competence on intrinsic motivation: A test of cognitive evaluation theory. *Journal of Sport Psychology* 6: 94–102.

Vanek, M., and B. J. Cratty. 1970. *Psychology and the superior athlete.* New York: Macmillan.

Weiner, B. 1974. *Achievement motivation and attribution theory.* Morristown, NJ: General Learning Press.

White, R. W. 1959. Motivation reconsidered: The concept of competence. *Psychological Review* 66: 297–331.

Yukelson, D. P. 1984. Group motivation in sport teams. In *Psychological foundations of sport*, ed. J. M. Silva and R. S. Weinberg, pp. 229–40. Champaign, IL: Human Kinetics.

6

Aggression in Sport

I tell you that in the arts of life man invents nothing; but in the arts of death he outdoes Nature herself, and produces by chemistry and machinery all the slaughter of plague, pestilence, and famine. The peasant I tempt today eats and drinks what was eaten and drunk by the peasants of ten thousand years ago. But when he goes out to slay, he carries a marvel of mechanism that lets loose at the touch of his finger all the hidden molecular energies, and leaves the javelin, the arrow, and the blowpipe of his fathers far behind. In the art of peace, man is a bungler. Man measures his strength by solely, it seems, his destructiveness."

(George Bernard Shaw, *Man and Superman*)

Defensive end Charles Martin of the Green Bay Packers football team was suspended for two games (with a loss of fifteen thousand dollars in pay) after "body slamming" to the ground Chicago Bears quarterback Jim McMahon in a game. In another incident one week later, Chicago Bears linebacker Otis Wilson hit Pittsburgh Steelers receiver Louis Lipps in the jaw with his forearm and was subsequently suspended for one game (with a loss in pay). And professional ice hockey is a sport well known for flagrant and expected use of violent behavior by the athletes. In fact, the frequency of physical abuse in hockey has moved politicians to outlaw it (as noted in *USA Today*, 11 December 1986):

Boston Mayor Raymond F. Flynn, angered by a recent bench-clearing brawl between the NHL's (Boston) Bruins and Montreal (Canadiens), said Wednesday he will send a letter to the city's professional sports teams to put them on notice that violence will not be tolerated.

The purpose of this chapter is to gain a better understanding of aggressive behavior, one of the most common yet least understood aspects of human behavior in competitive sport. Many coaches, under the false belief that "more is better," encourage athletes to be increasingly aggressive. As we'll see later in this chapter, aggression is the wrong strategy when it is used in a blind and irrational manner. Silva (1980) and others have argued that sport aggression tends to decrease athletic performance rather than to help it. Specific sports, skills, and situations require different levels of aggression. Often, in fact, even the slightest aggressive act is inappropriate (e.g., in golf putting, bowling, or shooting). But in many sports, aggression is an integral part of the competition and is an important component of player and team success. Of primary importance to the athlete is the extent to which aggressive behavior leads to success in one's specific sport experiences.

In addition to defining the concept of aggression, in this chapter we will (1) review aggression theory to understand and explain the possible causes of aggressive behavior in humans, (2) examine the relationship between aggression and sport performance, and (3) discuss the implications of aggression in sport for the coach and the competitor.

WHAT IS AGGRESSION?

Sometimes to understand a concept, it helps to know what it is not. For example, contrary to popular opinion, thinking negative thoughts or expressing a desire to hurt someone is not aggression. Aggression is not defined by feelings such as anger or any other emotion. Aggression is behavior. Alderman (1974, pp. 225) defines *aggression* as "the intentional response a person makes to inflict pain or harm on another person." This definition is contrary to the concept of what Husman and Silva (1984) call *proactive assertion* — forceful yet acceptable behavior. For instance, blocking in football, checking in ice hockey, maintaining a defensive position for rebounding in basketball, and breaking up a double play in baseball are assertive behaviors if executed without malice and as integral parts of the contest. But these acts become aggressive when the player's intention is to injure the opponent or to behave in a more hostile manner than is necessary in meeting the performance objective.

A second characteristic of aggression, in addition to its behavioral content, is that it is intentional. Aggression does not happen by accident. The aggressor

must desire harm or injury to the intended victim. A third dimension is that harm or injury must actually occur. The unpleasant outcome need not be physical, however. Acts that intimidate, embarrass, or deprive another person of something are also aggression. And fourth, aggression must involve interacting with another living being. Hurting a person or animal is aggression; kicking a chair is not.

Aggression has been categorized as being either *instrumental* or *goal reactive*. The purpose of instrumental aggression is to achieve some goal. Harm to another person might occur accidentally in the process of attempting to reach a goal. Instrumental aggression differs from Husman and Silva's concept of proactive assertion in that the latter does not usually result in harm or injury to an opponent. Although an athlete exhibiting instrumentally aggressive behavior may not seek to injure an opponent, such an outcome is still viewed as an integral part of the game. For instance, baseball pitchers may want to throw the ball inside to a batter who is crowding the plate in order to prevent him or her from hitting pitches on the outside corner. A proactive assertive action would be a pitch that is thrown inside, but at a slower than maximal speed so as to greatly reduce the chance of hitting the batter. An instrumentally aggressive act would be to throw the ball inside at a fast speed to intimidate the batter; if the batter is hit, this is viewed as part of the game. Next time, the hitter will not likely stand as close to the plate and will be more vulnerable to strikes on the outside corner. Purposely injuring the batter, however, is not intended.

Goal reactive aggression, on the other hand, has as its purpose injury or harm to another person. The "brush-back" pitch in baseball serves as a good example. Skilled pitchers might intentionally throw the ball inside either to psychologically intimidate or to "jam" the hitter to prevent solid bat contact with the ball. Both reasons for the inside pitch serve the goal of reducing the opponent's success, an example of instrumental aggression. However, if the pitcher intended to hit the batter with the thrown ball, then this attempt at injuring an opponent would be goal or reactive aggression.

Typically, the type of aggression most commonly associated with sport is instrumental. This may be for three reasons. First, purposely injuring another player is often met with some punitive measure by the sport arbiter, the umpire or referee. Penalties effectively prevent or stall the meeting of performance goals. As one coach put it, "I tell my players, 'In the end you lose when you abuse.'" The second reason comes from laboratory research findings in which athletes, both males (Figler 1978) and females (Finn 1978; Thirer 1978) have been found to react less aggressively to violent visual stimuli than nonathletes. In fact, even when they are provoked, athletes tend to react with less hostility than nonathletes (Zillman, Johnson, and Day 1974) and usually refrain from intentionally injuring an opponent. And third, based on their interviews with the 1984 Canadian Olympic team, Orlick and Partington (1986) found that highly skilled athletes want to perceive their success as due to their high ability rather than to an opponent's injury (in which the outcome is perceived as a function of luck or lower task difficulty; see chapter 4).

Apparently, despite some aggressive moments during the contest, skilled athletes respect one another. For example, even in contact sports, such as boxing, wrestling, and football, players will interact with one another immediately after the contest in a warm and sincere manner. The objective of their actions during the contest was not to hurt or to maim their opponents, but rather to win the contest. In fact, athletes are generally uncomfortable with deliberately trying to injure an opponent. As a consultant with a collegiate football team, I would hear the coach, in his pregame talks, urge the players to "hurt" the opposing team. "Tear their heads off," he said before one game, which was subsequently lost by a large margin. The athletes did not respond enthusiastically to the suggestion. After practice sessions, I asked the players about the directive to injure an opponent. Not a single team member indicated his willingness to consciously hurt another player.

■■■■

THEORETICAL BASES OF AGGRESSION

To explain or predict behavior, it is necessary to understand its probable causes. For many years, scientists have offered biological and psycho-sociological explanations for aggressive behavior in humans. These theories suggest how to control and to direct the expression of aggression in a productive and positive manner if, in fact, it can be controlled and directed. For example, observing and participating in sports competition has been viewed as an outlet for a person's innate need to express his or her aggression. But some individuals seem to need this outlet more than others. This leads to an important question: Is aggression genetically determined? If so, is it possible to predict a person's tendencies to aggress and, subsequently, to anticipate such behavior and to channel it in a productive direction? Or is aggression a reaction to some psychosocial phenomenon such as frustration (inability to avoid that rush-hour traffic) or learned social behavior ("You mean I can't fight in ice hockey just like the pros?"). The areas that have received most attention in the scientific literature include the biological (or instinct) theories, the frustration-aggression hypothesis, and the social learning theories.

Biological/Instinct Theories

The claim that human beings are genetically programmed is not a popular or acceptable theory to some people because it implies that environmental and social factors have no role in human behavior. In sport, for example, the role of proper training and skill acquisition would be neglected if coaches and athletes assumed that elite athletes were "born and not made." It may also be assumed in genetic theory that aggressive behavior is inevitable and a "normal" response in sport. Biological/instinct theories assume that aggression is a natural, innate characteristic of all persons and that this characteristic developed through evolution. The "proof " of this assertion, originally postulated by Konrad Lorenz (1966) in his famous book *On Aggression*, is the tendency of living beings to fight for survival, especially for territory. Territory is a foremost objective after the primary needs of food and procreation have been fulfilled. In fact, the birth and rearing of offspring provide a fundamental purpose for territorial possession, especially in animals. Another "innatist," Robert Ardrey (1961), has originated the concept of the *territorial imperative* to explain aggressive behavior as a means for survival. He asserts,

If we defend the title to our land or to the sovereignty of our country, we do it for

reasons no different, no less innate, no less ineradicable than do the lower animals.
. . . All of us will give everything we are for a place of our own (p. 161).

However, to Montagu (1968) and Morris (1967), the extrapolation of animal behavior to humankind is a fatal flaw in the biological/genetic explanation for aggression in humans. As Montagu asserts, "With the exception of the instinctoid reactions in infants to sudden withdrawals of support and to sudden loud noises, the human being is entirely instinctless" (p. 11). And Morris reminds us that not all animals, even primates, are territorial, and that the interaction among primate groups are less defensive and less aggressive than among carnivores.

Still, relatively recent studies, particularly at the Minnesota Center for Twin and Adoption Research and at the University of Southern California (USC), have shown that personality in general, and aggressive — even criminal — behaviors, in particular, follow striking hereditary patterns. For example, scientists at USC have found that children whose biological parents were convicts were much more likely to become criminals themselves. They agree that child rearing and other social factors certainly help to determine who becomes a criminal, but they contend that a strong hereditary component makes some individuals more likely to behave in socially unacceptable ways. Some scientists firmly believe that aggression, criminal tendencies, and intellectual ability may be biologically inevitable.

Suppose Lorenz, Ardrey, and other proponents of the biological basis for aggressive behavior are right. The implications of such thinking worry social scientists. Do we "throw away the key" rather than rehabilitate people whose heredity "hard-wires" them to become aggressive? Should so-called "predictive tests" be used to diagnose certain personality types, particularly those with a disposition toward aggression? Would society respond to the "future aggressor" in a manner that might actually cause or facilitate the occurrence of undesirable behaviors? In other words, would a person who was "diagnosed" as aggressive tend to become so? We know, for example, that people often act according to the expectations of "significant" others — people whose opinions and impressions they care about (a phenomenon referred to as the *self-fulfilling prophecy*). And, in a worst-case scenario, would some cultures and races be perceived as superior to others under such a testing program?

On the other hand, if a genetic/biological basis for aggression were confirmed and accepted, perhaps the small percentage of children with genetic traits likely to predispose them to aggressive behavior could be screened out and given special attention, diverting these children from criminal activities to more productive and happy lives. Perhaps all members of society would benefit if a genetic disposition to aggress were recognized.

According to innate theory, there is a natural buildup of aggression that requires its release through productive, acceptable channels (that must be why they invented ice hockey). Thus, daily activities could be structured that would allow the "release" of tension. Purging of the need to aggress is called *catharsis*.

The catharsis hypothesis (from the Greek word *katharsis*, "to cleanse or purify") was derived from the work of Leonard Berkowitz at the University of Wisconsin (1970). He suggested that the buildup of anger, tension, and other unpleasant feelings does not subside unless these emotions can be discharged in aggressive action. Berkowitz concluded that engaging in various activities, including competitive sports, lowers the person's inclination to attack others. In partial support of Berkowitz, Jack Hokanson and his colleagues at Florida State University (1962, 1963) found that the systolic blood pressure of male subjects who had an opportunity to give electric shock to a frustrator returned to normal more rapidly than it did in those subjects who were rewarded, did not have an opportunity to respond, or were in the control group. However, according to Husman (1980), this conclusion assumes, perhaps erroneously, that blood pressure is the best measure of arousal (especially in the absence of measuring an emotional counterpart such as anger or frustration). Theoretically, then, a sport performer or a person who participates in competitive sports should demonstrate less aggressive behavior than nonparticipants and observers. Right?

Wrong! The research literature does not support the catharsis hypothesis. On a global basis, scientists know that children who watch great amounts of violent television programs tend to show more hostility than infrequent viewers (Larsen 1968). In sport, Cox (1985) reports of several studies that do not support cathartic effect upon the observance of athletic contests. In fact, pre- and postmeasures of aggression, using paper-and-pencil inventories, show that state aggression tends to rise after the observance of competitive sporting events.

Another indictment of the biological/innate explanation of aggression is that it does not contribute to explaining the phenomenon. According to Alderman (1974, p. 231),

> To argue that aggressiveness is a universal instinct — that everyone possesses it — innate in man, allows us to explain and understand very little about the construct. . . . It provides us with no new information. When something happens it is ascribed to an instinct; when it doesn't happen, the instinct is said to be lacking. This explains nothing.

Alderman's argument is similar to the position of persons who think that the nature-versus-nurture debate regarding other characteristics (such as intelligence, personality, and motor ability) is pointless. If each person has a predetermined genetic disposition, so what? If, in fact, a person's capacity cannot be altered — if one person's capability is different from someone else's — why not get on with the business of using every social and psychological means available to influence the person's environment? Why not "grease the wheels" to help each individual have a better chance of reaching that inherited capacity? The one thing that scientists (naturists and nurturists) do agree on is that certain situations or stimuli seem to trigger aggression. And one of the most common emotions that initiates an aggressive response is frustration.

Frustration-Aggression Hypothesis

The English poet John Keats said, "There is no fiercer hell than failure in a great attempt." Most skilled sport competitors would agree. Because of their intense desire to achieve in sport, athletes are probably more susceptible than most others to making "great attempts" and suffering unpleasant emotions when they don't succeed at them. The frustration of not meeting goals and not satisfying personal needs can make a person angry. This is the basis for the frustration-aggression hypothesis developed by Dollard and his colleagues at Yale University (1939). The authors contend that aggressive behavior is a logical and expected consequence of frustration.

Take, for example, two basketball players attempting to rebound the ball. Both are positioning themselves near the basket, which sometimes leads to pushing and shoving. The player who does not get the rebound is frustrated and will likely be more assertive the next time. This frustration can build up and lead to either goal aggression (for the purpose of hurting the opponent) or instrumental aggression (the opponent might get injured accidentally while the frustrated player is legally pursuing the ball). Thus, if the player intentionally shoves the opponent to get better floor location and the rebound, instrumental aggression has occurred. If, however, repeated attempts to rebound the ball are constantly unsuccessful, resulting in a buildup of frustration, the frustrated athlete is more likely to attempt to injure the opponent. This would be an example of goal aggression. This is exactly what happened when, in 1982, Washington Bullets forward Kermit Washington severely injured opponent Rudy Tomjanovich of the Houston Rockets with a direct punch to the face.

But what happens when you can't retaliate directly against the frustrating opponent, for instance, when a soccer or hockey goalie continually prevents shot after shot from going into the net? If other conditions prohibit the destruction or removal of the source of frustration, aggression may be carried out on other objects. This behavior is called *displaced aggression*. Thus, teammates of this skilled goalie might experience heightened aggression in the frustrated athlete's attempts to score a goal. In another common example, baseball pitchers who have just given up a home run have been known to hit, or pitch inside to, the next batter due to their frustration. Retaliation is yet another example of displaced aggression. When an opponent injures one of your teammates, someone on your team might attempt to injure one of their players. Staying with our baseball example, it's common to see a pitcher hit an opponent with a pitch in retaliation for one of his or her teammates being struck by the opposing pitcher.

It is more than mere frustration that dictates an aggressive response. The strength and intensity of a person's frustration, the frequency of occurrence, and the degree of interference associated with the frustration response directly influence aggressive behavior. A scenario that will likely lead to aggression in sport might be a player who has repeatedly attempted to meet a desirable performance goal and has been repeatedly thwarted by the opponent; perhaps a defensive lineman is unable to overpower his offensive lineman opponent and stop the other team's offense. The coach then urges him to "get tough and knock his block off" or he won't be permitted to continue to play. The intensity of a contact sport, the frequency of failure to meet performance goals, and the low degree of punishment anticipated as a response to aggression (the coach is condoning aggression) all work together to maximize an aggressive response.

The frustration-aggression hypothesis is not without its critics. Detractors argue that not all frustration leads to aggression. For instance, many frustrated individuals, especially persons with low self-esteem or low ability, tend to withdraw from the activity or to reduce their efforts in it (i.e., they mentally drop out). Another limitation is the assumption that if aggression is the response to frustration, then the release of this frustration, through competing in sports or watching a violent movie, should have a cathartic effect. Yet, as was indicated earlier, this outcome has not been supported in the literature. In fact, aggression often increases rather than decreases after subjects observe others engaging in aggressive activity.

But in a reformulation of the frustration-aggression hypothesis, Berkowitz (1969) contends that rather than explaining the cause of, or directly leading to, aggression, frustration only heightens the predisposition to it. Further, the response to frustration can be modified by learning. Thus, an athlete can learn to have some other, more productive and less aggressive response to frustration.

Another limitation of the frustration-aggression theory is one of definition. As Husman and Silva (1984, p. 254) point out:

> Is frustration interference with a goal response, task failure, lack of reinforcement, internal arousal, or continued failure resulting in low self-esteem? With the acceptance of (social) learning as an intervening variable influencing the frustration-aggression relationship, frustration itself has become harder to define. Today the frustration-aggression hypothesis is of more interest as a historical document than a definitive statement about aggression.

Social Learning Theory

Is aggression a learned social behavior similar to other behaviors? In Albert Bandura's (1973) social learning theory, aggressive behaviors are acquired and maintained by two modes: modeling and vicarious processes (direct reinforcement). The *modeling* effect is based on a person's tendency to imitate the actions of the observed individual. Thus, according to the theory, observing an individual perform aggressive acts will likely lead one to demonstrate similar behaviors. *Vicarious processes* occur when observers are exposed to models who are rewarded for aggressive behavior as opposed to models who are punished for aggressive behavior. The observers are more likely to aggress after watching persons who are rewarded rather than punished for acting aggressively. When a child hears the crowd cheer after an athlete has injured an opponent, observes the success of the more "aggressive" team, or is offered adulation after performing an aggressive act ("Way to knock his block off, son"), vicarious processes and direct reinforcement are encouraging future aggressive actions.

Research, much of it by Bandura and his colleagues, has supported social learning theory to help explain human aggression. Two studies were concerned with the effect of modeling adult aggression on children's aggressive behavior. Bandura and Huston (1961) asked adult models to demonstrate aggressive behaviors in reaction to solving problems. When the children were asked to solve a problem, they imitated the adults' aggressive reactions even though they were unrelated to the solution. Bandura, Ross, and Ross (1963) asked children to observe four groups under different conditions: (1) a live adult modeling aggressive behavior, (2) adult aggression on closed-circuit television, (3) aggression as performed by an animal (cat), and (4) nonaggressive behavior of a model during play. The researchers found that exposure to aggressive models increased both the verbal and physical aggression of the young observers. Further, watching television aggression had a similarly effective influence in behavior as watching adult behavior in person. The animal model had less effect.

Other studies have been concerned with the effect of home environment on aggression. Bandura and Walters (1959) interviewed twenty-six delinquent white adolescent males and compared them to a random group of nondelinquent males of a similar race, age, and family socioeconomic status. They concluded that both groups had similar affectionate feelings toward their mothers, but that the delinquent group exhibited considerable hostility toward their fathers. Mothers of the delinquent group often displayed a lack of warmth for their spouses, and this feeling was usually reciprocated. Delinquent boys showed less guilt for wrongdoing, and their behavior was maintained by fear rather than by moral standards. The researchers characterized delinquent boys by a lack of appropriate modeling after the father and a failure to develop a personal conscience.

McCord (1962), in a study of 174 male adolescents and their parents examined over a five-year period, found direct correlations between degree of aggressiveness of the adolescent and aggressiveness in the family environment. Aggressive males had parents who were aggressive, punitive, rejecting, and inconsistent in their guidance. Also, the parents were characterized as being often hostile with each other and as often undermining each other's values. Nonaggressive boys were reared in a warm, far less punitive environment. Parents were consistent in providing guidance and displayed mutual respect for all family members.

The examination of social learning in competitive sport has received relatively scant attention in the literature. Mugno and Feltz (1985) compared high school (aged fifteen to eighteen years) and youth league (aged twelve to fourteen years) football athletes and nonathletes on the extent to which they learned about, and subsequently practiced, illegal aggressive actions through observing college and professional football. Among other results, they found (1) that athletes consumed more football through the media than nonathletes, (2) that athletes learned merely one more illegal aggressive action through their observations and reading about football than nonathletes, a negligible difference, (3) that significant correlations existed between the number of illegal aggressive acts that players observed and the number of those acts used in their own games for both high school ($r = .62$) and youth league ($r = .50$) participants, and (4) that high school and youth league athletes were similarly aware of illegal aggressive acts and the use of those acts in their games. In support of social learning theory, then, the authors found a modest relationship for young players between learning about illegal aggressive behaviors through observing collegiate and professional football athletes and using those actions in games.

Perhaps nowhere is social learning theory more validated in real-life sport situations than in ice hockey. Canadian sport psychologist Michael Smith (1980, p. 188) contends that violence in hockey is inevitable because it's an integral part of the "system." "One of the most important (professional standards to be promoted in hockey) is the willingness and ability to employ, and withstand, illegal physical coercion," he asserts. Further, youngsters who play organized hockey in Canada know what type of behavior is required to succeed. Smith reported that 76 percent of 274 players in a survey agreed that the following statement applied to their leagues: "If you want to get personal recognition in hockey, it helps to play rough. People in hockey look for this." And 68 percent of the players agreed that in their leagues, "To be successful most hockey teams need at least one or two tough guys who are always ready to fight." Apparently, aggression, particularly in sport, is indeed a learned phenomenon and is practiced in some situations and by certain individuals more than others.

Which situations? Which individuals? Schneider and Eitzen (1986) hypothesize that a competitor's violent behavior in sport is related to (1) the amount of scoring in the particular sport, (2) the amount of body contact allowed within the rules of the sport, (3) the amount of retaliatory power players have in the sport, and (4) whether the structure of the sport has high or low rewards throughout the contest. These characteristics, they contend, work in combination to help to explain the rationale for illegitimate violence by sport participants. But whether aggressive behavior hurts or helps sport performance is less certain.

AGGRESSION AND SPORT PERFORMANCE

When examining the issue of how aggression affects performance, to recall how aggression is defined is important. The question becomes whether inflicting harm or injury to another person (a sport opponent, in this case), either intentionally (goal aggression) or accidentally while pursuing successful performance (instrumental aggression), is desirable. Is there such a thing as a desirable threshold of aggression beyond which success is less likely? And to what extent does the type of sport and specific skills being performed in certain situations warrant a particular aggressive response?

Unfortunately, research on the effect of aggression on sport performance is not abundant. But coaches are in general agreement that in certain situations, aggressive acts are warranted. For example, several collegiate football coaches indicated to me in an interview that the primary means of deciding whether a player with "good size" plays on the offensive or the defensive line is the degree of aggression he exhibits in drills. Big, angry, hostile types are usually asked to play defense, while less assertive players of about the same size are assigned to the offense. It's no secret that coaches often advise their athletes to "get physical" with opponents. Smith (1980, p. 189) reports the pregame words of one hockey coach: "Look, if this character starts anything, take him out early. We can't have him charging around hammering people. Somebody's going to have to straighten him out. Just remember, get the gloves off and do it in a fair fight."

Does such an aggressive approach to competition help or hinder performance? We will answer this question with a brief look at the arousal-performance (inverted-U) relationship and at the pros and cons of aggressive sport performance.

Arousal, Aggression, and Sport Performance

In chapter 2, the relationship between arousal (both physiological and emotional) and sport performance was discussed. Performance improved as the person's arousal level increased and then deteriorated when the athlete became overaroused. Every sport, and skill and situation within that sport, had an optimal arousal level that would result in the individual's best performance.

In 1979, Dr. John Silva at the University of North Carolina tested the arousal-aggression-performance relationship. Silva asked actors (called confederates) to provoke hostility in subjects playing pegboard and basketball. The provoked participants exhibited less concentration and poorer performance than nonprovoked individuals for both tasks. Silva concluded that the players' level of concentration and their performance were impaired owing to their hostile reaction and an arousal level that was likely too high for the given task. Silva surmised that the players' hostility led to heightened arousal, both of which combined to inhibit performance.

Hostile aggression is more likely to occur when the person is excited, or aroused. Russell (1981) studied the effect of violent behavior by ice hockey players on the emotional arousal level of spectators in Alberta, Canada. Adult spectators completed a mood-state test after each of two games, one high in hostility (142 minutes in penalties) and the other with relatively little violence (46 minutes in penalties). The spectators scored significantly higher in aggression and emotional arousal (both measured by paper-and-pencil tests) after the game that featured more hostility.

Pros and Cons of Aggressive Performance

Certainly not all coaches promote aggressive behavior in competition, nor does every sport warrant it. In fact, many coaches prefer (and many sports warrant) a rather sedate, relaxed environment, one that is as low in arousal and hostility as possible. Golf, bowling, and even baseball come to mind. Presently, there are apparently no guidelines in the literature indicating desirable aggression levels for optimal performance. In the literature on arousal, for example, Oxendine (1970) suggests a range of desirable arousal levels for optimal performance (e.g., 1 = archery and basketball free throw, and 5 = football blocking or tackling and weight lifting). No such guidelines exist for aggressive behavior.

Widmeyer (1984) suggests three reasons that explain the difficulty in deriving such a scale for aggression in sport:

1. Aggression cannot be directly measured. Its partial definition, "the intent to do harm," is not observable and, therefore, must either be inferred from the athlete's behavior or determined by asking the athletes to describe and interpret their actions. The most common means of determining aggression has been measuring rule infractions observed by game officials.

2. There is no consensus about what constitutes an aggressive penalty. Not all infractions indicate the athlete's intended harm to an opponent.

3. In examining the aggression-performance relationship, how is performance distinguished from performance outcome or success? Widmeyer defines performance as overt goal-directed behavior, whereas performance outcome is the consequence of such behaviors. Success is subjective in that each athlete makes his or her own decision as to what constitutes success for the particular situation.

Common sense dictates that in some sports and in certain situations, aggressive behavior is desirable, at least if it is within the rules. The basketball athlete or hockey player who shuns body contact will not be successful. On the other hand, athletes who break the contest's rules are likely to be penalized for it, and this will hinder rather than lead to success. Further, the aggressive act is often a reflection of, or leads to, heightened arousal levels that reduce concentration, misdirect the player's attention, and diminish performance quality. Silva (1980, p. 184), based on his review of related literature, concluded that "Anger or heightened hostility directed toward the self or another can often create an attentional conflict for the performer. Thoughts about anger or injuring an opponent compete with and distract the player from fully focusing upon the skill task. In most sports this situation tends to create a skill decrement."

How much aggression is required for successful performance? The answer

might lie with the same paradigm documented in the arousal literature, the inverted-U. This makes sense if we agree that aggression and arousal are highly related. Every sport and sport skill probably includes a desirable level of aggression—high or low. Too little aggression will not allow the athlete to compete with the necessary energy, speed, and "mental toughness" (coaches love to use those words). And too much aggression will lead to penalties, misdirected attention, and reduced concentration, especially when the purpose of aggression is to retaliate against, and injure, opponents. The trick is to find the level of aggression that is optimal for a given sport situation.

On the other hand, if we closely observe the definition of aggression as inflicting physical harm or injury on another person who is motivated to avoid such treatment, then perhaps no level of aggression is acceptable. This is especially true in youth sports, in which participants closely monitor and imitate the behaviors of older, more-skilled athletes. Child athletes should be concerned with learning skills and performing those skills efficiently and consistently in competitive situations. Sport leaders should concern themselves with helping the children to develop mental skills to control anxiety and enhance self-esteem. And all athletic participation should occur in an environment that stresses sportsmanship and effort. Moreover, athletes of all ages are generally uncomfortable with their own aggressive behaviors. They actually feel guilty after exhibiting hostile aggression, losing their temper, and "playing dirty" (Kroll 1979).

IMPLICATIONS FOR COACHES AND ATHLETES

To suggest that aggression should not occur in competitive sport would be unrealistic, perhaps even incorrect. It would be more appropriate to discuss controlling goal-aggressive acts and promoting proactive assertion or instrumental aggression. Here are some guidelines on the appropriate and selective use of proactive assertion or instrumental aggression in sport (according to Cox 1985; Silva 1980; Widmeyer 1984; and Alderman 1974).

1. If winning is an important goal, aggressive behavior, if used at all, is more effective early in the contest.
2. If the athlete is already psyched up, to provoke him or her to "get tough" or to be more aggressive is unwise. This will likely reduce performance quality.
3. Coaches have to state their expectations of appropriate athlete behaviors at the first meeting period. If the object of the program is to have fun and to learn skills, the participants should understand that hostility is out of place.
4. Athletes who abuse rules and aggress when such behaviors are not sanctioned must be immediately reprimanded. If such acts reoccur repeatedly, the threat of dismissal from the team is indicated.
5. If aggression is desirable, then instrumental rather than goal aggression should be promoted. Injury to an opponent should not be the objective. In fact, most athletes are extremely uncomfortable with purposely hurting an opponent. But when aggressive behavior is seen as a way to enhance performance, it is more acceptable. As Alderman (1974, p. 244) states, "To raise levels of aggressiveness . . . is to place high incentive value on the action itself rather than its outcome."
6. Expose athletes to models, or examples, of individuals who have succeeded without hostility by using good skills.

7.   The game arbiters — umpires and referees — have an important role in controlling the aggression of players and spectators. They can reduce the embarrassment an athlete feels after committing an infraction. Often, the official will point at the athlete and loudly vocalize the penalty. For example, a boisterous "Stri-i-i-ke thre-e-e-e, your-r-r ou-u-u-t!" can embarrass and anger the batter. A less dramatic message that still communicates the message effectively might be desirable. Also, an official who responds to an angry coach in a relatively relaxed manner will tend to reduce the aggressor's hostility.

8.   Teach athletes to cope with failure and abusive treatment, especially when it's of a nonphysical nature. For example, an opponent who says terrible things about the player's family or team should be ignored. Or the athlete can be taught to "retaliate" with heightened arousal directed toward productive performance (e.g., by swinging hard at a pitch, leaping for the rebound, making a solid tackle in football, and always giving full concentration to the task. Above all, athletes should learn that physically abusing an opponent will reduce performance effectiveness and diminish team success.

9.   Coaches should provide positive reinforcement to athletes who control their temper, especially in highly emotional situations. A player who sustains physical abuse, either accidentally or on purpose, and does not respond in a hostile manner yet performs at an optimal level should be praised, especially in the presence of teammates.

10.   Keep assertive behaviors, when they must be used, within the competitive environment. Verbally or physically abusing opponents before or after the contest only raises anger and arousal to levels that inhibit performance. And it wastes the players' energy that might otherwise be spent during the contest.

11.   Encourage interactions between opposing teams. As Cox (1985, p. 235) suggests, "Sport is not combat. Sport is a highly significant event that promotes fitness and achievement. It's much easier to be aggressive against a feared enemy than against a respected and liked opponent."

12.   The athletes' family members should be encouraged to attend contests and to reinforce at home what the coach communicates during competition; to play at one's best within the rules and with minimal or no hostility.

Are male and female athletes similar in their aggression responses? In their review of the experimental literature, Frodi, Macaulay, and Thome (1977) from the University of Wisconsin concluded from nonsport research that the sexes can exhibit similar aggressive actions if females (1) do not feel empathy toward their opponent, (2) are not anxious about being aggressive, and (3) if an aggressive response appears justified. And although both males and females may be equally angered by insult, women are more likely to act on that anger if they reflect their feelings — an internal attentional focus. Males, on the other hand, are more likely to act if they attend to, and evaluate, the insulter — a more external attentional set.

What about the female athlete? Scientific studies are not conclusive, although personality studies (criticisms of their validity notwithstanding) indicate that female athletes measure higher on aggression than female nonathletes. However, in my own interviews with numerous intercollegiate women athletes, they indicated that: (1) yes, aggression can be a legitimate response in sport under the proper circumstances (i.e., when it is warranted), but (2) there is no room for hostility or purposely injuring an opponent (goal aggression) at any time. Apparently, all athletes are uncomfortable with a coach's request to dive through others to reach a ball, hit the batter with a pitch, or in some way hurt the opponent. But this is even more true for females. The women competitors whom I interviewed vowed that they would never purposely injure another player, even if told to do so by their coach.

Aggression in sport will not go away, especially when hostility is sanctioned by sport administrators, team owners, and of course, the coaches. This is often the case. For instance, John Ziegler, president of the National Hockey League, defended violence in hockey, as reported in *USA Today*, 13 May 1987. Ziegler contended that "violence sells"; the fans want to see the players fight and use physical intimidation. According to *Sports Illustrated*, 17 February 1986, "Many NHL executives are scared to death that if fighting were banned from hockey, thousands of season-ticket holders who get their jollies from watching grown men in short pants do quasi-legal, bare-knuckle battle would bail out on the spot." Even NHL referees have been accused by sportswriters in the media of being more tolerant of aggressive behaviors (resulting in fewer penalties) in the playoffs.

But many of the NHL hockey players would like to see more sanctions against overt aggression on the ice. Montreal Canadiens General Manager Serge Savard says, "Our club feels that fights should be banned from hockey. . . . Stop it altogether. After one fight, you're out of the game. If you fight in the last five minutes, you're out of the next game, too." A player from the Los Angeles Kings (NHL) hockey team was put on waivers — essentially cut from the team — because he refused to participate in a brawl on the ice with his teammates. This player was ostracized from his profession (no other team in the NHL signed him to play) because he did not follow the expected behavior.

In the final analysis, athletes do what they are taught and required to do. The athletes themselves are not at fault, but the coaches, sport administrators, and even parents who dictate inappropriate behaviors are. Athletes respond to the expectations of others. They have to, if they want to play. The adult leaders are responsible for separating assertiveness (instrumental aggression) from violence and hostility (goal aggression) in sport. Ironically, failing to control aggression actually decreases the team's and the player's chances of succeeding.

Nevertheless, despite these conclusions, the area of aggression in sport is in tremendous need of additional research. The relationship that we observe between hostile behavior and the ability to learn and to perform sport skills is strictly correlational. That is, we are not certain that aggression, especially of the goal or reactive nature, actually causes or directly leads to poorer performance. We also know very little about the factors that contribute to aggressive behavior in sport, why some participants have a greater propensity to aggress than others given the same sport situation. And we certainly know little about differences between male and female sport participants on this topic. What we do know, however, is that despite disagreement about the sources of aggression, coaches have the moral obligation to help athletes redirect their energies and aggressive behaviors in a positive, self-fulfilling, and socially acceptable direction.

SUMMARY

Aggression is the intentional response a person makes to inflict pain or harm on another person. Two types of aggression have been identified. *Instrumental aggression* occurs when the athlete's intention is to meet a performance goal, whereas *goal* or *reactive aggression* is related to purposely injuring or harming an opponent. The concept of proactive assertion, often confused with aggression, means performing acts that are forceful yet acceptable — an integral part of the sport (such as blocking and tackling in football or checking in ice hockey).

Different theories attempt to explain aggression. *Biological* or *instinct theories* claim that human aggression is inevitable because it is a component of our survival instincts. According to the *frustration-aggression hypothesis*, aggression is a logical and expected consequence of frustration. The *catharsis hypothesis* indicates that human aggressive tendencies are related to available outlets for expressing it. Ostensibly, then, sports fans should be less aggressive than nonviewers of competitive sport. However, researchers have found just the opposite effect of viewing aggression in sport. Perhaps the most acceptable theory of aggression is based on *social learning*. Modeling and child-rearing experiences appear to markedly dictate the extent to which a person possesses aggressive tendencies.

Aggression is difficult to measure. Defining aggressive behaviors and measuring them directly are among the problems. Somewhat more certain, though in greater need of research, is that sport performance for each sport, skill, and individual athlete is related to an optimal degree of aggression. That is, some degree of aggressive or assertive behavior is good, but too much inhibits performance. This concept is similar to the inverted-U hypothesis in the arousal literature. The athlete's best interests would be served by the use of instrumental aggression or proactive assertion rather than goal or reactive aggression.

REVIEW QUESTIONS

1. How would you define and differentiate between *hostility* and *proactive assertion*? Which of the following terms are most similar? Explain why: *violent behavior, instrumental aggression, proactive assertion, goal aggression,* and *hostility*.

2. Two football players on opposite teams both reach for a pass thrown by the quarterback. They collide, resulting in an injury to one of the players. What type of aggression has occurred, and why would it be classified as this type?

3. Based on chapter content, are athletes more likely or less likely to respond aggressively after observing violent behavior as compared to nonathletes? Defend your answer.

4. Briefly describe each of the three theories of aggression. How can aspects of each theory be supported and contradicted in a sport setting?

5. What is the catharsis hypothesis? Does research support it? In what way, or why not?

6. How are aggression and arousal related? Based on what you know about the effect of arousal on performing sport skills, how does aggression affect sport performance?

7. Should a coach ever want to promote aggression on the team? If so, under what conditions? When should aggression not be promoted?

8. What are some of the problems in measuring aggressive behavior?

9. Describe two coaching strategies that should increase aggression in athletes and two strategies that should decrease it.

10. Describe five guidelines athletes should consider for using aggression in sport.

REFERENCES

Alderman, R. B. 1974. *Psychological behavior in sport.* Philadelphia: W. B. Saunders.

Ardrey, R. 1961. *The territorial imperative.* New York: Atheneum Press.

Bandura, A. 1973. *Aggression: A social learning analysis.* Englewood Cliffs, NJ: Prentice-Hall.

Bandura, A., and A. C. Huston. 1961. Identification as a process of incidental learning. *Journal of Abnormal Social Psychology* 63: 311–18.

Bandura, A., and R. Walters. 1959. *Adolescent aggression.* New York: Ronald Press.

Bandura, A., D. Ross, and S. A. Ross. 1963. Imitation of film-mediated aggression models. *Journal of Abnormal Social Psychology* 66: 3–11.

Berkowitz, L. 1969. The frustration-aggression hypothesis revisted. In *Roots of aggression*, ed. L. Berkowitz, pp. 1–29. New York: Atherton.

Berkowitz, L. 1970. Experimental investigations of hostility catharsis. *Journal of Consulting and Clinical Psychology* 35: 1–7.

Cox, R. 1985. *Sport psychology: Concepts and applications*. Dubuque, IA: Wm. C. Brown.

Dollard, J., N. Miller, L. Doob, O. H. Mourer, and R. R. Sears. 1939. *Frustration and aggression*. New Haven, CT: Yale University Press.

Figler, S. K. 1978. Aggressive response to frustration among athletes and non-athletes. In *Motor learning, sport psychology, pedagogy, and didactics of physical activity*, ed. F. Landry and W. Orban, pp. 289–96. Miami, FL: Symposium Specialists.

Finn, J. A. 1978. Perception of violence among high-hostile and low-hostile women athletes and nonathletes before and after exposure to sport films. In *Motor learning, sport psychology, pedagogy, and didactics of physical activity* , ed. F. Landry and W. Orban, pp. 283–88. Miami, FL: Symposium Specialists.

Fisher, A. C. 1976. Psych up, psych down, psych out: Relationship of arousal to sport performance. In *Psychology of sport*, ed. A. C. Fisher, 136–44. Palo Alto, CA: Mayfield.

Frodi, A., J. Macaulay, and P. R. Thome. 1977. Are women always less aggressive than men? A review of the experimental literature. *Psychological Review* 34: 634–60.

Hokanson, J., and M. Burgess. 1962. The effects of three types of aggression on the vascular process. *Journal of Abnormal and Social Psychology* 64: 14–24.

Hokanson, J., M. Burgess, and M. Cohen. 1963. Effects of displaced aggression on systolic blood pressure. *Journal of Abnormal and Social Psychology* 67: 38–51.

Husman, B. F. 1980. Aggression: An historical perspective. In *Sport psychology: An analysis of athlete behavior*, ed. W. F. Straub, 166–76. Ithaca, NY: Mouvement.

Husman, B. F., and J. M. Silva. 1984. Aggression in sport: Definitional and theoretical considerations. In *Psychological foundations of sport*, ed. J. M. Silva and R. S. Weinberg, 246–60. Champaign, IL: Human Kinetics.

Kroll, W. 1979. The stress of high performance athletics. In *Coach, athlete, and the sport psychologist*, ed. P. Klavora and J. V. Daniel, pp. 211–19. Champaign, IL: Human Kinetics.

Larsen, O. N. 1968. *Violence and the mass media*. New York: Harper and Row.

Lorenz, K. 1966. *On aggression*. New York: Harcourt, Brace & World.

McCord, J., W. McCord, and E. Thurber. 1962. Some effects of parental absence on male children. *Journal of Abnormal Social Psychology* 64: 361–69.

Montagu, M. F. A. 1968. The new litany of "innate depravity," or original sin revisited. In *Man and aggression*, ed. M. F. A. Montagu, pp. 3–17. New York: Oxford University Press.

Morris, D. 1967. *The naked ape*. New York: McGraw-Hill.

Mugno, D. A., and D. L. Feltz. 1985. The social learning of aggression in youth football in the United States. *Canadian Journal of Applied Sport Sciences* 10: 26–35.

Orlick, T., and J. Partington. 1986. *Psyched: Inner views of winning*. Ottawa, Ontario: Coaching Association of Canada.

Oxendine, J. B. 1970. Emotional arousal and motor performance. *Quest* 13: 23–30.

Russell, G. W. 1981. Spectator moods at an aggressive sports event. *Journal of Sport Psychology* 3: 217–27.

Schneider, J., and D. S. Eitzen. 1986. The structure of sport and participant violence. In *Fractured focus: Sport as a reflection of society,* ed. R. E. Lapchick, pp. 229–44. Lexington, MA: Lexington Books.

Silva, J. M. 1980. Understanding aggressive behavior and its effects upon athletic performance. In *Sport psychology: An analysis of athlete behavior*. 2d ed., ed. W. F. Straub, pp. 177–86. Ithaca, NY: Mouvement.

Smith, M. D. 1980. Hockey violence: Interring some myths. In *Sport psychology: An analysis of athlete behavior,* 2d. ed., ed. W. F. Straub, pp. 187–92. Ithaca, NY: Mouvement.

Thirer, J. 1978. The effect of observing filmed violence on the aggressive attitudes of female athletes and non-athletes. *Journal of Sport Behavior* 1: 28–36.

Widmeyer, W. N. 1984. Aggression-performance relationships in sport. In *Psychological foundations of sport*, ed. by J. M. Silva and R. S. Weinberg, pp. 274–86. Champaign, IL: Human Kinetics.

Zillman, D., R.C. Johnson, and K. D. Day. 1974. Provoked and unprovoked aggressiveness in athletes. *Journal of Research in Personality* 8: 139–52.

7

Leadership in Sport: A Matter of Style

Fiedler (1964, p. 153) defines a leader as "the individual in the group who directs and coordinates task-relevant group activities, or who, in the absence of a designated leader, automatically performs these functions in the group." If a leader is to be effective, he or she must be recognized as the most influential on the behavior of group members and either appointed or elected to the position. But a leader who is not capable of altering the behaviors and attitudes of group members (in other words, who has no influence) is not effective in the position.

This chapter is about predicting and describing effective leadership in sport with respect to a person's traits and attributes. Of particular concern in this chapter is the degree to which the coach actually makes a difference between winning and losing. Can the coach be held responsible for the team's (or a player's) performance? Can the contest's outcome be influenced by the coach's leadership skills? Is effective sport leadership really dependent on the team's win-loss record, as is commonly depicted in the media? Or, instead, is effective coaching more often a matter of having the better players?

It is contended in this chapter that *leadership skills count*. After reading it, the student should be able to identify techniques that effective leaders use. As the literature reviewed in this chapter will show, the coach *can* make a difference in sport performance and team success. Athletes are human beings, not machines. Consequently, they are affected by the coach's attitudes, behaviors, perceptions, and decisions. Essentially, then, athletes react to their leader. The team leader's job is to help each competitor to reach his or her potential. The coach can, in fact, influence the quality of a player's performance. To do this, the coach must take on an array of roles.

ROLES OF THE COACH

Being responsible for influencing the behaviors and actions of the many different individuals on a team, and usually at the same time, is no easy task. Athletes differ as to the type of personal approach with which they are most comfortable. Not all coaches are prepared to meet these individual needs. Coaches who are less effective say, "I can't do that; it's not me" or "Everyone gets treated alike, regardless of their needs or preferences." Effective coaches, on the other hand, say, "I'll work at changing this behavior (habit)" or "I'm not good at doing 'that' so I'll ask someone with better skills in this area to do it." The best coaches are secure individuals. They recognize their strengths and limitations. Sometimes they'll attend workshops or seminars and read literature in an attempt to improve their skills or to change a particular approach. The coaching profession demands the mastery of many personal and technical skills. Leaders in sport maintain a variety of roles to meet each of these skills.

Leader
When a group of individuals is attempting to meet a goal, usually someone has to be in charge. In sport situations, that's the coach. Perhaps some coaches practice this role too authoritatively. Nevertheless, competitors assume that their coach will provide a sense of leadership — direction with a purpose — to achieve group success. Some examples of effective leadership include taking responsibility for team failure; giving direction during practice; devising and communicating pregame, game, and postgame strategies; and articulating expectations to each team member.

Follower
Hold it! If coaches are expected to provide strong leadership, how can they be followers? Because good leaders know when *not* to lead, when to respect and be sensitive to the needs and decisions of others, and when to respond sincerely and honestly to input from others. Following is not a weakness but rather a sign of *strength and security*. The group leader should not need to constantly demonstrate dominance, for the role is, by definition, the most powerful position on the team. The coach can be more effective by allowing assistant coaches and team captains to be responsible for certain team-related tasks. Examples include

leading warm-up exercises, recommending and implementing strategies in practice and during the contest, and making limited decisions, on and off the field or court.

Teacher

Effective coaches are educators. How else could participants learn and improve their skills? Athletes who make progress in developing their skills become more creative, self-assured, and successful. Part of the educational process in sport is to teach athletes to think independently of the coach's directions and to respond creatively to unanticipated actions of their opponents. Effective coaches are knowledgeable about the skills and strategies of their sport. But just as important is that they are able to communicate this knowledge to their players so that it can be applied proficiently in competitive situations. The best coaches also work at upgrading their expertise by reading relevant literature, attending seminars, and soliciting feedback from others as to their teaching effectiveness. The coach who is an effective teacher (1) asks athletes about the effectiveness of his or her teaching, (2) uses a variety of modes of communication, such as videotape to model skills and to provide a visual form of information feedback, (3) provides specific feedback that athletes can use in a relatively low-key, nonhostile manner, and (4) does not teach new skills and strategies during the contest but, instead, rehearses them in practice until the participants can perform them comfortably and consistently.

Role Model

"Model" is defined in the Random House College Dictionary as "a standard or example for imitation or comparison." Coaches serve as models for their athletes in demonstrating proper behaviors. Coaches must be consistent in following the same rules and expectations in their own actions and attitudes that they expect of their players. The rules that forbid profanity, alcohol abuse, intake of illegal drugs, and that demand a 100 percent effort should hold true for coaches and athletes alike. To maintain a double standard in regard to team policies is to invite distrust and a loss of credibility. For example, if the coach requests that all team members refrain from berating game officials, the coach must express feelings and ask for decision interpretations in a low-key, mature manner. Similarly, if the coach expresses anger occasionally, then players should be allowed to express anger as long as it is not directed at another player, excludes damage to property, occurs infrequently, and is quickly controlled. The coach should keep a neat, professional appearance commensurate with the demands on each player.

Limit Setter

Effective coaches have realistic but high expectations of their athletes. Demands on athletes include maintaining proper training and conforming to team policies.

Sometimes the coach must restrict certain behaviors and set limits to ensure the proper preparation of players for maximal game performance. Guidelines and specific procedures for monitoring the players' adherence to them need to be developed and implemented.

Often, athletes find limit setting to be necessary — even desirable — in helping them to control certain actions. Peer pressure to test rules and to "go along with the gang" is sometimes overwhelming. One good example is the pressure to experiment with illegal drugs. Athletes have told me in confidence that social gatherings often offer the opportunity to take drugs. Accompanied by the intake of alcohol and a rather seductive environment, the temptation to "try it" is almost overwhelming. But athletes who are warned about the dire consequences of ingesting drugs and breaking other team rules (and the law) have "an excuse" for refusing the drug. "If my coach finds out ("If my drug test is positive"), I'll be dismissed from the team" is a face-saving and justifiable reason to "just say no." For instance, if the team's star player breaks a team rule that was explained to the athletes before the season, the athlete should be disciplined accordingly. The coach should remind the team, verbally as well as through his or her actions, that starters and nonstarters play under the same rules. On the other hand, if a player criticizes an aspect of team rules in a group meeting, instead of making threats, admonishing the critical player, or "losing it," the coach should acknowledge the player's feelings, and his or her right to voice them. Depending on the nature of the complaint, the coach has several choices as the limit setter. He or she can decide to amend the rule, ask for more player input, promise to think about the matter, or explain why the issue is not negotiable.

Psychologist or Counselor

Effective coaches are approachable. They are not threatening to their athletes, and the players, in turn, feel that they can risk communicating their thoughts to the team leader. In this atmosphere, the coach can listen and respond to the needs of each athlete, which is important if the coach wants players to perform without thoughts and feelings that interfere with performance preparation and participation. The "airing out" of feelings that might inhibit full concentration to the task at hand is desirable. Instead of responding angrily to an athlete who is consistently lazy and performs erratically, the counseling coach first discusses his or her concerns with the player and seeks to find the reasons for this behavior. The coach would approach the athlete in the privacy of his or her office rather than in front of peers. In another typical situation, the coach may receive information that a player is struggling in class; the student's grades are low, and his future in this course look ominous. The counseling coach would immediately seek to meet with the athlete's teacher to discuss the problem. The coach would then meet with the athlete to jointly (1) decide on selected strategies to overcome the poor classroom performance, (2) set specific realistic goals of academic improvement, and (3) agree on a weekly follow-up of progress.

Friend

Can a coach ever really be an athlete's friend? Should coaches and athletes relate to one another as though they are in the same peer group, have similar interests, and share the same friends? The answer is a simple no. Athletes want to admire and respect their coaches. The athlete views the older, more experienced coach in a very different light than a teammate or friend. And the player's expectations of the coach's behaviors and attitudes are also different from the player's expectations of a peer. Athletes tend to be uncomfortable with the coach who tries to be "best buddies" with his or her players.

However, an element of friendship does exist in a healthy player-coach relationship. Coaches should be available to interact in a meaningful way with every player, even away from the sport arena. Jones and her colleagues (1982, p. 22) suggest that "Coaches can get players out of trouble, lend them money, pat them on the back, laugh, cry, and cheer with them, and not let anyone else talk about them." Thus, a relationship built on trust, honesty, disclosure of feelings, support, and to a degree, nurturance can be a healthy friendship. A coach might politely decline the players' invitation to a party but respond in a friendly manner when he or she is the "victim" of a friendly prank by the players. (New York Giants coach Bill Parcells received a Gatorade bath near the conclusion of a victory during the 1986 season.) In the role of friend, a coach might place his or her arm around the shoulders of a player just to say, "How are ya doin'?" or "I'm sorry to hear about your dad's operation. How is he?"

Parent Substitute

According to Jones et al. (1982, p. 25), "Stable children must have someone who cares about them who is important in their life...one must have the love and concern of a significant other — someone who really matters." The coach's role is not to *be* the parent but rather to support the same goals that parents have for their athlete sons and daughters. As the role model for players, the coach carries out a host of parental functions. This role is magnified when the athlete has a single parent. After discovering academic problems with an athlete, the coach would act as a parent in meeting with school personnel to schedule tutorial sessions. After finding out that a team member has cut class, the coach might give the athlete a choice between attending every future class session or leaving the team. No abusive language, embarrassing and insulting comments, or disclosures to parents should be necessary. To build trust and mutual respect, agreements about future behaviors should be conducted exclusively between coach and athlete.

Family Member

The coach who has a spouse and, perhaps, children must acknowledge family responsibilities. Working a sixty- to seventy-hour week, as some coaches do, may be destructive to one's home life. Is team and professional success directly proportional to the number of hours spent per week in game preparation and player development? An analysis of the effectiveness of such extreme coaching behaviors goes beyond the purpose of this discussion. Although on the one hand, spouses of coaches have to be supportive of the required work that goes into the coaching profession, especially if recruiting is a job component; on the other hand, families should be a rewarding and pleasant component of a coach's life: a source of pleasure and a means of preventing burnout and loneliness. The right perspective between sport leadership and home life is needed. For example, a coach should fulfill an obligation to engage in family activities at least one day per week. Coaches should keep in touch with their spouses and children, at least by telephone. And coaches should articulate the words "I love you" to each family member regularly.

THEORIES OF LEADERSHIP IN SPORT

What constitutes effective leadership? Several theories have been supported by researchers and educators. Some writers claim that effective leadership is an inherited skill, but others contend that it is learned. Still others assert that the combination of natural ability and an environment that nurtures this ability is required to lead successfully. The following sections explain a few of the more popular theories of effective leadership with reference to sport.

Fiedler's Contingency Model

Fiedler (1964) suggested that the effectiveness of any single leadership style is dependent on the type of situation. An authoritative approach might be more functional in the military than it would be in a factory where the manager's goal is to promote worker productivity. Sometimes the appropriate leadership style might depend on the skill level, age, and maturity of group members as well as on their expectations of proper leader behavior. For example, most athletes would typically expect their coach to make unilateral decisions during the contest, but they might also expect the coach to solicit their input when setting individual performance goals. The key to Fiedler's model is maintaining a favorable situation. The various components of such situations include (1) personal relations with group members, (2) the structure of the group's task, and (3) the power and authority inherent in the leader's position. Each of these components will be examined in the context of competitive sport.

Personal relations with group members. Fiedler contended that the personal relationships between the leader and key group members (e.g., team captains and starters) are an important factor affecting team performance. This view supports the findings of sport researchers that coaches of winning teams are viewed by their players as honest, receptive, good communicators, and effective teachers of sport skills (Anshel 1978; Mechikoff and Kozar 1983). Hence, "The liked and respected leader does not need formal power. . . .(his or her) interpersonal attitudes influence group performance to a significantly greater degree than similar attitudes of a leader who is not accepted by his group" (Fiedler 1964, p. 159).

Task structure.   The leader's job is easier when the task is highly structured, that is, when group roles and objectives are identified and accepted by members. However, when a group is given an unstructured task such as planning an event or jointly establishing group policies, the leader is relatively less powerful to affect group activity. What many leaders fail to realize is that this holds true even in situations where the leader holds considerable power. Think about it. How much cooperation will a boss (coach) receive if he or she makes overpowering, perhaps unfair, demands on employees (athletes)? The result may be poor, inefficient productivity.

An effective leader uses task structure to his or her advantage without coercion and without deceit toward subordinates. Task structure in competitive sport may be analyzed in four areas:

1.   *Decision verifiability:* Determining the degree to which decisions were correct by examining the consequences of these decisions or by obtaining information feedback from persons who were directly affected by the decisions.

2.   *Goal clarity:* The extent to which task requirements were clearly stated or known to group members. For example, did coaches explain to athletes the purposes for engaging in certain strategies and exercises in preparing for the contest?

3.   *Goal-path multiplicity:* Is there only one way to meet goals and to become successful at the task? Could alternative approaches be discussed? In sport, a good idea might be to solicit the opinions of coaching assistants and selected players to establish a joint commitment toward meeting team and individual goals.

4.   *Solution specificity:* Is there more than one "correct" solution to a problem? Must the coach always have the answers (or be expected to)? Are other group members allowed to express different points of view? Is there room for disagreement and negotiation off the field or court, during practice, and even throughout the contest?

Position power.   How much influence does the leader have over group members? It may be significant between workers and their immediate supervisor and

and between players and their coach. However, administrators, including athletic directors and the owners of businesses and sports teams, who "go over the coach's (supervisor's) head" in making team-related decisions are usurping the team leader's responsibility and effectiveness. Members of task- and goal-oriented groups, such as sports teams, should understand that the role of making decisions and influencing member behaviors and attitudes belongs to one person — the team leader.

There is little doubt that power is inherent in sport leadership. But the effectiveness of this power in a sport context raises a few provocative questions. Are coaches more successful at winning contests and maximizing the athletes' performance if they exhibit relatively more power and allow their players to have relatively less of it? Are coaches who make virtually all team-related decisions without the participation of team members more influential over the behaviors and attitudes of players than coaches who allow athletes to maintain a decision-making role? Is the extent of power in coaching related to team success? If the answer to each of these questions is yes, then coaching is a less sophisticated skill than researchers think. Fiedler's contingency model would not support the notion that more leadership power is always, or even usually, better.

The *ideal* situation, using Fiedler's model, would be one in which a trusted, respected leader (1) interacts with a homogeneous work group (for instance, a team of skilled athletes who share common goals), and (2) has a significant degree of influence over members' actions, in a program governed by standard procedures (e.g., conditioning, practice, and game schedules). The *least favorable* situation is where the coach (1) is disliked by a mixed group (say, for instance, team members who differ greatly in skills and goals, or do not like one another), (2) is managing an ill-defined task, e.g., directing a physical conditioning program or a practice session, and (3) has relatively little power to influence behavior. In this latter situation, the coach would lack credibility and loyalty.

Team sport leaders can use one of four alternatives to increase the probability of successful coaching:

1. *Use the appropriate style.* A coach's leadership style should be compatible with the situation. Citizens expect the head of their country to demonstrate strong decision-making capability, but the president of a labor union is expected to solicit the advice and voting participation of union boards, committees, and members. In sport, coaches in high-pressure situations (winning is often an expectation or even a mandate to keep their job) should not use the same leadership style as the coach of a junior high school or little league team. The needs and expectations of athletes in these situations differ.

2. *Meet situational needs.* Effective coaches can alter their behaviors to meet the needs of a given situation. Younger, less skilled players, for instance, might be treated differently than older, better skilled competitors. It is *not* realistic, perhaps not even possible, for a coach to change his or her personality per se. After all, personality traits are stable and are established early in life. But

a person's actions are changeable. Developing the ability to change the content and manner of one's communication style is both possible and characteristic of successful leaders.

3.   *Make the job fit the person.* The leader should seek a position that is suitable to his or her personality or natural leadership style. Fiedler (1964) asserts that this may be the most realistic approach to being a successful leader or coach. If the coach's personality is more compatible with a smaller group of players or is better suited to the achievement of relatively fewer tasks than governing a large group of players, then coaching golf, archery, and other teams with relatively few participants might be a good choice, or assuming an assistant coach's job might allow a more focused approach.

4.   *Learn to change styles.* Coaches can be trained to alter their styles. Seminars, conferences, in-service instruction, and published literature can promote professional and personal growth and can help one to upgrade leadership and administrative skills. The mentality of "I am who I am" rather than a willingness to adapt to various environments has very limited validity in effective leadership.

The Life Cycle Theory

Effective leaders perform two functions: They complete the group's goal or goals (task-oriented behavior), and they facilitate positive interaction between group members (people-oriented behavior). The main feature of the life cycle theory is the development of *task-relevant maturity* in the group, essentially the coordination of people-oriented and task-oriented behaviors (Hersey and Blanchard 1977).

The leader's actions are partially dependent on the maturity of group members, specifically *job maturity* and *psychological maturity*. Job maturity comprises three components: (1) the group's capacity to set and reach goals, (2) the group's willingness and ability to assume responsibility, and (3) the extent of group education and experience — in a word, competence. Psychological maturity indicates the level of self-respect, self-confidence, and self-esteem that each member brings to the group. As maturity increases, the need for task-structured behavior decreases. Leader behaviors go from a more directive style to placing an increased emphasis on developing the leader-subordinate relationship. In the latter stages of the life cycle (with extensive psychological maturity) the leader assumes a consultant role; people are allowed more independence to get the job done. Decisions tend to be more negotiable than directed.

Effective coaches, in implementing the life cycle approach, will:

- *Begin with a strict approach.* In the beginning stages of group development, before or early in the season, the coach should assess the maturity level of each performer prior to determining the needed leadership style. Typically, however, the team leader should maintain a relatively authoritative, structured posture, reducing the intensity level on selected occasions or when necessary. Expectations for player behaviors within and outside the sport setting should be communicated at this time.

- *Build self-confidence and mutual respect with each player.* Player achievement, constructive feedback on performance, honesty and sincerity, sensitivity to the feelings of others, and skill development (performance improvement) are needed here.

- *Nurture team leadership.* The opportunity to develop and exhibit leadership is inherent in the team captain position. But coaches may also want to give opportunities for leadership to other team members as well. To develop leadership qualities in *all* players is desirable. Leaders tend to be self-motivated, to take responsibility for their performance, and to remain loyal to the group.

- *Establish trust.* To build the coach-player relationship, trust between these parties should be established as soon as possible because this is a time-consuming process. Strategies to gain trust are covered in chapter 8 on communication. In a leadership context, the ability to establish trust with one team member has the advantage of spreading to others — athletes talk to one another. Conversely, being mistrusted by a player also leads to more resistance to openness by others. Rarely is a leader trusted by some group members but not by others.

The focus of life cycle theory is on the situation created by the subordinates' maturity level. One limitation of this theory is taking into account the age and experience of group members. The life cycle may not begin and mature in the same way for different groups. After all, older, more experienced workers have different needs and expectations of a leader than their younger, less experienced counterparts. This issue is addressed in the multidimensional model.

The Multidimensional Model

Athletes of different ages and skill levels do not have the same needs. Older, more experienced competitors differ from their younger counterparts with respect to their needs and their reasons for participating in sport. Chelladurai and Carron (1978) found that child competitors preferred a relationship-oriented coaching style rather than a task-related approach. In other words, kids need the coach's friendship as an integral part of the leadership role. College-age athletes, on the other hand, were found to have relatively low relationship needs and, instead, preferred more task-oriented coaching behaviors.

The multidimensional model, as depicted in Table 7.1, shows that professional athletes, persons whose careers and salaries are dependent on performance, are very task-oriented. Although a positive relationship between the coach and player certainly contributes to effective performance, professionals

Table 7.1 Leadership preferences by athletes of different maturation/age levels

Leader Behavior Level	Task-Oriented	Relationship-Oriented
Professional	High	Low
College	Moderate to high	Moderate to low
High school	Moderate to high	Moderate to high
Elementary—youth sports	Low	Very high

expect a leader to exert marked influence on the team through insight, intelligence, and the ability to communicate their knowledge. Notice that college competitors also have high needs for a task-oriented approach. However, the importance of getting along with the coach is more prominent here as compared to the professional athlete. High school athletes would tend to mentally withdraw or even drop out if the relationship with their coach were unsatisfactory. Child athletes would almost surely quit the team without warm coach-athlete interaction unless pressured by parents to do otherwise.

In summary, the multidimensional model focuses on three aspects of leadership: (1) actual leader behavior, (2) leader behavior that is preferred by subordinates, and (3) required leader behavior — i.e., behavior that is dictated by the organization or team. Chelladurai and Carron predict that performance outcomes and group member satisfaction will be positively related to the compatibility of these three components.

Theory X and Y

McGregor (1967) asserts that individuals in leadership positions typically formulate one of two sets of basic assumptions (referred to as *Theory X* and *Theory Y*) about subordinates. The assumptions of *Theory X* are that:

- Workers inherently dislike their jobs and will avoid working whenever possible.

- Subordinates must be coerced, controlled, directed, and even threatened to work at optimal efficiency.

- Followers mostly prefer to be directed; they avoid responsibility and have relatively little ambition to achieve or in any way to get ahead

In the opposite direction, *Theory Y* acknowledges workers who:

- Perceive physical and mental effort on the job as natural and necessary.
- Are capable of exercising self-direction and self-control to meet group objectives to which they feel committed.
- For the most part, learn to perform their jobs under appropriate conditions.
- Accept and actually *seek* responsibility.

Theory X is more comparable to an authoritative coaching style in which task completion comes first and warm relationships between coach and athlete are least critical to success. Personal concerns of subordinates almost always take a back seat to the objective at hand. The coach often believes, rightly or wrongly, that players *want* a tough leader who will direct and control all activity.

In fact, the leader's negative perception of team members is often fulfilled by the players' actions, a phenomenon called the Pygmalion Effect or the self-fulfilling prophecy (discussed throughout this text). The coach's behaviors and attitutes toward team members are condescending, insensitive, mistrusting, and disrespectful. The players then react to the coach in accordance with his or her expectations and perceptions just as the coach predicted (Rejeski, Darracott, and Hutslar 1979).

Theory Y reflects a coaching style more compatible with developing positive relationships and communication with players. Such "person-oriented" coaches are concerned about (1) team morale, (2) personal feelings — in addition to each player's attitude toward team goals, (3) relationships and affiliation among players, (4) discovering and attempting to meet the athlete's personal goals for participating, and (5) the general level of team member satisfaction.

Clearly, Theory Y is a more humanistic approach to leadership. However, extraordinarily high concern for personal feelings might be at the expense of meeting team goals and task productivity (Straub 1980). Many coaches are convinced about the need to be strictly task oriented and are quite naive about the need to be sensitive to the emotional needs of players. Ignoring this component often leads to a lack of player loyalty toward the coach, and the motivation to exhibit high effort decreases over time.

One weakness of Theory X and Theory Y in their relation to sport is the dichotomous nature of team leadership. Most coaches are rarely all X or all Y in style. A coach who assumes a posture of total domination at all times will rarely be successful. A firm hand in directing player behavior is often desirable, especially when the task is clear and player incentive is low (Chelladurai and Carron 1978). A military drill sergeant, on the other hand, might be able to get away with a continually authoritative style, at least during the training period. But otherwise, leaders must interact with others in a respectful manner, no matter what the situation, if they are to have the credibility and loyalty of subordinates. Without these feelings, no one will be left to lead.

Tannenbaum and Schmidt's Model

Similar to Fiedler's theory, Tannenbaum and Schmidt's (1973) view of effective leadership comprises three areas: (1) forces in the manager, (2) forces in the work group, and (3) forces in the situation.

Forces in the manager. The central issue here is the degree to which a manager (coach) has the power to make decisions and to influence the behaviors and attitudes of group members. Tannenbaum and Schmidt place this role on a continuum from leader-centered to group member–centered decision making. In a sport context, this role is decided by the extent to which players make team-related decisions. This is illustrated in Figure 7.1, in which the coach slowly allows more and more player involvement in the decision-making process. The sequence indicates a maturation of leadership based on time, and the age, maturity, and skill level of group participants. Older athletes, in particular, want to have, and feel that they deserve, additional freedom to at least partially determine team strategies, contest-related decisions, and performance outcomes.

Figure 7.1   Continuum of decision-making role and power of coach and athlete

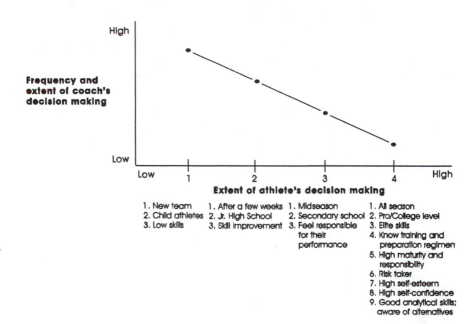

1. New team   1. After a few weeks 1. Midseason   1. All season
2. Child athletes   2. Jr. High School   2. Secondary school   2. Pro/College level
3. Low skills   3. Skill improvement 3. Feel responsible   3. Elite skills
                                              for their   4. Know training and
                                              performance   preparation regimen
                                                                  5. High maturity and
                                                                     responsibility
                                                                  6. Risk taker
                                                                  7. High self-esteem
                                                                  8. High self-confidence
                                                                  9. Good analytical skills;
                                                                     aware of alternatives

Coaches of older, more advanced competitors tend to have the personal security and flexibility to take risks and to share power.

Forces in the work group. Effective leaders "tune in to" group members. Leadership style is determined *after* a coach ascertains the maturity and skill level of the team. Higher skilled, more mature players respond better to a laissez-faire approach with greater allowance for decision-making and independence toward preparing for the contest than younger, less skilled performers. Intuitive coaches ask:

- What are the players' expectations of me as a coach?

- How ready are these athletes to assume responsibilities? For example, are they committed to conducting themselves off the field or court in a mature manner? Is it wise to closely monitor them when the team travels?

- What is their skill level? Do they need close supervision and instruction?

- What is their emotional maturity? Are they able to handle sport-related stress and anxiety? Can they use close emotional support?

- To what extent can the players tolerate ambiguity? Do they need clear, persistent direction — to be told when and how to do everything?

- Are they happy to be members of this team? Is there a sense of pride? Or are they embarrassed, timid, or stressed about their identification as athletes? Are they admired by others who are not on the team?

The answers to these, and perhaps other, questions will assist the coach in determining his or her expectations toward player behavior and the extent of monitoring, supervision, and guidance that will be necessary to lead effectively.

Forces in the situation. Only poor leaders are oblivious to their surroundings. One coach of a college team did not have the ability to stop, look, and listen to what his athletes were "saying" both verbally and nonverbally. Consequently, he couldn't possibly realize that his athletes were not responsive to his leadership. His words had no meaning because he was not trusted. With little or no credibility, he did not have their respect. He may as well have been arranging the chairs on the Titanic. Yet he maintained that the players were happy, as long as discussions were not held about "team problems." Intelligent managing is based on the ability to take an objective look at a situation, to gather information, and then to react accordingly. Understanding the group's immediate history (past successes and failures, for instance), and the backgrounds and current needs of group participants might partially dictate a certain leadership style.

Here are a few questions that coaches should ask when assessing forces in the situation:

- What is the nature of problems within the group? Are they racial in nature? Are athletes getting along?
- What is the group climate? Are players pleased to be members of the team?
- Are there any time restraints that may require certain leadership behaviors? Preparing for a game in two days necessitates a different approach to some issues than resolving certain issues between seasons.
- Does the team or league have a philosophy that should be adhered to? Youth sports leagues might require a relatively less intense atmosphere for winning than other situations. In some circumstances, all team members are required to play in each contest. To what extent are school grades connected to further sport participation? The coach should communicate his or her philosophy so that the expectations of each athlete will be formed realistically.
- Are there any group traditions that promote enjoyment and positive feelings that should be maintained?
- Finally, is the group effective? Is the situation under control in terms of meeting group goals? Is it best to leave well enough alone? As former U.S. President Harry Truman said, "If the plumbing ain't broke, don't fix it."

What Leadership Theories Do and Do Not Tell Us

Effective leadership behavior is impossible to dictate for all situations and populations. Scholars who examine the interactions between a group leader and the group's members are unable to prescribe any single best leadership approach. This is particularly true in sport, where participants who differ in age, skill, maturation, expectations, and personality must interact. Various types of sport also require different approaches. Not only is attempting to predict success based on certain leadership characteristics extremely difficult (and one purpose of developing a theory is to be able to make accurate predictions), but the very definition of "success" differs from situation to situation. Do we mean that a leader is successful if group members are satisfied? Or is the team's win-loss record a more accurate indicator of successful leadership? Nevertheless, several recommendations can be derived from these leadership theories.

- *There is no "best" way to lead for all situations.* Coaches in golf and football differ markedly as to the leadership style that best fosters athletic performance. Coaches should make critical assessments of their unique situations and surroundings prior to charging head-on into a style that may or may not be compatible with their players, assistants, administrators, their players' parents, and the community. For example, a coach who uses a particular approach successfully at one location (or with one particular team) needs to consider the effectiveness of using the same technique at a new location *before* implementing it.

- *Effective managers of groups "tune in" to the needs of members.* In addition to making their own plans, decisions, and strategies, coaches have to take the time to listen and react to the feelings of their athletes. Members of any group — and sport is no exception — tend to feel greater identification with group goals if they have played a part, however minor, in creating and carrying out group goals, rules, and behaviors. Athletes need not create and implement all of them, of course. Athletes want to respect their coach's ability to be a competent leader. But they also have feelings, needs, and skills that team leaders should not ignore. Virtually all theories of leadership tend to suggest the need for a time and place to get group members involved in certain decisions that will affect their performance.

- *There is a balance between task- and relationship-oriented styles.* Members of a sports team could probably function to some extent if they did not like one another. But member satisfaction through affiliation — getting along and developing some degree of friendship — helps teammates to support one another. Receiving recognition, respect, and support from teammates is an important need for most athletes. The point is that *completing tasks to reach goals and maintaining healthy relationships among group members are not mutually exclusive.* This is especially true for younger athletes who have a greater need to establish meaningful relationships with their coach as compared to older, higher skilled performers (Chelladurai and Carron 1983). Effective leadership consists of developing the proper balance between these two objectives.

- *Leaders must enhance their subordinates' skills.* Athletes are able, and want, to learn. Very few competitors come to the sport arena with the necessary sport skills and proper attitude and mental training to compete successfully. Effective leaders have the ability to teach mental and physical skills and to offer personal guidance and instruction to players. They take the necessary time and exert the required energy to ensure the player's personal growth and maturation. But the coach who is patient and willing to meet this challenge will develop a team of very loyal and motivated players.

- *There is a difference between a facilitator and a power broker.* Good leaders have skilled and motivated subordinates. But such desirable outcomes do not happen on demand. A coach cannot simply command and expect to receive respect, loyalty, and credibility. As Fiedler (1964) asserts, "The liked and respected leader does not need formal power." In other words, leadership is not built on intimidation, fear, and the mere completion of tasks. Instead, effective leaders have earned the respect of their subordinates through honesty, sincerity, mutual respect, fairness, empathy, and the ability to teach skills.

The style that a leader projects is perhaps the single most important characteristic that influences how he or she is perceived by the group. According to Cribben (1981), the group's *perception* of their leader is more important than the effectiveness of the leader's behaviors. In sport, often the players' perception of their coach dictates loyalty and respect (whether the coach seems to be fair and to treat each athlete with dignity, for example). "Images, not people, interact," Cribben asserts (p. 82).

Before examining the different leadership styles in sport, a few points should be made. First, some leadership styles are not included here because they are more related to business and industry rather than to sport. For example, Cribben calls one type "the climber," a person who is extremely self-oriented and not loyal to the organization (although occasionally an assistant coach fits this description). Second, it is important to recognize that leadership styles are not mutually exclusive — they interact. Rarely would you find someone who exhibits only a single leadership style but no others. And third, there is a difference between "successful" and "effective" leadership. Although some coaches in sport are only concerned about winning, most others understand the importance of the components of good coaching that underlie the final outcome.

SUCCESSFUL VERSUS EFFECTIVE LEADERSHIP

Successful leadership has been defined as the ability to get others to behave as the manager intends them to behave (Zaleznik 1977). The job may get done, and the coach's needs may be satisfied, but the players' needs are ignored. Perhaps the coach attends only to starters while ignoring substitutes. In *effective leadership,* the athletes perform in accordance with the coach's intentions and, at the same time, find their own needs satisfied. As Cribben (1981, p. 35) points out, "Success has to do only with getting the job done, whereas effectiveness adds the concept of satisfaction on the part of those who do the job." In this way, the positive feelings of subordinates usually contribute to long-term benefits such as team loyalty, support, and enjoyment of participation, an important component of intrinsic (or inner) motivation. For instance, team captains might feel better about their role — and would be more helpful to the team — if the coach gave them a sense of importance, perhaps a significant responsibility. And resolving conflicts in the privacy of a coach's office rather than in the presence of teammates certainly contributes to team and coach loyalty. Thus, effective coaches are concerned with maintaining good relations with team members over several months, even years, rather than with just winning a specific contest.

Successful (but Ineffective) Coaches

Mechikoff and Kozar (1983) interviewed twenty-three coaches with highly respectable winning records in various sports at the high school and collegiate levels. None of these coaches intimidated, ignored, deceived, or embarrassed an athlete to evoke some desirable mental state or to enhance physical performance. For example, University of Nebraska head football coach Tom Osborne reinforced the importance of honesty and being "genuine" with athletes. Terry Donahue, head football coach at UCLA, praised the use of nonverbal cues in effective communication. And John Robinson, head coach of the Los Angeles Rams, suggested that coaches should "Treat your players with respect." Table 7.2 includes a few styles that fit the so-called successful leader who is not necessarily effective.

Table 7.2   Leaders who are successful

Style	Characteristics	Typical Behavior
Bureaucrat	Formal, disciplined, impersonal.	Product more important than process. Tasks necessary to win more important than family and personal needs of athletes.
Zealot	Impatient, outspoken, very confident, demanding, domineering.	Very task-oriented, little concern for meeting personal needs of others, aggressive, works best with weaker assistants who do not challenge authority.
Machiavellian	Self-oriented, devious, manipulative. Cold but can be charming.	Takes advantage of others' weaknesses; exploits others; must win at any price.

(continued)

Style	Characteristics	Typical Behavior
Missionary	Too concerned with people and what they think of him or her. Likable but tries too hard to be liked. Superb interpersonal skills but not highly respected.	Prizes harmony over conflict. Low task orientation, gets emotionally involved, does what is popular, ignores "tough" decisions, extreme humanist.
Climber	Striving, driving, energetic, self-oriented; polished and smooth but always aggressive; little or no loyalty to organization, team, nor players; competent but is motivated by self-glory and own achievement.	Able to maneuver into the limelight; high task-orientation but for self-serving purposes, not for the team's good. Relates well to others but has no interest in them.
Exploiter	Arrogant, insistent, abusive, demeaning, coercive, vindictive, domineering, rigid, prejudiced, makes snap judgments, yet competent. Exploits others' weaknesses.	Exerts constrictive control, hurts anyone who is vulnerable, uses pressure and fear to get things done. Demands subserviance.
Glad-Hander	Superficial, deceptively friendly, extroverted, top interpersonal skills, lacks depth and substance, minimally competent, good survival instincts, talkative, and humorous.	Sells him/herself very well. Low modest task orientation, gets by on "personality," unconcerned with people but excellent in dealing with them, seeks to impress others.

These are traits of "successful" leaders. Their teams *may* win more often than not, and they may even be well liked or respected by some of their athletes, depending on the personal expectations and needs of each player. On the other hand, they might intimidate or hurt the feelings of their players, thereby limiting the achievement of each player's potential. What these leaders have in common is the *appearance* of success. The leader's needs are satisfied because goals are being met. Usually team members are performing tasks in a manner intended by the leader. Often the missing link, however, is the somewhat low level of satisfaction the subordinates feel in being a part of the group.

If these leaders want to continue winning, they should ask a few important questions. These include: (1) What is the long-term effect of my style? (2) How motivated are my players to perform well and win? (3) Are my athletes persistent in their efforts to achieve team and individual goals? (4) Do the athletes even care about team goals? (5) To what extent do they exhibit loyalty toward the team, school (or sponsor), or to each other? And, (6) if loyalty is lacking, why?

The answers to these questions separate the successful leader from the effective one. The next section indicates why another approach to leadership results in even better outcomes for the coach and team.

Effective Leaders

The renowned scientist Albert Einstein once said, "I have received excessive admiration and respect from my fellow men through no fault of my own." This is a man who "made it" without stepping on the toes of others. He created, initiated, and produced. He led by example. Einstein was not only successful in meeting his own goals, he was an effective leader of the whole international scientific community. His scientific research made him a model others wanted to emulate. His hard work, determination, and incredible perseverance to gain knowledge were never at the expense of the "other fellow." In fact, Einstein is reputed to have assisted others in their work to help ensure their success.

It might be said about effective coaches that they receive excessive admiration and respect from their players because (1) they have a genuine concern for people, (2) they have the ability to teach, (3) they demonstrate their knowledge and intelligence in sport, and (4) they communicate well. They respect others and, in turn, get it back several times over. Phoniness and intimidation are not part of the profile. Relationships are based on a long-term commitment to the program and the desire to reach team and individual goals. Some examples of effective leadership styles are described in Table 7.3.

All coaches in sport want to win. The coach's objective is to lead in a manner that not only will ensure a desirable outcome but also will ensure that the participants learn from, and are satisfied with, their sport experiences. The effective coach knows that *athletes are people*. These leaders are genuinely concerned about the human component — the feelings — of their athletes, in contrast to coaches who are "merely" successful (that is, their teams tend to win

Table 7.3   Leaders who are effective

Style	Characteristics	Typical Behavior
Entrepreneur	Extremely competent, forceful, dominant, self-confident, high need to achieve, can be very loyal, protective, and generous to team. Firm-minded, innovative, often a loner. Creative.	Commands great loyalty, unable to function well in a subordinate position. Offers challenges and opportunities to succeed. Motivates by example, rewards, and fear.
Corporateur	Quite directive but gives people freedom; cordial to others but keeps a certain distance.	Concerned about the good of the team; wins respect; high task orientation; polished and professional; makes people feel needed; delegates tasks and authority and consults, yet keeps effective control.
Developer	Trusts subordinates, wants to help them reach their potential, superb human relations skills; wins personal loyalty; builds a supportive achieving climate. Good counselor.	High people orientation; people considerations may take precedence over achievement, although is very productive. Supportive and emotionally involved with subordinates.

(continued)

Table 7.3   Leaders who are effective *(continued)*

Style	Characteristics	Typical Behavior
Craftsman	Amiable, very conscientious, bright, highly task-oriented, honest, straightforward, mild-mannered, analytical. Proud of competence. Perfectionistic.	Likes to innovate, build, and try out new ideas. Not overly concerned with status; motivated by desire for excellence. Prefers to solve problems alone or in a small group. Supports subordinates.
Integrator	Excellent interpersonal skills; good insight into people. A team builder; prefers group decision-making.	Shares the leadership role. Thinks in terms of associates rather than subordinates. Welcomes the ideas of others. Gives great freedom and authority to others.
Gamesman	Fast-moving, flexible, very bright, skilled. Takes risks, assertive, intent on winning, but not petty; does not try to hurt or "get back at" others. Will not purposely hurt another player or team. Very ethical, but will take advantage of good opportunities to succeed.	Wants to win from good strategy; enjoys fair competition. A tough leader to outsmart who challenges and rewards a person's contributions. Eliminates the weak and nonachievers.

more games than they lose). Examples of well-known coaches with winning records who have been known for their hot tempers and aggressive leadership styles include Bobby Knight (basketball, University of Indiana), the late Woody Hayes (football, Ohio State University), Billy Martin (baseball, New York Yankees and others), and Frank Kush (football, formerly at Arizona State University). These coaches have maintained high winning percentages year after year, yet do not fit the description of effective coaches. Perhaps this is because they were able to recruit elite athletes who, like most top performers, could mentally overcome a more assertive communication style. In addition, it is quite likely that these coaches interacted with the players in a more mild and sensitive manner outside of the competitive arena. Therefore, the players did not take the occasional verbal assault personally. Finally, the most aggressive leaders in sport are in competitive sports that demand relatively higher arousal levels, such as basketball and football. Almost never would you hear of a coach in golf or tennis (sports in which lower arousal levels are necessary) rant and rave in an aggressive, angry manner. The sport, then, partially dictates the type of leadership style that is most beneficial to the participant.

LEADERSHIP STYLES

This is not to suggest that a coach's habits should follow only one style at the exclusion of all others. In his review of the leadership literature as a guest lecturer at New Mexico State University, sport psychologist and sociologist George Sage concluded that coaching in sport is too complex for the use of only one approach. In fact, he postulated that effective coaches use each of the four major styles at one time or another, sometimes in rapid succession. Some styles are more appropriate in certain situations than others. For example, authoritative techniques are less effective with smaller teams than with larger ones and more effective with males than females. This is why identifying the characteristics of each style, describing their advantages and disadvantages, and determining the time at which each would be most appropriate are useful exercises. Many of the traits described in the preceding successful and effective categories are included in the four major leadership styles that have received considerable attention in the sport literature. These are referred to as authoritative, behavioristic, humanistic, and democratic approaches.

The Authoritarian

Do nice guys finish last, as former major league manager Leo Durocher is quoted as saying? Must good coaches be tough, demanding, overtly powerful, and dominant? These are some of the stereotypes of the coaching profession. In fact, research dating back to 1966 by Drs. Bruce Ogilvie and Thomas Tutko reinforce this image. From their sample, they derived a profile of the "typical" coach. The traits of the typical coach were (1) being highly success driven with an outstanding need to be on top, (2) feeling free to express aggressive tendencies in a manner appropriate to the role of coach, and (3) being a dominant, take-charge type of person who would actively seek roles of leadership. These traits describe aspects of authoritarian leadership behavior. Whether these data are accurate reflections of successful coaches is far from conclusive.

The authoritarian (sometimes called autocratic) leader is characterized as achievement-oriented and impervious to criticism (he or she projects an image of knowing all the answers). He or she feels that athletes want and need a "tough guy" approach. Authoritarians have great confidence that they can finish what they start and that they can do so successfully. They rarely doubt their actions. In all probability, autocrats were exposed to similar models either in their father or a former coach. "If it was good enough for me, it's good enough for my players" is their motto.

Sport psychologists Tutko and Ogilvie (1967) believe that coaches have a need to control others and gravitate to a sport situation to satisfy this need. But they also believe that athletes perceive the coach's role as an authority figure and, thus, expect authoritarian behaviors. Authoritarians believe that *athletes actually seek dominance from the coach.*

Power, if used effectively, represents direction; it facilitates action, especially with relatively younger and less skilled performers. In the literature on management, Hersey and Blanchard (1977) found that when the level of group member maturity is low, a high task-oriented leadership style is most effective. Thus, participants in youth sports or in physical education classes, for instance, need and prefer a high-task approach. But be careful: This is not to suggest that using a highly authoritative, commanding, and critical style of leadership is appropriate with these individuals. Instead, an approach in which the participants' behaviors are purposeful and highly directed is needed.

Power in leading others can have long-term benefits of facilitating action rather than inhibiting it. Fromm (1941) believes that persons who wish to be powerless do so to escape the responsibility that comes with independent thinking and decision making. Young, unskilled, less mature sport competitors might fall into this category. Fromm suggests that:

> Most people are convinced that as long as they are not overtly forced to do something by an outside power, their decisions are theirs, and that if they want something, it is they who want it. But this is one of the great illusions we have about ourselves. A great number of our decisions are not really our own but are suggested to us from the outside; we have succeeded in persuading ourselves that it is we who have made the decision, whereas we have actually conformed with expectations of others, driven by the fear of isolation and by more direct threats to our life, freedom, and comfort (p. 200).

In sport, power is a tool used by coaches to reach goals. But an authoritative approach to coaching need not always take the form of a repressive drill sergeant. The alternative might be what Sabock (1985) calls "the benevolent dictator." This coach makes demands and decisions based on the athletes' best interests. A vigorous conditioning program to get everyone in shape, raising one's voice to increase the players' arousal level, and making sudden and important decisions during the contest are examples. Sabock believes that "a good leader will tolerate uncertainty only up to a point" (p. 106). Tutko and Ogilvie describe four benefits of an authoritative coaching style.

1. *The athletes feel secure.* The insecure athlete may feel more protected with a strong leader, one who makes virtually all the decisions.

2. *Aggression can be redirected.* Theoretically, an authoritative approach may heighten aggression in the athlete, perhaps by increasing his or her frustration, essentially the frustration-aggression hypothesis that was more popular several years ago than it is in current thinking (see chapter 6). The intended result of this strategy is to translate these feelings into heightened aggression, which in turn is redirected toward an opponent. One limitation of this technique is that many sports (and individual performers) require relatively low levels of arousal and aggression. Arousal can be too high, which hinders rather than improves effectiveness. Further, not all individuals react to frustration in the same manner; some persons pout or withdraw. Others do not enjoy such treatment and quit the team. Sometimes a theory accurately predicts behavior, and sometimes it doesn't.

3. *The coach's needs are met.* An authoritative style can be an expression of the coach's needs and personality. As a result, he or she is most effective when these needs are met. However, subordinates such as assistant coaches and players might find an authoritative style contradictory to their own needs. Certainly, golfers, tennis players, and many other athletes whose sports demand relatively low arousal and high concentration could not function optimally with an angry, demanding coach. Clearly, authoritative behaviors are more appropriate in some situations than others.

4. *The authoritarian is viewed as efficient and decisive.* Nothing is more expeditious than a one-person system of decision making. However, if the decisions are the wrong ones or if the leader fails to meet goals, he or she can expect little support from group members and assistants. If coaches take responsibility for all decisions, then they also take responsibility for the outcomes.

Certainly authoritative behavior has a place in sport leadership. However, because power is literally inherent in the coaching position, there should be less reason to assert it than many coaches realize. The literature does not support the contention that athletes want and need a "tough guy" leadership style. Even effective authoritative coaches understand the importance of respecting the character and integrity of athletes. And to recognize the time and place for exhibiting power is also important. The expression of authoritative behavior, whether it is in decision making or in reprimanding, is clearly more useful with only selected competitors and conditions. One objective of effective coaching is to determine when and with whom this style is best suited.

The Behaviorist

Coaches who pat a player on the back after making a good play or express disappointment or anger after an unwelcomed performance are practicing a style of leadership called *behaviorism* or the use of a strategy referred to as *behavior modification*. This approach is based on the contention that human behavior is shaped or reinforced by its consequences. Reaching a goal or receiving a reward, then, is dependent on performing certain desirable behaviors. For example, an athlete who clearly gives a 100 percent effort during some task may be rewarded by the coach's words, "Nice going, Susan. Way to hustle." Ignoring the athlete who performs poorly, who is clearly not giving a 100 percent effort, or who behaves in an inappropriate manner is another example. This process is called *contingency management*. Desirable responses from the coach are contingent on expected, desirable performance. The desire to receive positive recognition, an integral part of human nature, is well understood by the coaching profession as a tool to influence sport performance and motivation.

A behavioristic approach in group leadership, including sport, can be a sophisticated science if conducted properly. Rather than merely giving orders and directing the behaviors of subordinates (more common with autocrats), the behaviorist sets up conditions in the environment that either (1) cause certain behaviors that have a desirable outcome (see Example 1 below) or (2) reinforce certain behaviors that either increase or decrease the probability of similar behaviors occurring in the future (see Example 2 below).

Example 1. A Behavioristic Strategy to Improve Group Cohesion

The coach of a baseball team noticed that many of the players were forming their own subgroups (cliques) during their free time and ignoring other teammates. The cliques consisted of personal friends but, surprisingly, did not consist of only starters or only substitutes. Playing status was not an issue in forming these groups. The coach, worried that subgrouping would weaken the athletes' commitment to support one another and to reach team goals, planned two programs, one on the field and one off the field, designed to weaken the subgroups (or at least some of them) and to bring the team closer together.

The objective of the on-field strategy was to have the different cliques work together in fielding drills. Three practices were planned. The strategy, planned before the first practice, consisted of:

1. Writing down names of players who formed the various cliques.
2. Listing the athletes in each subgroup who would make up the practice groups (the coach was careful not to include the same subgroup members in any practice group). The practice groups comprised members of different racial and ethnic backgrounds, starters and nonstarters, players from different positions and of various skill levels, and leaders and isolates.
3. Creating practice tasks that mandated interacting. Catching a fly ball and throwing it to the second baseperson would not allow players to interact with the desired intensity. The athletes had to actually depend on each other during the practice interaction. Sample drills included a first baseperson fielding a ground ball and tossing it to the pitcher, who would cover first base; or a second baseperson running toward the outfield to help to determine which of two outfielders should catch a fly ball (after the ball is caught, the outfielder would throw it to the second baseperson, who would then relay it to the shortstop covering second base. Each subgroup was assigned a different practice drill. The objective was to get players who normally did not congregate to interact around a common goal and literally to work together to meet that goal.
4. Offer verbal ("Excellent catch/throw/call") and nonverbal (smile, thumbs up, and so forth) congratulatory cues after each successful performance.

Due partly to this drill, players began to feel more comfortable with one another. In fact, they learned one another's first names and began to use them. Further, the players helped one another to reach the desired outcomes. This carried over into games, where they supported teammates after errors or striking out as well as after making great plays and getting hits. The team grew closer.

The off-field strategy consisted of assigning athletes to committees that were responsible for meeting a certain goal. These goals included planning a team workout, leading a team meeting (without the coach's presence), arranging for a guest speaker, planning a team party, and a grievance committee which informs the coach about the athletes' need to promote the interaction of particular players. Individuals who were usually quiet or tended to isolate themselves were invited to interact with other players who were more outgoing (e.g., positive leaders), and the groups were purposely intersocial. In other words, players were assigned to groups rather than volunteering for them, and every team member participated on one committee. Opportunities to meet were scheduled. Deadlines to provide information or to meet some objective from the group's activity were announced. The outcome of this strategy was that players became further acquainted with each other and, consequently, interacted in a more supportive, less "cliquish" (territorial) manner. The athletes actually enjoyed each other's company. Team harmony improved dramatically.

Example 2. A Behavioristic Strategy to Improve Risk-Taking in Basketball

A collegiate women's basketball coach was concerned about a player who played the forward position. He complained to a team consultant about the inability or unwillingness of this athlete to take open shots, to go after rebounds, or to maintain control of the ball. The player, in her first year with the team, was clearly uptight. The coach asked her to see the consultant, and true to her word, she was on time for her appointment. The consultant asked her about her past successes in basketball and what she did to deserve this success. He also asked about her perceptions of the present situation; specifically about the coach's habits and personality characteristics, her relationships with other players, and her general feelings about her social life, academic status, and adjustment to being a new team member.

Two things emerged from the conversation. First, this young woman was being pressured to do new things on the court that her previous coach did not require, such as scoring more points and exhibiting better ball control. Second, the coach's loud and aggressive manner made her uncomfortable and anxious. She realized that she was making mistakes on the floor and didn't need to be constantly reminded of this by the coach. However, the coach was openly critical of her errors on the court. His remarks carried over after the game. He was not hostile, but the assertiveness of his approach made her feel uncomfortable. She was simply afraid of her coach. As a result, her strategy became, "If I don't try, I can't fail." This young athlete was in great need of success and complimentary feedback from her team leader.

The consultant was given license in advance by the coach to make an agreement with the player concerning future behaviors. The coach agreed — also in advance — to abide by the contract. The agreement was that the athlete would relax, take more risks on the court, and have fun. In particular, she would shoot when she had the opportunity rather than pass the ball and would be generally more aggressive on the court. This was to be carried out in both practice and game situations (she was not a starter and only entered the game when the outcome was not in jeopardy). It was understood that the coach would congratulate these new risk-taking behaviors *regardless of the outcome*. He would voice approval in response to the behaviors, whether or not they were successful. The coach and the athlete were to understand that all the parties were working on the process of establishing the player's mental set, not on the end product — at least not at this time.

The process established a risk-free environment in which the player could perform the skills that she was able to demonstrate during the preseason and in previous seasons as a superb high school athlete. The strategy was to let the player "be herself"; to let her have fun as though the coach weren't even watching. The coach and consultant decided to let the physical performance errors take care of themselves; with time and more opportunity to play, the athlete would gain confidence and improve. Meanwhile, the right time to criticize performance had not arrived. In fact, for the next few weeks, she received no critical feedback whatsoever. After three weeks, the coach began to suggest alternatives and to throw in a few reminders about technique.

The use of behaviorism in this example served the purpose of extinguishing some feelings and behaviors while promoting others. The athlete's anxieties over the coach's actions and attitudes were real. Ironically, the coach didn't even realize that he was influencing the player in such a derogatory manner (which, by the way, is not uncommon). The use of complimentary remarks after the athlete's change in performance (regardless of outcome) served to reinforce certain desirable behaviors, which increased the probability of their reoccurrence. By refraining from criticizing the athlete's performance outcome after she risked a more liberal playing strategy, the coach reduced and eventually extinguished her anxieties by dissolving the association between risking and failing. She began to relax, to have more fun, to perform up to her capabilities (and her coach's expectations), and to feel more comfortable with the coach's critique of her play—both positive and negative. Her ability to handle negative feedback was based on more successful experiences, which built up her confidence.

The behavioristic approach in coaching can be used inappropriately, however. Two incorrect uses of behaviorism in coaching are punishment and threatening statements. Coaches love to discipline athletes and to control behavior by admonishing the athletes (yelling and screaming) and ordering them to do extra running. Threatening statements such as "If you can't do 'such and such,' you'll sit on the bench" are supposed to increase the athlete's motivation and, perhaps, aggression level. In fact, they may—but only for a short time. But often, such statements have the opposite effect. Exposure to threats may result in withdrawal and diminished incentive. Athletes may feel insulted, embarrassed, or angry at the source of this input—usually the coach. Risk taking and effort may plummet. In the behaviorism literature, both forms of punishment are called *aversive stimulation* to modify a player's behavior. Do these methods work? They must, or coaches would stop using them. But the reason they work is that they cause a sudden increase in the athlete's level of arousal (a physiological response) and motivation (its psychological counterpart) as the athlete attempts to avoid unpleasant future consequences. Because such techniques appear to result in desirable changes in player behavior, coaches are sold on their value and continue to use them. Of course, threatening someone's life will also result in very rapid behavioral changes. But does this make it an effective way to motivate people?

This approach to behaviorism has a few very serious drawbacks. First, the fact that *immediate* changes in behavior are evident does not necessarily mean that *future* behaviors will be affected. Rushall and Siedentop (1972) and Dickinson (1977) have surveyed the behaviorism literature and have applied it to sport contexts. The authors report that punishment (negative reinforcement) has an immediate effect on performance but that its impact fails to carry over to future situations. In fact, many athletes rebel at such treatment and, in response to their frustration, either quit the team or carry on at submaximal effort levels. In addition, aversive stimulation reportedly reduces risk-taking behaviors. The athlete is less inclined to attempt skills that do not virtually assure successful outcomes. This is not desirable because good sport performers are risk-takers (Vanek and Cratty 1970).

A second problem with punishment as a mechanism to control behavior is that it reduces the coach's ability to give positive reinforcement later on. The coach's effectiveness in positively arousing and motivating athletes is reduced because the team leader is perceived as a source of unpleasant input. Even the coach's nonthreatening suggestions become less credible. According to Dickinson (1977, p. 127):

> It is very possible that since the coach himself is a stimulus to the player, that his dispensing of aversive stimulation may result in the coach being able to act as a less effective positive reinforcer on subsequent occasions. However, aversive stimulation may bring about a rapid and significant improvement in the performance of the player. This will constitute an immediate reinforcement for the coach, hence making this kind of behavior more probable in the future and further reducing his capacity to act as a positive reinforcer.

There are several advantages and disadvantages of using a behavioristic approach exclusively and in the absence of other styles in sport situations.

Advantages of the behavioristic approach

1.   *The carryover effect.* Unrelated reinforcers such as playing well and winning the contest occur partly as a result of using immediate reinforcers in practice situations. Players who are given a pat on the back after running a series of forty-yard wind sprints will be motivated to prepare well and to be in better physical condition during the contest. As a result, they will likely be more successful competitors.

2.   *The teamwide effect.* Behavioristic techniques can be used with all team members simultaneously. Every team member should help to determine team goals and should work toward meeting them. In this way, each member will feel partly responsible for the team's success, even if less emphasis is placed on meeting certain personal goals.

3.   *Greater internal motivation.* Sometimes giving external rewards such as payment or a trophy actually increases internal motivation, the type that a

person feels when the task is performed because it is enjoyable. Not all types of rewards have this impact. Quite often externally derived rewards such as a high salary or other job-related benefits become the only reasons a person engages in a task. For example, if the rewards were removed, the person would not continue in the activity for enjoyment alone. However, if an external reward increases a person's feelings of self-competence, then the activity becomes increasingly pleasant. Self-esteem and self-confidence rise, and so does intrinsic motivation. In sport, then, if a coach offers an athlete rewards indicating improved competence (such as verbal encouragement or a favorable change in playing status), the athlete will likely feel more successful. These feelings tend to increase internal (intrinsic) motivation.

Disadvantages of the behavioristic approach

1.   *Extinction.* What if the athlete expects that certain responses will elicit particular desirable outcomes but, in fact, does *not* experience them as anticipated? If responses are dependent on a reward such as recognition from a coach, parents, or teammates; selection to the league's all-star team, or some other anticipated outcome, and in fact, these expectancies are not met, the contingencies become weakened or nonexistent. This process is called *extinction* (Dickinson 1977).

Take, for example, the effect of weight lifting on performance and game outcome. Let's assume that football players understand the importance of building muscular strength to being a successful athlete. If the players were rewarded for reaching certain goals in weight training, one would expect this activity to continue. But if their skills were not improving or they were not winning more games after achieving strength gain, their motivation to persist at this activity would decrease, perhaps even cease. The contingency for weight lifting (the belief that it will lead to winning) would be markedly reduced. The effects of extinction are illustrated in Figure 7.2.

2.   *Disparity between player and leader values.* If the goal is perceived as unimportant by the performer, the value of any reinforcement will be diminished appreciably. For instance, an athlete who rarely receives an opportunity to compete may feel undermotivated to participate in an intense conditioning program because he or she cannot identify any sport-related benefit to getting into top shape. Tasks that lead to accomplishing a goal (better performance, for instance) would not be performed unless the external motivating factors (getting into the game) were present. The coach should be sure (if possible) that the athlete understands and identifies with his or her own performance goals and the activities that are necessary to reach them.

3.   *The responsibility factor.* Unless an athlete feels responsible for his or her actions, the behavioristic approach will be of only limited value. Ensuring

Figure 7.2   The effects of reinforcement and extinction on future performance; when success in sport is contingent on strength building

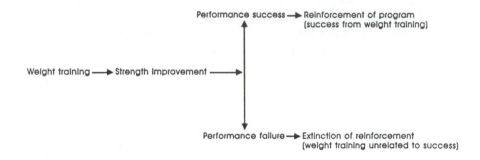

that performers attribute performance outcomes to effort (e.g., "I succeeded because I tried hard") is desirable and a challenge for any coach.

4.   *Not meeting long-term goals.* It was indicated earlier that one way to abuse behavioristic strategies is to implement noxious or punishing responses to control behavior (running extra laps around the field or gym, for example). One danger in using this approach—and I do not use the term "danger" flippantly, for punishment is subsequently demotivating and counterproductive—is that aversive control has been shown to meet short-term but not long-term goals. The athlete might get "pumped up" and perform better after the coach insults him or her in front of teammates, but the player might also never forgive the coach for this insulting experience and never play at optimal levels. Quitting the team is also possible.

5.   *What's reinforcing?* Finally, to predict what the athlete will consider to be a "valuable" reinforcer is very difficult. A good example is the use of decals on the helmets of football players as a form of recognition, which many athletes do not consider motivating, regardless of what many coaches think. My own interviews with over two hundred football players in high school and college support this claim. Sixty-five percent said the decals were not considered an important goal and did not heighten future performance.

Some coaches at the college level have a weekly award for the best "scout team" player, a nonstarter who plays the role of this week's opponent during practice sessions and mimics the opponent's offensive or defensive alignment. The players were actually embarrassed to receive recognition for this role. It signified and reinforced, after all, the athlete's nonstarting status. Such award recipients are "recognized" as third or fourth string at their position, not exactly a compliment to their skills.

Guidelines for using the behavioristic style

The behavioristic approach is based on (1) tangible performance-based achievement, (2) successful participation followed by reinforcement, and (3) responsibility for one's own actions. According to Anshel (1978), Dickinson (1977), and Rushall and Siedentop (1972), the proper use of behaviorism in coaching entails the following guidelines:

- Create a situation in which players are achieving desirable outcomes from their own efforts. Have athletes compete against individuals or teams of similar caliber, particularly in practice.
- Remain aware of the performances of all team members — starters and substitutes alike — especially in practice sessions. Successes should be reinforced through recognition, praise, and occasional (intermittent) tangible reward — reward that players find meaningful and desirable.
- Behavioral objectives of player performance should be (1) attainable, (2) based on past experiences and performance outcomes, (3) realistic, (4) meaningful to the participant, (5) positively stated (what the athletes should do rather than what they shouldn't do), (6) both short term and long term, and (7) set jointly by coach and athlete. If disagreement exists and it can't be negotiated, the best course often is to let the player's goal be met first to optimize future motivation (if it is not detrimental to the team's success). One collegiate swimmer interviewed for this book indicated that her coach set a goal of attaining a swim speed that was far in excess of the performer's own beliefs. Consequently, her motivation to reach the coach's goal decreased markedly. She felt helpless and was unable to make an all-out effort. The coach failed to negotiate a goal that the performer felt was within her ability. Remember that objectives should also be alterable. They're not written in stone. If the goal proves to be too easy or too difficult, it should be changed.
- The coach and team should agree on rules and regulations *before* the season starts to strengthen contingencies. For example, if the players understand that curfew is at a certain time and that breaking curfew will result in a particular unpleasant outcome, the contingency of maintaining this policy will be stronger. Players will be more responsible in supporting it. Another example: If the players communicate the minimal impact of a "sub of the week" award, to bestow such an award makes no sense. In fact, inundating the team with too many recognition awards ultimately weakens the intended effect.

The behaviorist coach may be manipulative, but he or she can also be bright, insightful, very goal-directed, and sincere. It's one thing to regulate the behavior of athletes both on and off the field or court based on a predetermined selection of rewards and punishments. But it's a feather in the coach's cap to be able to

(1) really understand the needs of each player or the team as a whole and (2) make sincere attempts to assist each person to meet his or her needs. Setting up environmental reinforcers that occur *in a natural setting or situation* is a complex procedure that entails planning and insight. Is it worth it? Authors Dickinson (1977) and Rushall and Siedentop (1972) contend that it can make the difference between the team's success and failure. This style has the added benefit of eliminating the authoritative, power-laden approach to directing the behaviors of athletes who rightfully feel that they deserve their coach's respect as human beings as well as sport participants. A sense of respect and sensitivity to the player's needs is the focus of the next leadership style, humanism.

The Humanist

The essential difference between authoritarianism or behaviorism and humanism is expressed by the contrast between viewing the team as a group of players or viewing the team as a group of individuals who play a given sport. According to Sage (1980, p. 224), "The goal of school sports . . . for the humanist is the production of increasing uniqueness and independence, and this cannot be achieved in an autocratic atmosphere in which the team is built around an omniscient authority figure where all decisions are made by the coach while players are relegated to passive followers of orders." Humanism explains behavior in terms of the relationship between the individual and the environment. It implies the leader's desire to understand the athlete's emotional and psychological makeup and how these factors affect the player's sport performance. The thrust of this style is to treat each player in the way that the coach feels the player would like to be (and needs to be) treated (i.e., with respect, sensitivity, and fairness). According to Sage, "The humanistic coach starts with the basic premise that the sport is for the players, not the coaches."

Mechikoff and Kozar (1983, p. 81) describe the frequent use of humanistic strategies by former Western Illinois University head cross-country and track coach Dick Abbot:

> He was very concerned about his athletes as students and citizens as well as athletes. He tried to communicate with his athletes not just on the track but between classes, visiting them at the residence, etc. . . . He sought the help of other athletes in giving psychological and emotional help and guidance to the athlete. . . . One of the most important techniques he had . . . was his attempt to listen to athletes and allow them opportunities to vent their feelings. . . . He feels the simple process of having someone care and providing them the opportunity to vent their concerns perhaps reduced some feelings of anxiety and tension and thus allowed them to perform well.

The humanistic coach cares about meeting the competitor's needs as well as achieving the outcome. In fact, the former should benefit the latter. Caring about the athlete's feelings and attempting to establish warm, trusting relationships with players should result in heightened loyalty, physical effort, and self-esteem. Smith, Smoll, and Curtis (1979) found that children who played for highly reinforcing and encouraging coaches had significantly higher levels of postseason self-esteem than did those who were exposed to coaches who did not behave in this manner.

The coach wants results. *Winning* is the name of the game, especially when retaining one's job depends on it. In their pursuit of team success, some coaches give little thought to the importance of tasks and goals that are unrelated to game outcomes. Humanism, however, places the individual before all other considerations, including the game outcome. The most effective coaches understand that an unhappy athlete has feelings that need to be exposed, feelings that may interfere with the player's concentration and motivation, directly inhibiting performance intensity and skill. This athlete will not approach the game with the proper mental preparation. Concentration and motivation will be suboptimal.

Humanism may also be extended to coaching assistants. Coaches have an obligation to solicit the input of assistants when making many team-related decisions. The sharing of authority and decision making gives assistant coaches a sense of meaningfulness and responsibility on the team. This aspect of humanism is referred to as the *participative approach.* In this way, the head coach uses the capabilities of each assistant and maintains "the congruence between [team] goals and the assistant's personal aspirations" (Magnotta 1986, p. 78). Thus, an important objective of humanistic coaching is to disprove a statement from former major league baseball manager Leo Durocher, that "nice guys finish last."

Characteristics of humanistic coaching

The humanist:

- Communicates in a sincere, honest manner with team members
- Acknowledges, understands, and responds to individual differences among players
- Is aware of the nature of relationships and interactions among the players and between player and coach (i.e., the group dynamics)
- Shows a sincere interest in meeting the players' personal needs as team members (e.g., being successful, learning new skills, establishing meaningful relationships with teammates, and maturing as a person) in addition to the ultimate objective of winning

In addition to these behavioral traits, the humanist is approachable. Players can confide in a humanistic coach and disclose their feelings to him or her. No question from a player is regarded as "stupid" (whatever that word means). The humanist understands that inquiries from athletes are desirable; they show interest and curiosity. Because this coach invests in the growth and learning of his or her players, typical responses from performers such as making mistakes, not remembering information, asking questions, and even having trouble making friends on the team are dealt with in a constructive and positive manner.

Humanism is the "fundamental concern for the human person . . . having a measure of autonomy, choice, and self-determination" (Sage 1980, p. 219). Humanistic coaches try to allow players the freedom to experiment, to take risks, to make decisions, and to learn from their decisions. The objective is personal growth.

Another aspect of enhancing personal growth in humanistic coaching is encouraging athletes to think at a higher level, to develop a sense of sophistication, maturity, and intelligence. For example, athletes tend to form closely knit peer groups that demand conformity to certain rules. Team members who do not conform are isolated rather than respected for their individuality, especially in the preadolescent and adolescent age groups. The humanistic coach, observing team members isolating or even scapegoating another teammate, would bring the parties together and help to resolve the conflict for the good of the team. More importantly, players would be encouraged to discuss their feelings about the pressures to conform to peer expectations. The coach would elaborate on the importance of accepting others, especially teammates who have the same goal of helping the team win. The coach can help competitors take an honest look at themselves—at their strengths, weaknesses, and aspirations, and what to do about them.

The following are some examples of humanistic coaching that illustrate the characteristics of this style.

Example 1

Athlete:	Hey, coach, what is the signal for stealing second base?
Authoritarian:	How many times do I have to tell you, kid? Are you deaf?
Humanist:	Let's go over it one more time, then you show me the signs, OK?

The humanist simply answers the question. No harsh words are used to criticize and generally weaken the person's self-concept. The issue is dealt with in a straightforward, mature manner. The authoritative response will cause athletes to avoid asking questions altogether, which means that more errors will be made, both mentally (forgetting strategies) and physically (fearing failure and avoiding necessary risks).

Example 2

An athlete makes a third mistake within a span of a few minutes.

Authoritarian: Darn it, Ed, catch the ball. How many times are you going to mess up? No more mistakes or we'll put someone else in there.

Humanist: (No anger in tone of voice) This isn't your day, Ed. You might be tensing up a bit. Take a short break and relax. I'll get you back in shortly.

Example 3

After the game, instead of ignoring substitutes, the coach approaches a player who did not get into the game.

Coach: Hey, Molly, I'm sure you wanted to get into the game today. I'll try to get you in at the next game. But I just want to let you know you've been a great help to the team. You give it your best shot at every practice, and because of you, our starting players are better prepared for game competition. Just want to say "thanks, and keep up the good work."

Example 4

A coach's team just won, but she wasn't happy about the way one of her players displayed discourteous behavior toward the referee. Humanistic coaches help their athletes to mature.

Coach: Debbie, I thought you played a fine game tonight. But there is one thing I'm concerned about that we should discuss. When the ref called a foul on you in the fourth quarter, you really blew up. You were obviously very upset.

Athlete: I sure was. No way did I foul the ball handler when she went for a lay-up.

Coach: Maybe not. But even more important is how you reacted to the call. Your outburst did not show maturity. In addition, you would have hurt the team if the ref had called a technical foul on you because of your mouth. Debbie, if you want to be a good athlete, you'll have to adapt to the ref's calls, whether they're for you or against you. Try to put those calls behind you and get on with the game, OK? If you're upset about a call, talk to me about it. Let me speak to the ref if I think it's a good idea. What do you say?

Athlete: I'll do my best, coach. Thanks for speaking to me
                        about it.

Advantages of the humanistic approach

Let's face it, many coaches and noncoaches have little patience for the humanistic style. To these individuals, effective coaching entails a "tough-guy" approach; don't give the players an inch, or they'll take advantage of you. Perhaps. But if done right, the proper use of humanistic strategies can add significantly to the quality of team performance. Consider these advantages of humanism in sport leadership:

1.   *It improves the athlete's internal motivation.* The desire to play and improve comes from within, from personal gratification and feelings of competence and self-direction. Instead of being governed by external reinforcement such as either punishment or reward, players assume responsibility for their own performance and, for that matter, for the caliber of team play.

2.   *The players' concentration and attention improve.* Coaches can put this outcome in the bank. The humanistic coach helps players to resolve personal issues so that they can focus totally and clearly on performance-related tasks. Many forces in an athlete's life have the potential to detract from learning sport skills and developing proper mental habits. An unhappy player is undermotivated to do his or her best against opponents. He or she is also less concerned about team performance and game outcome.

3.   *Players experience personal growth.* Some coaches might not feel that furthering the athlete's personal development should be a concern. After all, competitive sport is based on success; that is, winning. But, hold on. Don't coaches (the same ones who want to win) also want to work with mature athletes, with participants who perform all of the necessary tasks (mental and physical) to play at their best? Don't coaches prefer athletes who not only will do what the coach asks but also will pursue many of these activities on their own without being told what to do? What about coping with failure? The humanistic coach can help develop each player's ability to deal with the more stressful aspects of competitive sport. Clearly, then, personal growth does transfer to the sport arena.

4.   *Development of coach loyalty.* Let me discuss this issue with a tidbit about the infamous and successful Woody Hayes, former football coach of the Ohio State University Buckeyes. Hayes received considerable media coverage for his assertive behavior toward players. What is less well known is the degree to which his athletes felt admiration and loyalty toward him. Why? Because he invested in each player's personal growth as well as in their athletic development. Hayes used to have long discussions with athletes, even sometimes in the stadium shower facility, about issues totally unrelated to football. He was very knowledgeable about contemporary United States history and politics, and often engaged in discussions with the athletes on such topics. He was also concerned

about school grades and about adjustment to life on campus. The players believed in this man because they were correctly convinced that he believed in them. They wanted to win for Woody. Coach Hayes often followed an authoritarian coaching style, but he was more of a humanist than many would have thought.

5.   *Leader charisma*. The term *charisma* is difficult to define and even more difficult to describe. Mitchell (1979) described the charismatic leader as one who is confident, dominant, and purposeful. He or she articulates goals and builds an image, and effects in followers devotion, unquestioning support, and radical change. These qualities are also reflected in a humanistic leadership style.

Disadvantages of humanistic approach

Alas, not all is happy and fruitful in the land of humanism. What, you might ask, can possibly be wrong with being sensitive to the feelings of players and wanting each performer to feel fulfilled as a sport participant? Not much, in fact. But no system is perfect. Here's why.

1.   *It's not for elite performers*. Humanistic leadership might be incompatible with the requirements of advanced athletic competition. Chelladurai and Arnott (1985) found that when the coach was perceived by male and female collegiate basketball players as having the necessary information to make the best decision or when the type of decision to be made was based on a complex issue, the athletes preferred an autocratic leadership style. Successful participation in sport requires discipline, group cohesion, strategic planning, and the control of complex motor processes. A highly task-oriented approach to sport leadership is warranted. Relatively little time is available for meeting the personal (and often complex) needs of individual athletes.

2.   *Outcome is not a priority*. The coach who practices humanism tends not to be consumed with achievement and winning, which seems incompatible with the nature and objectives of competitive sport. Concern for personal feelings and emotional problems will not, by itself, lead to successful game outcomes. Sage (1980, p. 226), in reflecting the humanist philosophy in sport, asserts that "Using victory as the only end, the goal of sport competition, is too limiting, confining, too shallow, too short-sighted for humanism. . . .The end in sport is the joy, exhilaration, and self-fulfillment that one obtains from movement." Indeed, humanists are not afraid to diminish the importance of keeping score. The score is a means, not an end. For coaches who view the final score as the most important outcome of sport competition, the humanistic approach offers relatively little gratification.

3.   *No success may lead to dropping out*. If meeting the personal needs of each athlete is more important to the coach than winning (an example is making sure that all players on the team play in every game, regardless of the score), and as a result, the team tends to be unsuccessful, players might lose

interest and quit the team. Everyone wants to win, especially at higher skill levels. This is not to suggest that the humanist should necessarily consider winning to be the only important outcome of sport participation. However, certain strategies and situations might require an approach that neglects meeting every individual's needs.

Some games might not allow the second-string catcher or goalie to enter the game. Feelings might be hurt as a result. In youth sports, for example, where the humanistic approach is probably most warranted, every player gets a chance to play, regardless of the game status or possible outcome. But at a more advanced level of competition, a different coaching response would likely be warranted. Winning the game simply takes precedence over making athletes happy.

Guidelines for using the humanistic style

Here are a few coaching suggestions for using a humanistic leadership style:

- Interact with the athlete in a warm, trusting manner. This doesn't mean that less pleasant emotions should never be expected to enter the relationship, because after all, the parties are human. But mutual trust, respect, and sincerity result in mutual admiration. Under such circumstances, athletes become more "coachable," and coaches make better use of their expertise.

- Respect individual differences. Effective coaches do *not* treat all players in the same way. They understand that some athletes are more sensitive and need more patience than others. Athletes differ in the manner in which they prefer to mentally prepare for a game. Coaches should not bend team rules and policies, but they should be aware that the concept of T-E-A-M has its limitations.

- Engage in off-season interaction. Humanistic coaches care about their players' welfare year round, not just during the season. Issues such as school grades, physical conditioning, and perhaps the player's social or family life might need input or reinforcement from the coach. Certainly the recent concerns about drug abuse in sport should keep coaches interested in their athletes' recreational pursuits. The key here is a genuine concern for the total individual, a person who's more than just a sport competitor.

- Take an active part in practice. It's very common for coaches to bark their commands from a designated point and rarely become actively involved in the practice or conditioning program. Henderson (1971) suggests that, at least in the early part of the season, the coach should take an active part in practice. He or she might put on workout clothing and lift weights or run a few laps with the team. In this way, the athletes can meet their coach on common ground. A closer identification with the performers results.

- Promote mass participation. Coaches and players alike want to win. To do so often means playing the team's best athletes. But it's clearly a mistake to ignore substitutes who, by the way, are only one injury away from starting. To raise team morale, the humanist attempts to have as many team members as possible participating in the game. In fact, substitutes should be given tasks in practice as a technique to help them to feel more closely responsible for the team's game preparation and performance — and to improve their own skills if possible. Examples of such tasks include throwing batting practice, refereeing practice intrasquad games, keeping statistics, sharing observations with a starter playing the same position, providing moral support, or in some way assisting the coach. Actual game participation is more desirable, but realistically, not all players will get into the game. Having some meaningful identification with game preparation, however, gives the nonstarting participant a feeling of contributing to the game outcome.

Athletes do not want to be treated disrespectfully. They are uncomfortable with being perceived by their coach exclusively as athletes rather than as human beings. Lanning (1979) claims that the coach must take the responsibility to know and relate to each athlete based on his or her psychological needs. In other words, the fundamental objective in sport should be humanism: treating each athlete as a unique individual. To do this effectively, the coach must make the effort to do two things: (1) know the individual athlete and (2) have the introspection to see themselves as others see them. According to Lanning, "The coach *must* consider the effect of his or her personality on each athlete. Coaches can do this by understanding more about themselves and their influence on others. It is imperative that coaches know themselves very well" (p. 263). Clearly, a coach can take his or her role as power broker or troubleshooter only so far before loyalty begins to erode.

The Democrat

Any team with elected captains is exercising a *democratic* (also called *delegative*) leadership style. Holding team and individual player discussions prior to making rules that will affect the participants also employs a democratic philosophy. Is this an effective way to govern? It is, according to Litwin and Stringer (1968), who found that when group members desire participation in decision making, their performance and group member satisfaction is affected either positively or negatively, depending on whether this need is met. But whereas the authoritarian leader is efficient and decisive, the democrat is sometimes viewed as slow, inefficient, and confused. *Slow* because allowing a group of individuals to make decisions or policies takes time and patience. *Inefficient* because groups can make decisions that are counterproductive and not well thought out, decisions that meet short-term needs at the expense of long-term benefits. Sometimes athletes prefer that the coach make the decisions, deferring to his or her apparent knowledge and past experience. And *confused* because a coach who does not act decisively is not viewed by the players as "in control" or knowledgeable, which can cause player anxiety. Nevertheless, this leadership style can be inconspicuously effective.

The best way to elicit strong cooperation among group members is to have them participate in the decision-making process. The advantage of democratic leadership is the consensus of policy established among group members and the strong personal commitment by members that motivates them to act legitimately, to implement group decisions rather than to subvert them.

The democratic leader need not leave all decision making to the team. Decisions may have to be made quickly and without input from players and assistants (for example, in the rapid deployment of game strategy). Chelladurai and Haggerty (1978) argue that in solving complex problems in sport the coach is more likely to make the best decision for the group. In fact, under certain circumstances, the players actually prefer that the coach make the decision.

Chelladurai and Arnott (1985) examined when the democratic (delegative) approach is most and least preferred by athletes, using a sample of seventy-seven female and sixty-seven male collegiate basketball players. They compared four styles of decision making: (1) autocratic (coach makes the decision alone), (2) consultative (coach makes the decision after soliciting input from players), (3) participative (coach and athletes jointly make the decision), and (4) delegative (coach asks one or more players to make the decision). The researchers then identified four factors that affect the choice of a decision style in a group context: (1) quality requirement, e.g., selecting the team's quarterback, (2) information, e.g., coach knows weaknesses of opposition and decides on strategy based on this knowledge, (3) problem complexity, e.g., selecting plays to be used in competition, and (4) group integration, e.g., the cohesiveness of the group (it is better to involve a cohesive unit in decision making than a group with low interpersonal relations).

The study's results indicated that females were more oriented toward participatory decision making than males. The delegative style was uniformly rejected by all athletes, and the autocratic and consultive styles were substantially endorsed by both sexes. Members were prepared to sacrifice their influence in favor of the coach rather than in favor of teammates. Delegation to a few athletes was interpreted as unfair preferential treatment by other team members. The optimal situation for preferring an autocratic coaching style was when a high-quality resolution was required and when the coach was perceived as being knowledgeable (i.e., when he or she had the information to make the best decision). However, for simple problems (e.g., what color to paint the locker room or whether to swing at a certain pitch), the athletes preferred to have more input. Finally, the athletes did not view group integration as an important factor in decision making, although groups that were highly cohesive felt more strongly about participating in decisions.

How can the democratic coach make the most effective decisions? According to Harold Geneen, former president and chief executive officer of ITT, in his book entitled *Managing*, the leader should maintain open communications within the organization (team). Players and coaches should talk and *actively listen* to each other. All parties should feel completely free to disagree with one another and with their bosses. The leader must make it clear in meetings that the "messenger of bad news" will not be chastised. He asserts that the success of people (athletes) ultimately reflects the leader's (coach's) success.

Examples of democratic strategies in coaching include allowing participants to:

- Nominate and elect team captains, members of the all-star team, and recipients of other individual player awards.
- Make decisions about certain team policies, which the coach must be able to support. For example, whether the players can bring a partner to the team party might be a negotiable item, but whether team members should be allowed to smoke may not be negotiable.
- Choose the team mascot.
- Choose from three alternatives the team's drink during practice and games.
- Choose which plays to practice.
- Choose sides for an intrasquad game.
- Set practice times.

Clearly, numerous opportunities lend themselves to using a democratic approach with the athletes. Given the investment of time and planning by the coach required the democratic form of team participation in decisions and strategies, there must be certain advantages to this coaching style. A review of the advantages and disadvantages of the democratic approach to sport leadership follows:

Advantages of the democratic approach

1. *It is nonthreatening to athletes*. The coach who follows a democratic style is typically more approachable and a better communicator to players than coaches who follow other styles. The reason is simply because democratic leaders are good listeners; they respect the views—even the criticisms—of subordinates, and they offer advice only when it is either solicited or absolutely necessary. Consequently, this type of coach is perceived by players as being nonthreatening.

2. *Individual initiative*. Players feel that they have some control, either directly or indirectly, in the team's operation. Consequently, they are more apt to volunteer ideas, to demonstrate independence (presumably for the good of the

team, although this is not always the case), and to feel less dependent on the coach in stressful situations. For example, how many times have you seen a quarterback approach the ball only to stop and use a valuable time-out to discuss the offensive strategy with the coach due to the opponent's defensive alignment? To save the time-out to stop the clock when time is a critical factor, the democratic coach might train the quarterback to be able to recognize certain tendencies of the other team's defense and to call an "audible" at the line (i.e., make a sudden change from the play called in the huddle and verbally communicate it in code to the other players on the offense). Many quarterbacks with whom I've spoken would love to have the opportunity to call their own plays, at least some of the time or even in practice. The democratic coach is more willing to train the athletes to do this.

3. *Promotion of mature behavior*. All coaches desire maturity and personal growth in their players. By giving the players a role in decisions, the democratic approach helps to ensure that players take responsibility for performance outcomes. Few participants will abuse a coach's respect, which he or she shows by delegating decision-making powers.

4. *Greater flexibility and risk-taking*. When players are in the midst of game competition, sometimes they need to know that it's OK to take a chance. A batter can bunt if the third baseperson is playing deep, or a quarterback can throw when the defense anticipates a run. Players adapt more quickly to new and different situations if the coach's style says, "Go ahead, take a chance — but also take responsibility for the outcome." Players should not be overprogrammed to perform in a certain manner because the obstacles that lie ahead can change.

Disadvantages of the democratic approach

1. *The sham democracy*. When is a democratic approach to governing a group not a democracy? When the group leader does not live up to his or her end of the bargain. Let's take voting as an example. Just because the team votes on a decision does not mean the process is democratic. The vote outcome must be supported and carried out by the leader. Even authoritative leaders use voting to support their personal decisions. How democratic is it if the coach does not approve of the players' choice for team captain and appoints a different choice?

Another factor that defeats the democratic style is intimidation. Using the voting for team captain as an example again, what if the coach were to list all of the qualifications for team captain, thereby effectively eliminating 80 to 90 percent of the team? Is that a true democratic process? Or if the coach were to say "This is what I believe" just prior to a team-related decision, will players feel comfortable in not meeting the coach's expectations or wishes?

Intimidation also comes in the form of asking subordinates for their "honest" opinion. According to former ITT president and author Harold Geneen, "People are often reluctant to report unpleasant facts, especially if they contradict the viewpoints of the boss. It is human nature not to want to 'kick the gorilla.'"

Geneen suggests that the leader make it clear in meetings that he or she will not "shoot the messenger." If the players or assistants have a different opinion from that of the head coach, they should be heard and their views seriously considered.

2.   *Leading from a distance.* The democrat might have little actual contact with the team. Former University of Alabama football coach Bear Bryant, among others, reportedly observed practice from a tower and did not interact with players to a great extent. According to Jerry Pettibone, head football coach at Northern Illinois University and former assistant coach to winning coaches Barry Switzer, Jackie Sherrill, Tom Osborne, and Chuck Fairbanks, "My first recruiting job here was to recruit great staff. The main purpose of a head coach is not to coach. He should be an organizer, motivator, and recruiter."

Nevertheless, leading from a distance can have the disadvantage of supervising athletes through the "eyes" and guidance of assistants. Instead of having contact only with an assistant coach, some athletes desire and would benefit from the expertise of the team leader. The head coach is ostensibly the most knowledgeable person about the sport. If he or she chooses a strong democratic leadership style, the athletes will be less affected by this expertise.

3.   *Watching others suffer.* Adherence to strong democratic principles demands a philosophy of noninterference. Interference might impede the progress of the group toward its goals. Thus, a democratic coach must have the ability to stand by and watch a degree of human failure and suffering without imposing on the situation. Democratic leaders must not be more loyal to one individual than to the group. For instance, a player or assistant with a violent temper might have to be rewarded or favorably recognized because of contributions in helping the team despite unpleasant personality traits. Examples include players who produce outstanding results yet do not relate well to teammates or athletes who tend to argue with game officials. A subordinate who is well liked, even a good friend, might have to be fired or dropped from the team. The democratic leader must consider decisions in light of their ramifications for the greatest number of team members.

4.   *Slow decision making.* It's highly doubtful that a coach would call for a team vote with seconds to make a decision about game strategy while the game is in progress. For the most part, making decisions on a group basis is certainly slower than other leadership approaches. Thus, the coach should be careful that when a group decision is warranted, sufficient time is granted for this process.

APPLICATION OF DIFFERENT COACHING STYLES IN SPORT

A considerable number of choices of styles is evident. Some of these approaches are more effective than others, but the thing to remember is that several styles can be adopted. No single approach results in optimal success all the time. Situations dictate various ways of working with group members. An athlete who has just made an error might need a humanistic coach who can be sensitive to the player's injured feelings. An unmotivated, underaroused team might be more responsive to an authoritarian style in which players are admonished for improper conduct and attitude. A democratic vote might be the best way to decide certain team preferences if the coach can, in fact, live with the decision and if the players' adherence to the policy is crucial to its influence on behavior.

A number of criteria should be considered before a coach determines his or her fundamental leadership style:

The coach's personality. Nothing is less effective than a team leader who tries to be someone he or she is not. This doesn't mean that a tyrant should continue to be abusive at the expense of the players. This individual should make every possible attempt to be compatible with the athletes' needs and to mature as an individual. But a person has to be comfortable with himself or herself.

The athletes' characteristics. Younger athletes need more direction, yet they are not responsive to authoritative mannerisms. They are playing because it's fun, and the level of seriousness given competition for children must reflect this need. Hostile coaches need not apply. Older, higher skilled players (remember, age and skill level are not always synonymous) are more amenable to a firm, direct, task-oriented approach. Because of their superior skills, they are more susceptible to boredom and burnout. Innovation and creativity are important strategies here.

Player perception of the coach. How the athletes view the coach is more important than how the coach views himself or herself. If a coach is perceived by players as honest, sincere, intelligent, and sensitive to the athletes' needs, the coach will be significantly more effective than if the coach is perceived to manifest the opposite characteristics. Perhaps one of the biggest obstacles coaches face in sport is to understand the importance of the image that they project to the athletes.

WHAT WE DON'T KNOW ABOUT SPORT LEADERSHIP

Although much research needs to be completed in the area of effective sport leadership, two very important questions that have to be answered are: First, to what extent does the coach really influence player behavior? Coaches are using many different leadership styles currently in the sportworld — many successfully. Does the use of any one style tend to benefit the players' performance more than another coaching style? Second, does the athlete's feeling of team member satisfaction have anything to do with his or her performance? In other words, does it really matter if an athlete relates positively (or for that matter, interacts at all) with his or her teammates?

The Coach's Influence on Player Behavior

Despite the frequent assumption that "good" coaches win and "poor" coaches lose, researchers have yet to prove the existence of a coaching profile or "recipe" that will have a marked influence on the athlete's performance. The styles of coaches differ significantly. Lanning (1979, p. 265) notes the "striking differences in the programs and personalities of coaches; but they all developed highly successful programs. . . . Each of [these very successful] coaches put together successful programs with certain *types* of athletes." Lanning's point is that perhaps the compatibility between the coach's and the athlete's personalities is what underlies quality sport performance rather than only the behaviors and techniques of the coach. All of the styles mentioned in this chapter have resulted in performance success at one time or another. But despite the descriptions, prescriptions, suggestions, and warnings about the "do's and don'ts" of certain coaching practices, researchers still aren't certain whether a coach's style really matters, as long as the performance-related areas of leadership — teaching skills and using game strategies effectively — are conducted correctly.

What about the relationship between the coach and the athlete? In terms of game outcome, does it matter whether the two parties establish a sensitive, meaningful relationship? Should the coach be concerned about what every player thinks of him or her? Must a player like his or her coach to be a quality competitor? Apparently, the manner in which a coach addresses his or her players may not enhance or deteriorate their performance, given the track record of many coaches with winning records.

Perhaps of more value to the athletes' and the team's success is not so much that the coach and athlete like each other, but that the coach is an effective educator of sports skills and team strategies (Martin and Hrycaiko 1983). Athletes are learners; coaches are teachers. Effective coaches communicate team and player strategies that are clear, relatively simple to follow, repeated in practice under game conditions, and are based on the team's strengths and the opponent's weaknesses.

Perhaps effective coaching is a function of the "right" person coaching the "right" athletes in the "right" situation. This means that team leaders: (1) choose to coach sports that are compatible with their personality and past experience, (2) work with athletes who can respond effectively to the coach's style, and (3) use a leadership approach that is most effective for the situation — either authoritative, democratic, or humanistic under the proper circumstances. Mitchell (1979, p. 265) concluded, based on his extensive review of the leadership literature, that "successful leadership is contingent upon a variety of factors and what we must determine is the best match between leaders and the situation."

Group Satisfaction and Performance

Much has been written in the sport and social psychology literature about the effects of a group member's satisfaction on individual and group performance. Perhaps the business world, as an unstructured environment, is more susceptible to the individual's feelings and level of motivation to perform tasks with optimal efficiency. But sport situations may present a different, more structured environment in which attitudes among players affect their performance in a far less dynamic way. And in some sports the degree of interaction is relatively small (e.g., individual sports such as golf and singles tennis or a team sport like baseball). Perhaps in sports that require a significant amount of personal exchange, where trust and security among teammates affect attitudes and physical responses (e.g., basketball, football, or volleyball), having a positive attitude toward teammates might facilitate performance. But researchers still do not know for sure.

Theoretically, if a player feels a strong affiliation or identity toward the team, his or her attitude as a competitor will be more positive. As a result, performance will be enhanced. But what about players who are motivated to play well, who want to reach personal goals, and who receive recognition as quality athletes? Does it matter whether they like their teammates? Does the habit of socializing with teammates have anything to do with performance effectiveness? Sport researchers don't know.

Certainly professional athletes with families tend to spend less time with teammates than do nonprofessional competitors. And many of these players perform admirably, sometimes without establishing close personal ties with teammates. Effective coaching includes adapting to new situations and intelligently reacting to unanticipated events or strategies of the opponent. None of these requisites for team success are directly related to the type of relationship established between coach and athlete or whether the player likes his or her teammates. But, conjecture aside, further research is warranted in this area as well.

■■■■■■■

LEADERSHIP STYLE: A FINAL WORD

Effective leadership in sport is not learned exclusively in the classroom. Relatively few coaches ever take a school course in coaching and even fewer are familiar with the professional literature in sport psychology. Coaches learn their trade through participating in sport, first as an athlete and then as a coaching assistant. Many coaches have informed me that their techniques and strategies, even their leadership styles and personalities, are derived from models from their pasts—coaches they have known or observed. "If it worked for me, I guess it'll work for my athletes" is the common response. "If that coach (or school) is successful with this approach, why shouldn't I be?" is another frequent thought.

How receptive are coaches to recommendations based on sport psychology literature? Anshel (1985) studied the receptivity to sport psychology consulting of one collegiate football coach. Suggestions were based mainly on the professional literature (48 percent) and the feelings of the players (41 percent). He found that only 14 percent (27 of 165) of the suggestions were used. Of these, 22 suggestions were implemented in practice, not in the game. The coach's reasons for not using the recommendations were mainly that they were incongruent with the practices of other teams (48 percent) or that the coach lacked time to implement the suggestions (36 percent). Thus, regardless of the players' feelings or performance achievements, coaches follow a traditional, somewhat conservative path to leadership style. They have typically remained obstinate in thinking about a better way to do the job. There are many exceptions, of course. Many coaches invest in, and actually learn from, critical feedback, just as one invests in education or in buying a new home. These sport leaders are the real winners.

SUMMARY

Effective leadership in sport is a function of performing a variety of roles and styles to meet the needs of athletes and to reach team objectives. Coaches are leaders, followers, teachers, role models, limit setters, counselors, friends, and parent substitutes for their athletes. (They also have responsibilities as members of their own families.) These roles are conducted at different times and in various degrees with each team member. Leadership styles differ as a function of the sport situation, the nature of the coach-athlete relationship, and the preferences of the athletes. Sometimes the players desire a more dominant, authoritative style, especially in task-oriented rather than relationship-oriented situations. Humanistic coaching, on the other hand, holds that positive sport experiences and the feelings of the athletes are priorities. Behavioristic approaches do not ignore the athletes' feelings; instead, they use environmental situations and selective reinforcement to guide the feelings and behaviors of the players. Finally, democratic leadership consists of a more laissez-faire approach in which athletes are given reign to make many team-related and some contest-related decisions. Although athletes often take greater responsibility for their actions when they make their own decisions, this approach is usually slower and less efficient than the other styles. The players may sense confusion or a lack of leadership on the team.

Leadership theories most allied with sport include Fiedler's contingency model, the life cycle theory, the multidimensional model, McGregor's Theory X and Y, and Tannenbaum and Schmidt's leadership model. Despite the array of theories for effective leadership, little is known about the effect of different styles on player performance and group member satisfaction. These areas are in need of future research.

REVIEW QUESTIONS

1. Describe the various roles that a coach assumes, and provide an example of each role.
2. Five leadership theories were reviewed in the chapter. Name two ways in which all the theories are similar and two ways in which they differ.
3. You are the coach. Select a sport, and apply one of the theories that explains effective sport leadership.
4. Describe five differences between "successful" and "effective" coaches. As a coach, in what ways would you follow an "effective" coaching style?
5. The four primary leadership styles discussed in this chapter were authoritarianism, humanism, behaviorism, and the democratic style. Provide an example of how a coach would implement each style.
6. Describe two advantages and two disadvantages of the behaviorist, the authoritarian, the humanist, and the democrat.
7. What coaching style or styles would you employ as a leader of child athletes between the ages of nine and ten years? How might your style or styles differ if you were coaching senior high school athletes?
8. Power is inherent in coaching. The respective positions of coach and athlete dictate certain roles and expectations. Therefore, a coach can choose to make demands on athletes or to use authoritative means to influence behaviors. In this chapter, such an approach is judged to be not particularly sophisticated and ineffective in the long run. Describe the potential disadvantages of exercising the power of the coach's position as the sole means of controlling the team and the individual players.
9. One coaching style not covered in this chapter was laissez-faire, a style characterized by a deliberate abstention from direction or interference. The leader allows group members to function almost independently of the leader's influence unless his or her input is solicited. This is quite rare in sport. However, certain circumstances might warrant such an approach. Given what you've read about the other leadership

styles, in what ways and under what conditions could a laissez-faire approach be practiced in a coaching situation?

REFERENCES

Anshel, M. H. 1978. Behaviorism versus humanism: An approach to effective team leadership in sport. *Motor Skills: Theory into Practice* 2: 83–91.

Anshel, M. H. 1985. Examination of a college coach's receptivity to sport psychology consulting: A two year case study. Paper presented at a conference of the North American Society of Psychology of Sport and Physical Activity, May, at Gulfport, Mississippi.

Chelladurai, P., and M. Arnott. 1985. Decision styles in coaching: Preferences of basketball players. *Research Quarterly for Exercise and Sport* 56: 15–24.

Chelladurai, P., and A. V. Carron. 1978. *Leadership*. Ottawa, Ontario: Canadian Association of Health, Physical Education, and Recreation (Monograph).

Chelladurai, P., and A. V. Carron. 1983. Athletic maturity and preferred leadership. *Journal of Sport Psychology* 5: 371–80.

Chelladurai, P., and T. R. Haggerty. 1978. A normative model of decision styles in coaching. *Athletic Administrator* 13: 6–9.

Cribben, J. J. 1981. *Leadership: Strategies for organizational effectiveness.* New York: AMACOM.

Dickinson, J. 1977. *A behavioral analysis of sport*. Princeton, NJ: Princeton Book Company.

Fiedler, F. E. 1964. A contingency model of leadership effectiveness. In *Advances in Experimental Social Psychology*. Vol. 1, ed. L. Berkowitz, pp. 149–90. New York: Academic Press.

Fromm, E. 1941. *Escape from freedom*. NY: Holt, Rinehart & Winston.

Henderson, B. 1971. The intangibles of baseball coaching. *The Coaching Clinic* (April): 2–4.

Hersey, P., and K. H. Blanchard. 1977. *Management of organizational behavior*. 3d ed. Englewood Cliffs, NJ: Prentice-Hall.

Jones, B. J., L. J. Wells, R. E. Peters, and D. J. Johnson. 1982. *Guide to effective coaching*. Boston: Allyn and Bacon.

Lanning, W. 1979. Coach and athlete personality interaction: A critical variable in athletic success. *Journal of Sport Psychology* 1: 262–67.

Litwin, G. H., and R. A. Stringer. 1968. *Motivation and organizational climate*. Boston: Graduate School of Business Administration, Harvard University.

Magnotta, J. R. 1986. Positive motivational techniques: A key to teaching excellence. *Journal of Health, Physical Education, Recreation, and Dance* (August).

Martin, G., and D. Hrycaiko. 1983. Effective behavioral coaching: What's it all about? *Journal of Sport Psychology* 5: 8–20.

McGregor, D. 1967. *The professional manager*. New York: McGraw-Hill.

Mechikoff, R. A., and B. Kozar. 1983. *Sport psychology: The coach's perspective*. Springfield, IL: Thomas.

Mitchell, T. R. 1979. Organizational behavior. *Annual Review of Psychology* 30: 243–81.

Rejeski, W., C. Darracott, and S. Hutslar. 1979. Pygmalion in sport: A field study. *Journal of Sport Psychology* 1: 311–19.

Rushall, B. S., and D. Siedentop. 1972. *The development and control of behavior in sport and physical education*. Philadelphia: Lea and Febiger.

Sabock, R. J. 1985. *The coach*. 3d ed. Champaign, IL: Human Kinetics.

Sage, G. H. 1980. Humanistic psychology and coaching. In *Sport psychology: An analysis of athlete behavior*, ed. W. F. Straub, pp. 215–28. Ithaca, NY: Mouvement.

Smith, R. E., F. L. Smoll, and B. Curtis. 1979. Coach effectiveness training: A cognitive-behavioral approach to enhancing relationship skills in youth sport coaches. *Journal of Sport Psychology* 1: 59–75.

Straub, W. F. 1980. How to be an effective leader. In *Sport psychology: An analysis of athlete behavior*, ed. W. F. Straub, pp. 382–91. Ithaca, NY: Mouvement.

Tannenbaum, R., and W. H. Schmidt. 1973. How to choose a leadership pattern. *Harvard Business Review* (May–June).

Tutko, T. A., and B. C. Ogilvie. 1967. The role of the coach in motivation of athletes. In *Motivations in play, games, and sports*, ed. R. Slovenko and J. A. Knight. Springfield, IL: Thomas.

Vanek, M., and B. J. Cratty. 1970. *Psychology and the superior athlete*. New York: Macmillan.

Zaleznik, A. 1977. Managers and leaders: Are they different? *Harvard Business Review* (May–June): 67–68.

8

Communication
Techniques

Many fine coaches are geniuses at planning strategy, teaching techniques in performance, and knowing the details of their sport. But how effective and successful can such coaches be unless they can communicate their knowledge effectively? How important is communication in coaching? This brief story makes the point nicely:

A high-class sophisticate was crossing the river on a small boat. The sophisticate asked the uneducated boatman, "Tell me, sir, have you ever attended live theatre?"

"No," said the boatman, "can't say that I have."

"You've lost one-third of your life," answered the high-class person. "Tell me," the sophisticate said again, "have you ever seen a ballet?"

"Can't say that I have," said the boatman.

"You lost two-thirds of your life," said the high-class passenger. At that moment, the boat hit a large rock and started to sink.

"Tell me," the boatman said to the sophisticate, "can you swim?"

"No," said the passenger."

"Looks like you've just lost your whole life," said the boatman.

The point of this story is that no matter how brilliant a coach might be in planning strategy and knowing the technical aspects of his or her game, success depends on the coach's ability to communicate effectively with the athletes.

Communication may be *the* essential skill without which the coach's efforts are doomed. Very little has been written in the sport literature about effective communication techniques. It is little wonder that coaches develop their style of addressing the athletes through modeling — imitating the mannerisms and styles of their own coaches from the past.

The purpose of this chapter is to offer guidelines about effective communication — the art and science of helping athletes feel good about themselves, raising the performer's self-image, effectively teaching sport skills, and gaining the athletes' respect and loyalty. It doesn't happen automatically. The techniques must be learned and used "naturally" without thinking about them, or statements will appear to be contrived and insincere. A coach cannot sound honest when his or her actions and words appear programmed and stiff. We will review some of the most common situations in which communication becomes an integral part of coaching responsibilities. These examples illustrate the need for dialogue in developing an effective communication style.

THE NEED FOR DIALOGUE

Consider all of the people with whom coaches must interact if they are to be successful. The list would include players, assistant coaches, coaches from other teams, parents of the athletes, referees, teachers of the athletes, the media, and the coach's own supervisor or employer.

Players. Communicating with players can be both verbal and nonverbal. Teaching and practicing sport skills, presenting rules and team policies, interpreting strategies, disciplining the athletes, and using nonverbal techniques such as smiling, patting players on the back, and just noticing player performance are all examples of positive communication with athletes.

Assistant coaches. Soliciting information from assistants about the performance of various players on the team as well as on opposing teams, developing game strategy, receiving feedback from assistants about the head coach's own performance, offering input to assistant coaches about their performances, and engaging in informal verbal exchanges in a social context off the field or court all require effective communication.

Other coaches. Coaches on both sides of the court or field talk to each other about scheduling, defining rules for game play, exchanging team films, working out schedules, attending seminars, and exchanging information on techniques and strategies. The coach who cannot communicate effectively will not be approached and will receive little more than a casual response from his or her peers.

Parents. Coaches are accountable only to their supervisors — legally, that is. But if the coach wants to gain the loyalty of the athletes and, in many instances, keep the athletes playing on the team, then communication with parents is both inevitable and a good idea. Speaking with a player's parents can be enjoyable. To know some background on each player is helpful, and this information is most easily attained by interacting with the parents. However, parental involvement can also be challenging to the coach. Explanations as to why the athlete is not playing or starting and other issues about his or her participation can test the patience of many coaches. The ability to deal constructively with the concerns of parents is important.

Referees. Constructive dialogue with the arbiter is both necessary and desirable. Coaches are models to their athletes and are responsible for conducting themselves in a manner that demonstrates maturity and logic. Contrary to the view of many coaches, evidence suggests that it is *not* an effective strategy to argue with an arbiter in order to excite and motivate the team.

Teachers. All athletes except professionals attend school. Possibly, perhaps probably, the coach will need to secure information from the players' teachers about grades, problem behaviors, permission to miss class due to games, and so on. Quality coaching includes concern about the athlete's academic performance as well as his or her quality effort on the field or court. Teachers can help athletes to succeed on the field by reducing their anxiety about classwork and grades. Coaches need to work jointly with teachers to enhance the athlete's mental preparation for competition.

The media. Newspapers, television, and radio form the link between the fans and players. Proper communication with the media is crucial because athletes are very sensitive about how they are perceived by others. Players typically read and hear about their coach's remarks concerning members of the team. Derogatory statements by the coach are usually demotivating and embarrassing to athletes, whereas complimentary remarks improve self-confidence and effort.

Supervisor or employer. Coaches can lose their jobs if they cannot get along with "the boss." Sometimes a coach will feel frustrated with the demands of a supervisor that may or may not be fair. But the good news is that the use of correct communication techniques can help to eliminate any friction that may develop in this relationship. Some very fine coaches have lost their jobs because the two parties could not talk out or negotiate their differences.

All of these sources of communication are simply a part of the job of coaching. Each presents its own set of *potential* problems that may develop if the team leader does not use effective verbal skills. Inversely, the proper use of verbal and nonverbal communication may prevent, eliminate, or at least minimize potential problems among team participants. Let's begin by looking at a three-step approach developed by Miller (1982) for an effective communication style by the coach.

The objective of Miller's approach is to express appropriate thoughts and feelings without injuring the athletes' self-esteem; that is, without demeaning others. The three steps include (1) describing the situation, (2) explaining how it affects the team, and (3) telling what you think should be done. For example, if a football player fails to complete his blocking assignment, which results in a loss of yards, the coach might say, "Your assignment was to cover the halfback on that trap. When you follow your assignment, that type of coverage stops the play. I'd appreciate it if you would learn your assignment and follow the strategy correctly in this coverage at all times."

Using Miller's model, statements are made *without accusation*. The situation is described without evaluation. Emotions such as anger and guilt do not get in the way. The message is received by the athlete clearly, and future tasks and expectations of the coach are identified. This type of approach to communication between coach and athlete brings about the trust and loyalty that coaches need from their players to be effective team leaders. Techniques such as these form an integral part of what I call the ten commandments of effective communication (Anshel 1987). The use of these guidelines on the style and content of communication with athletes separates the talented and skilled leader of a team from the less capable, inarticulate leader. These "commandments" are based on hundreds of interviews and conversations with athletes, numerous interviews with and written commentary about coaches, and my own observations in the sport domain.

THE TEN COMMANDMENTS OF EFFECTIVE COMMUNICATION IN SPORT

For years I've been observing coaches interacting verbally and nonverbally with athletes, some with greater success than others. Based on these observations, interviews with athletes, the professional sport psychology literature, and media reports, I have concluded that effective communication consists essentially of ten guidelines. These recommendations are so important in the process of affecting the athletes' attitudes, feelings, and behaviors that I refer to them as "commandments," or "must do" practices for effective communication. They are: (1) Thou shalt be honest, (2) Thou shalt not be defensive, (3) Thou shalt be consistent, (4) Thou shalt be empathetic, (5) Thou shalt not be sarcastic, (6) Thou shalt praise and criticize behavior, not personality, (7) Thou shalt express feelings constructively, (8) Thou shalt use positive nonverbal cues, (9) Thou shalt teach skills, and (10) Thou shalt interact consistently with all team members.

I. Thou Shalt Be Honest

If coaches are to be effective, they must have credibility. They must be believed; otherwise, how can coaches do their jobs? This commandment goes against the old adage "Never say never." The coach should *never* be dishonest. Sometimes dishonesty is used purposefully to make an athlete feel better. Being untruthful may also occur by accident. A coach may make a promise that later cannot be, or is not, kept. But in any case, dishonesty destroys credibility. Here are a few examples that actually happened. The names have been changed.

Example 1: Dishonesty Ruins Credibility

Bill was the starting first baseman on his high school baseball team. After he batted fifth and had difficulty hitting the ball, the coach moved him into the ninth batting position. The coach told Bill that he wanted his power at the end of the lineup. Bill knew differently. No one had to tell him that he was having trouble batting. Instead of telling Bill that the fifth batter in a lineup must hit the ball more consistently, the coach lied. The coach could have told Bill that together they would try to work out of the slump and that he was moving Bill down the order to take some pressure off. Bill had trouble believing the coach after that and, in fact, grew increasingly frustrated with his own lack of success. He hit .191 that year and almost quit the team.

Example 2: A Promise That Could Not Be Kept

Willie, a punter on the college football team, injured his arm in a freak accident unrelated to sport. He lost the punting job to a first-year player. Into the fourth game of the year, the new punter was beginning to kick less and less consistently, which at times hurt the team's performance. In the meantime, Willie's arm was mending fast, but the coach decided to stick with the new punter. Finally, during practice after some poor punting in the fifth game, the coach told Willie, "If Joe kicks one punt poorly, you're going in to do the kicking." Willie was excited and looking forward to his opportunity. Indeed, the new punter kicked the first one off the side of his foot, and it landed all of twenty-four yards away. The coach, caught up in the excitement of the game and carrying out his usual array of responsibilities, forgot about the promise. In this instance, a promise was made that was not kept. Willie was so heartbroken that he quit the team after the game. The team lost an athlete with potential to be among the best (as his statistics the previous year had indicated).

Example 3: The model

Susan was not starting on her volleyball team. She attended all practices and felt good about her progress. The coach was, in fact, providing very positive feedback to her on her fine play in practice. After the fourth game of the season, she went to the coach and said she felt like quitting because she never got a chance to play during games. "Even Jan gets to play ahead of me, Coach, and all the players know I'm better than she is," she complained. The coach responded, "Susan, I can understand your frustration. You've made tremendous improvements in your play, particularly on your passing. You have every right to feel frustrated, as I might be if I were in your shoes. I just want you to know that I'm really proud of the way you've been playing in practice and how you have supported the other players. I will do my best to give you a chance to play. Let's work together to help you become the best volleyball player you can be. I know you can help us win. Hang in there. I'm on your side."

Notice that the coach avoided referring to any other players. Instead, the coach reflected Susan's feelings of frustration and anger. The coach also was realistic in projecting the future. No promises were made about playing — promises that may have satisfied the athlete for the moment but would have led to an emotional disaster if they were not kept. The coach's honesty focused on realistic expectations for the immediate future — practicing, learning, and improving. The coach was not condescending (Susan's feelings were taken seriously), sarcastic ("If you were half as good with your hands as you are with your mouth, you'd be an all star"), sexist ("Oh, my poor baby is sad"), or dishonest

("As soon as Jan makes a mistake, you're going in"). And the coach was not defensive. Instead, the coach was compassionate, honest, and sensitive of the athlete's feelings.

Of course, honesty can be taken too far. Do coaches want to tell athletes what they *really* think at *all* times? Absolutely not! Imagine this conversation with an athlete whom the coach evaluates as having little chance of starting.

Athlete:	Hey, coach, when do you think I'll get a chance to start?
Coach:	Well, to be perfectly honest with you, Frank, I think you're about as good as you are going to get. I doubt you'll ever be as good as Ed. He just plays better than you do. So, if I were you, I'd forget about starting and just be happy to fill in when we need you.

Why is this form of communication destructive? Why can honesty be taken too far? Because the coach has an obligation to teach skills to athletes and to see to it that the participation of every athlete is as fulfilling as possible. The coach's role is not to predict an athlete's future level of performance, especially if the forecast is a pessimistic one. Several reasons exist for coaches to avoid predicting the athlete's future or potential in sport.

First, how can anyone know to what degree an athlete will develop, grow, and improve? Coaches are not prophets. Is it the coach's duty to predict the future about the athlete's growth and development? And if all signs lead to the conclusion that this sport participant will never break into the starting lineup nor make it to the pros or the college team, is it the coach's obligation to break the news (assuming, of course, that the coach can predict the future)? Voltaire said, "Truth is a fruit which should not be plucked until it is ripe." Honesty is necessary if the coach is to be credible (i.e., believable) and if he or she wishes to gain the athlete's loyalty. But, honesty is also a matter of timing and tact.

In my experience as a sport psychologist, I have never seen an athlete feel so distrustful, disloyal, and unmotivated as in response to a coach who has proven to be dishonest. Successful coaches can be honest without stepping on someone's toes or ego. First, be honest and verbalize your thoughts when you think that it will make the listener feel better or improve performance. Second, avoid statements, even honest ones, that will hurt someone's feelings or will produce a sense of hopelessness (e.g., "I'd forget about starting if I were you"). In the words of the French philosopher Marquis, "Honesty is a good thing, but it is not profitable to its possessor unless it is kept under control."

II. Thou Shalt Not Be Defensive

Perhaps another way to word this commandment is "Thou shalt be a good listener" or "Thou wilt be receptive to the opinions of others." They all say the same thing. The literature, consisting mostly of research and opinion papers in sport psychology, counseling psychology, and management (coaches manage people), is filled with the notion that successful coaches and administrators have one thing in common: They are open to new ideas and receptive to feedback on their own performance. They are *not* defensive about who is the expert and the know-it-all. The components of this commandment include: (1) being open to the ideas and opinions of others — players, parents, assistants, and (naturally) supervisors, (2) engaging in *active listening* during discussions with other parties, and (3) soliciting the opinions of players and other coaches — get assistance from your assistants.

Be open to the ideas and opinions of others. As a sports psychologist to a college football team, I agreed to observe the behaviors of coaches and players during practice and at games and to submit written weekly reports. Included in these reports were recommendations on new and different strategies that the coach might want to use in the teaching of football skills and in mental and physical preparation for the game. Most of these suggestions were based on the sport psychology literature or feelings of the players. I decided to collect data on the tendency of the coach to implement or to ignore the recommendations and his reasons for not using them. The purpose of this case study, conducted over two years, was to see whether college coaches, at least in football, would be generally receptive to the application of sport psychology research. Just to be sure that my suggestions were realistic and valid, I asked a football coach from another team and a physical education teacher who coaches football in high school to review the suggestions. They thought that 192 of the 196 suggestions were justified. These suggestions, I might emphasize, were made at the invitation of the head coach, and they were provided on a volunteer basis.

The results indicated that of the 192 "valid" suggestions, 14 percent (27) were used and 86 percent (165) were ignored. Further, 22 of the 27 recommendations that were used were implemented during *practice* rather than before, during, or after a game, despite the fact that 64 percent (124) of the 192 recommendations were based on game-related observations. These results might be interpreted to mean that the coach was not very receptive to new and different approaches and, instead, conducted his job in the way in which he felt most comfortable — based on the coaches he learned from and techniques used in the past. Reasons for not using the advice related to (1) the head coach's comparisons with other teams ("Winning teams don't do it that way"), (2) a lack of time ("We don't have enough time to do it"), (3) not agreeing with the players' feelings ("The players here don't know what it takes to win"), and other reasons.

This case study may or may not reflect the attitudes of most coaches. But as an example, what does this say about being defensive? This coach chose to use excuses instead of innovative techniques that might have improved the morale and loyalty of the athletes. Essentially, he ignored the needs of the players because many of the suggestions were based on their input. The result was a team low in morale, loyalty, and success. Although not necessarily due to ignoring the suggestions, this team did not have a winning record for each of the two seasons it was studied.

Aside from attending to input from sport psychologists, even more important is for the coach to be receptive to the opinions and suggestions of assistants. This source is, perhaps, more knowledgeable about team personnel and strategies than anyone else. The inclusion of their opinions in the decision-making process will lead to greater collegial support and accountability for the outcome from those decisions. Coaching doesn't have to be "lonely at the top." The head coach does make the final decisions, but the use of all available resources to gather information before the decision is made will result in a more intelligent choice that assistants will support. Essentially, when leaders (coaches) are not defensive, they become active listeners.

Be an active listener. Probably the best way to avoid appearing defensive and to succeed at appearing to be receptive to the feelings or attitudes of others is to listen to what others have to say before you answer. When a coach listens to a player, parent, referee, or an assistant, the active listener shows sensitivity toward them or toward their child athletes. Sometimes, just sitting back and allowing the other party to speak their mind is enough to solve part of the problem. Keeping feelings inside when you aren't given a chance to communicate them can be very frustrating. Allowing a person to vent their feelings is much more constructive. The failure to respond or to show attentiveness toward another's feelings is called *passive listening*. It doesn't work. *Active listening* occurs when someone engages in a dialogue with another person in response to what the person is saying and feeling. See chapter 9 for guidelines on active listening.

Get assistance from assistants. Coaches cannot win games by themselves. They need assistance from their assistants. Coaches who choose to "go it alone" or claim to have "all the answers" place themselves apart from the rest of the team. They do not receive the support of team members. Worse, others do not feel accountable for the team's success or failure because there is a sense of little contribution. Still worse, some assistants and players want to see a coach who "knows it all" fail.

Doesn't a coach need to receive input from the people who are closest to the competition—the athletes themselves? Doesn't he or she need information from assistants who can offer insight into a player's physical or mental condition, which can help to explain the reasons behind certain performance outcomes? Should the coach be interested in hearing the method a colleague would use in approaching the game, given his knowledge about the opponent or the mental state of the team?

An important role for assistant coaches is to initiate and maintain close personal ties with the athletes. Mechikoff and Kozar (1983, p. 10) found through interviews with successful coaches (i.e., coaches who had winning records) that successful coaches encourage their assistant coaches "to promote and nurture close personal ties with the players while (the head coach) cooperates in a critical objective manner during practice and games."

III. Thou Shalt Be Consistent

Fred was having a pleasant conversation with his tennis coach in the coach's office about the use of certain strategies against his next opponent. The conversation ended as the coach told Fred to see him anytime he had any questions or concerns related to tennis or anything else. Fred felt great, having a sense of closeness and trust toward his coach. Then two days later after practice, Fred asked the coach to look at a few of his serves with which he was having some difficulty that day. To Fred's utter shock, his coach retorted, "After the practice you had today, young man, you need to work on much more than your serve." Fred was devastated. Where was the coach whom he had visited in the office just two days earlier? One day it's "How ya doin', buddy?" if the coach is in a good mood, and the next day it's "Don't come near me."

The confidence and security that athletes feel toward their coach can be destroyed by inconsistency. If athletes do not know how their coach will respond to an issue, most often they will choose to ignore the coach altogether. An important objective of coaches who are truly interested in fostering communication is to *be consistent* in the manner in which they come across. If coaches invite their athletes to visit them in their office yet close the door on them (literally or attitudinally) when they arrive, the coach is giving mixed messages. Perhaps he or she was being insincere to invite the athlete to visit in the first place. This tendency affects a coach's credibility.

What is credibility, and why is it important in coaching? Without it, you cannot coach. Credibility means believability: "worthy of belief or confidence; trustworthy," according to *Webster's Dictionary*. If an athlete does not trust or have confidence in the coach, how "coachable" can he or she be? Would you take advice on health and fitness from a person who was obese and smoked? How about legal advice from a convicted felon? Would you believe someone who changed the rules in the middle of the game? Similarly, to expect an athlete to believe a coach who is kind, considerate, and sensitive one day but sarcastic, insensitive, and unfriendly the next is unrealistic. An inconsistent person might go out of his or her way to say "hello" to someone on Monday, then choose to ignore the same person on Tuesday. Such a person would be viewed as rather insecure, and most persons would prefer not to risk having a negative encounter with someone whom they could not trust. This is one possible reason why some athletes tend to ignore rather than communicate with their coaches.

Here are a few guidelines to show consistency in coaching (remember, you can't coach effectively without it).

1.   Columnist Ann Landers recommends never letting an opportunity pass to say a kind and encouraging word to or about someone. Praise good athletic performance. Even acknowledging the quality performance of opponents after (but not during) the game will confirm your admiration and respect for sport excellence.

2.   Always recognize the greetings of others. "Hi" and a smile go a long way toward being viewed as a good, considerate person — and it costs nothing. Avoid being nice and friendly one day, then being stern, uncommunicative, and inconsiderate toward others the next. People will avoid you like the plague.

3.   If you have an open-door policy for your athletes and assistants (and you should, of course), show that you are sincere about it. Gil, a high school linebacker, visited his coach during the office hours that were designated for athletes. Upon Gil's arrival, the coach looked up from his notepad with a look of annoyance and said, "Yea, what can I do for *you*, son?" Gil was turned off immediately. "Sorry to bother you, Coach," he said. "See you later at practice. Bye!" Gil never felt comfortable about visiting his coach again. Naturally, a coach may excuse himself or herself if the time to talk to an athlete is truly not convenient. But show the athlete that not meeting with him or her is due to an issue unrelated to your interest in the individual or your sincerity of having an open-door policy. Make an appointment to meet with the athlete again, *soon*.

4.   Try to show the same compassion on the field (at least as often as possible) as you do in the locker room or office. Yes, anger is a very natural, human response. But don't ask an athlete to play psychiatrist and try to figure out when and how to approach you and how to handle possible negative responses. No one is suggesting that coaches should not raise their voices or that they should never display irritation and frustration. However, such feelings can be both controlled and communicated nondestructively.

5.   What about discipline? Here too, be consistent. If the team's policy is no smoking, and the punishment for smoking has been clearly communicated to the players, the coach must follow through with the punishment when players are found smoking. Again, what credibility can a coach maintain if rules and the results of breaking those rules are not carried out? Should the coach allow exceptions to a rule? Yes. Coaches must take on the role of judge and jury. Sometimes a verdict of "not guilty" is appropriate when the "defendant" has a legitimate reason to break a rule. It's a subjective call, and nothing short of common sense (as opposed to blind discipline) will succeed.

The bottom line on being consistent with one's behavior is really a function of respecting the feelings of others. Treat others as you would like to be treated, which leads us to the fourth commandment.

IV. Thou Shalt Be Empathetic

How many times have you heard the phrase, "How would *you* feel if. . . ?" Well, how *do* you think it feels to be ignored, lied to, rejected, blamed, teased, ridiculed, and injured? Inversely, how does it feel to be recognized, praised, accepted, depended upon, popular, and smiled at? The answers are obvious, aren't they? Yet what do we commonly do to others? Exactly what we wouldn't want done to ourselves. Some individuals are not capable of putting themselves in the shoes of another. Such persons do not recognize that they can get so much more out of athletes who feel that they are important and that they contribute to the welfare of the team than from participants who feel worthless, unskilled, or neglected. The ability to both understand and to respond to the feelings of others is a characteristic that will pay the coach many dividends. Sadly, this personality trait, called empathy, is often missing from the repertoire of techniques and strategies used by some team leaders.

Sharing and thinking about other people's feelings does not come naturally to children, according to Dr. Fitzhugh Dodson, a child psychologist. They need to learn these traits from their parents. Children imitate the kind, joyful, loving manner of their parents. In homes in which such parental behavior is absent or scant, no learning of these types of responses occurs. Children who haven't learned by age ten to share, to play by the rules, or to put themselves in another person's shoes usually are very troubled and not very well accepted by their peers, asserts Dr. Leo Kron, an assistant clinical professor of psychiatry at Columbia University. Many adults do not know what it feels like to be on the receiving end of many of their comments, and consequently, they make statements that hurt, offend, and even may destroy the aspirations and feelings of others.

Effective coaches remember how they felt when their feelings were hurt as athletes. The secure team leader says, "I don't want these athletes to be hurt and suffer the way I did as an athlete." Ineffective (insecure) coaches say, "If it was good enough for me, it's good enough for them." Was it really "good enough" then? Could it ever feel good to be emotionally distraught? We often get caught between celebrating our survival of tragic events from the past and thinking that such events actually allowed us to learn, to grow, and to become emotionally stable.

The empathetic coach follows three guidelines: (1) do not attack the athlete's character, (2) be sensitive to the feelings of others, and (3) do not allow peers or teammates to become verbally destructive toward one another. The key objective is *loyalty* to the coach and team. Do coaches prefer athletes who want to experience team success or ones who become occupied with individual success? Do coaches prefer athletes to be responsive to their words, or do they want to be ignored? Do coaches want to have a team full of players who believe in themselves and feel confident in playing better than the opposition? The difference between coach loyalty and the athlete's desire to see the coach fail becomes obvious. Empathy makes good sense, and one of the best ways to show it is to follow the next commandment.

V. Thou Shalt Not Be Sarcastic

A coach who has an acid tongue does not win. Why not? According to psychologist Haim Ginott in his book *Teacher and Child,* adults who use sarcastic remarks erect a sound barrier to effective communication with children and athletes. "Sarcasm . . . destroys their self-confidence and self-esteem. Bitter irony and biting sarcasm only reinforce the traits they (coaches, teachers, and parents) attack" (p. 55). An athlete who is physically fatigued should not be called "lazy." A participant who asks a question about the team strategy must never be labeled "brainless."

Coach Fred was observing his team run through several trials of a new play in football. He turned to his left and saw the team punter talking with a female student. "Hey, Lance," he yelled, "if you want to fool around with the ladies, do it on your own time. Pay attention to what we're doing on the field. Maybe you'll learn something." Lance was embarrassed, of course. Several players and other observers were also embarrassed for him. The coach, in the meantime, lost the respect of this athlete and diminished any chance of establishing a communication link for the future.

Fran was running wind sprints with her softball teammates. Suddenly, she felt a sharp pain in her side and could not continue. "What's wrong, Fran, you out of shape?" the coach bellowed. "Too many pizzas, huh?" This sarcastic response from the coach angered the athlete because she was in pain and was not trying to remove herself from the drill. And, in fact, Fran was in very good condition. Further, Fran perceived by the coach's remarks that her discomfort was not being taken seriously. Perhaps she was faking, the coach might be thinking.

Have you ever heard someone verbalize any of the following remarks? What do they have in common?

"Can't you even hold onto the ball?"
"Nice catch, butterfingers."
" That was the wrong play, Sam. How did you ever make it through school?"
" You run as if you have cement in your shoes. Come on, move!"

Each of these sarcastic remarks serves a common purpose. They destroy self-confidence and eliminate any existing respect between the speaker and the object of the statement. (Notice that I did not label the person to whom the statements were addressed as the "listener" because sarcastic remarks are often ignored, especially if the player expects the coach to use such statements.) Remarks that insult the player poison communication. How can an athlete be expected to feel competent, motivated, and loyal to the coach after receiving messages whose contents serve to deflate his or her status as a person, athlete, and teammate. I have concluded, based on hundreds of conversations with athletes of all ages, that one of the biggest mistakes a coach can make, next to communicating the actual insult, is making a sarcastic statement to the player in the presence of other team members. That's a sin in the eyes of an athlete that is almost unforgivable and certainly unforgettable.

Two primary guidelines about the use of sarcasm are helpful. First, *avoid sarcasm at all times.* Such statements are *never* humorous, whether or not laughter follows the statement. Laughter after a statement used to ridicule a person serves as a defense against embarrassment. Laughter in this context is almost never genuine. The speaker of a sarcastic remark may think that he or she is entertaining the "victim" or other listeners, but often just the opposite is true. My discussions with over one hundred athletes on this issue clearly indicate that more respect, admiration, and loyalty is never an outcome from such statements.

The second guideline is to use statements that *convey sincerity.* After observing a player fall and scrape her knees on the floor, the coach should simply ask the player if she is all right. The coach should not laugh and say, "Hey, nice balance," nor make some other remark that would embarrass the person. After a coach explains the strategy for the second half, a player may ask the coach to repeat something. The coach should wisely comply, rewording his or her original statements so that the athlete is certain of the strategies. The coach should not say, "What's wrong, Al, can't you listen the first time?" Sincerity says, "I care about you," and it is inherent in effective communication. Sarcasm says, "I don't respect you." Such statements attack the individual's personality, a habit that is detrimental to open communication, as indicated in the sixth commandment.

VI. Thou Shalt Praise and Criticize Behavior, but Not Personality

Author and child psychologist Haim Ginott asserts that praising and criticizing character or personality is never constructive. Why? Because it offers the listener no information and, therefore, does not allow him or her to make a realistic judgment about actions. Yet this is often the most common form of feedback that we give athletes.

The correct use of praise.   This is, perhaps, one of the most difficult skills to develop because, first, we don't offer praise as often as we should, and second, when we do offer praise, it's usually based on emotions of excitement and happiness, which means that we use statements that are hyperbolic (i.e., exaggerated). Examples include, "You're the *best* batter, the *nicest* kid, the *greatest* athlete," and so on.

The coach was very pleased about Bill's defensive skills in a recent basketball game. Certainly praise was in order, but it was not of a personal nature.

The coach avoided saying, "Bill, you're wonderful. What a great ballplayer you can be." Instead, he described what Bill had accomplished: "I liked the way you stayed with your man, Bill. You prevented him from scoring at his average. Nice going."

Barbara hit a double in softball, scoring the runner at second base. After the game, the coach said to her, "Solid contact on that double, Barb. It's great that you were able to bring home that runner." The coach avoided: "Super hitting, Barb. I knew you could do it."

Telling athletes that they (1) are "the best," (2) played a great game, (3) are better than someone else, or (4) did a "super" job might make an athlete feel good for the moment, but such statements fail to reinforce the *behaviors* that were responsible for the desirable outcomes. Another reason statements that praise character are better off avoided is because they create dependence on the coach for approval. The athlete might conclude, "If the coach says I'm good (or the best), then he likes me." Inversely, if the coach does not give the athlete similar praise on a given day, the competitor might feel differently about the coach, "I guess the coach doesn't like me today." It may never be the coach's intention to use praise as a means of conveying subjective feelings about the athlete (e.g., "I like you because you're a good player"), yet this is often what happens when praise becomes personally based rather than behavior-based. Personal feelings about an athlete should not be based on the person's sport skills; this disrupts team unity. The second type of praise that should be avoided is called *judgmental praise*.

Judgmental praise creates anxiety and evokes defensiveness. It does not lead to the athlete's sense of self-reliance, self-direction, or self-control. Applauding the athlete's efforts with superlatives such as "great" or "the best" brings on feelings of discomfort. The athlete gains little understanding about what he or she did to deserve such a comment. Praise of this nature also may be incompatible with the athlete's own self-image or perception of the situation. Finally, praising personality tells sport performers that they are accepted and liked only when they perform well but are not deserving of such recognition when they don't. These expectations are very difficult for the player to meet. Ginott (1965, p. 106) suggests, "Avoid praise that attaches adjectives to an athlete's character." He further states that avoiding praise that judges character or evaluates personality allows the person (athlete) to feel more secure in making mistakes and taking risks without fear. This, in turn, raises self-confidence.

The cardinal rules of praising are:

- Describe without evaluating.
- Report, do not judge.
- Let athletes evaluate themselves.

The correct use of praise has been demonstrated in a model by Smith, Smoll, and Curtis (1977). Their "sandwich approach" is a model for offering praise while teaching skills and is especially effective when providing instructional feedback after an error. The underlying philosophy of this approach is to ignore the past mistake — or at least not to make a big deal about it — and, instead, to focus on future performance.

The sandwich approach. This technique is used to offer constructive feedback to athletes in a sensitive, yet effective, manner. It consists of three elements that are verbalized in the proper sequence: (1) a positive statement, (2) future-oriented positive feedback, and (3) a compliment (as illustrated in Figure 8.1).

The positive statement. After an athlete makes an error, he or she typically anticipates a negative remark from the coach. To "survive" the predicted verbal assault, the player will usually avoid listening — will literally tune out the unpleasant message. It's the coach's job in using the sandwich approach to dispel this fear. Otherwise, the information feedback will never be heard. Instead of a negative message, the player needs to acknowledge a positive one. Once he or she is receptive to the opening (positive) statement, the athlete will also be listening to the next, instructional segment. Examples of appropriate positive statements are: "Good try, Gene." "Nice effort, Mary." "That was a tough ball to hit." "Not your fault, Barb." Notice the use of the player's first name. Athletes are more attentive to the speaker when their first name is used. And this use shows sensitivity toward the individual.

Future-oriented positive feedback. This is, well, the "meat" of the matter. The athlete should now feel no threat after the opening statement. At this time, the coach instructs the athlete about behaviors or strategies that should be attempted *next time*. The reason for keeping instruction future-oriented is to *avoid* having the competitor think about the error (thinking about the mishap actually increases the chance of repeating it). And the message should be positive in content. Learners remember positive information better than negative information. Coaches should say, in effect, "Next time, do this." No ridicule, guilt, threats, or anger. Examples include: "Next time the ball goes to your right, cross your left leg over the right leg" or "You'll have a better chance of catching the ball, Tanya, if you follow the ball into your hands."

The compliment. There is a phenomenon in cognitive psychology called the *recency effect.* It means that the most recent information is better remembered than messages presented before it. In the sandwich approach, it is important that the athlete reflect favorably on his or her interaction with the coach, especially when receiving constructive feedback on performance. To end the interaction on a positive note will (1) improve the retention of the information — we remember positive input better than negative input, (2) result in more trust and loyalty toward the coach and team, (3) reinforce actions that are being performed correctly — athletes need to remember what they are doing well, and (4) help the player to perceive learning skills as far less traumatic than if the coach's emotions got in the way. Examples of compliments include "I like the way you ran that

Figure 8.1   Elements of the sandwich approach for constructive feedback in sport

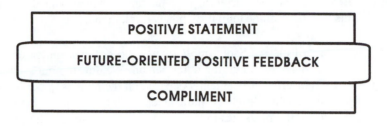

pass pattern," "Way to keep your eye on the ball," and "You almost got it. Good improvement, Doug."

Now let's put the three components together in a few contrived examples.

Example 1

Jennifer bobbled a ground ball hit hard to her left. "OK, Jennifer. Good effort. That was a tough one. On those grounders, try to keep your glove down a bit more. I liked the way you kept your eye on the ball. Stay with it."

Example 2

Gary dropped a pass from the quarterback. "All right, Gary, way to hustle out there. On the next toss, try not to run this pattern too deep. Go only about five yards, and watch the ball into your hands. You're showing me good speed, Gary. Stick with it. It'll come."

Three additional suggestions about the sandwich approach are in order. First, do not say "but" before a statement. "Nice try, Bob, but next time do 'this'" tells the athlete that the positive statement was insincere. It's like saying, "I really like you, Sherry, but . . ." which is another way of saying, "I really *don't* like you, Sherry."

The second recommendation is that statements to athletes must be honest. Insincerity is easy to spot. If the athlete really made a poor judgment in executing a task, then a stronger form of feedback might be in order. It's better to say nothing than to say something without meaning it.

The third recommendation is in response to many coaches who tell me that the sandwich approach is more applicable in practice than during the contest. I respectfully disagree — and so do the authors Smith, Smoll, and Curtis. This technique should be a habit that is used consistently in most situations. In fact, the contest presents additional pressure for athletes. Making an error is more anxiety-provoking, embarrassing, and stressful than at any other time. What better opportunity to present information in a relatively calm, factual manner so that the athlete learns and adapts to new demands than during the contest? Practice this technique alone until it sounds natural, then use it.

Constructive criticism. Sadly, most of us who criticize others do so for sinister reasons — usually to hurt the other person. We develop our vocabulary and our habits in offering critical remarks based on the models in our lives. We hear our parents, coaches, teachers, and friends criticize us and each other, and we, in turn, use similar messages in the way we criticize others. But too often, the goal is to hurt the feelings of another person. And we succeed in this goal too frequently.

In coaching, criticism is often used to give feedback on performance or to express anger or frustration. It isn't that criticism is so bad in itself but, rather, that the manner in which it is communicated can have negative ramifications. Most critical remarks bring on anger, resentment, and a desire for revenge. When an athlete is criticized, particularly if the criticism is constant, he or she learns to condemn himself or herself and to find fault with others. The athlete becomes suspect of others (say good-bye to trust). Ironically, the *last* thing an athlete needs is to have his or her character chastised; success in sport requires self-confidence.

Janice, a high school volleyball player, hit a spike stroke out of bounds, resulting in victory for the other team. The outraged coach reacted, "What the hell did you do that for, Janice. What a dumb mistake. If you can't hit the ball where you're supposed to, get off the court." The player's feelings were terribly hurt. This form of criticism condemned Janice's attempt to risk an offensive shot that could (and often does) score a point. In the future, she may well concentrate on merely returning the ball in bounds with a weaker, less risky shot. But winners are risk-takers. Chronic criticism reduces risk-taking behaviors in sport.

As indicated earlier, the problem lies not so much in the concept of criticism but, rather, in its content. Psychologist and author Haim Ginott asserts that the main function of *constructive criticism* is to indicate what must be done in the situation. Helpful criticism never addresses itself to the player's personality. Remarks are aimed toward the conditions in the environment — what has to be done — and do not attack the person. There *is* a right way to criticize.

Let's review what psychologists call the cardinal rule of criticizing a person.

Talk to the situation, not to the person's (athlete's) character or personality.

Example 1

Willie arrived ten minutes late for the warm-up segment of practice. The coach said, "Willie, all members of the team need to be here on time for the warm-up. If it's impossible, speak to me earlier in the day and tell me you will be late."

The coach did not ridicule, engage in name-calling, or offend the athlete. The coach also did not ask the athlete his reason for being late. This conscious psychological ploy was designed to communicate to the participant the necessity of warming up. No damage was done.

Example 2

The coach, speaking to his quarterback, remarked, "Conrad, I want you to run the play we just practiced — a 'z-out' pass pattern." The player looked down for a second, trying to remember whether he should throw to the split end or to the tight end on this play. He hesitantly asked the coach. The coach responded, "A z-out is always thrown to the sideline, so it should be thrown to the receiver closest to the sideline — the split end." Conrad was relieved that the coach did not explode. No name-calling, no temper tantrum, and no guilt-ridden statements were used to undermine the athlete's intelligence and self-concept (e.g., "You should know better than to ask me that question"). The coach simply responded with the requested information.

What if the quarterback forgot a play that was used in an earlier game and one that he should have remembered? The coach might want to offer constructive criticism *after practice* in this manner: "Conrad, I'm happy to answer your question about the play, but don't forget that the quarterback *must* remember the plays. Try to take some additional time to study them, and if you have any questions or want to review the plays before practice, let's do so. You are the leader of the offense out here." The coach communicated his feelings by dealing with the situation without attacking the player's character. No statements were made that said, "You're stupid."

Speaking of the word *stupid*, some words are so damaging to the listener that perhaps they should be deleted from the English vocabulary. Words such as *stupid*, *dumb*, *fool*, *idiot*, and *jerk* serve one purpose — to hurt the feelings and lower the self-image of others. They are terms that say nothing about the inappropriate *behavior* of the person but instead focus on degrading character and personality. As Ginott suggests in his book *Between Parent and Teenager*, "When a person is drowning, it is not a good time to teach him to swim, or to ask him questions, or to criticize his performance. It is time for help." Criticizing personality is like performing surgery: It always hurts, and at times it can be fatal.

Discharging character-destroying criticism to athletes misses its intended purpose. In fact, instead of having a motivating and arousal-inducing effect, the use of such terms destroys motivation, excitation, and the willingness to learn new skills, take risks during competition, and support teammates. The coach is now viewed in a more hostile manner and has lost the loyalty of the athlete, which he or she has been trying to attain all year.

In summary, the advice on criticism is:

- Don't attack personality attributes.

- Don't criticize character traits.
- Attend to the situation that faces you. Decide "Where do we go from here?"

VII. Thou Shalt Express Feelings Constructively

A philosopher by the name of Herbert once said, "He that respects not is not respected." To be an effective communicator, the coach must show respect when interacting with the players. Respect entails an awareness of the athlete as a unique and distinct individual. Respect for others must include respecting their feelings, opinions, privacy, and individual differences derived from both environmental and genetic sources. Dishonesty, pontification, sarcasm, and a lack of communication are examples of disrespectful ways of relating to others. If the coach communicates to the players with the same respect that he or she expects from them, loyalty toward the team leader should be optimal. Some of the feelings that are almost inherent in coaching include anger, frustration, and disappointment, among others. An effective coach learns how to express those feelings without losing respect for the athlete.

Expressing anger. It has been said that if people speak when they're angry, they will make the best speech they'll ever regret. Typically, anger is based on irrational statements and behaviors. A temper is lost; so is a little sanity. Coaches have been known to say and do things without thinking of the consequences, like anyone else. The angry coach will insult, hit below the belt, fly into a rampage, swear, and perhaps (albeit very rarely) physically strike at the source of his or her irritation.

Anger is a fact of life. Like the common cold, anger is a recurrent state that rarely feels good. Anger is used to "release" strong emotional feelings and tension, and this venting of feelings might relax the person. But usually, our response to anger is guilt, an upset stomach, or a headache. Of course, many coaches use anger as a technique to arouse, motivate, or condemn. Does it work? It may. The important point is that, as in giving praise and criticism, there is a right way and a wrong way to use and express anger.

The good news about anger in coaching is that anger *does* have its time and place. In fact, failure to express anger at certain times during practice or a game would convey to the athlete indifference, not approval and reinforcement. Coaches who care about the athletes cannot altogether shun anger. This does not mean that sport competitors can withstand a deluge of violence and hostility. It only means that the athlete should expect the wrath of the coach that says, "There are limits to my tolerance toward the level of your play."

It is crucial to remember that the medication must not be worse than the disease. For example, many coaches believe that getting angry, particularly at an umpire or referee, has an emotional effect on the team that may have its time and place. But this inspirational technique is not a panacea to arouse the team.

Anger should be used as an honest means of communicating feelings based on actual performance. Coach Bill was meeting with his basketball team at halftime. His team was not using the defensive patterns that they had practiced during the week. He was genuinely angry that the athletes seemed to forget what they had spent hours practicing in preparation for the game. The coach told them, in no uncertain terms, the following in this order:

1.   The specific performances that he had observed so that the athletes were made aware of the same situations and events as the coach.
2.   What the team had to do to counter the opponent's offense — sometimes position by position.
3.   What the team had practiced in preparation for this game and how these plays related strongly to the necessary strategy during the game.
4.   What he had observed during the first half of play that was contrary to what they had practiced.
5.   His feelings of anger and frustration about the incongruence between what the team must do on defense to win and what it had been doing in the first half.

Coach Bill did two things that made his halftime talk effective. First, his anger (which, by the way, *was* justified) was directed at specific behaviors of the athletes. He engaged in no name-calling and no hollering just for effect. Sometimes a coach will try to communicate feelings of sorrow and disappointment to make the athletes feel guilty, which the coach hopes will result in subsequent superior performance. Sometimes this approach works, although not if the players lack optimal loyalty toward the coach. A second problem with the "guilt approach" is that its effect, if it works, is short term. It does not breed self-confidence and team loyalty. Players may become quickly aroused, but participants who are more concerned with not hurting the coach's feelings than with performing for personal satisfaction are quickly demotivated after the contest. Essentially, they are saying, "There, coach, I did it for *you*. Are you happy now?"

The second effective strategy used by Coach Bill occurred *after* his expressions of anger. He told the athletes of his confidence in their ability to perform according to the plans. "I know you men can do it because I saw you do it beautifully this week in practice," he hollered. The players felt more confident leaving the locker room. If the coach's message would have ended on a down note — that the players were doing a terrible job and had no business being out on the court or winning the game — the team would have been undermotivated and less confident.

Guidelines for the *constructive* use of anger are as follows:

▪   It's fine for the coach to express angry feelings provided the athlete's character and personality are not attacked. Sarcasm, name-calling, use of destructive adjectives, and physical abuse are *never* appropriate.

- The first step in handling emotional upheaval is to identify feelings verbally by name. "I am annoyed with you. I am very, very upset. I'm furious." Sometimes the mere statement of feelings changes behavior, according to psychologist Haim Ginott. Most athletes fully realize the rationale behind the coach's angry emotions.

- The next step, which, by the way, is not always necessary, is to give the reason for one's anger by stating inner thoughts and wishful actions.

This takes some practice and control, but here are a few true examples of the constructive use of anger:

A high school basketball team was making the same mistakes repeatedly during practice. It was obvious to the coach that her players were not concentrating, not motivated. After several more minutes of some less-than-inspirational play, the coach threw up her hands and said,

> I've had it. You women are obviously not in the mood to play basketball. I can't stand what I'm seeing. Several of you are out of position. Jane, you're not guarding your opponent. Barb, you are simply not hustling. Elaine, if you know where you are supposed to be on the play we just ran, you didn't show it. I'm extremely upset at your performance out there. I want to see 'this' happen. I want to see 'that' happen. I wish that you women had shown me that you wanted to practice today because that's the only way we can win. I just can't take your lack of concentration any longer. I'm leaving.

And sure enough, the coach stalked out of the gym, leaving the stunned players feeling sorry that they had played so halfheartedly. The coach had a right to be upset. The players were very upset about their coach's leaving practice. The rest of the week saw the team playing magnificently. Now *that's* player loyalty. The refusal of the coach to attack the character of any athlete made a big difference in how her message was received. The players felt no bitterness toward the coach in this example, only remorse.

The tennis coach noticed that a player on his team was using the wrong stroke on a few returns to his opponent during practice. "Leo, I am becoming very frustrated in trying to be a good coach. When you continue to use a lob instead of a drive when your opponent is playing deep, I feel like taking you off the court. I wish I could get you to realize that you have the ability to win if you use the right strokes and that your drive stroke is the best choice in that situation. If you refuse to follow instructions, perhaps you need more time to learn the game, and we'll let another player compete instead while you sit and watch."

The key message in the above examples is that the coaches *are giving information* while venting their anger. The coaches were attacking specific, identifiable behaviors of the athletes and told players the reasons for their emotions. The coaches also identified wishful actions, changes in the athletes' behaviors that they'd like to see occur. It's best to conclude by expressing wishful actions. "I want to see 'such and such' happening out there" is far more constructive than "Can't you do anything right?"

Although the above examples are centered on the feeling of anger, others such as frustration and disappointment are also inherent in coaching. These feelings should be handled in a similar manner. If the coach wants the players to respond to his or her comments with enthusiasm, to retain the skills that they have learned, to support teammates, and to play with a strong desire to win, then constructive communication is the answer. The coach's personality comes out most strongly on this commandment. Sensitive, informative, intelligent, mature, caring team leaders, through the use of constructive expression, train their players to believe (1) in the need to master certain techniques and (2) in the effort it takes to make these techniques work consistently.

VIII. Thou Shalt Use Positive Nonverbal Cues

Over the years, there have been some great coaches in sport who would say relatively little to their athletes. Nonetheless, they were inspiring and produced a tremendous sense of player loyalty. How could this be? In many cases, the coaches with relatively poor verbal skills were able to communicate nonverbally and, thus, could produce in their players the desired psychological benefits and performance outcomes. The meaning conveyed by nonverbal communication and the proper use of its techniques are the issues here.

Dr. Rainer Martens and the coauthors of *Coaching Young Athletes* (1981) classify nonverbal communication (or what is sometimes called *body language*) into six different categories:

1. *Body motion:* gestures or movements of body parts such as the hands, head, and feet. Tilting the head, shifting the eyes, or raising the eyebrows in the proper context can tell another person a great deal about what is on your mind.

2. *Physical characteristics:* physique, height, weight, body odors, and hairstyle. Fitness instructors must never be overweight, or they will lose all credibility toward what they are trying to teach. You can't preach cleanliness while looking sloppy.

3. *Touching behavior:* Examples include patting someone on the back or placing an arm around a player's shoulders. Studies have shown that Americans are less inclined to touch or to stand close to one another than Europeans. Yet, touching conveys one of the most sensitive, caring, and trusting messages that a coach can project to an athlete.

4. *Voice characteristics:* Sometimes our messages to others are reinforced by the manner in which we send them rather than only by their content. The pitch, rhythm, resonance, inflections, and amplitude of

our words and sounds often indicate the feelings that underlie them. "Nice play, Phil" can mean a sincere compliment when spoken with a smile or smart-alec sarcasm when spoken with a stern, cold face.

5.   *Body position:* How close do you stand to another person whether or not you are interacting? The personal space between you and others and position of your body offer an unspoken message about the intensity and importance of your information or the status and respect you feel toward the person.

6.   *Eye contact:* Although missing from the list in Martens's book, the tendency to look the intended listener in the eye makes a different impact on the sincerity and intensity of the message than speaking and looking away from the person simultaneously. Of course, eye contact can be a glance, a glare, or a gaze; each denoting a different message.

Of central importance is understanding how nonverbal communication can work either for or against the coach when he or she tries to send important messages to athletes. For example, the coach should not raise his or her voice in an angry manner when giving information to the athletes. The participant will become conscious of the coach's angry feelings and, either intentionally or more often unintentionally, will filter out the coach's message.

On the topic of body position, another important behavior to consider is whether the coach surrounds himself or herself with starting players or well-liked individuals. This habit sends messages to others about the status of certain individuals, which leads to resentment by persons not selected. It's important to avoid showing favoritism on the team. Coach John Thompson of the Georgetown University basketball team says that he makes a habit of sitting among the nonstarters and, by interacting with those around him, is in a favorable position for instructing and motivating this group of players who can have a very important impact on the team.

Another example of the effective use of body position between coach and athlete is the usefulness of standing relatively close to a player when offering instruction and feedback. Often, close proximity during communication increases attention of the listener. The coach who yells information across the gym floor (although this may be necessary at times) is less effective in receiving the attention and concentration of the intended listener than if he were to speak with the player only a few feet away.

Many people, including coaches, avoid eye contact. Desmond Morris, in his book *The Human Zoo,* claimed that our human ancestors often used eye contact to frighten enemies. Looking an animal or another person straight in the eye was accompanied with aggression and a willingness to challenge another being or to protect one's family or food. To this day, many people are uncomfortable with eye contact. Without prolonging the psychological explanations of "meeting eye to eye," it is sufficient to say that looking directly at players when they are addressed is very important for effective communication. Eye contact enhances the player's attention and interest in the coach's message because the person to whom the information is intended is clearly identified. Secondly, the coach appears to be more sincere with eye-to-eye contact. This greatly increases the message's meaningfulness to the listener.

Sometimes nonverbal communication can be even *more* effective than the use of words to get across a message. It is desirable for coaches to express themselves with feelings of sincerity, warmth, sensitivity, and sometimes assertiveness. A coach's smile can show empathy and understanding to an athlete whose feelings may be hurt due to an unsuccessful attempt or who feels "great" after performing admirably. A pat on the back tells the player, "Nice try, better luck next time. You did the best you could. I (the coach) still support you" among other messages. Use of a regular speaking voice, as opposed to a raised, excited vocal tone, communicates a sense of calm, sincerity, realistic appraisal of performance, offering valid information feedback or suggestions, and mutual respect. The player concentrates on and remembers more of the message when it is communicated calmly than when it is communicated in a highly aroused manner. The key issue is to make the best use of nonverbal communication through positive rather than negative channels.

IX. Thou Shalt Teach Skills

A national survey of coaches (640 returned questionnaires) was conducted by Dr. John Silva and reported in the *Journal of Physical Education, Recreation, and Dance* (September 1984) about which areas of sport psychology were viewed by coaches as most important and useful to them. Silva reported that the more current and fashionable areas of sport psychology, such as psychological preparation, anxiety, and imagery, were not ranked highly. The need to use improved methods in teaching sport skills was highly ranked. It was found that "the interest in motoric processes indicates that motor learning-performance researchers with applied interests may find the coaching community more open to their inquiry than previously assumed." My own experience with numerous coaches concurs with Silva's findings. They are more interested in having a sport psychologist assist them in becoming more effective educators of skills than in consulting in the areas of mental preparation or player counseling. Coaches need, and many want, to become better teachers of sport skills.

Teaching sport skills to competitive athletes is a science. It differs from instructing the novice, but less than one would think. Basic guidelines of effective instructional techniques must be applied if skills are to be learned, remembered, and applied in a game situation. Some of these techniques include:

- Communicating the goal of the instructional session (what the athlete has to do).
- Modeling the skill in correct form so that a visual representation of the skill is used by the athlete during practice to compare his or her performance with that of the "perfect" model.
- Reducing the amount of information that must be learned at one time (or risk a greater amount of forgetting). Highly skilled athletes can learn and remember skills with which they are familiar better than the novice can, of course. But information overload is still possible when new information is transmitted, especially in verbal form.
- Allowing skills and strategies to be learned in practice before they are used in a game. It is necessary to allow for numerous repetitions to improve retention of the information or skill. Due to the athlete's psychological state during competition, entailing anxiety and high arousal, teaching new skills should *not* be attempted during the game.
- Giving learners feedback on their performance. Informing the athlete as to which skills are or are not being performed correctly is more than

a matter of shouting, "Nice catch, Jack." The timing of such feedback, its content, the manner in which it is communicated, and allowance for repetition of the skill are just a few of the considerations that need to be applied for conditions of optimal learning.

Athletes can be effective only to the degree that they are taught strategies and skills by the coach. A member of the San Francisco 49ers football team, after winning the 1985 Super Bowl, claimed that the one outstanding trait of his coach, Bill Walsh, was his ability to teach. "He's such a great educator," the veteran lineman said. Learning is one of the facets of participating in sport that motivates the athlete. Several studies in the area of youth sports conclude that young participants view learning new skills as one of the main reasons they continue to participate in competitive sports. Nonstarters on sport teams view their status on the team as relatively pointless unless they are learning new skills. The nonstarter is more likely to quit if practice sessions are redundant and learning is virtually nonexistent.

Perhaps one issue that some coaches need to address and to do more thinking about is their tendency to make conclusive, long-term judgments about an athlete's skills and abilities based on initial, brief observations of performance with little regard to the benefits of skill instruction. All athletes need to learn and to improve sport skills, no matter at what level of play and expertise they begin the program. In addition, differences between individuals in their present skill levels, their desire to learn, and other psychological characteristics make it impossible to predict to what degree a player will improve or how he or she will perform during the competitive event.

Making judgments about the future of a person's performance is scientifically invalid, unreliable, and unfair to the aspiring athlete at best and psychologically crippling to the athlete at worst. Researchers in the area of motor learning agree that perfection is impossible in sport performance due to the complexity and speed of neuromuscular and psychological demands on the human organism.

Although the experienced coach often has good judgment about the required "tools" to compete successfully in a given sport, one must not judge hastily. The commandment to teach skills says to the coach two things: (1) do not assume that "what you see is what you get" because athletes improve dramatically with quality instruction, and (2) improvement in performance often takes time and patience on the part of the coach, and due to developmental differences, some athletes will learn and greatly improve faster than others. Do not give up on them prematurely.

X. Thou Shalt Interact Consistently with All Team Members

Goethe, a philosopher, said, "Treat people as though they were what they ought to be, and you help them to become what they are capable of being." A coach will receive maximal effort, concentration, commitment, and loyalty from virtually all players on the team if those players believe that the coach is interested in them both as athletes and as people. Probably the best way for coaches to communicate these feelings is to interact with all team members — starters and nonstarters — on a consistent basis.

A few definitions of terms will help to clarify this recommendation. First, *consistent* and *constant* interaction are *not* the same thing. Consistent interacting in the present context refers to demonstrating an ongoing, predictable pattern of communication with others, whereas a constant communication style requires interacting with others on an almost nonstop basis. The coach should not attempt to speak with all team members (starters and nonstarters) all the time, particularly not with large teams as in football. This would not be the best use of a coach's time. What *is* suggested is that the coach "keep in touch" on a regular basis to (1) be aware of the strong and weak points of each athlete, (2) point out the ways in which the athlete has shown improvement, (3) acknowledge specific skills that have been demonstrated efficiently, (4) remind individuals of the skills that they need to improve further, and (5) offer compliments to performers based on some aspect of their play from the recent past or the same day. The contact may also be based on a more personal level. Discussing sport-related topics or the athlete's performance does not always have to provide a reason to interact.

Athletes feel greater loyalty to the coach who shows a personal interest in their lives. I have heard several athletes comment that they resented "being used" by the coach to attain his (the coach's) own objectives. Coaches who only care about player performance but have little regard for the "human being" will not develop the athlete's long-term commitment to succeed. How can a coach earn a sense of loyalty from players who do not perceive their coach to be caring, honest, respectful, or sensitive to their needs? How can the coach be aware of the unique needs and feelings of the team if players are ignored? And to what extent should the coach commit time and energy toward interacting with nonstarters or players who have had, and will continue to have, relatively little impact on the outcome of contests?

The importance of the nonstarter. It's no secret that many, sometimes most, players do not receive an opportunity to play in the contest, particularly at more advanced levels of competition. Nor can everyone have an opportunity to play in every game. Due to the time required to teach and practice skills and strategies to athletes who *will* compete (80 to 90 percent of practice time, according to some collegiate coaches), coaches will often neglect the nonstarter. This is a terrible mistake and forms the rationale for the inclusion of this commandment.

It is *wrong* to ignore or to dismiss the importance of nonstarters on sports teams for several reasons. First, the nonstarter is only one injury away from becoming a starter. How many nonprofessional athletes enter a game and play as effectively as the starters? Not too many. Professional players notwithstanding, where skill differences between starters and nonstarters are relatively minimal, one possible reason why nonstarters do not perform at levels similar to starters among nonprofessionals may partly be due to differences in the time and effort coaches offer starting players relative to players who are not scheduled to play or start.

Other reasons why the nonstarter should receive the attention, respect, and consistent communication from the coach include (1) to avoid the appearance of a double standard between starters and nonstarters on team rules that, if perceived by the players, would divide the team, reduce or terminate team loyalty, and lead to feelings of helplessness about future game participation by nonstarters, (2) to allow the coach to observe improvements in skill and performance of a given athlete, and (3) to prevent the deterioration of team morale — a devastating psychological state that leads to the low self-image of participants, a lack or absence of motivation to learn and perform at optimal levels, and a conscious or unconscious desire by players to see their coach and, perhaps, their teammates fail. It is important to remember that members of sports teams are friends. Such friendships are not often composed of nor dictated by similar status on the team. If nonstarters are perceived by team participants as being treated unfairly, *all* team members are affected with only rare exceptions. The coach must treat the team as a unit of individuals who jointly serve the common purpose of performing all the necessary tasks to win.

The ten commandments of effective communication for coaches should make worthwhile and productive all of the time spent determining strategies, relying on the pregame pep talk to motivate the players, and developing community and school support for the team. Many coaches have forgotten how they felt when they were sport competitors. It's important to remember the common feelings of many athletes: frustration, disappointment, the need to be recognized and to succeed, a desire to learn new skills, the need to affiliate with peers, and the desire to be accepted as a part of the team (or peer group). Communication, however, is a two-way street. In the next section, we look at what athletes can do to foster the coach-athlete interaction.

APPROACHING THE COACH

Perhaps asking coaches to use perfect communication techniques is an unfair expectation. Coaches are human, too. No doubt they can use some help from the athletes if the coach-athlete interaction is to remain strong and consistent. My experiences as a team sport psychologist at a university and in youth sports lead me to conclude that there is an interesting paradox between the athlete's being confident with his or her own feelings and communicating these needs to the coach. Most athletes are, in fact, aware of the techniques that work best for them in the psychological preparation of sport competition. Athletes have specific preferences about choices of food in the pregame meal, their mood both hours and minutes prior to the game, the type of atmosphere with which they are most and least comfortable prior to the game, and the manner in which they are being utilized as an athlete (e.g., the position at which they play best or starting versus substitute status). However, the players are equally intimidated or unsure of themselves when it comes to approaching the coach about their needs. Whether it is the coach's manner that intimidates a player or the athlete's lack of confidence is a riddle. The obvious answer is that both parties need to develop communication skills and to *use* these skills if they are to resolve the issues that may potentially inhibit desirable performance outcomes.

The Athlete-Coach Interview

Athletes may want to follow all or some of the following guidelines on approaching the coach to discuss their feelings, whether positive or negative:

- Make an appointment to see the coach. In this way, the issues that you wish to discuss may be presented in a relaxed environment free from interruption. In addition, the coach will realize that your concerns or feelings are serious enough to warrant special attention.

- Decide, in advance, on only one or two issues that you wish to discuss. Keep the agenda short. You, the athlete, may have a dozen issues that warrant discussion. However, an avalanche of concerns will only place most coaches on the defensive and convey the feeling that "nothing is going right." This is not the impression you want to make.

- Be on time for your appointment with the coach. If you're even a minute late, you are sending a message that your concerns are not that important. Further, you are showing disrespect to a person who has cleared his or her busy calendar for you, and it *is* busy.

- Dress neatly and appropriately. There is no need for a tie and coat (or a dress and heels for women athletes), but a torn sweatshirt and blue jeans show a lack of respect for your audience. If you want to be taken seriously and respected, look like it.

- Bring along a notepad and pen or pencil for note taking. You would not be wise to interview or interrogate the coach while recording every word. However, it makes sense to record agreements or statements about the tasks that need to be completed if the issues are to be resolved. Never bring a tape recorder. This shows distrust and will cut off communication immediately. Again, the purpose of the paper and pencil is to help you clarify and remember some of the coach's recommendations or responses to resolve the issues. In fact, you may even be perceived as conscientious in your efforts to remember information.

- Upon entering the coach's office, shake hands (this shows sincerity, warmth, and a willingness to communicate in a positive manner), and begin your conversation (if you have a choice) on a topic unrelated to the reason for being there. Warm up, but only for a few minutes. Don't take up too much of his or her time. Get to the point rather quickly (within a few minutes). A good idea is to converse about other aspects of the coach's job: "Are you enjoying the health course you're teaching?" "That was a crazy road trip we took last week, wasn't it, coach? It took forever to get there."

- You (the athlete) make the first statement about the reason for coming, and make the opening statement positive. For example: "Coach, like everyone else, I'm really pleased about the way the team has been playing lately. I really hope it continues. The reason I needed to speak with you was that I've been concerned about my role with the team. I feel that I can contribute and . . ." By beginning with a positive statement, the athlete is tearing down the tendency of many coaches to feel and respond to a critical remark in a defensive manner. A person, any person, who is defensive cannot communicate effectively because they are occupied with explaining their views while ignoring the feelings of the other party. Again, start out with something positive, something that is going well or a good feeling you have about an issue. Then, bring up your concern.

- Use "I" statements; avoid "you" statements. You are there to voice how you feel about something. Fine. State your feelings in a manner that indicates how *you* feel. Once you begin to say, "You did this" or "You said that," the coach will become defensive and stop listening. An example of a desirable approach is, "Coach, I'm a bit confused about our agreement last week. I heard you say that I would play in the games we had this past week. Of course, I didn't play, and I'm concerned about my role with the team and what ways I need to improve to play more often. Can you help me get a handle on this?"

- Give specific, behavioral examples when making your point. Avoid discussing general perceptions of the coach's attitude or behavior toward you. Instead, refer to the exact times and behaviors of the coach (or any other source of your feelings) that affected you. It's fine to have these thoughts written down in front of you so that you may refer to them for the purpose of accuracy. Failure to be precise with the use of performance examples will often result in denial of how you feel ("Oh, no, I don't ignore you" or "You have it all wrong. You shouldn't feel unneeded on this team"). Tell the coach exactly what events and behaviors took place that gave you your perceptions.

- Accept the coach's answers (at least in the initial meeting) even if you disagree. Coaches might feel guilty or defensive about their behavior and, as a protective device, will offer the best immediate answer that gets them off the hook. Their response might also be honest, to the point, and painful to hear. It is of no value to argue, to engage in a duel of winner and loser, or to verbalize your doubt about the coach's honesty and integrity. Your point has been made. Despite the coach's denials, corrections of your perceptions or statements, or his or her interpretations of "the facts," expressing your feelings in a positive, mature manner may result in desirable changes. Again, do not challenge.

- If agreements or verbal contracts are completed, verbally review them in summary form before leaving the coach's office and agree to meet again if the need arises. To write down the agreement or agreements for your own records as soon as you can (in the coach's office or soon after the meeting) to remember exactly what was said is very helpful. If the agreement is not carried out as promised right away, do not remind the coach. Allow some time to pass, and give the coach the flexibility to fulfill his or her end of the bargain. The team leader may have a good reason for postponing or for not fulfilling the promise.

- End your meeting with (1) a handshake (female athletes, too), (2) a smile, (3) a statement of appreciation for the person's time and understanding, and (4) a positive statement about your future as an athlete. For example: "Coach, I'm really looking forward to doing everything I can to help us win. Thanks so much for taking the time to help me out."

- Finally, keep your conference confidential. This may be the toughest part of all. But, if word were to spread about the nature and content of your discussion among the players, the coach might feel obligated to refrain from carrying out the agreement so as not to look foolish or weak in the eyes of the other players and assistant coaches.

Written Feedback

The content of this chapter has focused mainly on verbal communication with a small segment on nonverbal mannerisms. Not discussed as yet is the written form of communication. Figure 8.2 is a feedback sheet that has been used by a few coaches with athletes at the high school and college levels. They have found the results of using the survey to be rewarding. The advantages of using the feedback sheet in written form include:

- Making available a vehicle for input from the players that can be used at any time during the season as an expression of feelings or attitudes

Figure 8.2   Feedback sheet for sports teams

(This can remain anonymous. No need to sign your name.)

To the Athletes: The purpose of this form is to gather your input about how *you feel* as a member of this team so you can play your best. Also, the coaches want you to enjoy your experiences on the team.

I.   Feelings about being a member of the team:

(a) I can enjoy being on the team: Yes___ No___
(b) I understand the reasons behind our conditioning: Yes___No___
(c) I understand the reasons for our training schedule: Yes___ No___

If you would like, expand on your answers here:

_____
_____
_____
_____

II.   About the coaches:

(a) I understand the function of each coach, head coach, and assistants: Yes___ No___

If no, what in particular do you not know?

_____
_____
_____
_____

(b) The things(s) I like best about the coaches are: _____
(1) _____
(2) _____
(3) _____
_____

(c) The thing(s) that concern(s) me most about the coaches are: _____
(1) _____
(2) _____
(3) _____

(continued)

Figure 8.2 Feedback sheet for sports teams (*continued*)

(d) I would like my *head* coach to be more _____

(e) I would like the *assistant* coaches _____
Name(s)

to be *more* _____

(f) I would like the head coach to be *less* _____

(g) I would like the assistant coaches _____
Name(s)

to be *less* _____

III. About you—the athlete:

(a) I am coached fairly: Yes___ No___

(b) The coaches like me: Yes___ No___

(c) Generally, I like the coaches: Yes___ No___

(d) My performance has improved due to my relationship with the coach: Yes___ No___

(e) I am now playing the best I can: Yes___ No___

If you have answered "no" to any of these questions, please include additional comments here:

_____
_____
_____

If you were coaching you, what would you do differently than the way you are now being coached? That is, how would you coach you?_____

_____

Any other comments?_____

_____
_____
_____

Thanks for taking the time to help create a
championship team.

- Allowing players a chance to vent their feelings instead of keeping them inside, which could interfere with concentration and mental preparation for competition
- Having an instrument that allows for anonymity so that the athlete can communicate feelings openly and honestly without fear of retribution
- Giving the coach a chance to ask athletes questions in a nonthreatening manner without the potential of intimidation from the coach's presence
- Allowing for the fact that some athletes prefer, and may be more effective in, writing rather than verbalizing their thoughts. The chance to write down one's feelings allows time for reflection and eliminates the possible inhibiting influence of trying to communicate sincere feelings nervously in the presence of another person.

SUMMARY

The amount of information and number of suggestions contained in this chapter may seem to be overwhelming. Coaches may feel justified in concluding that "I just want to be myself and forget this 'stuff' about how to talk to athletes." Others might say that they have coached a long time without resorting to psychological techniques and still have been quite successful. It is not suggested that coaches should dismiss their present modes and styles of communication and switch to a new set of behaviors. Instead, the content of this chapter offers the team leader a chance to examine the emotional impact that he or she has on athletes. These insights can help make the coach more successful. Developing new communication strategies could mean the difference between success and failure to a team or to a particular athlete.

Questions that coaches might want to ask are whether their use of certain words or emotions are effective in helping the athlete succeed or whether they are actually inhibiting the athlete from performing at peak levels. They might also consider whether their intentions are being perceived accurately, whether something about their demeanor fosters or inhibits open dialogue with team members, whether conversations with players and assistants easily turn into arguments, and whether they usually force their point of view on others without hearing the other side. Do players or assistants take advantage of their coach, or do they tend to avoid confrontations at all costs? The answers to these questions, and others, will help coaches take a close look—perhaps for the first time—at how they are perceived by others, which in turn will help point out areas for further personal growth.

Effective communication is a difficult assignment. It's an art to translate thoughts and feelings into words and actions. And it's virtually impossible to fake being a sensitive human being. Communication also involves effectively using certain techniques that meet the speaker's objectives in affecting the listener. Coaches cannot affect the thoughts, feelings, and actions of athletes and other team personnel unless they are aware of the manner in which they communicate information — verbally and nonverbally.

This chapter includes ten guidelines, or "commandments," that are very important to being an effective communicator — in sport and elsewhere. These include being honest, consistent, empathetic, and consistent with all team members, using positive nonverbal cues, teaching skills, praising and criticizing behavior and not personality, expressing feelings constructively, not being defensive, and avoiding sarcasm. The chapter also offers guidelines for athletes to use when communicating with their coach, verbally and in written form. In fact, coaches are urged to consider providing players and coaching assistants with an opportunity to express their views in writing in addition to face-to-face discussion.

———

REVIEW QUESTIONS

1.   Write down the three parts of the sandwich approach to effective communication and corrective feedback. Provide an example of a situation in which you would apply it.

2.   In this chapter, honesty, loyalty, and credibility are three of the most important characteristics that coaches should possess if they want to be effective motivators, educators, and communicators. Describe three behaviors of the coach that help to promote these traits and three behaviors that diminish or eliminate each of these traits.

3.   As a coach, how would you respond to an athlete who approaches you and expresses his or her negative feelings about not playing? He or she is certain that the teammate who plays his or her position is inferior. What strategies can a coach employ that would help to prevent the athlete from feeling this way in the first place? Remember to use some of the ten commandments.

4.   Interpret and apply this thought in the use of effective communication between coach and athlete: "A coach should always treat athletes as though they were the voters and the coach a candidate."

5.   Write a dialogue between coach and athlete that illustrates the coach's use of active listening.

6.   Describe the strategies an athlete might use in speaking with the coach privately.

References

Anshel, M. H. 1987. Ten commandments for effective communication. *Fundamentals of coaching and understanding sport*. Ottawa, Ontario: Coaching Association of Canada.

Ginott, H. 1965. *Between parent and child*. New York: Avon.

Ginott, H. 1969. *Between parent and teenager*. New York: Avon.

Ginott, H. 1972. *Teacher and child*. New York: Avon.

Martens, R., R. W. Christina, J. S. Harvey, and B. Sharkey. 1981. *Coaching young athletes*. Champaign, IL: Human Kinetics.

Mechikoff, R. A., and B. Kozar. 1983. *Sport psychology: The coach's perspective*. Springfield, IL: Thomas.

Miller, T. W. 1982. Assertiveness training for coaches: The issue of healthy communication between coaches and players. *Journal of Sport Psychology* 4: 107–14.

Orlick, T. 1982. *In pursuit of excellence*. Champaign, IL: Human Kinetics.

Silva, J. M. September 1984. The status of sport psychology: A national survey of coaches. *Journal of Physical Education, Recreation, and Dance* 55: 46–49.

Smith, R. E., F. L. Smoll, and B. Curtis. 1977. Coaching roles and relationships. In *Youth Sports Guide for Parents and Coaches*, ed. J. R. Thomas. Reston, VA: AAHPERD Publications.

9

The Counseling Coach

The previous chapter, on communication techniques, was concerned with general guidelines to coaches for interacting with other coaches and members of the team, and to athletes for approaching the coach. The objective of chapter 8 was not so much to suggest how to talk to others but, rather, to alert team leaders about the effects of verbal and nonverbal messages, often communicated unconsciously, on the listener's feelings, attitudes, and behaviors in sport. This chapter goes a step further in the area of communication than most coaches care to venture. Here we examine the use of a more formal approach to verbal interaction with athletes—a discipline called counseling. Although this term might create some anxiety in many sport leaders who contend that they know very little about counseling others (perhaps just using the term *counseling* creates a sense of discomfort), successful coaches counsel their players all the time, some more effectively than others. The objective of this chapter is to provide guidelines for the proper use of counseling techniques. After reading this chapter, the reader should acknowledge the importance of counseling between coach and athlete, and be able to apply fundamental principles of counseling strategies with players and coaching assistants on an individual and a group basis.

Perhaps some readers will conclude that counseling is not the coach's job. Should coaches offer counsel to their players? Shouldn't the role of counseling athletes be given to a professional? Doesn't a person have to be licensed to conduct counseling sessions? And should coaches delve into an area in which they are uncomfortable or have not been trained? Coaches are in a unique position to use counseling techniques. But some coaches are more willing to, and capable of, verbally interacting with their athletes regularly on personal issues than others. In fact, however, successful sport leaders "counsel" athletes regularly. They offer guidance to the players about making personal decisions related and unrelated to the team, they listen to personal problems, and they offer advice on alternatives from which the athletes may choose. Understanding the definition of counseling may clarify the coach's role of counseling in sport. This chapter also offers guidelines about applying fundamental counseling skills and about knowing when to refer an athlete for professional counseling.

WHAT IS COUNSELING?

Counseling is concerned with helping normal people to cope with normal problems and opportunities. It's a process — which is sometimes long term — that involves responding to the attitudes, feelings, and behaviors of each client. Also integral to the counseling process is the acceptance of the client's perceptions and feelings without personal prejudice and outside evaluation standards (Hackney and Nye 1973). This means that if the coach and athlete engage in an open, honest, and meaningful dialogue, the coach must accept the athlete's feelings ("I'm the best") and perceptions ("The coach doesn't like me") as real rather than denying that the athlete's feelings are legitimate ("You can't feel that way").

Coaches may be better counselors than they think, even without professional training. Counseling is similar to interviewing, and coaches interview players (and assistant coaches) all the time. Tasks of the counselor include (1) gathering information, which requires good listening skills, (2) helping the athlete to solve problems by looking at alternative approaches and solutions to issues, and (3) giving information or advice. Counseling about problems such as drug abuse, academic studies, and quitting school might necessitate referral to professional counseling services and staff, depending on the severity of the problem and the type of relationship between the coach and the athlete. Issues in which the coach needs to become involved are usually related to the athlete's participation on the team. However, topics unrelated to athletics such as grades, social life, and family concerns are certainly feasible — and sometimes necessary — for discussion.

Examples of topics with which athletes commonly confront the coach include: "I'm playing up to my potential"; "What should my goals be?"; "Will I ever get a chance to play?"; "I'm getting burned out"; "I've lost my confidence"; "I don't have any energy on the field (or court)"; "The players don't like me"; "I want to quit the team"; and "I broke up with my girlfriend (or boyfriend)."

When dealing with these issues, the counseling coach must honor the confidentiality and privacy of the client. Counseling sessions should never be conducted in public or in the presence of others.

If the focus of counseling is to make a change, however minor, then the process must be voluntary. The person must be willing to engage in meaningful dialogue — disclosing feelings, listening to feedback, and if necessary, making a commitment to change. For example, if a player is not performing up to the coach's (or his or her own) expectations, the coach may want to communicate his or her observations and concerns, and discuss some of the possible causes of the athlete's poor showing. The client must be prepared to listen and to act on this information.

Counseling is sometimes risky, especially for athletes, for two reasons. First, it requires one to expose deep-rooted, private attitudes that may be held against one. For instance, an athlete may feel that disclosing negative feelings may result in a nonplaying status or even dismissal from the team. Athletes need to feel secure about the benefits and outcomes of "opening up" with the coach prior to risking self-disclosure. The second risk lies in comparing one's own perceptions of a situation with another's views. For example, if an athlete is highly anxious and frustrated over his or her lack of playing time, the coach might feel compelled to be candid about the player's lack of necessary skills to start. The coach's role is to help players to feel secure about disclosing personal feelings and perceptions. Such disclosures may benefit the athlete emotionally and may lead to improved performance.

THE NEED TO COUNSEL ATHLETES

Although it is commonly called "a game," participation in organized competitive sport is stress inducing. In school situations, for example, athletes are asked to follow training and practice schedules that reduce time for academic studies. Despite the long hours of practice and other tasks for game preparation, athletes are required to maintain an acceptable scholastic record. Traveling exacerbates the problem.

Athletes need assistance in the areas of time management and study skills. Many athletes do not graduate from college because they have not been trained to manage the time restraints placed on them when they arrive on campus, and given the time for study, relatively few athletes have developed proper study skills (Lanning 1982). These problems often result in either lacking concentration in the sport or failing school grades. However, athletes care about their studies because being a sport participant in a school setting means maintaining academic standards. And sports participation is often the key to an athlete's self-image. Coaches should counsel athletes to help them to achieve academic as well as athletic success. The coach is certainly influential and empathetic about the daily pressures with which athletes are confronted.

The pressure to excel in sport and to live up to the expectations of others is often excessive. Playing first string, performing consistently at high levels, and, of course, winning are continuing sources of external pressure for the participants. Often the result is high anxiety, stress, and the tendency to prioritize sport before academic pursuits. Further, athletes set their own lofty, sometimes unrealistic, goals of playing professional sports. This is unfortunate because available data suggest that fulfilling the dream of competing as a professional athlete is quite rare.

For example, a report from the NCAA Intercollegiate Athletic, Physical Education, and Recreation *Progress of the Member Institutions*, Report No. 4 (1979), indicated that only 4.5 percent of high school football players will participate in college football, with only about 2 percent of those collegians going into professional ball. That means only about one of ten thousand high school football athletes realizes the dream of playing professionally. And if they get there, it likely won't be for long. The average career span for a player in the National Football League (NFL) is 4.5 years. Similar data are available in other sports. The need to prepare athletes academically and psychologically for a life that is independent of competitive sport participation is obvious. This is one of several reasons why coaches need to counsel their players.

THE NEED FOR TEAM COUNSELING

Winning is a team effort — and so is losing. If team members need to resolve issues among themselves, they will have less energy available for competition. Therefore, a positive group climate is essential to player satisfaction and, in many cases, to a favorable game outcome. Coaches, based on their observations, need to ask questions such as: Do the players on the team get along? Do some members isolate themselves from the others? Do players spend time with one another while away from team-related gatherings or tasks? Do arguments break out among teammates, particularly off the field or court? Is anyone deliberately ostracized by the others or teased (scapegoated) excessively? These are issues about which the coach should be aware despite occasional claims that "How the players get along off the field (or court) is their own business."

Is it important for coaches to be aware of each athlete's level of satisfaction? Absolutely, especially at nonprofessional levels! An unhappy player is an ineffective one. In visiting a women's collegiate volleyball team as a consultant, I recall the anxiety of one player who felt that she was being ignored by the team's setter. She lamented that this player rarely passed the ball to her. She felt that her teammate disliked her because of her poor ability. This perception was affecting her incentive and performance. When I raised this issue privately with the setter, I quickly learned that personal feelings had nothing to do with her strategy. Instead, I discovered that the net player was left-handed, forcing a spike at an awkward angle. The insulted player's feelings quickly dissipated when she learned of the setter's perceptions. She then positioned herself differently, which, in turn, resulted in more passes and an improved frame of mind. The important issue was not so much the correctness of the setter's explanation but, rather, the debilitating effects of the net player's feelings on her motivation and performance, which were resolved with the explanation.

Team counseling is needed for other reasons in addition to responding to personal problems or problems with interpersonal relationships. Coaches agree that cohesiveness and high morale are characteristics of a team that improve performance. For players to feel high group satisfaction and to mutually support one another is desirable. When cohesiveness and morale are not at preferred levels, counseling with all or part of the team to gain insight into the issues that cause team dissension is in order. Coaches cannot dictate heightened cohesion and morale. Although some coaches may try to mask the actual lack of satisfaction with shouting and speech making, the athletes' attitudes cannot be faked. Positive team outcomes will likely be minimal. The primary objective of team counseling, then, is to facilitate player discussion on an individual or group basis to solve problems or to confront and deal with issues.

FUNDAMENTAL COUNSELING SKILLS FOR THE COACH

People need not be licensed counselors to be effective in helping other people. Bartenders, hairstylists, and yes, coaches — people who are often in a position to hear the concerns and feelings of others — can be quite effective in the role of confidant. How is this possible without proper training? The untrained "counselor" can be effective if he or she has the ability to (1) listen, (2) show concern, (3) be supportive, (4) be honest, and (5) keep conversations private and confidential.

Listening

Professional counselors call listening *attending behaviors,* comprising several techniques to facilitate the client's need to talk. This is probably the most critical aspect of the counseling process (Ivey 1983). The basic approach for the nonprofessional is to sit back and listen — attentively.

Well, wait a minute. There's listening, and then there's *active listening.* Think about the mannerisms of people when they really care about what a person is saying as opposed to when they don't really care. People are quite effective at communicating interest or disinterest, empathy or apathy, sensitivity or insensitivity, trust or distrust. Effective coaches are active listeners. They (1) maintain constant — or at least frequent — eye contact, (2) face the speaker squarely with a slight forward trunk lean, (3) use encouraging gestures (such as nodding) or a reassuring "hum-mm" once in a while, (4) avoid distracting movements like manipulating an object or doodling on paper, giving full attention to the athlete, (5) avoid cutting off the speaker in midsentence or midthought, allowing the person to continue expressing his or her feelings, and (6) are nonjudgmental in response to the player's comments, at least initially.

Showing Concern

A coach must take the performer's feelings seriously regardless of any discrepancy between the coach's and the athlete's perceptions of the situation. If the athlete feels that the issue is serious, then it is serious, no matter what anyone else thinks. Responses that incorrectly minimize the importance of the other person's feelings include "Don't give me that," "How can you think that?" and "It's your own fault, now get yourself out of it." These statements show a lack of concern toward the athlete's problems, exactly opposite to the player's needs at this time. Whether or not the athlete is, indeed, at "fault" — we seem to be obsessed with pitting blame — coaches who ignore or do not show sincere concern about helping the player cannot expect to receive the athlete's loyalty. And disloyal players do not tend to contribute to the team effort.

Being Supportive

Whereas showing concern is a part of the listening phase of communication, giving support is the response phase. It doesn't take a degree in counseling to show empathy and understanding toward the player's feelings or situation, and that's exactly what is meant by "being supportive." It's fine to disagree with the athlete's point of view on a matter, but don't make him or her feel inadequate as a person for having a different perception or opinion. "I disagree with you about that" is more constructive than "You don't know what you're talking about." Support means "I understand" and "Let's try to work things out so that the situation is resolved." Support can also mean helping the athlete to "face facts."

Being Honest

Was it the player's fault that the defensive unit surrendered so many points and responded incorrectly to the opponent's offense? Were the communication between coach and athlete and the selection of strategies during game preparation accurate? In other words, is it fair to "fault" (there's that word again) the athlete for the contest's outcome? Could the coach have made an error in judgment that contributed to the outcome? The coach should try to assess these issues honestly. What about making promises to athletes? The counseling coach must have credibility and the trust of players; therefore, he or she *must* keep promises made.

Respecting Privacy

Conversations between the parties in counseling should invariably be without the presence of an audience. If an athlete comes into the office for a discussion and the coach fails to provide an environment that is free of interruptions and other listeners, the message is "What you have to say isn't important." It also indicates a lack of respect for the player's integrity, as though he or she were not important enough to warrant a private atmosphere. Where is the trust — or the respect? Eventually, the coach will be asking, "Where is the athlete?"

Maintaining Confidentiality

An important role of the counseling coach is the role of *confidant*. Keeping the coach-athlete interaction confidential is a cardinal rule of honest communication unless the issue requires including others to reach a solution. The athlete opens up to the coach with a feeling of trust and security. Once that trust is breached, it is almost never regained. Conversations should be based on the understanding that issues, agreements, and feelings are held in confidence between the two parties unless otherwise agreed upon in advance. "When will I get a chance to play?" might require speaking with an assistant coach who has more insight into the player's progress before an answer is offered. A player's complaint that "Susan never speaks to me off the court" might require a private discussion with Susan to ascertain her feelings toward the offended player.

When you think about it, the communication skills of listening, showing concern, being supportive and honest, and offering a sense of privacy and confidentiality are, for many people, very natural — almost common sense. Yet these are the most fundamental aspects of counseling. Everything beyond this point is simply a matter of additional sophistication in helping the client (athlete) to make the right choices in resolving problems or concerns (not every concern is a problem). We now turn to the development of these additional skills.

THE MICROSKILLS APPROACH TO COUNSELING

Identifying and selecting specific skills for use in counseling is called the *microskills approach* (Ivey and Simek-Downing 1980). Effective counseling requires using certain techniques that lie within broader types of skills. These broader skills are attending behaviors (listening) and influencing behaviors (speaking).

Attending behaviors involve three dimensions: (1) eye contact, (2) appropriate body language, and (3) verbal following. *Influencing behaviors* involve the coach in causing growth or change in the athlete. The coach needs to do more than listen and offer brief verbal exchanges if he or she wishes to influence a change in the player's behavior. At times, the coach will need to actively direct the interview process.

Attending-Behavior Strategies

Not every coach is comfortable with the task of discussing another person's feelings, or with discussing his or her own. Coaches who want to have nothing to do with counseling athletes in any form — those who resist listening and verbally responding to athletes' feelings — should avoid this role completely. Don't fake it. Athletes can clearly tell when a person is insincere, uncaring, or uncomfortable with the situation. However, it is very important that another responsible adult (an assistant coach, for instance) maintain this role. Athletes need someone with whom they can talk who is in an influential position with the team.

One head coach of a university women's basketball team evenly divides the team of twelve players into three groups. Then he and two assistant coaches meet privately with each athlete several times before, during, and after the season. They rotate these subgroups on three occasions so that each coach eventually meets with all the players. They discuss performance goals; exchange views about the player's role on the team; offer feedback on athletic performance, academic performance, and potential concerns in these areas; and engage in verbal exchanges on personal and social topics (e.g., relationships, goals, and family matters). The players also have the opportunity to offer their views about the team, teammates, and coaching behaviors and decisions. All information is respected, open for discussion, and held confidential. The players are convinced that they are respected by the staff and that they are perceived as students and adults in addition to their athletic roles and responsibilities.

Some individuals in positions of authority (such as supervisors, managers, school principals, teachers, and coaches) unknowingly "turn off" others. They appear to be unapproachable, demanding, condescending, overpowering, or insensitive. Often, these individuals do not realize the effects that they have on others. In coaching, the problem with this type of attending behavior is that it provokes a state of underarousal and decreased motivation. In discussing types of counselor behaviors, Hackney and Nye (1973) use three categories of erroneous communication patterns: (1) underparticipation, (2) overparticipation, and (3) distracting participation.

Underparticipators have the image of incompetence or insecurity or both. They convey to the client an unwillingness or an inability to offer assistance. In a sport setting, this lessens the player's faith in the coach. The typical underlying cause of underparticipation may be the coach's fear of involvement either with the player or a particular topic. The counselor withdraws in both verbal and nonverbal directions. Nonverbal examples include (1) appearing stiff with little body movement, (2) positioning the body away from the player, (3) directing the eyes downward and avoiding eye contact, (4) maintaining a stooped-shoulder position with frequent shrugging of shoulders during the conversation, and (5) using a very soft, weak tone of voice (responses sometimes trail off into silence).

Overparticipators may be covering up their anxiety as evident in the person who always has to be the center of attention and who is constantly talking or clowning. Typically, this is descriptive of an insecure person who's afraid to lose control of the environment and who desperately needs attention to reinforce his or her self-worth and to overcome self-doubts. Overparticipating is a way of exerting control, which, in turn, reduces anxiety.

Coaches who overparticipate usually confront the athlete and jump to conclusions with little awareness of the player's feelings. Examples of nonverbal traits include creating much body movement, gesturing frequently, or fidgeting and talking in a very animated and expressive manner, often to the point of being distracting. Verbal features are exhibited when the coach talks almost nonstop, includes much repetition and detail in his or her speech, talks far more than the athlete, and speaks rapidly and loudly.

The *distracting participator* overresponds to irrelevant issues, sometimes with loud (nervous) laughter. At times, the issues may never be addressed because the conversation becomes bogged down in trivia. Coaches should not carry on and on about the weather, who's going to win the pennant, and other trivia. Use only the first minute or so to get comfortable and exchange pleasant comments. This tends to reduce nervousness and defensiveness. Then, address the "gut" issues.

A second technique of the distracting participator is to shift topics hastily before the primary issue has been resolved or at least dealt with at length. A frequent change in topics tells the player that the main issue is either not being taken seriously by the coach or has not been adequately communicated. The counseling coach should get to the "nitty-gritty" and stay with the topic until a sense of closure is reached.

Coaches want to be approachable so that they can favorably affect the emotions and actions of athletes. To foster openness and honesty, effective coaches use some of the following strategies:

- *Facial animation.* Show interest and active mental involvement in the conversation through facial expressions.
- *Good eye contact.* Avoiding eye-to-eye contact and glancing everywhere but at the athlete shows disinterest, a lack of seriousness or sincerity, or low self-confidence.
- *Occasional head nodding.* This is used effectively to reinforce the

player's commitment to talk. It also shows that the coach is interested in the topic.

- *Soft, firm tone of voice.* Effective communicators avoid appearing defensive and, instead, remain in control and relaxed, which fosters honesty and communication.

- *Occasional smiling.* This relaxes the athlete and makes the coach appear compassionate, understanding, and "human."

- *Occasional gesturing with hands.* This helps the speaker to make a point and maintains the listener's attention.

- *Moderate rate of speech.* This prevents the listener from "tuning out" the speaker and facilitates getting the message across.

- *Occasional use of minimal verbal reinforcers.* A brief "hum-mm" or "interesting" fosters continued conversation and informs the speaker (athlete) that his or her message is being heard. It can also indicate agreement with the message.

The following is an example of proper attending skills:

Athlete: Coach, I don't feel I'm getting a fair shake with my lack of playing time.

Coach: *(Option 1)* Tell me about it.
               (Option 2) Could you tell me a little more about exactly what you feel is unfair?
               (Option 3) I can understand how you feel. Let's discuss what it will take to play more often.
               (Option 4) I've definitely noticed improvement in your skills. It's easy to see why you're frustrated.

The key element here is to address the player's feelings immediately. Athletes need to feel that the coach is listening and taking their feelings seriously. Here are a few examples of how *not* to respond.

Athlete: Coach, I'm really falling behind in my school work. It seems that the hours of practice time are making it difficult to keep up. Any suggestions?

Coach: *(Inappropriate response 1)* Tell me your favorite subject.
               (Inappropriate response 2) It doesn't look like you're any better at school than at remembering the plays.
               (Inappropriate response 3) Go ahead, quit the team.

In these examples, the athlete's feelings are not being taken seriously. And the real issue of schoolwork is not being addressed. The player is not saying that he wants to quit the team, only that he is worried about the effect of participating with the team on his grades. He needs help finding an alternative to quitting.

Proper Strategies for Influencing Behavior

Listening and verbally reacting are important. But what affect will these strategies have on the athlete's behavior? Influencing behavior is a function of the coach's making the "right" verbal responses. The counseling skill that will be discussed in this section is called *responding* (Carkhuff 1980). There are two types of responding: (1) responding to content and (2) responding to feelings.

Responding to content. What is the athlete saying? What is his or her message? Responding to content means that the coach communicates his or her understanding of the athlete's experience. It involves imagining another person's world as though the coach were the player. Coaches can best facilitate this empathetic understanding by encouraging the player to be specific about experiences or feelings, and by not indicating (the coach's) personal attitudes to the player — at least not for the time being. Athletes should feel that they can explore their feelings without fear of retaliation. For example, if a player remarks, "Coach, running wind sprints is a waste of time," the coach can respond, "Those wind sprints can be tough, no doubt about it. The reason we do them is. . . ." An inappropriate response would be: "Do them or leave the team" or "You don't know what you're talking about."

Responding to content also involves the coach's ability to show the player that he or she understands the player's situation or feelings. This is done by carefully listening to the details presented by the athlete and rephrasing the player's expression in a fresh way. Rather than "parrot" back the player's own words, respond with, "What I hear you saying is. . . ." or "In other words. . . ." For example:

> *Athlete*:   Coach, I'm really upset about being replaced in the second half just because I fumbled the ball one time in the second quarter. I thought I was playing really well, and I had a good week of practice. Then, all of a sudden, I'm on the bench because I made one mistake.

> *Coach*:   You're obviously upset and disappointed that you didn't play the whole game, especially after the fumble. And you feel that fumbling the ball was the reason you were taken out. I can understand your feelings. I'd feel uptight too in the same situation.

Responding to feelings. Athletes may express their feelings directly through their choice of words or indirectly by tone of voice, by describing a situation without stating their feelings, or by facial and body gestures. When a player says, "Hey, Coach, you wouldn't believe how tough my math course is," he or she is really asking for assistance. Perhaps the person needs tutoring in this subject. Athletes who walk in a dejected manner with head down or who isolate themselves from others after being taken out of the contest might also be making a strong, nonverbal statement about their feelings of disappointment. Whatever the form of expression, the coach's role is to respond to the speaker's underlying feelings.

The following true story actually occurs with some frequency. At the first practice, one athlete was particularly vocal about how easy it is to play the game and to perform a particular sport skill. The youngster was "mouthing off" (bragging) before he even took the field. "Eh, this is easy," the youngster said. "I already know how to catch a fly ball." Which of the following responses should the coach make?

1. "Oh, yeah? You think you're better than everyone else, big shot? Let's see you try to catch a few of these." (Coach then hits a long, towering fly ball to the player, who naturally doesn't come close to catching it.)
2. "You're no better than anyone else. Everyone does what I say. I'm the coach."
3. "I'm sure you can do a fine job. Some of us have more experience than others, but we all want to improve on what we can already do. Even the major leaguers practice daily. So, let's all practice catching a few fly balls."
4. "Good for you. A real major leaguer, eh? Why don't you go out there and show us just how good you are."

The third response is the correct one. Many coaches become upset when a player claims to "know it all," without realizing that the bragging player is often masking low self-confidence. What is important is listening to what the athlete is *not* saying. What he is not saying is, "If I boast and show how confident I am, maybe I don't have to prove it on the field because I'm scared to show my lack of skill to the others."

And what about the athlete who *can* play as well as she says but enjoys boasting? This youngster — and sometimes adults do the same thing — lacks general self-confidence and may not feel secure about her ability to make friends. Her approach to gaining respect from peers is to show off and demonstrate superior skills. Again, this person lacks a sense of security and needs to know that she will be accepted regardless of her skill level. And what about the coach's reaction? Criticizing the person only reinforces a low self-image. Instead, let the player know that good skills are evident and that she need not advertise them. Also, tell her, privately, that her bragging disturbs others and may prevent her from forming close friendships.

COUNSELING TECHNIQUES FOR THE
COACH-ATHLETE INTERVIEW

Ivey (1983) suggests that counselors use three strategies to help clients. Each is applicable to the counseling coach in sport. He suggests (1) asking the right questions, (2) confronting, and (3) summarizing.

Asking the Right Questions

Effective questioning techniques encourage the client to talk more freely and openly. Questions serve various purposes. They can:

- Help to begin the interview ("What would you like to discuss today?" or "How have things been going since we last spoke?").
- Help the player to elaborate on issues ("Could you tell me more about that?" or "How did you feel when one of the other players criticized you?").
- Help to bring out concrete examples about the player's feelings ("Could you give me a specific example of what I did that upset you?" or "What do you mean when you say our team meetings depress you?").
- Provide a diagnosis and assessment of a problem. The coach might ask: Who is responsible for these feelings? What is the player's concern and the specific details of the situation? When does the problem come up? When did it begin? Where does the problem occur? On the field? In the dormitory? At home with mom and dad? How do you (the athlete) react to the problem? How do you (the player) feel about the issue? Why does the problem occur? Are you (the player) doing something — intentionally or unintentionally — that is provoking the issue?

Different types of questions each have their own purpose. Used harmoniously, the different types of questions open new areas for discussion, assist in pinpointing and clarifying issues, and aid in the player's ability to self-explore feelings, attitudes, and behaviors (Ivey 1983). The important point is to ask questions selectively and in a nonthreatening manner. There are two types of questions, open and closed.

Open questions are those that can't be answered in just a few words, whereas closed questions require a relatively short response. Typically, open questions begin with *what, how, why*, or *could*. For example, "Could you tell me why you didn't bunt after I gave the bunt signal?" Such questions encourage others to talk. *Closed questions* often begin with *is, are*, or *do*. An example is, "Do you expect a passing grade in all of your courses?" The advantage of a closed question is that it focuses the interview and elicits specific information from the client.

In the following examples of closed questions, the coach is asking for specific information. This approach is used when there is no time to get into long discussions.

Coach:	Hi, Sue. Is your injured knee feeling better today?
Athlete:	Well, it still bothers me. Seems that it gets inflamed after a few minutes of running.
Coach:	Is the trainer aware of your discomfort?
Athlete:	Oh, sure. I still see him for daily treatments.
Coach:	Do you think you can practice with it?
Athlete:	As of now, I might have to wait a day or two until the swelling goes down a bit. I can't seem to put too much pressure on it for more than a few minutes.
Coach:	I'm sure it's best not to take a chance. I'll get a report on it from the trainer this afternoon. In the meantime, do you think you can attend and observe practice, or should you stay off the leg completely?
Athlete:	Even if I'm walking with a cane, Coach, I'll be there.
Coach:	That's great! Hang in there.

Now, let's take a look at the open-question technique with the same situation. Notice that the athlete is asked to express her feelings no matter which direction they take. There is also no time urgency; sufficient time is allowed for interacting with the player even though the topic is specific and answers are needed.

Coach:	Hi, Sue. How's your injured knee today?
Athlete:	Well, coach, it's still a little tender. Seems to swell up on me after a few minutes of running.
Coach:	How does it feel when you're not playing and just walking around on it?
Athlete:	Not too bad. As long as I don't put too much pressure on it.
Coach:	Our next game is in two days. What is your feeling about playing if we maintain treatment and the trainer says it's OK?
Athlete:	I'll sure give it a try. In the meantime, I'll rest it until practice and continue to see the trainer for therapy.
Coach:	That's all either one of us can ask. We'll just take it one day at a time. Don't get too discouraged. No use in taking a risk. Just give it your best shot.

Questioning strategies, like all techniques, have certain limitations, especially when used by an untrained counselor. The following problems should be avoided:

- *Posing multiple questions.* The coach may confuse the athlete by tossing out several questions at once.

- *Bombarding or grilling.* Too many questions tend to put the athlete on the defensive. And some individuals might feel an invasion of privacy.

- *Asking questions as statements.* For example, "Don't you think your contribution to the team would be more helpful if you remembered your assignment?" (could be viewed as either sarcastic or condescending). Or, "What do you think of using imagery techniques every night?" (traps the athlete because it is a suggestion cloaked in question form). As Ivey (1983, p. 47) suggests, "If you are going to make a statement, it is best not to frame it as a question."

- *Asking "why" questions more often than necessary.* These questions often put people on the defensive, sometimes producing the feeling of being grilled or trapped.

- *Rapid-fire questioning.* This leads to distrust of the questioner because the person doesn't seem really interested in the answers.

Confrontation

What should the coach do when an athlete offers mixed messages, discrepancies, untruths, or is simply not making sense? Should the player be labeled a liar? Should the "truth" be communicated in no uncertain terms with crude candor such as, "You're not starting, Bob, because you don't have very good skills. You might as well know the truth." Instead, a very powerful tool called *confrontation* might be used very carefully and sensitively. It is a technique that allows the client to understand the issues more clearly without feeling undue stress, guilt, and inadequacy. That's right, confrontation is *not* a "street fight."

Confrontation involves three steps. First, the athlete's mixed messages, lies, and incongruities have to be identified by the coach. Second, the player's messages must be pointed out clearly to him or her. Third, the coach and athlete must jointly work through the issues to a constructive conclusion. No one should leave the coach's office in tears, in anger, or in frustration. Effective confrontation includes the use of questioning, reflective listening, and feedback.

Identifying incongruities and mixed messages. When athletes behave in a manner that is inconsistent with what they say, then incongruent, contradictory, and mixed messages are being conveyed. How to identify the incongruity is the trick. Here's an example:

Athlete: Coach, I think I should get more playing time.
Coach: Could you tell me why you think so?

Athlete: I've been on the team longer than Jeff who's starting, and quite honestly, I think I can do a better job. I even know the plays better than he does.

Coach: Bill, do you think your feeling of having more talent and the desire to play more is consistent with the number of times you've arrived late to practice, run at half-speed during wind sprints, and failed to cheer on your teammates during games? How do these habits square with deserving to play more? Where's the dedication?

Athlete: OK, Coach. I hear what you're saying. I'll show you a different approach in the future.

In this contrived example, the obvious inconsistency was between the athlete's feelings versus his behaviors, which the coach was compelled to point out — quickly. There was no attempt to tell the athlete that he was a bad person, a poor performer, or wrong. The coach merely pointed out discrepancies between the athlete's wishes and his behaviors. Other ways in which a person can display incongruities and inconsistencies include these examples:

- *Between two statements*. An athlete might say at one point how much he or she supports the team, yet indicate later that reaching his or her own personal goals is most important. For example, "I'll do whatever it takes to help this team to win. But I want to keep up my scoring average."

- *Between what one says and what one does*. An athlete may voice full loyalty to the coach yet miss team meetings, clown around at inappropriate times, or not make the effort to support his or her teammates.

- *Between statements and nonverbal behaviors*. A player might claim to be motivated and excited at some point before the game but act withdrawn (not maintaining eye contact when communicating this "excitement") and show nervousness and tension. In another example, some coaches may talk to their players about the importance of having fun when they compete. However, they do so in a loud and serious tone of voice without smiling. The message and the manner in which it is communicated are not consistent.

- *Between two nonverbal behaviors*. The athlete may be breaking out in a nervous sweat or looking pale while smiling or telling the coach that everything feels fine when he or she is in pain.

- *Between statements and the context*. A player may claim that he or she will be the game hero when, in fact, the player may have neither the skill nor the playing opportunity to live up to this expectation. Or a team may feel confident of victory prior to playing a far superior opponent. This is not to suggest that the team should not show up at the game. But having unrealistically high expectations could augment the disappointment of losing.

- *Between statements in different contexts.* The coach may say positive things to a player but then make negative statements to others about the same player.

Techniques for Confrontation

How should the coach handle the apparent discrepancy between fact and fiction? The most blunt technique is to simply tell the athlete about the difference in perception between the parties. A more sophisticated approach would be to follow these four steps:

1.   Identify the incongruity clearly by leading the athlete to self-confrontation. "You say you want 'this,' but you're doing 'that.' How do you match what you say with what you're actually doing?"

2.   With the use of questioning skills, draw out the specifics of the conflict. Give attention to each segment of the mixed message without appearing judgmental. Aim for facts. "OK, John, you say you never forget your field assignment. Let's review what happened on the touchdown they scored in the last quarter last week." The counselor would then ask one or more of the following questions to gather information, establish facts, and clarify perceptions, not to instill guilt and cause embarrassment (the athlete must not be "grilled" as though a crime had been committed; tone of voice should be low-key and nonthreatening):

     "Where were you lined up?" "What formation were they using on the touchdown play?" "Where are you supposed to go on this play?" "Where did the film indicate that you went?" "Were you playing the correct man?"

3.   Periodically summarize the different dimensions of the discrepancy. For instance, you can say, "On the one hand . . .but on the other hand . . . ." Then add, "How does that sound to you? Am I on target? What would you think?"

4.   The coach may want to provide feedback with his or her opinions and observations about the discrepancies. Here's an example:

     Janice, it is becoming increasingly difficult for me to believe that you really want to play volleyball, given the way you're going about preparing for the game. When I speak to the team, your eyes start to wander and you appear to be bored. At least that's my perception. For example, I asked each player to submit to me suggestions for making practice more exciting, and I received nothing from you. The message I get from you is that you don't want to be here. If I'm wrong, then help me to be a better coach by understanding the meaning of your actions. Nothing would make me happier than to help you out because I think you can contribute to this team, but only if you want to be here.

In this example, the coach is fostering decision-making by the player whether or not she stays with the team. But most importantly, the athlete is being confronted with the realities of her behavior. The coach is risking losing this player by going into an area that raises serious questions about the player's willingness to be there. The door is now left open for her to leave the team. But, if she does, she has probably wanted to leave for quite some time.

Summarization

The technique of gathering together the client's words, behaviors, and feelings, and then presenting them to the client in outline form is called *summarization*. Its purpose is to review the significant content of the conversation, to clarify the issues, and to agree on the athlete's message—before the coach responds. Summarizing is similar to paraphrasing but covers a longer time span and more information. Whereas a paraphrase might reflect a sentence or a few minutes of conversation, summarizations might be used to begin or end a complete interview, to act as a transition into a new topic, or to clarify lengthy and complex client issues.

Summarizing techniques can be used at the beginning, middle, and conclusion of the interview. Here are some examples:

Beginning a session. "Let's see, last time we talked about your feelings of not caring about school and not knowing what you wanted to do in your professional career. You were even afraid of flunking off the team. Your grades were not good, and you rarely felt like studying. However, you thought you might enjoy owning your own business if you didn't have to complete all of those college business courses and had the money to open up your own place. We discussed a plan of action to give you new insight into how to get you moving in the right direction, which we were going to discuss today. How did it go?"

Midway in the interview. "So far, it appears that the plan has not worked out too well. I commend you for following up on our agreement to speak to the job counselor and to find academic help with tutoring. But you still feel unmotivated in class and doubt your ability to graduate with a degree. I'll tell you one thing: The fact that you care enough to discuss it is half the battle. So things can't be all bad because it bothers you. That's a good sign. Let's discuss your conversation with the job counselor. How did it go?"

At the end of the session. "Let's summarize where we've come in this meeting. We've taken a look at some of the problems you've been having with schoolwork and your attitudes toward succeeding academically. We know that things have not been going well and that you're concerned about it — especially if it means not remaining eligible to stay on the team. We agreed that succeeding in school allows you to play sports and will help you to reach your goal of owning your own business. We also agreed that you're going to do three things in the coming week which should start things rolling in the right direction. You will. . . . When we meet again next week, we agreed to take a new look at the situation and perhaps decide if staying with the team is in your best interests. Is that right? Anything else?"

Review of Counseling Techniques

In the following verbal exchange, let's identify the strategies that have been discussed earlier.

(Athlete knocks on coach's door at appointed time.)

Coach:	Hi, Jim. Come in. (*Coach is smiling.*) Have a seat right here. I'm glad you could make it. How's the day going? (*Smiling reduces tension and potential defensiveness of player, relaxes atmosphere.*)
Athlete:	Pretty good, Coach. I'll be looking forward to the end of midterm exams.
Coach:	Those math courses are tough, no doubt about it. *(Use of empathy.)* How is school going in general? Are you pleased with the other courses? *(Use of open questions that show coach is interested in other aspects of Jim's life in addition to sport.)*
Athlete:	Pretty well. French is a bit tough, but I'm reading some neat stuff in English.
Coach:	Tell me, Jim, how are things going for you on the team, I mean from your point of view? *(Open question allows athlete opportunity to get into the topic at his own pace and depth. Coach avoids appearing defensive and uptight.)*
Athlete:	Well, to be perfectly honest, Coach, things aren't going too well, and that's why I'm here to see you. I'm down about not getting more playing time. In fact, I thought I'd be starting this year, and I haven't even played more than ten minutes in our first five games. It seems like I'm going nowhere. I know I can play better than Mike. I don't think I'm getting a fair

	chance. *(Coach nods, indicating his understanding of Jim's feelings.)*
Coach:	You're disappointed about not starting or at least playing more than you have, is that right? *(Coach paraphrases in reflecting player's feelings.)*
Athlete:	Right. I'm hustling in practice and not making many mistakes. I'm playing good defense and getting along with everybody on the team. Even the other players don't understand why I'm not playing.
Coach:	So, in your view, your ability should mean more playing time, and it's not fair that you're not starting or at least not playing more, right? *(Summarizing.)* I can understand your frustration. *(Empathy.)* I'd probably feel the same way if I were you. Let's take a few minutes and discuss your strengths as we both see them, the areas you can further improve upon *(notice the coach is not using the term "weakness")*, and what it will take to get you into the game more often. First, Jim, tell me about the areas in which you excel. What do you do well? *(The coach does not want to compare Jim's strengths with the other players. The main issue is Jim's desire to play, not defending or criticizing the other players.)*
Athlete:	Well, first of all, I can move well; I've got speed. Also, I move the ball well.
Coach:	So, speed of movement and dribbling skills top the list, right? *(Summarization.)*
Athlete:	Yeah. And I think my shot is pretty good, and it's getting better.
Coach:	Anything else you think you can improve upon? *(The coach takes Jim's cue about weak skill areas and pursues it without "announcing" this topic of discussion as a "weakness." It's a smooth transition to a difficult area where athletes tend to get defensive.)*
Athlete:	Well, as I said, my shot could be better. I think I'm hitting at about 48 percent. And, I wish I was taller. I'm a guard, but if I would grow a few more inches, I could snag a few more rebounds.
Coach:	Anything else? *(Athlete shakes his head.)* Could you comment about your assessment of playing defense? *(Coach is leading athlete into an area for further discussion. The athlete's recognition of his own*

weaknesses will greatly improve the coach's success at explaining decisions and will allow the athlete to make accurate judgments. When it comes to getting the athlete to list areas for improvement, only open questions will do.)

Athlete: No, I think that's it. Oh, I suppose I could guard my man a bit closer on defense sometimes, but usually I do a pretty good job.

Coach: Uh-huh. *(Nonverbal attending: supportive of athlete's answers.)* OK, now describe for me your opinion of an outstanding basketball player. What should a starting player be able to do consistently to be successful and help the team win? *(Coach is getting closer to confrontation between what the athlete says and what he actually does.)*

Athlete: You have to be able to shoot and score points. And you have to get the ball down court in a hurry and pass the ball, like on a fast break.

Coach: OK, so far you've said a good player has to dribble, pass, and shoot well. What else? *(Combination of summarization followed by an open question to facilitate discussion in the right direction; athlete is encouraged to be held accountable to his own set of desirable standards of a quality athlete rather than believing they are the coach's standards.)*

Athlete: He's got to get more than his share of rebounds.

Coach: So jumping high is important?

Athlete: Yes.

Coach: What about playing defense? Is it important for a starting player to guard his man closely? To prevent his opponent from getting off a good, clear shot? Occasionally to steal a pass? To keep himself between his opponent and the basket? *(Here the coach is asking closed questions to gain information quickly and accurately. A second objective here is to alert Jim to important basketball skills that he is not performing well.)*

Athlete: Yes, I'd say those things are important. I do those things.

Coach: Well, let's talk about it. *(To avoid a defensive posture, the coach does not deny the athlete's feelings by saying, "No, you don't." Instead, the issues are still open to discussion. But it appears clear that only confrontation will work in getting the athlete to see the problem.)* Let's evaluate your basketball skills based on what you and I agree is important in basketball and what you are and are not currently doing on the court. *(The coach plans to note the incongruity between what the athlete says is important as opposed to his actual performance.)*

The key strategies in dealing with Jim in this situation included (1) making the atmosphere pleasant (being warm and polite) and private (in the coach's office), (2) allowing the athlete to express his views without the coach interrupting and maintaining a defensive posture, (3) respecting the athlete's point of view (sensitivity to feelings) regardless of its accuracy, (4) asking open questions that allow the athlete to reflect on his own performance and to articulate good performance standards, and (5) respectfully pointing out the discrepancies between the athlete's and the coach's perceptions of the performer's actions on the court. The session should end on a hopeful note: thanking the athlete for coming in, offering sincere compliments on certain aspects of the athlete's performance, summarizing the issues that were discussed, and articulating the actions that are expected in the future to change the status quo. A conference between coach and athlete should have a sense of closure or accomplishment.

SHORT-TERM TEAM COUNSELING

A university football coach once told me that team meetings should never focus on the personal feelings of players because "it turns into a gripe session." In fact, this coach contends that when one player voices a complaint, the atmosphere snowballs into a widespread negative feeling on the team that did not exist before the meeting. In other words, he contends that complaints in groups have a bandwagon effect. Is this coach's view accurate? Do team meetings in which feelings and future team directions are discussed undermine team morale and cohesion? Are players more apt to complain in a team-meeting situation, and does vocalizing personal feelings — particularly if they are negative — fuel team dissent and reinforce unpleasant issues that may otherwise be left alone and accepted?

There is a school of thought in the coaching ranks that argues against player feedback, especially in groups, resulting in no "open" discussions between the team and its coach. It is the major premise of this section that group discussions about feelings of players (on various issues) are essential to team cohesion and morale. Team-related unresolved issues must surface and be confronted with the proper attention of all concerned parties. Otherwise, the athlete's full and proper attention and concentration will be diminished and redirected away from game preparation and skill development.

What Is Short-Term Team Counseling?

Sometimes a person will approach a friend who looks depressed or unhappy and ask, "Hey, what's wrong? Anything I can do to help?" Well, imagine asking a group of people the same thing. Team (group) counseling involves meeting in relatively small groups to share concerns; to explore common problems; to gain insight, knowledge, or understanding about issues; and to share these thoughts with each other (Grayson 1978). In addition, attempts are made to meet the objectives of the sessions in relatively short order so that issues can be quickly resolved and team members can give their proper concentration to preparing for the contest.

Team counseling does not involve addressing individual or personal issues, although exceptions to this rule exist. One exception is when a player is unable to establish a positive relationship with any other team member, an issue that affects the attitudes or performances of others. A second exception is when an issue concerns relatively few team members at which time it is better to interact in a small group or individually with the affected individuals. Drug abuse, academic problems, lack of social contacts, personal feelings of dissatisfaction, concerns about the team or coach, and questions about a player's role on the. team are all examples of items that do not belong on the team counseling agenda.

However, examples of issues that are open for discussion on a group basis might include the pervasive use of drugs by many team members, team rules and policies, choosing of team captains, widespread feelings of dissension, displeasure, lack of motivation (boredom), the team schedule, and concerns about other facets of the team affecting more than just a few team members. In short, group counseling, in addition to individual counseling, provides another vehicle for delivering help to athletes who need it. The trick of using team counseling as a constructive, rather than a destructive, tool is structuring the sessions so that issues are addressed positively (no shouting allowed) and are resolved to the satisfaction of all concerned.

Reaching the Goals
of Short-Term Team Counseling

Probably group counseling is most usefully applied in establishing and examining group values. Examples of group values include:

- Being supportive to all team members under all conditions (when winning, losing, making an error, playing well, and so on)

- Engaging in group prayer before and after every game
- Avoiding behaviors that could harm performance, such as smoking, drug ingestion, excessive alcohol, or late-night socializing
- Eliminating behaviors that might prove embarrassing to the team and school, such as reckless driving, improper social conduct, committing infractions of school rules, breaking the law, or cheating
- Maintaining sound study habits to achieve high academic grades
- Always giving it your best during the season
- Staying in good physical condition year-round

The coach's role is to work with team members to establish team values and to work toward translating the values into actions. As Grayson (1978, p. 9) suggests: "By helping them connect values with acts, and acts with outcomes, they are helped to learn to connect effects with causes—to learn that how they think and what they do are related to what has been happening to them." Coaches want their players to be held accountable—to take responsibility—for their actions. If this is to happen, the team and coach should jointly establish codes of proper conduct, standards by which all team members and coaches hold one another accountable. Thus, the process of team counseling aids in the development of standards and values that are more positive, effective, and acceptable to all parties.

The Atmosphere for Short-Term Counseling

If the purpose of having a team meeting is to share feelings, discuss concerns, offer opinions, and exchange information, then the participants must feel secure in the meeting environment. Having an open group dialogue means that the opinions of every group member must be accepted (not followed, necessarily, but at least tolerated and allowed to be communicated) without judgment, vindictiveness, and recrimination. For instance, if an athlete feels that there should be no curfew or bed checks, the opinion should be respected, dealt with, and resolved during the meeting. The player should not be criticized, nor should the recommendation be ignored. This is not to say that the team should have a role in making every team policy; the coach also has an obligation to set limits and rules that are nonnegotiable. But the feelings of the players need to be exposed, and concerns resolved. Sometimes the team should be informed about the reasons for a particular nonnegotiable policy.

Unless otherwise stated by the coach prior to the meeting, the purpose of a counseling session should be to share . . . to fulfill the athletes' needs to communicate feelings; perhaps to examine present team policies and strategies; and to entertain alternatives to the status quo. Another purpose of the session is to assist the coach in exposing and resolving issues that ultimately might be deleterious to team performance.

An example of a team counseling session in youth sports involved a player who was disliked by all of his teammates. Not only was this player, aged twelve, being unmercifully scapegoated, but other team members seemed to be giving more of their attention to criticizing and blaming him for the team's problems than to learning skills and improving their performance. The coach, noting the constant ridicule and lack of attention to game preparation, called a meeting to resolve the issue. I was brought in as an observer to offer feedback to the coach regarding his conduct during the meeting.

The coach began the meeting by stating concerns about his observations of the players' scapegoating behaviors and their lack of full concentration in game preparation. The meeting's purpose, then, was to resolve these concerns. Each player was given a chance to state his feelings about the ridicule and the reasons behind it. Some of the accusations were simply unfair (e.g., "I don't like the way Bill wears his hat"). But others were based on valid points about inappropriate behaviors (such as "Bill swears every time he doesn't get a hit").

The coach reacted to the views of each player with respect, allowing the speaker to complete all statements before moving on to the next athlete. No player was interrupted, although occasionally statements were clarified and summarized. Further, no single issue was dealt with until all players had an opportunity to speak. Then, the subject under discussion, the scapegoated player, had a chance to offer his input by responding to the issues and asserting his own feelings about how it feels to receive constant ridicule from his teammates.

After input from all of the players was completed, the coach addressed each issue separately without making any value judgments about "good" versus "bad" responses. He did indicate, however, how unfair it is to criticize other persons based on the way they wear their hats or comb their hair. The session ended with several agreements among the coach, the players, and the scapegoat. This meeting not only helped a young athlete to have a more pleasant experience in sport but also redirected the team's energy away from ganging up on one youngster to playing the game. The atmosphere of the meeting was devoid of fear of retribution, moral "preaching," threats, criticism of a point of view, and continuation of name-calling. The meeting was not a forum for additional scapegoating. Figure 9.1 includes suggestions for providing the proper environment for a team meeting and suggestions for what not to do.

Group counseling has the dual role of (1) exposing and exploring the feelings of group members in an open atmosphere and (2) supporting those participants who need support to help them handle or cope with their current predicament. According to Grayson (1978, p. 24):

> Another supportive potential in group counseling is derived from the possibility that, when a member feels uneasy, anxious or threatened, for whatever reason, he or she may take refuge in the group. He or she can . . . melt into the group mass and not venture forth until he or she feels ready and secure. A good [coach] will sense this and will seek to provide the encouragement and warmth that will motivate the person to venture forth and risk making a contribution to the group process.

Figure 9.1 Do's and don'ts for creating a healthy meeting environment

Do:
- Be at the meeting location at least a few minutes in advance.
- Inform all invited players of the meeting's correct time and location.
- Be warm to the arriving players. Let them see a coach who is relaxed.
- Meet at a location that is familiar and easily accessible to the players and that encourages privacy.
- State the meeting's purpose and goals—and stick to them; don't be influenced by extraneous issues.
- Accept all points of view no matter how irrational. Remember that acceptance doesn't mean that you agree with others but, rather, that you respect them enough to allow them to express their opinions freely.
- Allow for a free exchange of opinions.
- Solicit the opinions of all members present.
- Be patient. Let the athletes do most of the talking. Then respond in a relaxed, sensitive, and mature (nondefensive) manner. And hold off on reacting to an opinion unless it is more constructive and informative to deal with the player's statement immediately. When in doubt, it's best to keep quiet.
- Use nonverbal positive feedback to the players' input with signals that indicate understanding of the message.
- Write down important points on a chalkboard or other surface visible to the group, particularly if the input needs to be reviewed and discussed further.
- Communicate to everyone the purpose, objectives, and format of the meeting. Will players be allowed to "barge in" with their opinions, or must they first raise their hands? Some counselors feel that formal approaches to group sessions stifle a warm, free communication style.

Don't:
- Show anger if a player arrives late; deal with the tardiness later.
- Become visibly upset if a player disagrees with your opinion.
- Dominate the conversation.
- Voice your own opinions first. This "cuts off" the comments of the players, especially if they disagree with yours.

(continued)

- Raise your voice; it puts listeners on the defensive.
- Patronize the athletes. Address them with the same respect as you would adults.
- Try to be "one of the guys" or close friends with the players. They need a leader and someone to turn to for help.
- Be sarcastic. There's no room for appearing to be funny at the expense of a person's feelings.
- Be humorous if the situation is serious, although professional counselors suggest that some humor, perhaps at the start of a meeting if it's handled in a mature manner, could facilitate discussion.
- Allow any group member to be insulted or offended in any way by another group member.
- Let a few participants dominate the discussion. They'll tend to "turn off" the others.

If the coach perceives the use of team counseling as meaningful and potentially effective, then the chance of a warm, cordial atmosphere will be highly probable. Coaches, many of whom are inexperienced in working with groups under the conditions of free and open expression, may not feel comfortable in a group setting that might appear to undermine their authority. But coaches, whether or not they are experienced at open group discussions, can look to the following advantages of short-term team counseling.

1. *To gauge group feelings.* In team counseling, coaches can spot group problems before they have a chance to spread among the players and undermine morale. Ultimately, the honesty and openness that develops between coach and athlete can be transformed into a highly effective tool to enhance player loyalty to the coach and the team.

2. *To provide information and insight.* From group counseling sessions, the coach can obtain information on the thoughts, feelings, needs, motives, and problems of the team members. The coach, therefore, becomes more effective owing to his or her understanding of "what's happening behind the scenes."

3. *To humanize player-coach relationships.* Coaches should welcome the opportunity to interact with the players on an informal, non-threatening basis rather than only in a sport-related context. Athletes are markedly more loyal to coaches who relate to them in ways beyond the roles of coach and player. Many athletes have told me of their warm feelings toward a coach who treated them as a mature, thinking human being rather than as a "mindless jock." Group counseling is a

process that allows a coach to be "human," to say "I don't know," or to look into previously undiscovered issues. Even more importantly, the players have a chance to disclose their insecurities, questions, fears, and feelings on a variety of issues.

Planning the Group Meeting

Surgeons don't walk into the operating room before examining the patient's condition. Lawyers never enter a courtroom prior to extensive preparation of the case. And, just as effective coaches would never approach a contest without a game plan, neither should they approach a team meeting unprepared. Several questions should be addressed. What is the meeting's purpose? Does a specific topic need attention, or is this a gathering with an open agenda? What outcomes need to be derived from the meeting? Is there a time limitation on completing the agenda? Who will lead the meeting? What will be the roles of the players, coach, team captains, and assistant coaches? If a follow-up session is necessary, will the coach be able to indicate the time and place before the meeting is adjourned? The following are a few specific considerations in planning a successful team counseling session:

For whom is the meeting intended? Determine with other responsible parties (such as assistant coaches and team captains) who will attend the meeting. Should it be for the full team or only for a subgroup of players? Does the agenda require that only particular players attend but not others? Is privacy among selected players required?

What's there to discuss? The coach should have a fair idea about the meeting's content before it starts so that the manner of presenting an issue and responding to verbal input from players is planned — or at least given some thought — in advance. This does not suggest that a coach should always anticipate his or her responses to projected questions and statements before the meeting. However, the meeting presents a golden opportunity for the coach to demonstrate that he or she is "in control" and comfortable with team policies, yet secure with discussing change. The coach should be knowledgeable about the alternatives available to him or her on any given issue. One response that players do *not* want to hear is, "We do it this way because I'm the coach, that's why."

Be prepared to be put on the spot. It's not uncommon for coaches to be asked some provocative questions — some of which do not require (indeed, should not receive) an answer. For example, during discussion of a no smoking team policy, one high school athlete asked his coach, "Why can't we smoke if you smoke?" A college player quizzed her coach on the hypocrisy of a rule against smoking marijuana when the coach was accused of trying it in the past.

How should the coach respond to such testing of authority (or challenging the double standard, as some have put it)?

Preplanning responses to challenging questions will help to prevent the coach from having nothing (or worse, the wrong thing) to say. According to most authorities in counseling, coaches should avoid talking about themselves; their role is to foster communication among group members and not allow the group to control the session. Asking or challenging the coach to defend his or her personal habits and behaviors is an example of attempting to control the meeting. So, the first rule of thumb about responding to such personal questions is not to respond to the question at all. In other words, don't provide an answer beginning with "Because . . . ." Here are a few suggested responses to such provocative questions:

- "Frank, the issue here centers on your behaviors, not mine, and on what the members of this team need to do in order to win games."

- "Smoking marijuana is illegal, and it is my responsibility to prevent the athletes on this team from breaking the law."

- "Why do I smoke cigarettes? Because, as an adult, I've made a decision about what I find important and enjoyable. I understand the negative consequences of smoking and how bad it is for my health, but I've decided that I'm happier with it than without it."

- "I cannot give you permission to smoke for three reasons. First, it's bad for sport performance. You lose endurance. Second, I cannot allow you to maintain a habit that has proven to be so harmful to health until you are old enough to read about and understand the issues involved — then you can make a mature decision. And third, most people of your age smoke because of peer pressure, because it's the "in" thing to do. Young men and women need protection from this pressure by someone in an authority position. This removes the pressure to conform. Now you can say, 'Hey guys, I can't smoke because the coach won't allow us' or '. . . will kill us if he (or she) finds out.'"

Preplan to deal with silence. Some meetings have an open agenda; anyone can ask or raise concerns about anything. But what if there is silence! What if not a single hand or issue is raised? Is everything going perfectly? Are there no concerns or discord? The coach cannot assume that everything is just fine if no response is forthcoming. Coaching techniques include the following:

1. Be prepared with specific follow-up questions that will facilitate a response.
2. Break the group down into smaller units; perhaps the group is too large, which inhibits communication.
3. Work out a "game plan" with a few group members — perhaps, al-

though not necessarily, the team captain — for providing verbal input during the meeting if things get bogged down.

4. Be prepared to use visual aids such as films, videotapes, photos, or short documents, all of which make a point or provide information.

5. Perhaps the players are still too "cold" and uncomfortable and need to engage in light banter or a discussion unrelated to the team before addressing more serious, team-related issues.

6. Bring in an outside speaker or authority who might be able to elicit a more fruitful response from the athletes.

What is the role of team captains?   One of the surprises I've experienced as a sport psychologist is that coaches are less knowledgeable than I thought about the role of team captains. One college football coach (with ten years of experience as a high school coach) told me that "To this day, I don't know what a team captain should do beyond leading team exercises and working the coin toss before the game." Well, one very important role for a team captain is to lead team (or partial team) meetings — either in the presence of, or perhaps more comfortably, the absence of team coaches. Captains might lead sessions that partially determine the team meeting agenda.

Often, players are more apt to disclose feelings with their peers than in the presence of the coach. And they may more comfortably decide issues or determine policies that the coach has delegated to the team. For instance, should there be a team party after the season? If so, where will it be held, and should personal friends be invited? Of the list of movies the coach has provided, which one would the players like to see before the game? Coaches should be cautious in living up to these agreements. Giving responsibility to, and supporting, the team and team captain's decisions on selected issues is critical. Preplanning is essential to effective control and content of team meetings. Coaches should not have the team meet without goals and an agenda that is well thought out. The next step is implementation.

Implementing the Meeting

One way to avoid having a meeting that no one wants or that elicits virtually no active participation by the players is to be clear and honest with the group at the start. Remember that the purpose of the meeting may be to address a need, either of the team, an individual player, a group of players, or the coach. As the players enter the meeting area, allow a brief time for chitchat among them; perhaps the coach can also chat among a few players or with other team personnel. This is a time to loosen up and relax. Anxious group members do not talk; relaxed, secure members do. The coach is now ready to open the session, one in which an exchange of feelings is planned.

The meeting's purpose. Inform the players at the start about why you've gathered. Stating the meeting's purpose helps the participants to stay on track rather than trying to cover too much ground or discussing extraneous issues. For example: "The purpose of getting together is to review the strengths and weaknesses of our weekly practice schedule and to try to meet the needs of many of you who claim to need more time to study. If this meeting is going to be successful, it will require that the people in this room feel comfortable about voicing their opinions. That means you."

Expectations of the meeting. What are reasonable expectations of the meeting? Can players and coaches expect to reach decisions at the end of the gathering? Or is it more probable that the coaches will take the athletes' feelings (those generated in the meeting) into consideration and decide on a plan of action in the near future? To keep expectations about the meeting's outcome realistic and conservative is important. In most cases, change takes time, and deciding to make changes from previous habits takes even longer. Rarely should the coach promise a change or decision before the meeting ends unless the meeting's primary objective was to resolve an issue. Then, a decision is imperative.

Establishing the ground rules. If full participation is to take place, the players need to feel secure about several items. For instance, they should be made to feel that everything said in the meeting will remain confidential. To gain trust and credibility, the coach may need to promise not to tell mom or dad that their son or daughter engages in some behavior of which they would not approve. If it is learned that a player broke the law, the promise of confidentiality means that the coach will not consult the school principal or law officers. Of course, it is also against the law to hide information about a crime, and the coach does have an obligation to convince the athlete to approach school or legal authorities under extreme conditions.

Another ground rule is a promise not to use disclosed information against the athlete in future encounters. What would the team members' perception be if a player who said something at the meeting that may have offended the coach never or rarely had a chance to play thereafter, especially if that player received more playing time in contests before the meeting? Could the coach keep the team's loyalty and trust? Could the coach again be viewed as credible? Unlikely! So, it might be prudent to tell the players, "This is the time to get those feelings off your chest" or "I will respect all points of view at this meeting without feeling insulted or upset, as long as we talk to one another in a mature manner and with respect."

A third ground rule to be considered concerns the choice of topics under discussion. The coach may feel that it would be more productive to center the discussion on one or two issues at a given session and then discuss other issues at another meeting held at a later date. The coach might suggest: "Folks, let's keep the discussion limited to your feelings about practice time and game preparation. In this way, there's a better chance of reaching an agreement sooner than if we were to go off in different directions. At the next meeting, we can discuss other issues."

Another rule is to encourage the participation of all team members present, but not to force such participation. Players can be invited to send an anonymous note about their feelings at some future time if so desired. Also, participants should agree that one or more players may not dominate the conversation unless the players announce that one player is acting as the spokesperson for the group. However, the participation of relatively few players may defeat the purpose of a team meeting. Further, team counseling (expressing feelings, changing behavior, and so on) requires massive participation. Only in this way will each athlete feel responsible for fulfilling the agreement of the meeting.

Perhaps the group should agree before verbally interacting that no group member will be insulted, teased, ridiculed, abused, laughed at, or threatened and, in fact, that the point of view of each participant will be heard and respected. Everyone should be entitled to his or her point of view.

Finally, the time limitation of the meeting should be announced before beginning. For example: "Folks, we will adjourn in one hour" or "We need to conclude this meeting at 6 P.M. I will tell you when we have ten minutes left. After another five minutes, we will bring the discussion to a halt, and I'll summarize where we stand and review our options."

One coach from a high school in Wisconsin uses one additional agreement: Anyone who wishes to see the coach privately to discuss an issue raised during the meeting or who, for some reason, is not comfortable disclosing his or her feelings publicly may make an appointment to see the coach. This coach claims that shy players, especially in younger age groups, are intimidated by speaking in front of their friends and teammates. Private time should be set aside for these individuals.

The meeting's verbal content. Coaches can assume that group participants are going to be initially cautious about becoming involved too quickly. They'll want to "test the waters" by observing how the coach responds to other participants. Therefore, it is crucial that the discussion leader be very accepting of virtually all input, giving full recognition to all participants.

Grayson (1978) makes the following additional suggestions to keep the session moving:

1. Guard against going on unrelated tangents.
2. Give credit to individuals for all contributions, however minute.
3. Take time out at appropriate points in the session to summarize what has been said up to that point, being fair to each point of view.
4. Point out related areas or issues that the group might explore.
5. Encourage the expression of different points of view.

6. Tactfully discourage "soap box" oration, including that of the group leader.
7. Patiently help members to express themselves if they are floundering in the attempt.

Closing the session. As indicated earlier, the length of the meeting and ending time should be determined and communicated to all group members at the start. The coach should remember several points about terminating the session:

- *Give a warning before the meeting ends.* Depending on what the coach is planning at the meeting's conclusion, the participants need to be told when there are five or ten minutes remaining before the meeting is over. If you plan to do an extensive summary of the ideas exchanged during the meeting or to conduct a vote at the end, extra time may be needed. But regardless of such plans, to indicate to the participants in advance when the discussion part of the meeting will end is only fair.

- *Be prompt when ending the meeting.* If you said five more minutes before the meeting ends, mean it and do it.

- *Summarize.* At the time of termination, review the highlights of the session with the group. The summary should include a brief restatement of all points of view expressed by team members.

- *Attend to interesting issues.* Were there any particularly interesting issues raised or statements made during the session that are deserving of further comment? Group participants will feel a sense of closure, purpose, and accomplishment if the numerous comments and issues are crystallized into meaningful units. In this way, the meeting's contents and decisions will be better remembered and the basis for the decisions better understood. This means more support for carrying out these decisions.

- *Suggest further exploration.* Certain points may need additional discussion at subsequent meetings. Perhaps more information must be gathered or more exploration of established policies is needed before a decision can be made. The coach, in his or her concluding comments, can point out these needs, which will be the basis for further discussion.

- *Thank participants and offer special recognition.* The coach might recognize the group or certain individuals for making special contributions. There's nothing wrong with expressing gratitude to group members for their attendance and participation. At this time, the coach might want to suggest that certain positive outcomes were derived from the meeting. These may include a sense of fulfillment and accomplishment in expressing feelings and making decisions, feelings of team togetherness, improved team morale, an optimistic view of the team's future, better team member satisfaction, learning and sharing new ideas that might improve team or individual performance, and perhaps most important of all, the coach's sense of appreciation for the players' candor and honesty in expressing their sentiments.

- *Plan the next meeting.* The coach should inform the group when the next session will be held and, if possible, should provide some information about the possible agenda for that session. This allows the players time to think about the issues, to plan their responses, and to begin to make observations and notations that may serve as topics or ideas for further discussion.

After the session. When the meeting has concluded, the session leader should remain in the meeting area to discuss any personal or follow-up issues with group members. The coach should not socialize with the players at a club or restaurant after the meeting. Players need the opportunity and the "space" to share their feelings about the meeting and to discuss ideas about future directions of the team without the presence of an authority figure. After all, the coach is not the players' "buddy." The coach's job at this point is to insure the proper follow-through on issues and decisions that were discussed. It is crucial that decisions from the session be carried out as soon as possible (or when agreed upon) to support the coach's credibility.

The coach should be consistent in his or her behavior toward the athletes between meetings. Imagine the players' confusion if the coach espouses in meetings the need for players to be open and sensitive to one another, yet tends to ignore or reject certain players. Where is the trust and credibility? All the work it takes to gain the athletes' loyalty can go down the drain very quickly if coaches preach one set of actions yet demonstrate another set toward the participants.

Finally, it might be a good idea to have the participants evaluate the session. Have the players complete an anonymous form in response to specific questions about the session (with room for additional comments). In fact, to help establish a truly anonymous and confidential response, players should print (to disguise their handwriting) and an objective party (not the coach) should review and document the data in capsule form and then give a summary of the comments to the coach.

The questionnaire should be as specific as possible and should be administered during practice time (if you want a 100 percent return rate) by the team captain or some other player. Questions might be structured open ended (e.g, "Discuss your views about the way the meeting was conducted") or closed ended (e.g., "How well did you feel the meeting was conducted? —— excellent —— good ——fair —— poor"). Focus on attitudes related to the meeting's content, behavior of the participants, performance of the group leader (coach), degree of satisfaction about interaction among group participants, suggestions for change, positive aspects of the session, recommendations for future topics, and other issues deemed pertinent by the coach. Keep the questionnaire short so that it can be completed within ten to fifteen minutes.

GENERAL RECOMMENDATIONS

No one said counseling athletes was easy. But it can also be said that performing this role in a sport context does not require the expertise that some people think. Here are some simple guidelines for the amateur counseling coach offered by Chappell (1984):

1. Make personal contact with every athlete on the team — starters and substitutes. This includes establishing an open-door policy.
2. If the head coach is unwilling or unable to establish rapport with an athlete, make sure that at least another member of the staff can. The important thing is that all performers need someone with whom they can speak.
3. Talk regularly with support staff (such as athletic trainers, medical personnel, consultants, counselors, even family members) about the athletes. Their impressions can help to support or dispel the head coach's perceptions.
4. Be genuine. Even youngsters are aware of insincerity. Be yourself, and respond honestly — the athletes will respect this and will give their coach more credibility.
5. Be supportive and strive at all times to build the players' self-esteem. A positive self-image improves performance and other aspects of the players' lives. Criticisms related to skills and specific performance are necessary but can be done constructively.
6. Encourage outside interests and a balanced preparation for life beyond the sport experience. Coaches must communicate to the players that sport is only one facet of life, albeit an important one.
7. On a personal, one-on-one basis, do not treat all athletes alike. The psychological needs of each athlete differ. For instance, not all players respond to the same approach; some need — even expect — a stricter approach than others. Experts in industrial psychology suggest that managers think about treating others not so much the way they would want to be treated but, rather, the way they feel that their subordinates would want to be treated.
8. When it comes to team rules, however, all athletes should be treated alike. The starter should receive the same reprimand for breaking a rule as the substitute.
9. The individual's best interests should be put above the team's (many

coaches would find this suggestion controversial). Examples would include not playing an injured athlete, allowing an athlete to practice less in order to study, or taking the pressure off a key player in the big game because of extraordinarily high stress. This approach may appear to reduce the team's chances of winning the next contest, but it will more likely pay off in the long run. Perhaps a player who stays qualified academically or stays healthy and well adjusted will ultimately be of greater benefit to the team.

10.   Be aware of the way in which athletes relate to one another. Discourage cruel, nonsupportive behavior. The coach sets the example; to allow (or model) such behavior is to condone it.

11.   Try to meet each athlete's parents or other family members. They can serve as excellent sources of support in the attempt to enhance the player's attitude and performance if they are convinced that the coach's priority is their child's well-being.

SUMMARY

Counseling is helping normal people to cope with normal problems and opportunities. In coaching, it involves responding to the attitudes, feelings, and behaviors of the athletes (and, for that matter, all other team personnel). Counseling is based on the counselor's sincerity, honesty, warmth, and sensitivity in the communication process, and consists of an array of techniques that are enacted to help clients (individual athletes or the team) to resolve issues and to meet personal goals.

Fundamental counseling skills include listening, showing concern, respecting privacy and confidentiality, and being supportive and honest. With the microskills approach to counseling, the coach's primary objective is to interact with the athlete by using an array of listening and speaking skills. The counseling coach moves toward confronting the issue or issues and then, through the athlete's new insights, begins to help in resolving it (or them). The coach's role is to ask the right questions and respond appropriately to the player's answers. This chapter discusses in detail how to do this.

Team counseling is somewhat different in terms of the types of issues that need to be addressed and the techniques used to resolve them. Although the same fundamental communication skills are necessary in team sessions, the coach is faced with additional challenges such as dealing with team silence or confronting and resolving the feelings of several individuals. The players' feelings may or may not be compatible among themselves or with those of the coach on a given issue. Resolving (perhaps preventing) controversy involves the coach's use of strategies, from planning the meeting to preparing several approaches — in advance — for responding to the players' feelings. The fundamental imperative is that coaches respect the feelings of others during the counseling process, no matter how incompatible those feelings may be with those of the coach.

REVIEW QUESTIONS

1. What are attending and influencing behaviors? Provide an example of each.
2. Describe the nonverbal behaviors that counselors can use to facilitate client communication. Which nonverbal behaviors inhibit communication?
3. Encouraging, paraphrasing, and summarizing are three strategies for effective individual counseling. Create a dialogue between coach and athlete — perhaps two or three paragraphs in length — in which the coach is using each of these techniques.
4. Asking the right kinds of questions in a sensitive manner is important in counseling an athlete. Name and give an example of the two types of questions. How can questions be used incorrectly? Create a discussion in which the coach is asking both types of questions in order (a) to gain further insight into the situation, (b) to help the athlete become aware of his or her behaviors, and (c) to seek alternatives to the situation.
5. What is confrontation? How can it be used by coaches in a sensitive way to help an athlete understand certain behaviors or habits?
6. Describe each of the three techniques of counseling as described by Ivey (1983). Create a dialogue between the coach and the athlete. In this case, the coach has asked the athlete to come to his or her office to discuss an issue (which you decide upon).
7. Describe the steps a coach could take in preparing for a team counseling session.
8. How is team counseling different from individual counseling? How does the former differ from a meeting for game preparation?
9. How can the coach promote group interaction in a team meeting? What could a coach do if the interaction stalls?

REFERENCES

Carkhuff, R. R. 1980. The art of helping. Amherst, MA: Human Resources Development Press.

Chappell, A. J. 1984. Counseling your athletes. *Coaching Review* 34 (January–February): 46–48.

Grayson, E. S. 1978. The elements of short-term group counseling. College Park, MD: American Correctional Association.

Hackney, H., and S. Nye. 1973. Counseling strategies and objectives. Englewood Cliffs, NJ: Prentice-Hall.

Ivey, A. E. 1983. Intentional interviewing and counseling. Monterey, CA: Brooks/Cole.

Ivey, A. E., and L. Simek. 1980. *Counseling and psychotherapy: Skills, theories and practice.* Englewood Cliffs, NJ: Prentice-Hall.

Lanning, W. 1982. The privileged few: Special counseling needs of athletes. *Journal of Sport Psychology* 4: 19–23.

10

Team Climate: Is
Everybody Happy?

As discussed earlier in this text, coaches whose teams consistently win have different leadership styles, personalities, and philosophies. Apparently, no single approach to coaching is beneficial in all situations, nor does any one style always lead to failure. But coaches seem to agree that identifying a common purpose on which to focus the group's efforts is vital to success. The ability to "stick together" is a characteristic called *group cohesion* (Carron 1984). The feeling of togetherness is considered important by coaches in satisfying player needs, enhancing each player's loyalty to the team and coach, and gaining support among teammates. The purposes of this chapter are (1) to examine the extent to which team cohesion and the development of healthy player relationships contribute to group member satisfaction and sport performance, (2) to examine the roles that are common on sports teams and the coaching techniques that enhance some and diminish others, and (3) to suggest ways in which coaches can assess (measure) and promote a supportive and constructive team climate.

HOW A GROUP BECOMES A TEAM

Sports teams are groups. But many coaches and players think that any group of individuals that gets together, shares the common goal of winning, and attempts to meet that goal is automatically a team. But this is not always true. According to business and management consultants David Francis and Donald Young (1979), a team is more than a composite group of individuals who wear similar uniforms. These authors view a team as "an energetic group of people who are committed to achieving common objectives, who work well together and enjoy doing so, and who produce high quality results" (p. 8). No sport coach would find these characteristics undesirable on his or her team. How can the coach build a team concept of this nature?

A team of athletes, together with their coach, should seek the answers to seven questions posed by Francis and Young:

1.   What are we here to do? Learn skills? Improve performance? Win? Have fun?
2.   How shall we organize ourselves with respect to team roles, the playing position of each participant, and other issues?
3.   Who is in charge in terms of the roles of the coach, coaching assistants, and team captains?

4. Who cares about our success? Is school loyalty strong, and are members of the community, school officials, or parents involved?
5. How do we work through problems? Does the coach have an open-door policy? Are team meetings held?
6. How do we fit in with other groups? How do we compare with other teams, and what kind of recognition can we expect within the school and community in comparison to other sports teams?
7. What are the benefits of being a team member? Friendships? Affiliation? Recognition? Learning new skills? Having fun?

Working through these issues will help team leaders to overcome potential blockages and build a cohesive unit of athletes. *Clearing blockages* is a task that separates successful from less successful teams. This is not because some teams have more talent than others, but rather because there is more commitment and identification with some teams than with others. One of the greatest challenges to coaches in sport is making everyone on the team feel that his or her particular role contributes to team success.

Groups of athletes become a team via an evolutionary process. Although team development does not always follow a step-by-step sequence, a process exists by which a group of individuals comes together and, through a variety of actions and reactions, emerges as a cohesive unit—a team. Theorists refer to these normal evolutionary steps of team building as (1) *forming*, (2) *storming*, (3) *norming*, and (4) *performing* (Cartwright and Zander 1968). The coach's understanding of group formation in sport could lead to using strategies that promote harmony among team members.

Forming

The process of forming, referred to by Francis and Young as *testing*, is concerned with familiarizing group members with one another. At this time, the members of a team engage in social comparisons, assessing one another's strengths and weaknesses and the probability of playing. The first issue a person deals with is developing group identification: "Do I belong to this group?" "If so, how?" The failure to address this issue may result in a participant's social isolation.

To help prevent introversion and feelings of isolation on the team, Carron (1984) recommends that coaches try to limit the amount of turnover among team personnel. And for team newcomers, Carron suggests that established team members be assigned the tasks of introducing the new players to their teammates and engaging them in social exchanges. Still, the coach needs to be aware of the participants who do not feel group identification and who are unable to form positive relationships with other team members. Strategies should be enacted to facilitate group member familiarity and interaction at the early stages of team formation—even prior to the first practice if possible (Mechikoff and Kozar 1983).

Glen Patton, successful head swimming coach at the University of Iowa, engages in team-building sessions when the fall semester begins:

> The swimming team has several social get-togethers to help members get to know each other. Picnics . . . soccer games . . . and other social nonswimming events. . . . Team members interview each other at length and then report to the rest of the team what they have learned about the individual. . . . The concept of [these] team building [sessions] is to develop team awareness, communication, and interdependence, so that when a fellow swimmer is feeling the pressure of competitive stress, he can obtain some psychological security by knowing that team members understand his responses to the situation.

Storming

The second stage of group formation is a bit less hospitable. Also called *infighting* (Francis and Young 1979), this level of functioning is characterized by polarization, conflict, and rebellion — not exactly components of team cohesion. Sometimes the conflict is physical. For example, during preseason tryouts and training periods, a relatively high incidence of fights and other aggressive acts tends to occur among teammates, each of whom is trying to make the team or the starting lineup. This is especially the case in contact sports such as football and ice hockey. But usually the issues are socially based. Athletes typically fight for control, for status, and for the coach's attention. The amount of infighting (storming) is often related to the coach's ability to assess the strengths and weaknesses of each team member. When these assessments are objective and communicated to players, hostility tends to decrease because the participants are less concerned with the uncertainty of their role and status in the group (Carron 1984).

Norming

This is the "getting organized" stage in which the group comes together, resistance or "going your own way" is overcome, and cooperation among group members is improved. Teammates want to work together to establish success and improve satisfaction among team members. Whereas storming occurs most frequently in the early stages of a team's training period, norming is the quiet period after the storm. This stage is important because the concept of group cohesion is defined here. The team needs the support and interest of all members. If members become preoccupied with personal needs, the team will not grow stronger. Mutual support will be compromised.

Norming is a function of the group's respect for each member's unique contribution to the team. Instead of competing against a teammate, players become more concerned with economy of effort and task effectiveness. Without a healthy norming stage, the team will become satisfied with mere adequate performance instead of striving for excellence.

Performing

At this point, the group is prepared to direct its energy toward its goals. This fourth and final stage, referred to by Francis and Young as *mature closeness*, is characterized by a close rapport among group members. Roles of team members have been identified, and each person's contribution is distinct. Teammates sincerely want one another to succeed; they feel enjoyment and respect in response to each member's accomplishments. Group relationships are secure. Players interact informally with no artificial interpersonal behaviors. There is a willingness to help a teammate if needed. In order to reach this stage, coaches should avoid, rather than promote, intrateam competition and interpersonal aggression. Instead, the value of each athlete's contribution to the team should be reinforced verbally by giving positive feedback and by recognizing the special role of every team member.

A Who's Who of Team Personnel

Substitute players are simply not in a position to receive the same amount of practice and instruction as starters — although second stringers probably receive relatively less input from coaches than they should (Rotella 1985). On what basis does the coach prioritize the contribution of each team member? Francis and Young (1979) designate three levels of group membership that apply to sport: core team members, supportive team members, and temporary team members.

Core team members. The contribution of core team members is necessary over an extended period. This does not mean that core team members should receive superior treatment compared to the so-called "less essential" participants. Such treatment would undermine the coach's credibility. For example, Janice, a substitute, should not be punished for being late to practice while a starter, Ruth, is not. But it does mean that a coach needs to decide with whom to spend additional time in game preparation. Core team members should also serve as group leaders to help carry out team policies and demonstrate desirable behaviors, both on and off the field or court. Remember that a significant change in the content of core team members might occur if the team is consistently unsuccessful.

Supportive team members. These athletes help the team to function more effectively. Rather than having a direct impact on game performance, they support and provide assistance or information. They are very much needed, despite the infrequency of their competing in events, and the effect of their loss due to injury, poor school grades, or quitting should not be minimized. In fact, sometimes supportive team members carry even more "weight" with their peers than with the coach due to the high need of all athletes for affiliation, support, and recognition among teammates (Cratty 1983). Coaches should remember that supportive team members are only one injury away from becoming a starter.

Temporary team members. The contributions of temporary team members are specific to tasks and the time available to perform them. These individuals usually bring a skilled service to the team based on their professional qualifications outside of the sport domain. The team doctor, psychologist, publicist, and religious leader fall into this category. To have any one of these roles filled on a volunteer basis is not unusual, especially in a nonprofit organization such as a school or amateur sports program. Because of their prominence, unique skills, unpaid service, and low public profile, the coach *must* make temporary team members feel wanted, needed, and important. The best way to accomplish this is through recognition. Perhaps the coach should make it a point to express his or her appreciation and gratitude for their input, both privately and publicly. However, implementing their services, at least to some extent, reinforces their expertise and clearly demonstrates appreciation. The person who knows that his or her advice is being heeded — that it is making a difference and affecting others in a desirable way — feels rewarded. This will go a long way toward keeping the services of temporary team members for the future and contributing to the team's effectiveness.

TRAITS OF AN EFFECTIVE TEAM

A plethora of information exists describing the characteristics of "effective" groups that reach their goals consistently and efficiently while maintaining high member satisfaction and loyalty. Let's discuss the most critical of these traits (unranked) with sport teams.

Appropriate leadership. Effective coaches use a variety of leadership styles to help athletes perform to their capability on a consistent basis. But one sign of a secure, effective leader is knowing when *not* to lead. Team personnel other than the head coach (assistant coaches and team captains, for instance) should be occasionally assigned leadership tasks. Sharing the leadership role may actually enhance the effectiveness of the head coach.

Suitable membership. Effective teams consist of members who are proud of their affiliation and believe that their role will contribute in some way, large or small, to the group's success. Coaches need to be aware of specific strategies that facilitate the athletes' feelings of belonging on the team. For instance, when John Robinson was head football coach at the University of Southern California (USC), he developed a "USC Mystique" by placing photos of Heisman Trophy winners in highly observable places. His purpose was to remind current team participants of USC's elite history and the importance of maintaining the tradition of success.

Commitment of the team. In sport, commitment is associated with loyalty. In behavioral terms, it means that each athlete makes the effort to learn skills and to support other team members. Members of effective teams feel a sense of belonging to the group and are proud to represent the team outside of the sport arena. Ideally, each member should find pleasure in the success of other teammates.

Concern to achieve. Not only is the successful team aware of its objectives, but it is in total agreement with them. After all, if goal setting was conducted properly, the team should have had a role in establishing its objectives. Defining team standards is important so that performance levels and expectations can be set realistically and yet be as challenging as possible. Gerald Myers, highly successful head basketball coach at Texas Tech University, emphasizes team play over individual achievements. To Myers, team goals take precedence over individual goals. The role that the player is asked to play in optimizing team success sometimes requires the modification of individual goals (Mechikoff et al. 1983). For instance, the team's strategy that prioritizes defense supersedes a player's desire to score a given number of points.

Effective work methods. The team should develop a systematic and effective way of solving problems jointly between coach and athletes. To establish a sense of personal commitment in each team member is desirable. One way to do this is to broaden the base for making decisions that affect team members. There are advantages to making team members responsible for decision making.

Well-organized team procedures. Effective teams have clearly defined roles and well-developed communication patterns and administrative procedures. Players might be consulted before group goals are developed. However, the coach should make final decisions firmly and without equivocation. Yet, he or she should show flexibility in changing a decision that proves to be ineffective or unjust.

Critique without rancor. An effective team consists of secure members. This means being receptive to feedback for improved performance. Team and individual errors and weaknesses should be examined objectively without attacking any person's character or personality. The correct policy is to learn from past mistakes in order to improve future performance.

Creative strength. The effective team has the capacity and motivation to create new ideas through interactions with its members. Innovative risk taking is planned and often accepted and rewarded. Athletes show that they are capable of thinking quickly and creatively during game situations, especially in making rapid, unrehearsed decisions. Creativity, performed by highly skilled athletes, has been shown to improve team satisfaction (Fisher et al. 1982).

Positive intergroup relations.   Players should be aware that personal contact with other team members has its benefits. Sometimes assignments and strategies can be learned and remembered better under conditions of peer teaching (where the environment may be more relaxed) than if the coach provides the instruction. Teammates should be trusted to help one another.

Constructive climate.   When the atmosphere is relaxed and nonthreatening, athletes feel more comfortable in engaging in direct, honest communication with their coach and teammates. And they feel secure in taking logical risks in their performance, which is one component of success.

DEVELOPING AN EFFECTIVE TEAM CLIMATE

Think of the various ways in which the weather is described: sunny, bright, cloudy, stormy, clear, warm, cold, fair, and dry. Some of these adjectives can be used to describe how people in a group interact, communicate, and feel about their affiliation. The terms portray what sociologists call a group's (team's) *climate, atmosphere,* or *environment.*

Team climate is a psychological construct, an internal representation of how a person perceives the conditions and interrelationships among group members (James et al. 1977). The key issue is the group (team) members' perceptions; it is not the coach who evaluates and determines the team's climate but rather the players. Athletes make an assessment, or a *value judgment,* based on their own needs and priorities, in identifying and categorizing the team atmosphere. What is so important about these perceptions is that they have a significant impact on each athlete's attitude about being a team member. Researchers refer to this feeling as *team member satisfaction.*

The coach, the person in the most powerful position on the team, has the greatest influence on establishing team climate and insuring a healthy psychological environment (Fisher et al. 1982). Effective coaches, whose teams win and whose players have high group member satisfaction, follow certain guidelines that create a positive team climate. Much research has focused on determining these guidelines and strategies.

Factors that Most Affect Team Climate

DeCotiis and Koys (1980) found, based on their literature review in the area of organization and management, the use of fifty-four different dimensions of the concept of group climate. Using only subjective measures (i.e., terms used and feelings described by group members in the different studies), clusterings of eight dimensions of climate were uncovered. These were autonomy, support, pressure, recognition, trust, fairness, innovation, and cohesiveness.

For the athlete, *autonomy* is the opportunity to function independently of the group leader. Autonomous athletes might feel more satisfied if they were allowed to make decisions on their own—at least occasionally. For instance, many collegiate and professional quarterbacks would prefer to plan and implement at least some of the plays; common practice is for the coach to make all of the decisions. One of the negative outcomes of always having the quarterback follow the coach's play commands is the possibility of blaming the coach for performance failure (e.g., "He called the wrong play. If only he would have called 'this' play, we could have scored"). The players may not accept responsibility for the outcome. Also, occasionally allowing athletes to make their own decisions or, perhaps, to make them jointly with the coach can promote coach loyalty ("The coach trusts me and respects my opinion").

Perhaps no greater need exists for the athlete than emotional *support* from coaches and teammates, especially when the athlete's optimal effort in competition does not lead to success. This sense of "caring and sharing" provides participants with fundamental psychological needs such as recognition for a good effort and psychological comfort to help reduce the stress of nonsuccess (Fisher et al. 1982). Negative, inappropriate responses from group members, such as harsh criticism, sarcasm, nonrecognition of effort (ignoring the performer), and in extreme cases, wishing physical harm to a team member, can result in a cold, disloyal, nonsupportive team climate. The coach is the one agent in the group who makes a major impact on whether the atmosphere on a team is positive and supportive (Sage 1973). This is especially important in sport situations in which anxiety and pressure are inherent.

The *pressure* to succeed, to meet the coach's expectations, and to reach predetermined goals is an integral aspect of competition. Tension and stress are often inevitable. The team environment may be "tight," meaning that athletes are afraid to make a mistake. Or the climate may be one that pressures performers to go beyond their ability to beat superior opponents. The athlete's perception of pressure inevitably heightens anxiety. The consequence of this additional tension may be poorer, not better, performance (Martens 1977). One way to reduce these undesirable emotions is to help athletes to feel competent.

The coach's *recognition* of the athlete's efforts, improvements, and successes improves self-confidence, promotes feeling responsible for one's performance, establishes and maintains close personal friendships with peers, and fosters a supportive team climate. Further, the athlete's strengths are reinforced, which provides the participant with the personal security and confidence to be more receptive to critical feedback in order to improve weaknesses. The relationship between recognition and team climate is that more secure and satisfied athletes tend to be better prepared to support their teammates. Feelings of group member satisfaction and adequacy are heightened when athletes are given the proper recognition (Williams and Hacker 1982).

One of the most important components of team climate is *trust*. Each athlete on the team should feel that performing certain, perhaps risky, actions during competition is "allowed." The performer should not fear being emotionally and physically abandoned by teammates or losing group identity. The feeling of "You can count on me" or "We're in this together" is very motivating for most athletes. It creates a sense of fairness among teammates.

Fairness is in the eye of the beholder; it's based on the athlete's perceptions of the situation. This perception may be different from the coach's interpretation — and even different from reality. An athlete's interpretation of fairness is partly based on three issues:

1. The degree of compatibility between the coach's and the player's respective assessments of the performer's skills and contributions — or potential contributions — to the team. Why, for example, does the player not start or not receive more playing time?
2. The coach's manner in communicating — or not communicating — his or her views to the athlete.
3. Evidence of the coach's attempt to improve the athlete's skills and level of satisfaction as a team member.

The athlete's personal view of being treated fairly by the coach will have a strong and direct impact on the athlete's level of commitment, motivation, and satisfaction as a team member. This issue is capable of bringing a team very close together or driving its members far apart. Coaches rarely give much credence to the athlete's feelings of fairness, which is unfortunate given the degree to which these feelings transfer into action — even quitting the team. Therefore, an effective team climate must be based on the athlete's view of fair treatment. If this view differs from that of the coach, these two individuals must communicate directly to work it out. The answer in the negotiation between coach and athlete may lie in a more innovative approach to the sport experience.

One relevant issue in fostering *innovation*, or creativity, on the team is the group's and coach's willingness to tolerate — even to facilitate — diversity and change. At least occasionally, athletes should have a chance to be creative in planning and executing strategies. (Why do coaches feel absolutely compelled to be directive and to know all the "right" answers?) In football, for example, does the team always have to run on first down? Are the participants allowed to take risks? Is the coach responsible for calling all of the plays, or can the players occasionally do what they think is best in a certain situation? Does the coach offer new and exciting alternatives to practice schedules and drills? Are skills being learned during practice, or is the session a mere repetition of the past with great redundancy and little new ground covered? A positive, effective team climate is one in which change, creativity, input from athletes, and some risk taking are encouraged. In this way, the participants are cognitively involved in all aspects of the team's performance, feel accountable for the outcome, and are mutually supportive, all key aspects of group cohesion.

Cohesion is a measure of a person's attraction to, sense of belonging to, and desire to remain a part of the group (Carron 1984). A warm and enduring team climate reflects cohesion in that participants develop and maintain an atmosphere members find attractive and desirable. In a cohesive team climate, members are communicating, the members' collective personality is compatible with that of the coach, team goals reflect those of the individual members, and the roles of each member are clarified, understood, and agreed upon by all participants. Teams with the proper team climate provide players with the incentive to invest energy in meeting group goals.

Is the proper team climate related to, or does it actually cause, desirable performance? Dr. Craig Fisher and his colleagues at Ithaca College (1982) studied the effects of coach-athlete interactions on team climate. They video-taped and tape-recorded three groups of varsity high school basketball athletes. Coaches and athletes completed questionnaires that measured their respective views on the degree of team member satisfaction, which they labeled "social climate." It was found that:

- The satisfied athletes received more verbal and nonverbal praise and acceptance from their coach and responded to the coach's instructions with more verbal and nonverbal initiative. Satisfied athletes in general were more verbal than their less satisfied counterparts.
- Coaches of satisfied teams asked their athletes more questions during instruction but provided less feedback. The content, rather than the amount, of feedback appeared to be an important factor in promoting satisfaction.
- Athletes on less satisfied teams were more predictable and mechanical in their responses in drills and scrimmages. On satisfied teams, athletes had more freedom to experiment and to be creative.
- Coaches of less satisfied teams spent more time giving information and directions compared to coaches of satisfied teams. And much of it was negative. Feedback to dissatisfied players was excessive — 70 percent more than with satisfied teams.
- Satisfied teams were more cohesive and received more support from their coach.
- The coaches of both satisfied and dissatisfied players perceived their team's climate as matching what they considered to be an ideal climate.

However, less satisfied athletes perceived a less positive climate than did their coaches. Apparently, then, coaches of less satisfied players may not be "in touch" with their athletes' feelings, nor do they apparently comprehend the manner in which they affect their players.

The Fisher et al. (1982) study showed a strong relationship between player satisfaction and team climate. Not only was the coach-athlete interaction in a positive climate more trusting, sensitive, and supportive, but it involved more productive and effective use of practice time and instructional techniques. In addition, coaches on satisfied teams appeared to be more accurate in perceiving the feelings and attitudes of the players than leaders of unsatisfied teams.

A Team Climate Checklist for Athletes

What is the best way a coach can assess his or her team climate? Ask the athletes. The purpose of a team climate checklist is to ascertain the players' feelings about being members of the team and their perceptions of the coach's behaviors and attitudes. Its usefulness is dependent on the coach's willingness to read, reflect on, and react to these opinions in a positive and serious manner. The checklist was derived from Francis and Young (1979) and is applied here in a sport context.

There are three guidelines for its use. First, the checklist is without norms; no scale defines a "warm" or "cold" team climate or a "satisfied" or "dissatisfied" competitor. Everything is relative, so coaches should be interested in changes in scores over time. Thus, the checklist should be administered periodically, preferably before, during, and soon after the season so that the coach can ascertain team climate and *use* the information. Second, the players should be told that the checklist is not a test; there are no right or wrong answers. And third, anonymity is essential! Athletes need to feel that they can respond with complete honesty and without fear of repercussions from their answers. To avoid such fears, the coach might want to ask a player to distribute the checklist to each athlete, whose identity would be coded — perhaps his or her mother's birthday or by the selection of a number from a hat. The coach can compare scores based on the coded number on the different administrations of the checklist.

GROUP DYNAMICS: THE ROLES AND INTERACTIONS OF TEAM MEMBERS

Coaches should be aware of the need of most athletes to belong — to affiliate with other team members. The process of making friends and developing into a cohesive, supportive group is best understood as a process of *group dynamics*. This is an analysis of the ways in which group members interact and the development of certain roles within the group. Coaches should be aware of

Figure 10.1   Team Climate Checklist

Please use the following code, and write in the appropriate number after each statement:

1 = never occurs, 2 = sometimes occurs, 3 = usually occurs, 4 = always occurs

1. I make many of the decisions that affect the way I play. __
2. I can count on the coach to keep the things I say confidential. __
3. People on the coaching staff pitch in to help each other out. __
4. I have enough time to do the things the coach asks me to learn and perform. __
5. I can count on my coach to help me when I need it. __
6. I can count on being told when I play well. __
7. I can count on a fair shake from the coach. __
8. The coach encourages me to create and develop my ideas about any aspect of the team. __
9. I have a role in selecting my physical conditioning procedures, especially during the off season. __
10. The coaching staff tend to go along with each other. __
11. Practice sessions are relaxed places to learn and implement techniques. __
12. My coach is interested in me becoming the best player I can be. __
13. The feedback I receive from coaches is balanced (both positive and negative). __
14. The goals the coach feels I can reach are reasonable. __
15. The coach is open to alternative ways of getting the job done. __
16. I make decisions about my playing strategy—what to do and when. __
17. The coaching staff takes a personal interest in each other. __
18. I welcome having the coach observe me perform at any time. __
19. The coach is behind me 100 percent. __
20. The coach knows my strengths and lets me know it. __
21. The coach follows through on his or her commitments to me. __
22. The coach is honest with me in statements and actions. __
23. The coach is quick to recognize me when I perform well. __

(continued)

Figure 10.1   Team Climate Checklist (*continued*)

24. The coach is easy to talk to about personal, team-related problems. ___

25. The coach understands the players' need to get away from the same sport occasionally rather than being burned out. ___

26. I don't feel overworked and mentally drained. ___

27. I have an important role in setting my own performance standards.

28. The coach does not play favorites.___

29. The coach encourages me to find new ways around problems or strengths of our opponents. ___

30. My teammates do not get burned out from the practices and length of the season. ___

31. The coach talks to me (or the team) about new approaches to coaching. ___

32. The coach criticizes only players who deserve it. ___

33. The coach supports me and helps me learn after making a mistake. ___

34. I have a lot in common, and socialize, with my teammates. ___

35. The coach is not likely to give me bad advice. ___

36. The coach uses me as a positive example in front of other team members. ___

37. I am aware of my role on the team. ___

38. Practice sessions and drills change to prevent boredom. ___

39. The coach keeps in touch with my parents. ___

40. The coach is supported by his or her supervisor (boss). ___

Total Score: ____
Higher scores represent warmer team climate, better player satisfaction.

common traits of group behavior, particularly at the beginning stages, where team members make first impressions and judgments about others, and begin to develop a level of group satisfaction.

Everyone Has a Role

Coaches often stress to their players the importance of team unity and loyalty. However, they do very little about promoting it. A science of using strategies to establish these feelings exists. Unhappy athletes do not play consistently up to their potential. Coaches can identify the level of member satisfaction for each athlete and use techniques that further promote positive feelings. For example, Dean Smith, the very successful head basketball coach at the University of North Carolina at Chapel Hill, articulates each player's specific role with the team prior to the season — in fact, even when the athlete is initially recruited. In this way, the expectations and development of each player are acknowledged by all parties. This approach fosters team unity and helps to assure maximal effort by all players. Smith also diminishes the possibility that a player will feel isolated, unimportant, unwanted, or betrayed. Promoting or, in some cases, inhibiting, the player's role on the team contributes to team cohesion. As you will see shortly, some roles actually dampen the proper team climate. The roles most commonly observed on sports teams include the positive leader, negative leader, follower, isolate, scapegoat, and clown. The following sections provide a description of each of these roles, their advantages and disadvantages, and the coaching strategies that can improve team harmony.

The Positive Leader

The positive leader is a "dream come true" for the coach. Other names used to describe him or her include *facilitator*, *encourager*, *supporter*, or *rescuer*. The positive leader is like an assistant coach among peers. He or she is among the more mature and supportive athletes on the team. One would expect this person to be the team captain, but this is not always the case. Sometimes the role of captain is awarded to the most popular player or to the team's most productive player. Positive leaders are well liked and respected by their teammates. This is because they tend to be good listeners, are sensitive and empathetic, have good communication skills, support team policies and rules, usually do well in academic subjects, and establish mature relationships with authority figures. Coaches are drawn to positive leaders by their good problem-solving and decision-making skills, their willingness to set high and challenging goals, and their tendency to persist at activities with optimal effort; they just don't quit.

The positive leader is "in touch" with the "pulse" of the team and is aware of the personal problems of some athletes. The positive leader can be a confidant in that he or she will not divulge private or confidential information to others if asked not to. The coach may ask this person to befriend a team member who seems withdrawn from the group or to discourage inappropriate behaviors such as drinking, smoking, fighting, and others.

The positive leader is not without problems, however. This athlete wants to affiliate with teammates and be "one of the guys" just as much as any other team member. Yet, the coach might ask this person to assume responsibilities that appear authoritative and supervisory to fellow teammates — to take on the role of "pseudocoach." This person may lose friendships and acceptance by teammates if given too many supervisory responsibilities. The positive leader is still an athlete, not a coach, and should be perceived as one. However, the positive leader has talent that can be utilized by the coach — the talent to work and communicate with others. Sometimes athletes are more respondent to, and affected by, actions and statements of teammates than by those of coaches (Bird and Cripe 1986).

The Negative Leader

Negative leaders are a coach's nightmare because they depress team morale and unity, among other reasons. This person tends to act against the coach, either personally (in an antagonistic relationship), philosophically (by not following team rules), or both. Psychologically, negative leaders often have personal problems with authority. They do not like to be told what to do and, consequently, resent an authoritative leadership style. If their feelings were kept to themselves, this role might not be so potentially harmful to the team. But the real problem is that negative leaders are . . . well, leaders; others tend to follow their lack of cooperation and testing (breaking) of rules.

Negative leaders perform numerous potentially destructive functions. Sometimes they solicit other team members in generating a mutiny of anticoach sentiment. What makes this person especially dangerous is his or her ability to succeed at these goals, at least with a few teammates. Negative leaders possess enough charisma to cause less mature teammates to follow him or her down the wrong path. Breaking curfew, illegal drug ingestion, and dishonesty are examples.

Benne and Sheats (1970) describe negative leaders as aggressors, blockers, or playboys. *Aggressors* deflate the status of others; express disapproval of the values, acts, or feelings of others; attack the group or the group's objectives; joke aggressively, e.g., with pranks and other acts of hostility; or try to take credit for the contribution of other group members. *Blockers* are negativistic and stubbornly resistant; disagree with and oppose others without, or beyond, reason; and attempt to maintain or bring back an issue after the group or coach has rejected or bypassed it. *Playboys* display a lack of involvement in the group through cynicism, horseplay, and apathy.

So what can the coach do about it? Before the coach dismisses this person from the team, he or she should remember that this athlete possesses leadership qualities that a coach can use to the team's advantage. If the coach can turn these qualities into something more productive such as supporting the team's starters or motivating teammates, then everyone wins.

Here are a few recommendations for dealing with the negative team leader:

Problem recognition.   The most important step is to identify this person's counterproductive behaviors. Does the person demonstrate a tendency toward testing rules, chronically making excuses for inappropriate behavior, or not following instructions? Testing team rules may be a way of communicating doubt in the coach's leadership ability or a technique for gaining group acceptance (some athletes believe that this is the only way they can gain this respect).

Positive confrontation.   After certain behaviors or attitudes of the negative leader have surfaced, it's time for the coach to move quickly. The offending individual should be approached privately and quietly by the coach under relaxed conditions. This means no public confrontations. And the specific time and place of the meeting should be agreeable to both parties.

Conclusions and agreements.   The coach's initial step is to gather information from the player before reacting. The athlete may have feelings that underlie and help explain his or her behaviors. But the real objective of this meeting is to reach an agreement to stop the inappropriate behaviors immediately. For example (coach to athlete): "Teasing Sandra because she wears glasses will not be tolerated, Tanya. We are not here to hurt the feelings of others. I want it stopped now."

The conclusion from this meeting must be the athlete's agreement to stop the counterproductive behaviors. But it doesn't end there. If this issue is handled constructively, then agreements for future behaviors should be negotiated and concluded. This is what John Robinson (presently head coach of the Los Angeles Rams) refers to as "respecting the integrity of each athlete" (Mechikoff et al. 1983).

Sometimes the coach has no other choice and must suspend or dismiss an athlete from the team. Although giving the person an opportunity to make realistic changes in his or her actions is constructive, the athlete may not agree to the required changes in behavior or may not follow through on agreements. However, before athletes are dismissed from the team, they should be warned about the consequences of their actions. In this way, they make the choice and take responsibility for their own behaviors. For example, the possibility of dismissal from the team in response to committing certain acts should be announced before the season starts.

The Follower

This person can play any one of several roles. He or she is extremely susceptible to the suggestions and actions of others. Often the person follows directions or imitates the actions and attitudes of leaders. Usually, the follower seeks friendship with more popular, influential members of the team. Followers are not inherently "bad." A team cannot perform optimally with too many "generals" and no "soldiers." A team needs athletes who will follow the leader without questioning every strategy and policy. But in a less desirable way, followers may select the wrong team members to emulate, have low self-confidence and self-esteem (which is often associated with being afraid to take risks and initiate actions that may help their performance), be a noncontributor to building team cohesion, avoid taking responsibility for their performance ("I just do what I'm told" or "It's not my fault"), and lack the ability to support teammates.

In describing *help-seekers,* Benne and Sheats (1970) suggest that followers have the potential to drain the group's energy. They can solicit sympathy from other members through expressions of insecurity, personal confusion, or self-doubt. Followers, therefore, can possibly be a drain on the group.

Coaches can help the follower to mature by implementing strategies that develop leadership skills. These include (1) placing the follower in situations in which he or she will be seen by others as successful, (2) determining the follower's skills and using these skills to the team's advantage, (3) placing the competitor in a leadership role that the coach decides is within the follower's capability, (4) giving the person plenty of positive feedback on performance, (5) offering comments or assigning tasks that help the person to feel that he or she is an important part of the team, and (6) recognizing the follower's accomplishments to others.

The Isolate

If you were to ask a coach to describe the strengths, weaknesses, and personality characteristics of each player on the team, the people who would first come to mind would be those who get the coach's attention—leaders and starters. One type of individual who does not usually have a high profile on the team is the isolate. Isolates are, as suggested by the term, physically and mentally removed from other team members, at least more often than not. This response is typically self-imposed; they choose to be alone.

However, isolates do not always want this role. Sometimes they demonstrate certain habits or communicate in a manner that seems peculiar to other players and that makes teammates feel uncomfortable. It's entirely possible that isolates are rejected by the team rather than the other way around. For example, a junior high school baseball player verbally announced to several teammates who were taking batting practice that he was the best hitter on the team. He further suggested that only he possessed the skills necessary to make the high school team. The immediate and long-term response of his teammates was to ignore him. The other players rejected his requests for affiliation, both on and off the ball field. A team isolate was "born." Despite the seemingly deserving nature of the team's response in this situation, isolates rarely deserve or appreciate this role.

Researchers have not actually studied the personality characteristics of isolates in sport. But I have gathered anecdotal evidence from observations and conversations that suggests that causes range from a mild case of social maladjustment to more serious psychological problems with feelings of revenge, hostility, and destruction. A social worker with extensive experience in detention centers for adolescents once described the isolate as "a negative leader waiting to happen."

Typically, isolates (especially child athletes) may:

- Be less skilled as compared to other team members (but exceptions have occurred, particularly in professional sports)
- Be disloyal to team goals and, instead, be more concerned with their own performance quality and psychological survival, even at the team's expense
- Lack physical and psychological maturity for their age
- Feel rejected by others and sometimes think that they deserve such treatment
- Have a low self-image
- Lack effective communication skills
- Be critical of others (but may not typically voice this opinion except when asked by someone whom they consider to be nonthreatening)
- Rarely smile (a partial display of low self-esteem)
- Be chronic complainers
- Test authority by breaking team rules (perhaps to gain attention or for revenge)

Isolates, especially children and adolescents, should concern the coach. Children have a salient need for affiliation (Cratty 1983). It is the rare child who consciously chooses to remain alone, without the warmth and support of peers. Athletes are a particularly gregarious population (Iso-Ahola and Hatfield 1986). And probably the most common result of the isolate's behavioral tendencies is dropping out of sport (Gould 1984).

Coaching strategies can be initiated that will make the isolate feel more wanted, motivated, and most importantly, more connected — emotionally and behaviorally — to the team. The following true story includes several suggestions for dealing with the problem (and it is a problem):

Martin was a fifteen-year-old who played outfield on his high school's baseball team. His models were professional athletes, and he dreamed of making it to the major leagues. He was tall and lanky for his age, appearing awkward and clumsy, a sign that his body was growing too fast for his neuromuscular development. He possessed a strong arm (was a good thrower) and had above-average total body movement speed. His most glaring weakness was batting; he simply could not get the bat around quickly; he swung late and missed fast pitches. But one of Martin's most obvious characteristics was that he did not associate with any team members. In fact, the other players indicated that they rarely noticed him interacting with others off the field. Martin was the team isolate.

An outside observer noticed Martin and discussed his social status with the baseball coach. Not surprisingly, the coach knew relatively little about Martin. Usually, the athletic skills of isolates are below average. Consequently, coaches spend only minimal time with them.

Martin's coach agreed to let the observer study Martin as part of a research project concerned with identifying player roles and enhancing each individual's contribution to the team. The coach would help by implementing the following strategies over the next two weeks: He would (1) observe Martin's actions toward other teammates to determine whether he had any friends on the team, (2) include Martin in drills and offer instruction, (3) give him as much honest, performance-based, and positive feedback as possible, (4) ask one of the more mature, positive players on the team to befriend Martin; to get to know him and include him in activities in which other team members participated both on the field (playing catch) and off the field (going to a movie), (5) give Martin the responsibility of calculating the batting averages and earned run averages of each player each week, and finally, (6) engage Martin in verbal and nonverbal exchanges on an ongoing basis.

Follow-up observations of Martin's behavior two weeks after the implementation of these techniques revealed an incredible transformation. He started smiling occasionally at practice and, in a 180-degree change in demeanor, engaged in frequent conversations with his teammates. There was more. What surprised both the coach and the observer was the obvious increase in energy Martin exhibited on the field. This was a youngster who went from casual walking to running when going out to the outfield to shag fly balls in batting practice. Martin's skills were still below average, and the coach and observer agreed that either he would make a better basketball player than a baseball player (he towered over his teammates) or he would need to receive more instruction and plenty of practice to gain the necessary expertise.

One more positive outcome emerged from this project. Three team isolates (of which Martin was the most obvious) were identified. The coach implemented a plan to deal with each one in a relatively short time span. After one month, it became apparent that eliminating the roles of team isolates translated into three additional team supporters; three more players who cheered for the starters and displayed team loyalty, energy, and enthusiasm in helping others prepare for games; and three individuals who grew as athletes and matured as young men. Although it could not be proven that this change also resulted in more team victories, clearly the lives of three individuals became more enjoyable, on and off the field, and the whole team benefited.

The Scapegoat

The term *scapegoat* is defined as "a person made to bear the blame for others or to suffer in their place." The concept of a scapegoat has a biblical derivation (*Lev.* 16:8–22) in which a goat was sacrificed as the symbolic object of the people's sins. In contemporary social psychology, scapegoating is described as a phenomenon in which "aggression toward a frustrator is suppressed and displaced upon some nonparticipant bystander" (Harari and McDavid 1974, p. 357). Apparently, scapegoating has been around a long time and occurs in many different settings, including sport. But this does not make it a constructive form of communication. Ginott (1968, p. 67) refers to scapegoating (and sarcasm) as "sound barriers to learning."

Athletes might be teased by peers for a number of reasons (e.g., an awkward appearance, poor performance, peculiar habits, and statements perceived as "funny" or unusual). Although a scapegoat by definition is a victim who does not warrant such treatment, sometimes a person may appear to deserve it. For example, the scapegoat might behave in a manner that is so upsetting to others that they actively reject the targeted person. In one example, Dale had the disturbing habit of asking the coach to constantly repeat information in team meetings. This player made it obvious that either he was not listening to the coach or was confused by the coach's message. Either way, the group grew impatient with his habit, which disrupted meetings. Eventually, Dale became the target of crude remarks and pranks.

Another possible reason for scapegoating behavior is the insecurity of team members. Some individuals, especially those who are relatively younger or less skilled, have a psychological need to blame others due to their lack of self-confidence, self-esteem, and maturity. Persons who are uncomfortable with themselves tend to subconsciously blame others for their own inadequacies. Scapegoating fulfills this need; the abuser perceives the victim as less competent. Preadolescent and adolescent age groups are especially susceptible to scapegoating. Peer pressure and the need for group affiliation are present during the preteen and teenage years to a greater extent than at any other time in a person's life (Ginott 1969).

Sadly, one possible instigator of scapegoating behavior in sport is the coach. Sometimes the coach will unfairly blame the athlete or a small group of players for the team's continual lack of success or, in some cases, the failure to win a major event (choke). Despite the team's decisive loss, one participant might shoulder the blame for the entire team after failing to execute a single play successfully. Or in attempting to be popular or to improve the mood among the players, the coach may use "gallows humor" — invoking laughter at the expense of a person's character or self-esteem through sarcasm or teasing. The targeted individual does not find such comments humorous.

Scapegoating has a potentially negative impact on team success. First, teams with scapegoats do not comprise secure, satisfied individuals (Harari and McDavid 1974). The team climate lacks mutual support, trust, and warmth. And when a group of players scapegoats a teammate, it is likely that the players are not making accurate causal attributions for the team's lack of success. In other words, instead of taking responsibility for their own performance in explaining a poor team record, they are choosing to blame an "easy" target.

Scapegoating is inevitable because "boys will be boys," right? Wrong! The coach can, and should, do everything in his or her power to prevent and stop scapegoating behavior. It is harmful and unneeded.

Coaches should be aware of scapegoating tendencies on the team. Although some coaches contend that communication among team members is none of their business, scapegoating is another matter. The victim needs protection, and in sport, only the coach can supply it. This is why the coach should put a stop to scapegoating immediately when it's detected. Players should be warned that hurting the feelings of others will not be tolerated. But the coach's reaction shouldn't stop there.

Probably the most constructive approach is to try to understand the derivation of the scapegoating. Why is this particular athlete the victim? Who are the organizers, initiators, and leaders of this behavior, and what is their complaint or problem? Perhaps the coach can best handle the situation by getting at the root of the "attacker's" feelings. To avoid embarrassing the scapegoat and invoking hostile reactions from teammates, the coach's approach to the problem should be low key.

The coach must be able to separate scapegoating behavior from legitimate and normal teasing and joking. It would be inappropriate to overreact to the players' statements of friendly banter, which reduce anxiety and help to relax the participants. However, destructive sarcasm is a different message. How can the coach tell the difference? Look at the person's reaction to the statement. Is it genuine laughter? Is he or she able to return the teasing? Are statements accompanied by physical abuse or light playful interactions? Coaches must listen to the verbal and emotional messages of such responses. How consistent is the teasing? Is it a chronic habit? Is there a pattern of its occurrence, or does it happen rarely?

Coaches can help the scapegoat to cope with this problem. Scapegoats can be helped to understand how their own behaviors and comments affect others if they are, in fact, doing or saying something that triggers the scapegoating. In addition, the scapegoat can be informed about the emotional immaturity and undesirable personality traits of persons who engage in scapegoating (e.g., "They don't know any better"). This technique, called *psychological distancing*, helps the victim to gain perspective about the problem and to take the insults less personally. Journalist David Brinkley is quoted as saying, "A successful man is one who can lay a firm foundation with the bricks that others throw at him."

Sometimes the coach is actually the cause of the problem. Coaches should never join the players in scapegoating anyone, as harmless as it may seem. In one case, a coach walked in on a discussion among the players (ages eleven and twelve years) in which one person was being teased because of a spot on his uniform. The coach, thinking that such bantering was harmless, joined the laughter. The young athlete took one look at the laughing coach and immediately burst into tears; the frustration was too much to take. Tears were his only release. The victim's need to have the coach "save" him from the cruel remarks of others was not taken into account. And the coach should never tease an athlete for the sake of gaining popularity with other players or to foster humor in the group. A philosopher named Gough once said, "We constantly underrate the capacity of children to understand and to suffer." A primary role in coaching is to avoid this pitfall.

The Clown

Everyone on the team seems to need attention, but some are in far more need than others. In fact, certain team members seem to demand it — even if it means demonstrating behavior that is obnoxious, unpleasant, or perhaps humorous. The team clown (or clowns — many teams have more than one) has this need. What is it about the clown's personality that brings on the need to be so often "on stage"? Why does the person need attention and choose to obtain it in this manner?

Athletes who clown consistently do so for different reasons. The most salient of these is peer recognition (Ginott 1969). Any normal athlete needs recognition. However, this need should never be met at the expense of team goals. Athletes who continously "clown around" likely have certain psychological needs that mandate these behaviors. They may (1) feel unsure of their skills and contributions to the team, (2) be masking a low self-image and insecurity, (3) need attention to feel adequate, (4) feel negative toward authority figures such as the coach, (5) feel physically unattractive, in which case humor would be used to cover up a low body image, (6) display disloyalty toward the coach by using antics to disrupt the coach's goals and strategies, and (7) feel unwanted by others, in which case humor is used to gain love, recognition, and admiration.

Coaches must make accurate judgments about the timing and content when reacting to clowning. They must take into account whether clowning behaviors are harmless, whether the clown's actions are at the expense of hurting the feelings of others, and the timing of such behaviors (pregame humor is rarely conducive to establishing proper arousal and concentration levels). However, responding with a smile sometimes makes everyone feel more comfortable and less uptight.

How does the coach deal constructively with the "team comedian"? Rule number one is the old adage "An ounce of prevention is worth a pound of cure." This means that coaches may circumvent having to deal with clowning by stating their expectations and regulations of inappropriate behaviors before the season, specifying when clowning is off limits and when a more serious atmosphere is warranted. The second rule is to be certain that the cure is not worse than the disease. That is, the coach's reaction to clowning behavior should be appropriate for the situation. Overreacting may be less productive than no reaction at all. The coach's reactions to the clown could range from selectively ignoring the behavior or comment (especially if it is displayed rarely by the individual or is ignored by, or has minimal impact on, others) to verbally indicating disapproval immediately after the clowning action, followed by moving ahead on the task at hand. Coaches should make their point and get back on track as soon as possible. An explosive reaction will diminish the athletes' concentration and give the clown the attention and recognition that he or she seeks.

In fact, seeking recognition from the coach is often the primary rationale behind clowning behaviors. Perhaps the best response is to provide positive attention on occasions when the athlete is not clowning through skill instruction, feedback on performance, and mature conversation related and unrelated to sport — clowns often have difficulty in, or are incapable of, verbally communicating with others. Clowns seek approval. Coaches should try to give it to them in motivating ways.

That group members take on roles is a natural phenomenon of human behavior. Because teams are groups, this practice similarly exists in sport. The coach's job is to deal with this natural occurrence in an insightful and productive manner so that the unique personality and ability of each athlete contributes to the good of the team and improves team cohesion.

TEAM COHESION

For years coaches have assumed that positive feelings among team members result in better sport performance. Coaches contend that team unity is essential for success, and consequently, they have used techniques to help ensure an "esprit de corps" among the players. The pregame meal, physical conditioning programs, meetings, and pregame preparation traditionally occur as a group. Ostensibly, when the players interact and share team-related experiences, they develop closer interpersonal relationships and feelings of mutual support and trust. Researchers aren't certain that this is true.

For example, Carron (1984) and Widmeyer et al. (1985) reviewed several studies in which teams that were highly cohesive also achieved superior performance outcomes and other studies that indicated a low relationship between cohesion and team performance. In fact, in some instances, high cohesion may actually have hurt teams. For example, in a study by Fiedler (1967), close player friendships actually interfered with team success. Teammates on a basketball team who were very close friends chose to pass the ball to each other rather than to players in better shooting positions. In this case, team success was not a priority. Thus, coaches who try to promote cohesion might, under some circumstances, do more harm than good.

An example is the common strategy in team sports of requiring all athletes to be together and to follow the same protocol up to twenty-four hours before the contest. Anshel (1985) found that collegiate and high school football players were actually annoyed at following this procedure. Many players preferred to be alone with their thoughts or to have the option of attending team activities that did not relate directly to game preparation such as viewing a commercial film, engaging in mental imagery, and spending their "free time" with their position (assistant) coaches. Sport psychologists have also studied the extent to which this "we" feeling affects performance and whether the level of interpersonal attraction and feelings among athletes translates into improved individual performance.

What Is Group Cohesion, and What Factors Affect It?

Cohesiveness is a term used to describe feelings of interpersonal attraction and the sense of belonging to the group by its members. It also signifies the members' desire to remain in the group (Carron 1984). Two different types of cohesion have been identified by researchers: social (or sociometric) cohesion and task cohesion (Bird and Cripe 1986; Iso-Ahola and Hatfield 1986). *Social cohesion* is the degree of interpersonal attraction among group members, the extent to which the group allows a person to reach a desired goal. *Task cohesion* refers to the athletes' objective appraisal of their group's level of coordinated effort or teamwork. In other words, it is the degree to which the team and the individual member reach their respective goals. Acknowledging the differences between social and task cohesion is imperative in determining how each might affect a person's level of group satisfaction.

Several factors affect both social and task cohesion. As Table 10.1 shows, these include characteristics of team members, characteristics of the group, and situations experienced by the group (Widmeyer et al. 1985).

Measuring Team Cohesion and Player Roles

Sport literature gives relatively little attention to measuring team cohesion. If it's so important to have a cohesive team, as commonly assumed by coaches and sport psychologists, then we need to determine the extent of its presence on a particular team.

The sociogram. A sociogram is an "illustration" of affiliation and attraction among group members. It reveals (1) the degree to which group members are valued by teammates, (2) clusters (subgroups) and isolates, and (3) persons who are actively rejected by others. A coach or researcher can obtain this information in two ways. One approach is to ask team members (preferably in written form to ensure privacy and confidentiality, although child athletes may require an

Table 10.1   Factors that contribute to cohesion on sport teams

	Characteristics of Team Members	Characteristics of the Group	Situations Experienced by the Group
Social Cohesion Improved if:	1. Liking each other is a need among players	1. Small group size	1. Players perceive team is threatened
	2. Similar personalities exist among teammates	2. Democratic leadership style used	2. Athletes share blame for failure
	3. Athletes have similar social backgrounds	3. Team captains selected by team and have active role	3. Athletes make similar causal attributes for success and failure
	4. Being on team meets person's social needs	4. Structured to reward and recognize athletes equally	4. Group receives equal recognition and adulation for some achievement
	5. Players have become good friends off the field	5. Players choose to socialize among themselves	
	6. Each player feels accepted by teammates	6. Warm group atmosphere	
		7. Group leader supports each player	
Task Cohesion Improved if:	1. Players are satisfied with their performance	1. Members work together	1. Competition with another team

(continued)

Characteristics of Team Members	Characteristics of the Group	Situations Experienced by the Group
2. Players feel their sport skills are improving	2. Players are aware of and accept team role	2. Team has consistent success
3. Players demonstrate similar skill levels	3. Frequent practice helps players anticipate their teammates' moves	3. Intragroup competition (team rivalry) for team status, position, skill development, etc.
4. Each member perceives role on team as important to team's success	4. All athletes have similar work patterns	4. Social cohesion for indepen-dent-type sports detracts from intrateam rivalry, perhaps re-ducing individual optimal effort
	5. Team's goals are clear to each athlete	
	6. Team accepts group members	
	7. Path to meet team goals is clear	

interview format), and the other is through direct or indirect (videotaped) observation. In fact, to validate data accuracy, both methods can be used jointly.

The coach could create a questionnaire on which each athlete would indicate specific teammates with whom he or she would prefer to share a certain activity (e.g., tossing a ball) or situation (e.g., sharing a motel room on the road). Interpersonal attractions and repulsions within the team would be obtained. The data concerning "who chooses whom" would then be diagrammed as a sociogram in which individual team members and their choices are represented by the connection of circles by lines.

The coach should ask each athlete to respond in writing to a single question that best fits a particular situation. Sample items might include: "Name three people on the team whom you would most like to invite to a party and three people whom you would least like to invite" or "Name the one person on the team with whom you would most prefer to share a room when we're on the road and one person with whom you would least want to share a room." Sociogram questions, then, should be concrete, such as "a person with whom you would like to work," rather than abstract, such as "a person whom you like very much." They should also have real meaning with actual and direct consequences for the respondent. So, if the coach asks the players to select a teammate with whom they would prefer to share a room, it is best to assure the person, if possible, that actual room assignments will be based on his or her reply.

Two other issues in the gathering of such information are confidentiality and honesty, especially when the athlete is asked to indicate a person whom they do not like. Athletes must be told that all responses are confidential but *not* anonymous; after all, coaches must know who feels what about whom. Instead of saying, "Whom do you dislike on the team?" the question might read, "Whom do you like less than others on the team?" The coach can ask the athletes to rank order their responses to a predetermined number or to list as many teammates as they wish. The picture of the players' responses might look something like that in Figure 10.2.

The sociogram in Figure 10.2 reveals that Sam is well liked and very popular among his teammates. Fred, however, appears to be an isolate. (The term *appears* is important because a sociogram reflects feelings, not actual behaviors. The coach should follow up this data with direct observations.) Bill is not liked by several teammates. But interestingly, he has positive feelings toward two of the players who reject him. And apparently Joe and Mike do not care for each other. Based on the information provided on just a few of the team members, it appears that (1) Fred needs some attention, (2) Bill, a possible scapegoat, appears to desire acceptance from others but is apparently not a welcomed group member, and (3) the conflict between Joe and Mike should be resolved by the coach. If a friendship cannot be developed, at least attempts should be made to reduce discord. Finally, the mutual attraction of Mike, Steve, and Herb indicates the formation of a subgroup. The coach's direct observations of this threesome will indicate whether they need further attention.

The sociometric matrix.   Here, the observer makes pluses and minuses in a given box when two or more persons interact positively or negatively. Rows indicate the outgoing choices of, and columns indicate the choices received by, each person as indicated in Figure 10.3.

It can be seen in Figure 10.3 that Susan and Janice positively interact somewhat frequently, with Susan taking more initiative in the relationship. Gail, however, rejects the approaches of Marge. Sadly, Marge does not approach anyone else on the team. And Renee interacts with no one.

Figure 10.2   Sociogram illustrating type of feelings among group members

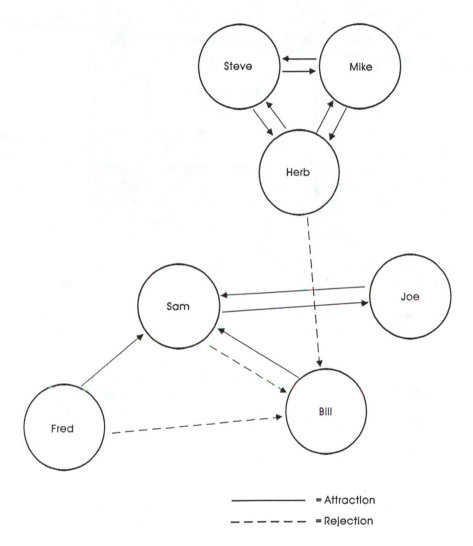

Clearly, one limitation to the use of sociograms in the absence of other information is that the nature of the interactions is not explained. Taking this last example, does Renee become the group isolate by choice, or is it imposed by her teammates? Does she behave in a manner that facilitates this role? How does Renee feel about the situation? Is she more comfortable keeping to herself? And of particular importance to the coach, is Renee's role detrimental to her perfor-

Figure 10.3   Sociogram indicating frequency of attraction or acceptance and rejection among group members

	Susan	Janice	Gail	Marge	Renee
Susan		++++	- -		
Janice	+		+		
Gail		+		- - -	
Renee					

mance? Only further observations and information gathering from others will help the coach to understand the dynamics of the relationships on the team.

The value of sociometry. Sociograms are rarely used by coaches, partly because most are not aware of their existence (they *are* well known among sociologists and social workers) and because very few people are trained to use them. But they can be a valuable tool in sport to better understand the extent of team togetherness. Sociograms allow the coach to observe his or her players objectively and in the context of a sport environment — although information used in constructing sociograms could be gathered at team social events as well.

Sociometry is particularly valuable for teams with many members. Researchers have shown that as group size increases, the level of member satisfaction decreases proportionately (Fiedler 1967). So, it is possible that fewer satisfied members (or more players who express lower satisfaction) will exist in football than in basketball. It is certainly possible that information derived from a sociogram could either improve team relations or work toward preventing a disruption in team cohesion. Sociograms can help the coach to answer some of the following questions:

- Who does and who doesn't have friends on the team?
- Is any one player being rejected by other team members? If so, could this be one reason for a player's lack of incentive, commitment, and effort?
- Who are the team leaders, and who's popular among the players?
- Who is and who is not a satisfied team member? Is everybody happy?

- Do subgroups (cliques) exist on this team? Who are they? Do these friendships help, hurt, or have no effect on team morale?
- Are the players communicating? Does a player in a key position, a quarterback or goalie, for instance, go his own way during practice? Are pitchers talking to each other or speaking with catchers about opposing hitters or pitching strategies? Does a particular player refuse to approach another player?

In summary, sociometric techniques measure (1) the ratio of friendship choices within or outside of the group, (2) group congeniality, (3) the presence or absence of cliques, (4) members' perceptions of group closeness, (5) the extent of group attraction, (6) social activity of the group, (7) the degree to which the athletes perceive interpersonal feelings and behaviors similarly, and (8) reciprocal sociometric choices (Widmeyer et al. 1985). There is debate in the literature as to the effectiveness of sociograms. They certainly alert the user to the manner in which group members interact and tendencies toward leadership, attraction, rejection, and isolation. However, according to Widmeyer et al. (1985, p. 8), sociograms have some disadvantages.

Operational measures of cohesion based upon interpersonal attraction: (a) under-represent the concept — there are other factors at work within the group in addition to attraction to other members which keep individuals in a group, (b) fail to account for cohesiveness in situations characterized by negative affect (i.e., dissatisfaction, dissention, hostility), (c) have not been supported empirically — interpersonal attractiveness has not been shown to correlate with other attractiveness measures in groups . . . and (d) do not totally account for the conditions necessary for group formation. In addition . . . interpersonal attraction may be synonymous with group cohesion in sociometric groups but be unrelated in task groups.

Widmeyer et al. also criticized other inventories that purportedly measure group cohesion because they "were not developed from a conceptual or theoretical model on which to make predictions and test hypotheses, were not tested extensively for its psychometric soundness, or were specific to one sport." Apparently, then, the coach should use as many tools as possible, particularly those with which he or she is most comfortable, in assessing the interactions and feelings of players.

Team cohesion questionnaires. Another way a coach can assess the extent of team unity is by using a psychological inventory developed by Yukelson, Weinberg, and Jackson (1984). Their assessment comprises forty-one questions indicating the best expression of the athlete's feelings. The coach totals the scores for each response by all the players to determine the team's feelings about the factors that contribute to team cohesion. For example, if the coach calculates a high score for "sense of pride" or "enjoyment playing with this particular team," then he or she can conclude that a rather high level of team satisfaction and affiliation exists in the group. In other words, the competitors enjoy playing together.

Another inventory, the Group Environment Questionnaire, was developed specifically for sport teams by Widmeyer, Brawley, and Carron (1985). The athletes are asked to complete eighteen questions related to their feelings about their "personal involvement with this team" and their perceptions of the "team as a whole" on a scale of one (strongly disagree) to nine (strongly agree). As with Yukelson, Weinberg, and Jackson's scale, a higher total for each question represents a greater level of the particular feeling or behavior.

Does Cohesion Affect Player Satisfaction?

How important is it for athletes to like one another, to be close friends, and to win consistently? Can teams be successful if some (or even most) of the players do not get along or if they compete among themselves for playing status? Does the coach need to be concerned about the players' social interactions in addition to teaching them sport skills and strategies?

Satisfaction is in the eyes of the beholder. Each individual athlete must define what he or she finds satisfying as a team member. Tennis professional and former college coach Bill Glaves contends that one important component of player satisfaction is being recognized for effort and talent (Mechikoff et al. 1983). One way in which he promoted this philosophy was to encourage the press to talk to the players rather than speaking only with him. In addition, he mounted press clippings on the team bulletin board and continually updated them. As Carron (1984, p. 349) asserts, "Whereas cohesion is a group construct, satisfaction is an individual one." Carron's review of related literature indicates "a strong positive relationship between cohesion and satisfaction."

If "happy" athletes feel closer to one another, does this mean that their level of satisfaction will also enhance performance success? Williams and Hacker (1982, p. 336) asked female intercollegiate field hockey players to complete questionnaires to obtain cohesion scores. They found no evidence that satisfaction led to an increase in performance success. However, successful performance did improve satisfaction. They concluded that "performance success and cohesiveness lead to greater satisfaction but satisfaction, in turn, does not lead to anything."

Does Cohesion Affect Team Performance?

Intuitively, we assume that cohesive teams win more games or, inversely, that teams lacking in cohesiveness (with more dissension and conflict) fail to live up to their potentials. Research findings are equivocal on this issue. Some investigators have found that cohesion is related to team success — that there is a high relationship between team cohesion and winning — but that it does not necessarily cause success (Iso-Ahola and Hatfield 1986). Others have found that team success is not related to whether or not the players like one another but, rather, the extent to which they can interact constructively during the contest to use proper skills and strategies (Carron 1984). Making any definite conclusions about cohesion and performance is difficult because researchers have studied different types of sport populations. Generalizations about the results of these studies for all teams and sports would be unsound. Much of the research on team cohesion has centered on university intramural teams.

Landers et al. (1982) examined the cohesion-performance relationship with collegiate intramural teams. They found a significant relationship between friendship and performance outcome. A particularly high relationship was found between friendships occurring in early to midseason with late-season performance. Specifically, the quality of play increased later in the season for the intramural athletes if their team was cohesive earlier in the season. Cohesion that was apparent before the season or near its end did not influence performance. Remember this was a study of intramural teams (whose members are often recruited by personal friends), not of organized competitive sport leagues.

In another study of intramural (college) male competitors, Martens and Peterson (1971) found that highly cohesive teams (identified by how participants rated the value of team membership, teamwork, and closeness) won significantly more games than did low cohesive teams. Similar advantages for cohesive teams were found in examining team success on postseason performance; high cohesive groups won more games (Peterson and Martens 1972).

Also of important interest is the extent to which the positive cohesion-performance relationship with intramural competitors is replicated with inter-collegiate athletes. In a review of related literature, Gill (1980) found that cohesiveness was positively related to team success (close teams won more games) in intercollegiate football, high school basketball, intercollegiate ice hockey, and ROTC rifle teams, and in a relatively rare study of female athletes, in intercollegiate volleyball. However, other studies have not only failed to show positive relationships, they have indicated just the opposite finding, that highly cohesive teams lost more games or had less satisfied members than did groups that were low in cohesion.

German sport scientist Hans Lenk (1969) studied two high-caliber rowing teams over four years (1960 through 1964). One team (1960) represented its country in the Olympics. The second team (1962) became a world champion. Before reviewing his research findings, keep in mind that rowing teams are classified as *coacting groups* (e.g., as in tennis, bowling, golf, or weight lifting) rather than *interacting groups* (e.g., as in basketball, baseball, or football). Therefore, Lenk's results may apply to some types of sport teams more than others.

Lenk studied the interactions and interpersonal relationships and attractions among team members, as measured by sociometric analyses (discussed earlier). His data were derived by directly observing the behaviors of the athletes and through self-report techniques. In his 1960 study, Lenk observed sharp conflicts among racing team members, especially between two unfriendly subgroups. He reported that the internal strife was so bad that the team was almost abandoned. Nevertheless, a performance deficit was not found as a result of group tension. Ironically, performance slightly improved as team members became increasingly combative toward one another over the two years of the team's existence. In fact, the team became an unbeaten Olympic champion. Lenk concluded that teams in sport are capable of achieving maximal performance outcomes in spite of strong internal conflicts.

The world champion rowers of 1962 were from a club team rather than a racing team. Lenk noticed a subgroup of four rowers that set itself apart from the others. Sociometric data indicated that the subgroup formed due to the mutual attraction of the team's four strongest rowers, leaving the remaining four members to affiliate among themselves. Moreover, the cliques resented each other for different reasons. Members of one subgroup thought of themselves as physically superior to the others, while the second subgroup resented the "second-class" treatment and one-upmanship attitude of their teammates. This led to infighting for team leadership. The intrateam rivalry intensified with time. Despite this lack of cohesion, the eight teammates won the European championship during the second year, the time at which intratime rivalry was strongest. The level of performance had not suffered from the conflicts over the players' status.

Perhaps, then, players need not like one another in order to succeed in sport. Some athletes in certain sports and situations are able to overcome conflict among teammates and be impervious to internal conflict. Consider two important and unique circumstances that surrounded Lenk's studies. First, these were world-class athletes, not exactly players from the local high school or little league. These men were highly skilled, had a history of past success, were self-confident in their ability, and were less reliant on teammates for recognition, support, and affiliation. Further, the team's relatively short life span — about two years — in which to train and compete combined with the unified purpose of representing its country successfully in international competition were likely more important in reaching their ultimate objective than establishing close relationships.

The second issue was discussed earlier; rowing is a coacting sport requiring less dependence for team success than other types of sports. As Lenk readily admitted, coacting group members can successfully meet their goals without extensively affiliating with others. Further, Lenk never claimed that low cohesion in teams was desirable. He only contended that his study found no decrease in performance.

In summary, cohesion does not appear to markedly improve sport performance, with the possible exception of collegiate intramural teams. However, team success appears to breed cohesion. As Williams and Hacker (1982) concluded, while coaches may not need to be concerned with building cohesiveness to enhance team success, cohesiveness still may be important since participation on cohesive teams appears to be more satisfying than participation on less cohesive teams. Thus, given a choice, perhaps coaches should consider the objective of establishing compatible, mutually enjoyable relationships among team members as highly desirable.

Suggestions for Improving Team Cohesion

If having a cohesive team is important to the coach, several strategies can help to make it happen. Sport psychologists (Carron 1984; Bird and Cripe 1986; Widmeyer et al. 1985) suggest the following:

1.   Acquaint players with the responsibilities of their teammates. This will help to develop support and empathy among the players. This can be facilitated by having players observe and record the efforts of other athletes at their positions. This will further improve the pride within the subunits of larger teams. If subunits naturally exist on the team, which is common in football, ice hockey, and track and field, coaches will want to develop pride within each of these subunits. Players need the support of their peers, especially of the same positions and in team sports where the interaction among athletes is required for success.

2.   The appropriate use of humor and praise in verbal and nonverbal forms is advantageous in generating feelings of mutual satisfaction and enjoyment. Athletes are especially responsive to recognition for special contributions.

3.   Coaches should be "in touch" with their players and should know something personal about each player. If a competitor has a problem that affects his or her play quality or, conversely, is celebrating some joyful event (e.g., a birthday or receiving a good grade in class), the coach can acknowledge it and perhaps respond to the athlete appropriately. How do the players feel about the team? What changes would they like to see? What explanations do they need that will help them to better understand the reasons for certain approaches toward game preparation?

4.   Goals should be based on performance, not only outcome. Playing effectively, yet losing, does not have to result in a hostile, negative response from other players and coaches. There should always be something to feel good about after the contest regardless of the final outcome.

5.   To promote motivation and team loyalty, players should be informed about their status on the team, given an explanation for this status, and told what they can do to upgrade or maintain it. Each athlete should feel that he or she has an important role with the team.

6.   Players should not be "allowed" to hurt the feelings of teammates. The coach has an obligation — one which is too often neglected — to protect the rights of each athlete on the team. As mentioned earlier, scapegoating, blaming, and chronic teasing must be stopped quickly, or cohesion will dissipate.

7.   Social cliques that benefit only a few athletes at the expense of alienating the majority of team members should be avoided. A plan should be developed to split up clique members, especially if they are evident during the competitive event.

8.   Disciplining players should be consistent for all team members. Starters or stars should not be treated differently than others with respect to setting limits.

9.   Excessive turnover of personnel is not helpful to cohesion. Establishing close rapport with a group when its members are unfamiliar with one another and are uncertain as to the longevity of maintaining the same group is difficult. Individuals avoid risking being close to teammates when they perceive the relationship to be short term. So, when a new member joins the team, established players should be asked to integrate the newcomer into the larger group and to help outline task expectations. The selected individuals should be warm, sensitive, mature, have good communication skills, be capable of establishing personal contact, and interact in a positive manner on and off the field or court.

10.   Group cohesion means, in part, open communication between coach and athlete. Therefore, it is wise to have player-selected team representatives (even from each subunit, if necessary) meet with the coach on a regular, prescheduled basis — perhaps weekly or biweekly — to discuss issues of concern.

11.   Leadership should be developed among team members. Coaches are mistaken in assuming that they are (and should be) the only team leader. Athletes respond favorably to peer leaders. Perhaps player leaders can lead discussions among themselves about developing or maintaining team cohesion. Such feelings and needs should be communicated between coach and athlete. Ultimately, the result of such interaction may be to make appropriate adjustments in strategies for team management.

SUMMARY

A warm, supportive climate on sport teams, of which group cohesion is a relevant component, is highly desirable for group member satisfaction, performance, and team success. Other aspects of a healthy team environment include autonomy, recognition, mutual trust among coaches and teammates, the players' perception of fairness, and opportunities for innovation.

The manner in which group members interact is referred to as *group dynamics*. Coaches should monitor the frequency with which players interact and the nature of these interactions. From this ongoing assessment, coaches can determine the role or roles of each player on the team. The common roles described in this chapter included the positive leader, negative leader, follower, isolate, scapegoat, and clown. After acknowledging these roles, coaches can (and should) initiate strategies to augment some (positive leadership, for instance) and attenuate others (such as isolates and scapegoats). The objective is to promote team cohesion and to build team member satisfaction.

For athletes to like one another appears to be desirable in terms of a warm, supportive team environment and the enjoyment of sport participation. Indeed, researchers have found that cohesiveness is associated with player satisfaction. What is less certain, however, is the extent to which team cohesion influences performance. In Lenk's examination of elite rowers, less cohesiveness was related to better success. Researchers have not yet been able to support the contention that team cohesion, even group member satisfaction, is significantly related to performance outcome. More research is needed in this area, particularly in comparing age groups and skill levels — whether child athletes, for instance, are affected differently by these factors than older, better skilled competitors.

REVIEW QUESTIONS

1.   The evolutionary stages of most groups include forming, storming, norming, and performing. Provide examples in which each of these steps are evident on a sport team.

2.   Describe five factors that contribute to a proper team climate in sport. What techniques can the coach use to ensure that each of these factors will be present?

3.   Describe the six roles of team members discussed in this chapter. What are the advantages and/or disadvantages of each role? What can the coach do to facilitate or reinforce some roles while inhibiting or preventing others?

4.   In your opinion, do you feel that it is appropriate for coaches to become involved with the athlete's interactions with other team members away from the sport environment? Why or why not?

5.   Does being a satisfied team member usually result in better sport performance? In other words, will the team play better if each member likes (or is friends with) other members?

6.   Describe the different types of group cohesion. Under which conditions is one type of cohesion preferable over another, if at all?

7.   Provide an example of using a sociogram to illustrate the degree of player affiliation or team cohesion using contrived information. In other words, assume that the players responded to a question about preferences or attraction toward another team member. What might their responses look like on a sociogram?

8.   Should the coach request that certain athletes interact with other team members to improve team cohesion or to help change an athlete's role

on the team? What are the advantages and disadvantages of this strategy?

9. Describe the techniques that coaches might use to improve team cohesion.

REFERENCES

Anshel, M. H. 1979. Effect of age, sex, and type of feedback on motor performance and locus of control. *Research Quarterly* 50: 305–17.

Anshel, M. H. 1985. *Examination of a college coach's receptivity to sport psychology consulting: A two-year case study.* A paper presented at the North American Society for Psychology of Sport and Physical Activity Conference, Gulfport, MS.

Benne, K. D., and P. Sheats. 1970. Functional roles of group members. In *Perspectives on the group process*, 2nd ed., ed. C. G. Kemp, pp. 271–75. Boston: Houghton-Mifflin.

Bird, A. M., and B. K. Cripe. 1986. *Psychology and sport behavior.* St. Louis, MO: Times Mirror/Mosby.

Carron, A. V. 1984. Cohesion in sport teams. In *Psychological foundations of sport*, ed. J. M. Silva and R. S. Weinberg, pp. 340–51. Champaign, IL: Human Kinetics.

Cartwright, D., and A. Zander. 1968. *Group dynamics: Research and theory.* 3rd ed. New York: Harper & Row.

Chelladurai, P. 1984. Discrepancy between preferences and perceptions of leadership behavior and satisfaction of athletes in varying sports. *Journal of Sport Psychology* 6: 27–41.

Cratty, B. J. 1973. *Psychology in contemporary sport.* Englewood Cliffs, NJ: Prentice-Hall.

Cratty, B. J. 1983. *Psychology in contemporary sport: Guidelines for coaches and athletes.* Englewood Cliffs, NJ: Prentice Hall.

DeCotiis, T. A., and D. J. Koys. The identification and measurement of the dimensions of organizational climate. *Academy of Management Proceedings.* Detroit, August 1980.

Fiedler, F. E. 1967. *A theory of leadership effectiveness.* New York: McGraw-Hill.

Fisher, A. C., U. H. Mancini, R. L. Hirsch, T. J. Proulx, and E. J. Staurowsky. 1982. Coach-athlete interactions and team climate. *Journal of Sport Psychology* 4: 388–404.

Francis, D., and D. Young. 1979. *Improving work groups: A practical manual for team building*. San Diego, CA: University Associates.

Gill, D. 1980. Cohesiveness and performance in sport teams. In *Sport Psychology: An analysis of athlete behavior*, ed. W. F. Straub, pp. 421–30.
Ithaca, NY: Mouvement.

Ginott, H. 1968. *Between parent and child*. New York: Avon.

Ginott, H. 1969. *Between parent and teenager*. New York: Avon.

Gould, D. 1984. Psychosocial development and children's sport. In *Motor development during childhood and adolescence*, ed. J. R. Thomas, pp. 212–36. Minneapolis, MN: Burgess.

Harari, H., and J. W. McDavid. 1974. *Psychology and social behavior*. New York: Harper & Row.

Iso-Ahola, S. E., and B. Hatfield. 1986. *Psychology of sports: A social psychological approach*. Dubuque, IA: Wm. C. Brown.

James, L. R., E. A. Hartman, M. W. Stebbins, and A. P. Jones. 1977. An examination of the relationships between psychological climate and VIE model for work motivation. *Personal Psychology* 30: 229–54.

Landers, D. M., M. O. Wilkinson, B. D. Hatfield, and H. Barber. 1982. Causality and the cohesion-performance relationship. *Journal of Sport Psychology* 4: 170–83.

Lefcourt, H. M. 1976. *Locus of control*. Hillsdale, NJ: Erlbaum.

Lenk, H. 1969. Top performance despite internal conflict: An antithesis to a functional proposition. In *Sport, culture and society: A reader on the sociology of sport*, ed. J. W. Loy and G. S. Kenyon, pp. 224–35. New York: Macmillan.

Martens, R. 1977. *Sport competition anxiety test*. Champaign, IL: Human Kinetics.

Martens, R., and J. A. Peterson. 1971. Group cohesiveness as a determinant of success and member satisfaction in team performance. *International Review of Sport Sociology* 6: 49–61.

Mechikoff, R. A., and B. Kozar. 1983. *Sport psychology: The coach's perspective*. Springfield, IL: Thomas.

Peterson, J. A., and R. Martens. 1972. Success and residential affiliation as determinants of team cohesiveness. *Research Quarterly* 43: 62–76.

Rotella, R. J. 1985. The successful coach: A leader who communicates. In *Sport psychology: Psychology considerations in maximizing sport performance*, ed. L. K. Bunker, R. J. Rotella, and A. S. Reilly, 19–26. Ithaca, NY: Mouvement.

Ryan, E. D. 1979. *Athletic scholarships and intrinsic motivation.* A paper presented at the North American Society for Psychology of Sport and Physical Activity Conference, Trois-Rivière, Quebec, Canada.

Sage, G. H. 1973. The coach as management: Organizational leadership in American sport. *Quest* 19: 35–40.

Widmeyer, W. N., L. R. Brawley, and A. V. Carron. 1985. *The measurement of cohesion in sport teams: The group environment questionnaire.* London, Ontario, Canada: Sports Dynamics.

Williams, J. M., and C. M. Hacker. 1982. Causal relationships among cohesion, satisfaction, and performance in women's intercollegiate field hockey teams. *Journal of Sport Psychology* 4: 324–37.

Yukelson, D., R. Weinberg, and A. Jackson. 1984. A multidimensional group cohesion instrument for intercollegiate basketball teams. *Journal of Sport Psychology* 6: 103–17.

11

Coaching Child Athletes: Special Needs

The volunteer coach for the city league was meeting just before the game with his young athletes, boys aged nine and ten years. He was talking about how important it was for everyone to play well and win; this was a "big game." Then he asked whether anyone had any questions. A youngster raised his hand and asked, "Coach, will everyone get a chance to play?" "What's more important," the coach snapped back, "everyone playing, or winning?" In a nutshell, this actual story illustrates two things; first, the problem with youth sport today, and second, the different needs and priorities of child athletes as compared with those of the "mature," grown sport competitor.

Youth sport typically pertain to children aged thirteen years and younger who are involved in adult-organized sport programs. Adult-organized programs are characterized by an arranged schedule of contests for children under a competitive environment using prescribed rules (Martens and Seefeldt 1979). They may be held within or outside of a school. This means that pickup games and other free-play situations are not considered youth sport. Approximately ten million children participate in North American youth sport programs that meet these criteria.

The purpose of this chapter is to take a close look at child athletes — at their needs as children and how being a sport competitor can meet these needs; the reasons why they participate in sport and why they drop out; how child athletes differ from older, higher skilled players; and finally, how coaches and parents of young performers should go about the business of helping the young athletes enjoy the experience of competitive sport. The first issue confronting a parent is whether the child really *wants* to compete. It's a matter of readiness.

WHEN ARE CHILDREN READY TO COMPETE?

I observed a father coaching his son, who was reputed to be a future Canadian Olympic swimmer. The young man, aged eleven, was swimming laps — plenty of them. After what must have been at least twenty minutes, the boy asked his father to rest. "I'm tired, Dad," he said. "Can I get out now?" Without missing a beat, the father  answered, "If you want daddy to love you, you'll keep swimming." This young lad was well known in the city of Montreal as an athlete of potential national caliber. But imagine the pressure he felt to maintain a highly intense, long-term commitment of time and energy in order to gain the love and acceptance of his most important fans — Mom and Dad.

Pat McInally, national newspaper columnist of youth sport and former professional football player for the Cincinnati Bengals, had this to say on "pushing" kids into sports prematurely:

> I think parents should try to judge their children's talents objectively and avoid pushing them into sports they're either ill-suited for or unenthusiastic about. . . . Instead of pressuring your child into sports, which he might be unequipped for, perhaps you . . . should introduce him to other sports. . . . There are so many sports available to kids these days and you should help your child find the one or ones which will allow him to best express himself and enjoy the experience most.

McInally goes on to suggest that parents should find out why their child is participating in a particular sport. If it's just to make a parent happy instead of for the fun of it, then the parents should help their child to find another sport — or for that matter, another recreational activity — while giving him or her full support. Inflicting feelings of guilt (e.g., urging the child to make his or her parents proud) is inappropriate. A more difficult task for parents is to know when their child is physically and mentally ready to engage in competitive sport.

The word *readiness* implies that a person has reached a certain point during his or her involvement in an ongoing process. How do physical education teachers, coaches, and parents know when that point has been reached? According to Dr. Vern Seefeldt (1982, p. 31), a leading researcher in children's motor development and director of the Youth Sports Institute at Michigan State University, specialists depend more on tradition rather than on developmental progressions: "(We) depend on the performer to tell us when the state of readiness exists." He suggests that the goal of early researchers, who were practitioners of learning motor and sport skills, was to be able to identify the primary factors that underlie a child's state of readiness (i.e., the abilities that allow for sport involvement) and to recognize the immediate signs of readiness for specific skill learning situations (e.g., when a youngster demonstrates a minimal degree of competence in entry behaviors, or "must have" skills, that allow for successful participation). An analysis of physical or anatomical considerations necessary for engaging in competitive sport is beyond the scope of this chapter. Our review will consist of issues concerning motor skill learning and performance.

Primary Factors of Readiness

Maturation, the most important determinant of readiness (Gagne 1977), is one of three primary considerations indicating when to introduce a skill to a young participant. Through interacting with the environment, a child assimilates new information and new experiences into existing cognitive structures. The child's prior experiences, or *learning,* is the second consideration. Learning simply occurs with greater efficiency at some period in life than in others (Magill 1982). The so-called "critical period" for learning sport skills is when sensory (mental) processing and motor responses are functioning at optimal levels (Scott 1962). The child must be able to understand and to identify the demands of a task — the speed and trajectory of a ball in flight, for example — and respond accordingly for a successful outcome. The third consideration is *motivation.* Learning theorists agree that skill acquisition is impossible unless the learner wants to learn; you "gotta wanna."

Thus, the child's greatest potential for achieving in sport is dependent on his or her maturation level, prior experiences or learning, and motivation. These factors, however, do not necessarily function independently of one another. For example, a youngster might have the incentive to play a competitive sport — perhaps to please parents or to emulate older athletes — but not possess the skills or experience to perform effectively. The result of premature participation could be failure and subsequently dropping out of sport. Children who *do* possess the proper skills might be afraid to fail, feel "burned out" from too much participation, or for some reason not have the motivation to continue. Thus, all of the readiness factors must be present if a skill is to be learned and performed successfully. Perhaps the most frequent example of mismatching the three primary components of readiness in sport concerns involvement in competition before the child is adequately mature.

Competition and cooperation, both central to sport competition, are learned behaviors; they are not inborn (Gould 1984). Further, children learn to compete in stages. Veroff (1969) has shown that children at about age four years exhibit more cooperative than competitive behavior. They have learned to compete by about age five or six. By seven or eight years, they compare themselves to others. This social-comparison process becomes increasingly intense with age. At about age twelve years, the child athlete associates losing with failure. Moreover, the young performer perceives the cause of this failure as his or her own lack of ability; the hope and desire to improve, to learn new skills, or to recognize the fun component in competitive sport is greatly diminished. The result is dropping out of sport.

In summary, two important issues emerge at this point concerning readiness in sport: (1) that children are not likely to be ready to compete in sport until they have acquired the necessary skills to become successful and (2) that the likelihood of skill learning and performance is dependent on the individual's level of cognitive (perceptual and sensory) and physical (movement speed and accuracy) maturation.

Meeting the needs and limitations of children as sport participants requires instruction and adaptations in the environment that will lead to successful experiences. Wise choices need to be made about the type of sport in which a particular child should engage, about changes in rules and equipment, and even about the dimensions of the playing surface that will accommodate the youngster. Magill (1982), for example, suggests that tee ball is an appropriate modification in baseball competition and that flag football should replace tackle football for the under-thirteen age groups. Other suggestions include lowering the height of the hoop in basketball or using lead-up games that make fewer complex demands on the players. Finally, equipment should be altered to promote fundamental motor skills such as climbing and throwing (Herkowitz 1984). Climbing equipment should accommodate children with limbs of all sizes; balls should not be too large, heavy, or hard to grasp. Striking movements should be aimed at stationary targets (bowling pins or a ball dangling from a string, for instance) rather than at balls in flight at high rates of speed.

Signs of Readiness for Learning Sport Skills

In order for a child to be ready to participate in sport, he or she must have the ability to learn and demonstrate competence in requisite skills. What "immediate signs" can parents look for before signing up their child in a sport program? One way to make accurate decisions is to determine the subordinate or prerequisite skills that must be effectively performed for the child to successfully engage in competitive sport.

What must an athlete be able to do in order to strike a thrown baseball? Some skills that demand mastery are holding the bat properly and directing the bat at the ball. In addition to physical skills, the child must be able to demonstrate competence in perceptual abilities. *Visually tracking* ball flight and accurately anticipating the time and point at which the ball will be contacted with the bat (*coincidence anticipation*) are two such abilities. Another ability inherent in striking a thrown ball is adequate *hand-eye coordination.* At what age do children usually attain proficiency at visual tracking, coincidence anticipation, and hand-eye coordination? It's not the same time for every child. But the age range for being able to demonstrate such skills — at least initially — is generally between the ages of nine and twelve years (Malina 1982). This means that a seven-year-old child should not be a Little League participant unless he or she can perform skills commensurate with the demands of the task.

Another approach parents and coaches can use to ensure that children are ready to participate in a sport program is to encourage youths to experience a variety of skills. Researchers (Magill 1982) have found it unwise to restrict a child's repertoire of skill development for several reasons. First, children who start early in one sport and rarely engage in others tend to burn out by the time they are adolescents (Cratty 1983). Stories abound of famous athletes who quit or took a prolonged "breather" from sport competition, most often in tennis and swimming. Either the youngsters were bored or were under too much pressure to be successful in the activity. Second, growth and maturation may dictate that the child is better suited for a sport other than the one that he or she experienced in early years. A boy who is an early maturer in junior high school may actually be too small to play football by the time he reaches high school or college. Third, children should be allowed to participate in areas that they enjoy; otherwise, they will not persist very long at the activity. How are children to know whether they enjoy badminton or some other sport until they try it? And finally, children, like individuals of all ages, tend to maintain interest and incentive to participate in activities in which they succeed. Why not allow each person to willingly experience as many different sports as possible to increase the probability of success in at least one of them?

Perhaps the most important factor that underlies acknowledging a child's readiness to play competitive sport (aside from physical or anatomical limitations) is that of competence. How well can the young participant perform the fundamental skills of the sport? Is he or she able to catch a hard baseball without fear? Can a rapidly pitched baseball be visually tracked and the bat swung at sufficient speed to contact the ball? Can the ball be thrown at the proper speed or distance to ensure a successful outcome? How many youngsters are playing shortstop who lack the physical maturity to toss the ball to first base on the fly? The acquisition of primary skills associated with the particular sport is an imperative, but often lacking, first step *before* children are involved in competition. When children *are* able to perform the necessary tasks successfully, then parents can consider enrolling them in a competitive sports program — given, of course, their wish to become involved in such a program. They may prefer to play the game but not participate in an organized league. Exactly why would they want to play competitively?

WHY CHILDREN PARTICIPATE IN SPORT

Youth sport involvement is becoming more and more popular across North America. Unfortunately, equally common is the degree to which children drop out of sport. The pattern of involvement obtained for the State of Michigan by researchers at Michigan State University (Gould 1984) indicates an increase in youth sport participation up to the ages of eleven, twelve, and thirteen, with a marked decline after that. If we can identify the reasons for participation, then adult leaders of teams and organizations can more adequately meet the needs of child participants and significantly lower the dropout rate.

Many studies have examined the reasons for sport participation. The age of subjects in these investigations ranged from six to eighteen years. In summary, the young athletes tended to rank their reasons for playing in the following order: (1) to have fun, (2) to learn and improve skills, (3) to be with friends and make new ones, (4) for excitement, (5) to succeed or win, and (6) to exercise and become physically fit (Gould 1984; Wankel and Kreisal 1985). A recent study by Wankel and Kreisal indicated that pleasing others, receiving rewards, and even winning the game — contrary to popular opinion — were consistently rated *least* important by their sample of 822 youth sport participants, aged seven to fourteen years. Of far greater importance were the excitement of the sport, personal accomplishment, improving one's skills, and testing skills against others.

Of great interest when reviewing children's responses about their reasons for participating in sport is the dichotomy between what adults *think* children want as opposed to what they *really* want. The use of rewards, the importance of winning, the benefits of competition, and pleasing others (parents, for example) are viewed by adult leaders in youth sport programs as imperative for a successful program. "The kids want this," they seem to be saying. Program leaders insist on providing elaborate rewards to participants (sometimes only to athletes on winning teams), stress the importance of being in first place or winning the championship, and convince parents of the need for children to "build character" through competitive sport. And what do the kids say? "No thanks!"

Wankel and Kreisal (1985) found that "getting rewards" and "pleasing others" ranked very low in importance as reasons for enjoying sport. Inversely, "fun," "improvement of skills," and "personal accomplishment" were rated high.

Of more moderate ranking were "excitement" and "to compete." The importance of "getting rewards" and "being on a team" were considerably more important for the enjoyment of the younger participants and become of decreasing importance with age. Apparently young children react more strongly to material reinforcers (i.e., rewards and recognition from "important" adults) than older players who, with age and maturity, find these reinforcers less important (Rushall and Siedentop 1972). Further, younger players identify with being part of a team — for many their first organized team experience — more strongly than do their older counterparts. Wankel and Kreisel concluded that "winning and receiving rewards for playing, aspects that are frequently given considerable emphasis by parents, coaches, and the media, are of secondary importance to the participants' enjoyment and accordingly should not be heavily emphasized" (p. 62).

WHY CHILDREN DROP OUT

Children approach the sport environment for different reasons and to meet various needs. These reasons are dependent on psychological factors (e.g., experiencing success), emotional factors (e.g., feeling competent), and social factors (e.g., affiliating with and meeting new friends). But regardless of the many characteristics of children that underlie their involvement in sport, for some reason (or reasons), they do not tend to "stick with it." The dropout rate in youth sport is soaring. Between the ages of twelve and seventeen years, about 80 percent of all children who are enrolled drop out of organized sport programs (Roberts 1984). Why? Because the needs mentioned earlier are not being met. In his review of related literature, Gould (1984) found that the primary reason for quitting was an overemphasis on winning. A lack of success, not playing, involvement in other activities, and "other interests" were also rated highly. Typical examples of reasons included in some studies were: "The coach yelled at me when I made a mistake," "I never got to play," and "I wasn't good enough."

Theorists have written extensively about the needs of young competitors and the factors that appear to be most responsible for discontinued involvement in sport. The causes of quitting sport fall into three areas: (1) comparative appraisal, (2) lack of perceived ability, and (3) low intrinsic motivation.

Comparative Appraisal

Children begin comparing themselves with others to determine their own relative status on motor ability starting at about ages four to five years and increasing in importance through the elementary years (Scanlon 1982). This process is called *comparative appraisal*. During grades four, five, and six, both appraisal and the number of children engaged in youth sport interact optimally. This means that children in sport are comparing themselves with the abilities of others more often at this time than at any other. The reason for this is that children have relatively little past experience on which to base accurate self-appraisals. Consequently, they become dependent on others for information about their own adequacy.

The competitive sport arena is filled with many public situations in which coaches, parents, teammates, and spectators provide the young athlete with feedback on performance. The input comes in verbal and nonverbal forms — both positive and negative. Positive verbal statements reflect pleasure, recognition, and praise, while negative verbal communication includes ridicule, reprimand, and sarcasm. Nonverbal cues, both intentional and unintentional, are emitted continuously. Parents telegraph pride and approval, or embarrassment and annoyance, by facial expressions, body language, eye contact, or ignoring the youngster. It is easy to see how comparative appraisal, at first externally derived from others, then internally defined by the athlete, can lead to either the athlete's persistence or withdrawal from the competitive sport experience.

The primary objective of working with child athletes should be to provide them with information that promotes a feeling of success at performing sport skills. When this happens, other needs are also met (such as enhancing self-concept, the feeling of mastering one's environment, receiving recognition for effort and improvement, and gaining a sense of competence and achievement). The following suggestions indicate how coaches and parents can help young participants to deal constructively with the process of comparative appraisal.

1.   *Avoid comparing children.* Every child has his or her own skills, strengths, and weaknesses. The role of the adult is to inform participants about their adequacies and to help them learn skills and improve performance. Statements such as "If Jimmy can do it, why can't you?" are unfair at best and destructive to a child's character at worst. To realize that children excel at different sports and skills is important. Give them the credit they deserve so that involvement in sport does not become uninvolvement in it.

2.   *Help children to realize that "different" doesn't mean "better."* Because of the social pressures exerted by parents, children will compare their performances with others. However, when a child believes that love and recognition from "significant others" (persons whose opinions are valued) depend on favorable performance outcomes such as getting a hit (baseball) or catching a pass (football), the youngster is apt to be more intense in the comparative appraisal process. Consequently, he or she will be more critical and will manifest insecure behaviors (Ginott 1968). One child might possess a set of skills different from that of another child. The important issue is that each person has something to feel good about.

3.   *Adults should be positive models for children.* If we expect our children to avoid criticizing peers, coaches and parents must do likewise.

Children's performances should be critiqued during practice (not during the game) and in private (not in public). Embarrassing a child in the presence of peers creates bitterness and resentment. The desirable outcomes of sport such as skill learning and fun become nonexistent.

4.   *Finally, help to prevent sport-related stress.* Adults can help children to make more positive appraisals of their sport experiences and to overcome stress in sport. The sport environment is filled with evaluative messages of approval (cheering or backslapping, for example) and disapproval (booing, ridicule, and ignoring). Coaches and parents, aside from the very important suggestion of not being the source of negative messages, can help children to deal with the unpleasant messages given by fans, opponents, and others. A pat on the back with a few kind words of support go a long way toward preventing depression — especially after the player has made an error or in some way contributed to an unfavorable team outcome (missing a shot, for instance). Teach children how to handle some of the unpleasant aspects of playing competitive sports such as insulting or angry remarks from others. Better yet, give the young victim of such verbal abuse an immediate heavy dose of emotional support and, if possible, put an end to the negative remarks.

Lack of Perceived Ability

The best advice for adult leaders of sport programs is to *focus on improvement and effort, not ability* in youth sports. Dr. Glyn Roberts (1984) from the University of Illinois, who has investigated and written extensively about the area of youth sport, has concluded that the primary reason why children drop out of sport is because they attribute failure (poor performance) to their lack of ability. Early in a child's athletic experience, successful performance is based on merely completing the task — just getting to the finish line in a fifty-yard dash, for example. Later, however, social approval becomes an important goal. If the athlete is to maintain participation in sport, he or she needs the approval of "significant others" such as the coach, teammates, friends, and parents. The young player soon realizes that the approval of the coach is dependent upon effort. "If I try hard, the coach will like and accept me," he or she feels. Therefore, trying hard becomes the criterion of success and failure.

However, starting at about the ages of eleven and twelve years (and sometimes younger), "perceived ability" becomes of paramount importance as the motivating factor for playing sport. Instead of completing a task (the goal of the six-, seven-, and eight-year-olds) or vying for social approval (common at the ages of eight, nine, and ten years), the youths' primary source of motivation in sport becomes the feeling of competence. The lack of competence is now attributed to low ability, instead of to a lack of effort or to task difficulty. Most kids who drop out of sport (as many as two-thirds in some studies) think that they are "not good enough." This is where the coach and parents enter the picture.

Coaches in particular can directly affect a child's feelings of competence in sport. To do this, they need to help the youngsters to interpret the causes of performance outcomes. Striking out, missing a shot, or making an error can be interpreted as due to a lack of ability ("You don't have a good eye for hitting") or lack of effort ("With more practice, performance will improve; keep trying"). Coaches and parents, then, need to offer feedback to young players that indicates three things:

1.   Doing the best they can — making the effort — is very important for success.
2.   Performance (any aspect of it that can be observed and identified) is, in fact, improving.
3.   Lack of ability has nothing to do with performance outcome.

Children should know that everyone is capable of improving. In youth sport, the accent should be on skill development and fun, not on winning contests. The game outcome is not an end in itself but merely an end result of learning, performance improvement, and improved self-confidence. Once a player feels that he or she lacks the ability to be successful, the probability of dropping out of sport increases dramatically. Adults can prevent this by doing the following:

1.   Help to focus the child's attention on how he or she is performing in relation to previous performances and away from comparing himself or herself with other children. To do this, orient the child to the use of performance goals within the sport rather than to the outcome of winning or losing.
2.   If assessing one's own ability is inherent in older children (around ten years and up), then coaches can encourage a positive perception of ability through sport mastery. Reinforce the specific skills that each athlete can perform competently while emphasizing improvement on weaker skills.
3.   Youngsters might view themselves as skilled in some areas and unskilled in others. To help children to develop accurate and stable views of their abilities, set performance goals for each individual that each is capable of achieving. Use *performance* as the standard for success and failure. The youths will be less apt to fail if goals are set realistically.
4.   Encourage children after failure. Children tend to have global perceptions of their abilities after success or failure — particularly after the latter. Making an error translates into "I'm a terrible player." Children need to be reminded that a good performer can experience a performance failure. They need to be reminded of their competence.
5.   Children need to know that people grow and mature at different rates. Comparing themselves to bigger, stronger peers may promote feelings

of inadequacy and low self-esteem. Coaches should communicate to young athletes about what is happening to their bodies and assure them that they will grow, become stronger, and improve in the performance. The message should be, "Be patient."

Young athletes drop out of sport to avoid feeling incompetent and to save face in front of peers and parents. One way to help these children to deal with athletic competition is to teach them how to ask the right questions and avoid others. Asking "How can I improve?" or "How can I improve this skill?" is a far more constructive strategy than "Can we win?" or "Am I good enough?" Children should be concerned with sport mastery and not ego-involving outcome assessments.

Low Intrinsic Motivation

As previously noted in chapter 5, the main reason why children want to participate in sport is to have fun. And the most common reason they offer for dropping out is "It's not fun." This fun component underlies the concept of intrinsic motivation. To feel motivated is to have the desire and drive to move toward some goal (Magill 1985). To feel *intrinsically motivated* is the desire to do something because it's enjoyable; the experience itself is enough to feel good about performing some task. Outside rewards and ultimate goals are not neccessary. The lack or absence of intrinsic motivation plays a significant role in withdrawal from sport. Sadly, parents and coaches, often unknowingly, contribute to this predicament.

Adult leaders in sport typically claim that children want and need a reward system (trophies, for instance) to maintain interest in, and derive pleasure from, playing competitive sport. Researchers have not found this to be the case. Reliance on rewards, a form of *extrinsic motivation*, turns play into work. Activity that is intrinsically motivating is often play activity (Siedentop and Ramy 1977). The important questions parents and coaches should be asking are: (1) "What can I do to maintain or increase intrinsic motivation in child athletes and reduce or prevent the onset of extrinsic motivation?" (2) "Does the use of all rewards undermine intrinsic motivation?" and (3) "Do kids want and enjoy receiving awards?"

The good news is that the selective use of awards in sport has been shown to benefit young athletes; rewarding play activity *can* actually increase intrinsic motivation under certain circumstances but can decrease it in others. It's a matter of how the child perceives the reason for the reward. Sometimes, however, a child's motivation for engaging in an activity goes from internal (e.g., fun) to external (e.g., a trophy). This process has been termed the *overjustification effect* (Lepper, Greene, and Nesbitt 1973). This occurs when the child receives an award that is expected, very obvious, and highly recognized — not just a pat on the back but a highly visible reward such as a trophy presented at a banquet. This effect is based on the assumption by adults that the child can't possibly want to participate in an activity simply for its enjoyment. "Doesn't every kid want a trophy?" they seem to ask. "Won't most-valuable-player awards and all-star team recognition motivate them to play better and have more fun?" they predict. The answer is an emphatic "no!" Adult leaders in sport and parents of child athletes "overjustify" the youngster's reasons for engaging in the activity by making an erroneous assumption: that kids can't possibly have the incentive to play sports in the absence of some tangible reward.

To increase intrinsic motivation through the use of rewards, consider the following suggestions:

1. Remember that children seek information about personal ability through sport performance. Therefore, the rewards derived from that performance should reflect the child's ability. A trophy, ribbon, certificate, or verbal recognition should reflect some accomplishment, improvement, or effort from their performance.

2. Rewards should be distributed to all players, but rewards should be based on some aspect of performance worth recognizing. Not every athlete can demonstrate efficiency in performance, but all athletes *can* exhibit improvement or effort. Recognize it.

3. Children should not be coerced into participating. Let the motive for playing be self-determined. The motive should not be to gain their parents' love but because they want to play.

4. Teach skills. Children can improve only if they are taught sport skills. It's unfair to expect better performance simply as the result of repetition in practice.

5. Help the team members to support one another. Point out good performance of one athlete to the team. Encourage mutual support by team members.

6. Often coaches are the models for desirable behaviors. As such, their statements and behaviors of positive verbal and nonverbal communication, support, and approval of others will facilitate similar responses by team members.

7. Whenever possible, give players an opportunity to make decisions that affect their play or the game. Choosing one's position, developing team strategy, and making other decisions can help participants to meet their needs for self-determination.

8. Try to have each youngster experience some degree of success as soon as possible in his or her career in competitive sport. The need for competence is most salient at the early stages of involvement when youngsters have the most doubts about their skills and make rapid judgments about further participation.

9. Awards should be unexpected, if possible. Researchers have found that children who receive rewards unexpectedly maintain a stable level

of intrinsic interest. Avoid promising some reward if they win; you will be setting them up for failure, and they will feel resentful. After a well-played game or practice session, surprise them with a treat. The effect will be much longer lasting. The participant will receive the reward as an outcome of competence rather than playing for the treat — although the reward is external, it is noncontrolling.

10.   Establish individual goals *jointly with the athlete* based on realistic expectations of the person's performance.

Why do kids drop out of sport? The comparative-appraisal process, the lack of perceived ability, and the lowering of intrinsic motivation are each — and in combination — primary causes. But in a word, the single condition that underlies each of these perceptual processes leading to withdrawal from competition is stress.

Competitive Stress in Youth Sport

Competitive sport is a game, and kids participate in sport to have fun — or at least that's the way it is supposed to be and for many children it is. Unfortunately, others find the sport experience unpleasant and even stressful. The negative emotional reaction of a child when his or her self-esteem is threatened is referred to as *competitive stress*. Sport psychologists, Tara Scanlon and Michael Passer (1978) from UCLA and the University of Washington, respectively, have jointly examined the topic of competitive stress in the child athlete. They found that competitive stress is based on the child's *perceptions* of inadequacy in meeting performance demands and his or her *perceptions* of the consequences of failure. The child's own appraisal of the situation is what determines whether his or her self-esteem is threatened. If the child predicts that not getting a base hit will result in negative consequences (e.g., being ignored by peers, reprimanded by parents or the coach, or booed by spectators), then competitive stress is heightened. If the child feels comfortable that doing his or her best — making an optimal effort at the task — is all that's necessary to succeed or to gain the approval of others, the perception of threat (i.e., competitive stress) is reduced or nonexistent.

Competitive stress can occur at any time: (1) before the competition in anticipation of poor performance, (2) during the contest if performance is viewed as inadequate, or (3) after the competition if the child has concluded that the completed performance did not meet expectations.

Further, in their 1984 published findings, Scanlon and Passer concluded that the most common cause of competitive stress, also referred to as *state anxiety*, is the threat of failure. This anxiety increases with age and is most prevalent at age twelve years, the time when dropping out of sport begins to peak. Children in sport fear failure because of the importance adults place on success and game outcome.

To combat competitive stress, less emphasis should be placed on requiring children to meet performance expectations, winning the contest, and comparing athletes on their abilities. At the same time, more attention should be given to teaching skills, emphasizing effort and performance improvement, training coaches to communicate with young athletes in a mature, nonthreatening manner, and deemphasizing championships and other forms of selective recognition that reward relatively few children while facilitating feelings of failure and inadequacy in a far greater number of child participants.

Gould (1984) suggests that coaches and parents should ask the following questions to become more aware of the characteristic symptoms of competitive stress or anxiety: (1) Does the athlete consistently perform better in practice than in actual competitive situations? (2) Is the player having trouble sleeping, especially the night before competition? (3) Does he or she have trouble "getting loose" before an event? (4) Are there marked personality changes just before competition? (5) Does the athlete complain of illness the evening before, or the day of, a contest on a regular basis? This tendency is referred to as "Little League Syndrome," in which the stress of anticipating an unpleasant sport experience is so great that the child either feigns illness or experiences psychosomatic effects of stress. These are issues that need to be discussed and resolved, should they become evident.

ADMINISTRATION OF YOUTH SPORT LEAGUES

It is rare to find a person who does not recall his or her experiences as a young athlete in a structured youth sport program. Being an athlete fulfills the fantasy of emulating our heroes and models in professional sport and provides an opportunity to enhance our self-images. The child's needs for recognition and achievement can be met. And being a sport participant can mean having fun, learning new skills, affiliating with peers, and getting physical exercise. Therefore, playing sport is an integral part of growing up in many communities. The administration of a youth sport program carries with it a tremendous responsibility in meeting the needs of so many children — and parents. All moms and dads want their child to have a positive experience through sport. Administering a quality youth sport program is extremely challenging, but very gratifying.

The Administrator's Role

Who "runs the show"? Is only one person responsible for developing and implementing the program? Is it a board of directors? A group of interested parents? The local government (the city recreation director, for example)? Whoever takes the responsibility for creating or supervising a youth sport program is accountable to its participants and their families to conduct a program that is safe and supervised by skilled, responsible adults, who view the child's welfare as their primary objective. The professional youth sport literature suggests effective strategies for the administration of children's sport programs. Assessing needs, developing a philosophy, structuring the organization, implementing operational procedures (including ongoing evaluation) and identifying key activities during the season are the administrative components.

Assessment of needs. Before jumping into a full-scale, expensive effort, determine what extracurricular programs are now available to the local community. It would be counterproductive to replicate an effective program already in progress. What sport programs are offered in the schools? Implementing the same skills that local physical educators are teaching is helpful. Under ideal conditions, teachers and volunteer coaches can get together and review these skills.

It is also wise to determine whether a similar program existed previously and, if so, why it was terminated. No need? No response?

Who will promote the program and what resources are available to assist? Perhaps local organizations such as the community recreation department, Girl or Boy Scouts, Young Men's or Women's Christian Association, or Jewish Community Center can provide opportunities to help promote and implement sports programs. The cost, available financial resources, affordability to consumers, and available facilities and equipment are other issues that should be addressed.

Philosophy. The program should emphasize helping children, promoting the opportunity for success for all participants, focusing on the pleasure of participation, learning new skills, and improving health. Local control of the program should also be emphasized.

Another important aspect of the program's philosophy concerns the benefits that participants should derive from the involvement. If, as most sport sociologists contend, sport is a microcosm of life in which young athletes can learn from and apply sport-related experiences to their own maturation, then several goals should be reached, including (1) learning to cooperate with others, (2) working persistently at long-term goals, (3) accepting one's strengths and weaknesses, (4) becoming self-assertive, (5) respecting others, (6) feeling motivated to achieve, and (7) coping with success and failure.

If the program truly meets the needs of its participants, then it is fun, builds self-confidence, develops sport skills, facilitates player interaction and building of friendships, provides additional play opportunities (which means everyone practices and plays, not just starters), develops lifelong patterns and habits of physical activity (athletes *never* run for punishment), and the program is safe (first aid supplies are available, supervisory personnel have skills in first aid, water is available to all participants, and the facilities and equipment are cared for and functional).

Organizational structure. How is the sport organization administered and implemented? An organizational flow chart of positions and responsibilities of key personnel should be created to illustrate the flow of communication and responsibility from the "bottom up" and the "top down." In addition, job descriptions of paid and volunteer positions should be written clearly and distributed. Ultimate responsibility for the program lies with a board of elected citizens.

Operational procedures. Three primary areas affect the implementation of the sport program. First, coaches, parents, and officials should be systematically involved in the decision-making process. This strategy broadens the base of support and is important in carrying out decisions. Second, all policies of the league's control board should be reviewed and supported by a committee or other body that represents the constituents. Third, all goals and policies of the program should exist and be distributed to selected individuals in written form.

Ongoing evaluation. The effectiveness of a sport league program can only be assessed if it is evaluated on a continual and systematic basis. Evaluations should be built into the program, including the objectives, timing, outcomes, the process, and how the information will be shared. Who does the evaluating? Who and what is evaluated? What is the procedure for objectively reviewing the assessments, suggesting changes, and gathering a consensus from selected personnel to implement changes? Typically, game officials, coaches, athletes, parents, security, and spectators should be included in the evaluation process.

Identify key activities. Another primary responsibility of the administrator is to provide leadership for activities during the season in addition to game schedules. Recommendations for organizing the season include conducting clinics for coaches and officials (i.e., referees, umpires); planning promotional strategies such as with newspapers, radio, television, flyers in schools and at recreational centers, at halftime in school sport programs, in churches and synagogues, and at businesses; registering players; making coaching equipment available; setting up dates for practices; making team rosters and game schedules available; planning to teach certain skills and putting them on a weekly calendar; planning parent meetings before and after the season, and, if possible, during the season as well to offer information and feedback on the program; planning postseason games, tournaments, and awards recognition banquets; and evaluating the program in written and verbal form based on input from players, coaches, parents, spectators, and officials.

If there is one key element to effective administration of a youth sport program, it's community involvement and support. Parents must believe that the program is governed by intelligent, conscientious, experienced individuals who are concerned with providing a quality, safe, and secure environment for child participants. In addition to the image that the league projects in its literature and advertisements, perhaps the most important feature of the program that makes the greatest impact on parents is the level of coaching expertise.

Training the Coach

Providing quality training for the leaders of youth sport programs is no easy task. To begin with, most coaches are volunteers — men and women who have full-time jobs and can offer relatively little time for player and team development. Attempts to require preseason training for coaching have met with little success. In many cases, hard and fast rules about such training programs have resulted in a lack of leadership on the field or court. The result could be cancellation of the program. Nevertheless, the training of coaches is a fundamental requirement of a quality sport program. Training the coaches should consist of six areas.

A.   **Formal Presentations/Workshops/Group Discussions**

A minimum of six topics should be covered prior to the season.

1. *Understanding and discussing the program objectives.* How important is winning? What is the Bill of Rights in youth sport (discussed later in this chapter)? How does one use effective communication techniques with parents, athletes, opponents, officials, and other coaches? Is there a reward system that the league endorses or ignores?
2. *Sport psychology.* What is the coach's role as a sport leader? How can the young athlete be motivated and be mentally prepared to play at optimal levels? How are goals set and measured? When is there too much or too little competitive stress, and how does one cope with too much of it? What can the coach do to build team cohesion and player friendships? What are good communication strategies? One technique to improve player input is to provide a written evaluation form that players can complete and submit anonymously to the coach.
3. *Exercise physiology.* How do males and females differ with respect to training in sport? How important is physical conditioning with child athletes, and what techniques are appropriate for the particular age group? What are the do's and don'ts of weight training? What is the proper way to warm up, stretch, and cool down? Are there some movements that are detrimental to good health? How does the athlete prepare for and participate in extreme heat, cold, humidity, and wind? How does eating right influence performance?

4. *Growth and development.* How do boys and girls differ in body size, strength, and movement mechanics? Why do children grow at different rates? And how might the size and maturity of children affect their athletic ability? When should competition begin for young athletes? What is the best way to equalize the teams for competition? Does intense physical activity influence growth and maturity? Are there any dangers in performing certain types of physical tasks — movements that could be potentially harmful to the child?

5. *Motor learning.* How does one teach sport skills so that they are remembered and performed efficiently in game situations? How does the coach organize a practice session? What are the correct skill progressions so that athletes progress smoothly from simple to more complex skills?

6. *First aid.* In what ways can the coach prevent injuries including those related to cold or hot weather? What is the immediate response to different first aid situations? What situations are emergencies that require medical assistance? Does each coach know the emergency telephone number by memory? Is first aid equipment readily available? Do coaches possess telephone numbers of parents and, if necessary, a second party for emergencies? Are coaches familiar with cardiopulmonary resuscitation? How does one communicate effectively with the victim?

B.   Outline the Sport Skills to be Taught

1. Determine which skills are required to participate successfully and how many to emphasize during the season.

2. List the subskills that should be mastered before skills can be used in a game. For example: Subskills in basketball include bouncing the ball while eyes are focused on others (without looking at the ball); in a tennis serve, subskills include the ball toss, racket movement, and arm extension at ball contact. To select the proper subskills, use these criteria:

   a. Physical capabilities of children (seven-year-olds cannot serve a tennis ball successfully; young children cannot perform an overhand volleyball serve)

   b. Previous experience (novice versus experienced)

   c. Length of season and the number of practices (prioritize and select a realistic number of skills or subskills that can be taught and mastered)

   d. Learning rates of children (do not expect child athletes to master skills quickly, especially those considered continuous, open, and complex)

C.   **Organize Skill Instruction**

1. Fundamental to complex (from putting to driving a golf ball)
2. Elements of a skill to its completion (subskills of a batting swing)
3. Single skill to skill combinations (dribbling a soccer ball to stop the ball, then dribbling and shooting)
4. Approximations to accurate execution (what is an acceptable level of mastery, given their age, experience, and so on?)
5. Go from partial to full speed (don't slow it down too much, or it becomes a different skill)

D.   **Construct a Weekly Calendar**

1. Identify all practice and game days
2. Enter the skill on which you intend to focus and the time allotment given to them at each practice

E.   **Prepare a List of Activities or Drills Appropriate for Each Skill**
Components of a good drill include:

1. A name
2. Purposefully planned prior to practice
3. Relatively short explanation required (talk less, do more)
4. Easily understood
5. Matches the plan and time needed to master the skill
6. Easily modified to prevent boredom or used differently according to age group and background of athletes
7. Facilitates the use of skills in a game situation
8. Provides repeated opportunities for skill analysis and feedback

F.   **Develop an Effective Practice Plan**

1. Plan well before practice
2. Try to stick with the plan, but be flexible
3. Include the following:

    a.   warm-up (less necessary with active children in warm weather)
    b.   series of short, intense drills
    c.   review skills previously taught
    d.   teach 1 or 2 new skills
    e.   game-type scrimmage (simulate game situations)
    f.   team meeting to provide additional feedback
    g.   evaluate the practice
    h.   record suggested changes for the practice

Parental Involvement

Without the support of parents, no program will exist. Program administrators sometimes think that the presence of parents at contests adds stress to an already anxiety-filled situation. It's true that some parents are sources of stress to their children (and to other players, too). And in some leagues around the country, parents have been barred from appearing at games; the kids play without spectators. However, to prevent parents from observing their children as they engage in sport competition is counterproductive; it does not resolve the issue of the overzealous parent spectator. The real issue is how can league officials get more cooperation from parents who receive considerable satisfaction from observing their child participate? In fact, many children enjoy having their mom and dad watch them play; the need for recognition is very real to these kids. What, then, can coaches and program administrators do to turn the situation around? How can parents become sources of strength and support for the participants?

Clearly the first priority for league officials is to engage in verbal and written exchanges with parents. Parents want and need information about the program's philosophy and approach to sport. The exchange of information is even more productive if it flows in both directions: Parental support is more forthcoming if opinions are solicited and if meetings are held to exchange information. The following recommendations concern both verbal (parent meetings) and written forms of input from the parents of players.

The parent orientation meeting. Youth sport league administrators need to understand that parents have a right to know as much about the program as possible. In fact, parents will be far more supportive of program objectives (and will conduct themselves accordingly) if the program is discussed *before* the season begins. The best way to communicate this information is through the parent orientation meeting. Here are a few guidelines:

1. The meeting should be at a time and location convenient to all concerned.
2. Children should not be prohibited from attending for two reasons: (a) content of the meeting should not be inappropriate for children anyway, and (b) many parents are unable or unwilling to pay a babysitter and, if required to do so, will not attend.
3. Be sure refreshments are available and indicated on all written advertising.
4. League officials should dress appropriately to project a professional image. Someone once said, "You have just one chance to make a good first impression." Sloppy dress says to the audience, "I don't respect you."
5. An example of an agenda for the meeting is:

a.   *Introductions.* The administrator, coach, and team sponsor should be introduced (including their telephone numbers). A plan to introduce parents to one another would also be helpful. The purpose of the meeting should be described, and any handouts distributed at this time.

b.   *Understanding the sport.* Parents need to have the same understanding about realistic expectations of the young players, game rules, demonstrating techniques, and perhaps a film depicting the skills. A coach or arbiter might be the best source to lead this segment of the meeting.

c.   *Dangers and risk of injury.* Let parents know if a medical examination is required before participation. What are the common injuries of the sport, and how should they be treated? Who pays for medical care? Is there a league accident insurance policy? What are the safety rules for games and practices, and what can parents do to promote these rules in the home?

d.   *Equipment needs.* What equipment does the league provide, and what must the players supply? Parents may need advice on the type and brand of equipment to purchase and the approximate cost of these items.

e.   *Coaching philosophy.* The goals of the program and coaches should be articulated. Is winning the most important thing? If having fun and learning skills take priority, it is crucial that parents realize that winning and losing are mere by-products of the child's involvement—not ends in themselves. Other rules concerning who starts; who plays; discipline; expectations about showing up for practice; and the rationale for, or existence of, awards, an all-star team, most valuable player, and other forms of recognition should be discussed now. If rewards are offered, are they contingent upon performance, or are they given to all participants regardless of achievements?

f.   *Emergency procedures.* Obtain a list of the names, addresses, and telephone numbers of parents, family physicians, and other adults if parents cannot be contacted in case of an injury. This information should be distributed to all parents of each team to facilitate contact between families. Emergency procedures should be outlined.

g.   *The child's responsibilities.* If children are to mature due to their sport experiences, they must assume certain responsibilities. These include: (a) reporting promptly to practice and games, (b) cooperating with coaches and teammates, (c) wearing the proper uniform at games, (d) following team rules, (e) making the proper effort to condition their bodies and learn sport skills, and (f) conducting themselves in a mature manner before, during, and after team-related functions. Parents should be asked to support these behavior expectations at home.

h. *The parents' responsibilities.* All of the programs related to effective youth sport programs agree on the importance of parental involvement as an integral part of the child's experience in competitive sport. And if the type of involvement cannot be positive — for example, if parents will not discipline their children to ensure that they meet their responsibilities as program participants — then it should be supportive, preferably both. Parents should: (1) learn what their children want from the sport—why they are participating in the first place, (2) determine if their children are ready to compete in sport and in the particular program they desire, (3) have realistic expectations and help their children to understand the time and effort that goes into quality sport performance, (4) help their children to understand the meaning of winning and losing, the probable outcomes from high versus low effort, the importance of personal improvement, the disadvantages of comparing themselves with others (especially older or more experienced players), (5) not interfere with their children's coach at any time, soliciting information about the child's progress or offering to assist the coach at practice are fine, but negative interactions such as blaming and arguing are not, and (6) conduct themselves in a mature manner at games. The competitive event presents a relatively tense atmosphere even without the presence of parents. What the children need is support and recognition in both verbal and nonverbal forms. What they do not need is ridicule, pressure to succeed, reprimand, blame, threats, and isolation. Often it is the parent's response to the athletic event that determines the type of experience sport will provide: fun or misery.

i. *The season's schedule.* At the parent meeting, provide written documentation of the locations and times of all games, practices, and other events that are scheduled before, during, and after the season.

Written input. Not everyone is able to attend meetings, nor are they comfortable expressing themselves verbally. There should also be a written outlet for expressing opinions and providing feedback. To enhance the support of parents, it is important to solicit their opinions about the program. In this way, parents begin to feel a sense of ownership toward program policies and activities. A follow-up to this input is advised, either a written response acknowledging the feedback or by making actual changes in some aspect of the operation that reflect the input. If parents and players feel their opinions are not valued, they will stop responding; league officials will lose credibility.

A final issue concerns the timing for parent meetings. There are good reasons to offer opportunities to meet with parents before, during, and after the season. Preseason meetings, of course, introduce the parents to the program. Meeting during the season provides a forum to offer feedback that can result in *immediate* changes or, at least, discussion about concerns from program experiences. After the season, it's time to reflect upon the season and discuss what went well and what did not; what to keep for next year and what to change. In addition to meeting times, it would be a good idea to hand out suggestion/feedback forms with a mailing address indicated. This would allow each parent or player an opportunity to communicate their feelings — both positive and negative — rather than holding them inside, which, under some circumstances, could be frustrating and raise the chances of hostilities among parents, coaches, and administrators.

COACHING CHILDREN

When coaching children, to keep in mind that they are not miniature adults is important. Their levels of physical and mental maturation do not allow them to perform complex skills and to withstand the pressures of winning. Success and failure are not defined the same way for child athletes as they are for their older counterparts. Success might be getting into the game; it might mean doing one's best or not making an error. Winning has nothing to do with a successful outcome to most kids. The objectives we have for child athletes are different as well. We want to help them to develop skills and positive attitudes about participating in sport. Successful experiences can improve each youngster's self-image and lead to a variety of other desirable personality attributes discussed earlier.

But if sport participation is to have these positive outcomes, the coach must understand the unique qualities of child athletes and respond accordingly. As Martens (1980, pp. 383–84) contends, "Children are unique in that not all respond the same way to criticism, perceive the same situations to be stressful, or seek the same outcomes from sport." One way that coaches can provide effective leadership to children is to understand their reasons for dropping out of sport.

Reason 1: Not getting to play. Researchers have found that given the choice, more children in sport would rather play on a losing team than remain on the bench of a winning team. Playing is valued much more than winning.

Therefore, coaches should be sure that skills are taught so that *all* players on the team can participate successfully. If arranging for game participation is difficult, then ensure that all players receive plenty of attention and positive feedback during practice. Make their affiliation with the team meaningful.

Reason 2: Negative reinforcement. Errors, for children and adults, are a normal part of learning, particularly with less skilled performers. Children are especially vulnerable to negative feedback and ridicule because it's so difficult for them to put the situation in perspective. Being a "poor" player also means being an inadequate person. Kids believe what adults tell them. But eventually, if insults don't stop, the kids will drop out. Coaches should focus their comments on performance, not character. Follow the "sandwich approach" discussed in chapter 8. Also, keep errors in perspective. The coach's reaction to an error has a direct relationship to the amount of learning gained from it.

Reason 3: Mismatching. When kids are mismatched in size and skills, the underdog finds little about which to feel successful and motivated. Boys of the same chronological age may differ by as much as five years anatomically. Try to provide a safe and enjoyable environment for each child. Each player should enter a program and be assigned a team that is compatible with his or her physical maturity and approximate skill level.

Reason 4: Psychological stress. Kids should not have to feel anxious before games. The competitive process should be challenging, but also rewarding and fun. The closer that practice situations simulate the games, the easier athletes will be able to adjust to game conditions. Also, coaches should avoid telling the players about the importance of winning, or reminding them of who's watching them. Coach, don't take the game too seriously.

Reason 5: Failure. If children want to derive a sense of satisfaction and fun from playing sports (it is, after all, a game), then chronic failure will diminish interest, generate anxiety, inhibit performance, and lower feelings of self-worth. This is particularly true as children move closer to adolescence. First, children feel that they've failed only when coaches and parents send messages indicating such. An error can be interpreted as failing or as making a good attempt and some improvement. Let's emphasize the positive aspects of performance. Second, errors can be minimized by teaching skills and engaging in efficient practice sessions. Coaches must know the correct skills and how to teach them.

Reason 6: Overorganization. Some studies show that children can receive more exercise in unorganized sports around the neighborhood than in structured programs. The kids simply do not get the chance to become physically active. A related comment by children is that practices are too regimented and sometimes far too reliant on physical conditioning rather than skill teaching.

Sometimes, kids are disciplined for not keeping in a straight line or for not giving the coach their full attention during the coach's explanation of the drill. But the reason why the children are "getting into trouble" is because the practice is boring and physically inactive. The fun component has been effectively removed. Follow the principles of effective skill instruction. In other words, talk less and do more. Keep the kids moving. Also, be creative. Avoid engaging in the same drills constantly. Simulate game conditions. Have contests among team members that utilize game-related skills. Another suggestion is promote fitness, but don't overwork them. Child athletes need skill development, not bigger muscles. Keep the conditioning regimen to a minimum.

BILL OF RIGHTS FOR YOUNG ATHLETES

In 1979, the National Association for Sport and Physical Education's Youth Sports Task Force prepared a set of guidelines to help millions of adults provide quality youth sport programs. The primary component of the guidelines was a Bill of Rights for Young Athletes that adults should acknowledge and respond to as leaders of youth sport programs. The ten rights included (1) the right to participate in sport, (2) the right to participate at a level commensurate with each child's maturity and ability, (3) the right to have qualified adult leadership, (4) the right to play as a child and not as an adult, (5) the right of children to share in the leadership and decision making of their sport participation, (6) the right to participate in safe and healthy environments, (7) the right to proper preparation for participation in sport, (8) the right to an equal opportunity to strive for success, (9) the right to be treated with dignity, and (10) the right to have fun in sport.

Right to Participate in Sports

Should only the gifted play while the unskilled are eliminated from the sport area? Should only the best be selected to participate, as in the professional and school models, while others are "cut" from the team? Every child should have the right to choose whether to participate and the opportunity to participate regardless of gender, race, or ability level.

Right to Participate at a Level Commensurate with Each Child's Maturity and Ability Level

According to the guidelines, "The use of age and sometimes weight as the only criteria for classifying children often denies late-maturing children the right to participate at a level commensurate with their maturity" (p. 18). The task force recommends that a greater variety of sports be offered to match children to the sport that best fits their physical statures, maturities, and abilities. Also, offering varying levels of competition within a sport will group children of comparable ability and maturity more homogeneously.

Right to Have Qualified Adult Leadership

Qualified leaders (1) understand children, (2) organize and conduct efficient practices where children learn, (3) keep it fun, (4) do not abuse their power, (5) understand the basic skills and strategies of the particular sport, and (6) do not abuse children and have no need to seek their own recognition.

Right to Play as a Child and Not as an Adult

Because children define success differently than adults, it is unnecessary to seek victory as the primary objective of youth sport. Merely contacting the ball is a far more important criterion for success than scoring runs. A quality soccer kick carries more weight than whether the ball goes into the goal. For children under ten years of age, merely completing a fifty-yard dash is the measure of success, not arriving first at the finish line. Sport is an experience or, better yet, a set of experiences that allows a youngster the opportunity to explore, experiment, and risk. Let them try.

Right of Children to Share in the Leadership and Decision Making of Their Sport Participation

This is a difficult objective for coaches who are consumed with the power to make decisions, dictate strategies, and have general control of the environment. Such persons should not, in fact, be leaders in youth sport programs. A quality youth sport experience should include the development of independence and accountability for the young player's behavior. Giving children the choice of whether to play sports, and the opportunity to decide the sports in which to participate, to jointly establish goals of their play, and to share their opinions with the coach about practices, games, and other aspects of their involvement helps to meet the objectives of the program.

Right to Participate in Safe and Healthy Environments

Parents are rightfully concerned for the safety of their children when participating in sports. Effective leadership in sport must do whatever possible to *prevent* injuries from occurring and use correct first aid procedures when they do occur. Safe equipment, safe facilities, and safe activities must be guaranteed components of the program. Equipment in disrepair should be discarded, and unsafe facilities rejected and ignored. Participants must learn performance techniques and, to an extent, engage in conditioning programs that reduce the probability of injury.

Right to Proper Preparation for Participation in Sport

Physical and mental readiness is an integral part of the sport experience. Tell the children what is expected of them and what they can expect from their efforts. Tasks such as obtaining a medical clearance for participation, leading proper physical conditioning, and teaching skills are responsibilities of the coach. Children should not be thrust into competition prematurely. Understanding the rules, accepting norms of behavior, and performing skills at even minimal levels are requisites for sport competition. Parents also have a role in ensuring that their child pursues proper nutrition and sleep habits so that engaging in athletics becomes a pleasant experience.

Right to Have an Equal Opportunity to Strive for Success

The issue here is not having a right to success, but the right to *strive* for it. "Children must be taught (and so must some adults) that success is not synonymous with winning, nor failure with losing. They must be helped to see success as progress towards achieving their potential" (Martens and Seefeldt 1979, p. 29). How are children denied an opportunity to strive for success? They are denied when they are given little or no instruction, when criticism of errors replaces constructive coaching, when they have little opportunity to practice skills or perform those skills in contests, and when they are thrust into competition at levels for which they are not prepared. As Martens and Seefeldt claim, children "must learn that winning and losing are not a reflection of their self-worth, but success and failure are." Although winning constantly is impossible, all children can succeed when success is viewed as progress toward meeting one's potential.

Right to Be Treated with Dignity

Children want and need respect. There is no place for the humiliation of children, particularly in an activity in which participation is voluntary and meant to be fun such as sport. Sadly, the competitive sport arena is fertile territory for abusive treatment, disparaging remarks, intimidation, and criticism owing to (1) the requirement of performing complex skills successfully and consistently and (2) the inherent component of athletes that always compares performers, viewing one as more skilled (the winner) than the other (the loser). Adults must always be self-conscious about prohibiting abusive treatment of the players. Even punishment, if necessary, can be carried out without destroying the child's dignity. "Through sport, adults need to help children build self-respect, not destroy it" (Martens and Seefeldt 1979, p. 30).

Right to Have Fun in Sport

As indicated earlier, "to have fun" is the most frequent reason why children play in sport settings. The components of fun include meeting individual needs, growth and maturation, and personal satisfaction. It is "fun" to feel comfortable risking attempts at new skills without fear of unpleasant ramifications such as rejection or ridicule. In fact, if the nine previous rights are obtained, then these fun components are virtually assured. If fun is lacking in sport involvement, then the child has every right to withdraw from the situation and to seek fun elsewhere. Too often this is exactly what happens. Ideally, adults should prevent stress from becoming a predominant component of the sport experience and respond immediately to stressful situations.

According to Seefeldt (1980), youth sport is too stressful when:

1. Children aren't having fun in practice and games.
2. Winning becomes the most important element of the competition.
3. Children return from practice or games emotionally upset because of what their coaches or teammates have said to them.
4. Practices or games interfere with scheduled meals or sleep.
5. Participation causes a change in the child's overall personality or attitude.
6. Children within an eligible age group are eliminated because of their gender, inadequate motor skills, or body size.
7. Children are asked to practice or play one position and are prevented from trying out for others that they prefer.
8. Children are asked to concentrate on one sport for the greater part of the calendar year, thus depriving them of learning the skills that are essential for other sports.
9. Parents coerce or compel children to participate in sports.

The beauty of being a leader among children is that they are so influenced by the forces that surround them. They view adults with respect and admiration — until they learn to feel otherwise. And what they learn is often a direct reflection of their experiences. In sport, it is the responsibility of each adult leader (and parent) to ensure that these experiences are as successful and pleasant as possible. Children learn what they live.

SUMMARY

Children are not miniature adults, and child athletes have needs that differ from their older, more skilled counterparts. First, children mature at vastly different rates. This means that at a given age, some youngsters will be better prepared to develop and perform sport skills proficiently than others. A second need of child athletes is to learn sport skills prior to the time that these skills are executed in competitive situations. Unlike older players, children are significantly less physiologically affected by vigorous physical training for strength and endurance. Another important need of child athletes is to participate in an environment that includes equipment size and dimensions that are commensurate with their smaller physical size, strength, and skill.

The primary reasons why children participate in sport are to have fun, followed by learning new skills, being with friends or making new ones, having excitement, succeeding, and maintaining physical fitness or exercise. Participation is optimal when children are intrinsically motivated. The primary reasons why they quit sports are due to a lack of fun, having something else to do, boredom, and not feeling competent. Winning is among the least important reasons for participating. Rather, the coach's emphasis on winning is a primary factor for *leaving* the sport experience. Probably the most important issue that underlies withdrawal from sport is the determination of low ability: "I'm not good enough" or "I'm not successful." To have a successful youth sport program, league administrators must be able to articulate their philosophy, train coaches in skill instruction and team management, and evaluate their operation on a regular basis. Contact among league officials, coaches, and parents is of paramount importance.

REVIEW QUESTIONS

1. If you were a parent, what issues would you consider before allowing your child to engage in competitive sport? (Hint: Focus on the areas of physical and mental maturity.)

2. What are the most important reasons that children give for engaging in sport? In what ways are the needs of children *not* met in many competitive sport programs?

3. Why do children drop out of sport? How can coaches *and* parents help to prevent this?

4. What are intrinsic and extrinsic motivation? What can adult sport leaders do to increase intrinsic and decrease extrinsic motivation?

5. Describe the differences between adults and children in their ability to process information during motor skill learning.
6. How would you teach sport skills differently to children as compared to teaching adults?
7. You are the administrator of a youth sport league. How would you develop and implement strategies to (1) involve and work with parents, (2) train coaches, and (3) receive evaluative feedback on your program?
8. Name five of the ten rights of children participating in youth sport, and describe how each should be protected in a sport setting.
9. Finally, how does coaching children differ from coaching older athletes? What are the specific considerations of being an adult leader in a youth sport program as opposed to coaching older athletes?

QUALITY YOUTH SPORT TRAINING PROGRAMS

1. *National Coaching Certification Programs*: Coaching Association of Canada, 333 River Road, Ottawa, Ontario, Canada K1L 8B9 (offers three books, Levels 1, 2, and 3).
2. *Coaching Effectiveness Program*: Dr. Rainer Martens, Director, Human Kinetics Publishers, P.O. Box 5076, Champaign, Illinois 61820. Films, videotapes, and leadership training available. Primary publication is *Coaching Young Athletes* by Martens, Christina, Harvey, and Sharkey.
3. *Youth Sports Institute*: Dr. Vern Seefeldt, Director, Michigan State University, Health and Physical Education Department, Intramural Sports Circle, East Lansing, Michigan 48824. Quarterly newsletter, leadership training, and list of reasonably priced publications available upon request.
4. *Coach Effectiveness Training*: Dr. Frank Smoll, Department of Psychology, University of Washington, Seattle, Washington 98195. Various materials, some of which are free of charge, and leadership training are available.

REFERENCES

Arnold, R. K. S. 1981. Developing sport skills: A dynamic interplay of task, learner, and teacher. *Motor Skills: Theory into Practice* (Monograph 2).

Chi, M. 1976. Short-term memory limitations in children: Capacity or processing deficits? *Memory and Cognition* 4: 559–72.

Chi, M. 1977. Age differences in the speed of processing: A critique. *Developmental Psychology* 13: 543–44.

Cratty, B. J. 1983. *Psychology in contemporary sport*. Englewood Cliffs, NJ: Prentice-Hall.

Deci, E. L. 1975. *Intrinsic motivation*. New York: Plenum.

Fitts, P., and M. I. Posner. 1967. *Human performance*. Belmont, CA: Brooks/Cole.

Gagne, R. M. 1977. *The conditions for learning*. 2d ed. New York: Holt, Rinehart & Winston.

Gentile, A. M. 1972. A working model of skill acquisition with application to teaching. *Quest* 17: 3–23.

Ginott, H. 1968. *Between parent and child*. New York: Avon.

Gould, D. 1984. Psychosocial development and children's sport. In *Motor development during childhood and adolescence*, ed. J. R. Thomas. Minneapolis: Burgess.

Herkowitz, J. 1984. *Motor development during childhood and adolescence*. New York: Macmillan.

Lepper, M. R., D. Greene, and R. E. Nesbitt. 1973. Undermining children's intrinsic interest with extrinsic reward. *Journal of Personality and Social Psychology* 28: 129–37.

Magill, R. A. 1982. Critical periods: Relation to youth sports. In *Children in sport*. 2d ed., ed. R. A. Magill, M. J. Ash, and F. L. Smoll. Champaign, IL: Human Kinetics.

Magill, R. A. 1985. *Motor learning: Concepts and applications*. 2d ed. Dubuque, IA: Wm. C. Brown.

Malina, R. M. 1982. Physical growth and maturity characteristics of young athletes. In *Children in sport*. 2d ed., ed. R. A. Magill, M. J. Ash, F. L. Smoll. Champaign, IL: Human Kinetics.

Marteniuk, R. 1976. *Information processing in motor skills*. New York: Holt, Rinehart & Winston.

Martens, R. 1980. The uniqueness of the young athlete: Psychologic considerations. *American Journal of Sports Medicine* 8: 382–85.

Martens, R., and V. Seefeldt. 1979. *Guidelines for children's sports*. Reston, VA: American Alliance for Health, Physical Education, Recreation, and Dance.

Passer, M. W. 1984. Competitive trait anxiety in children and adolescents. In *Psychological foundations of sport*, ed. J. M. Silva and R. S. Weinberg. Champaign, IL: Human Kinetics.

Roberts, G. C. 1984. Children's achievement motivation in sport. In *The development of achievement motivation*, ed. J. Nicholls. Greenwich, CT: JAI Press.

Rothstein, A. L. 1976. Information processing in children's skill acquisition. Paper presented at the North American Society for Psychology of Sport and Physical Activity Conference, May, at Austin, Texas.

Rushall, B. S., and D. Siedentop. 1972. *The development and control of behavior in sport and physical education*. Philadelphia: Lea and Febiger.

Scanlon, T. K. 1982. Social evaluation: A key developmental element in the competition process. In *Children in sport*, 2d ed., ed. R. A. Magill, M. J. Ash, F. L. Smoll. Champaign, IL: Human Kinetics.

Scanlon, T. K. 1984. Competitive stress and the child athlete. In *Psychological foundations of sport*, ed. J. M. Silva and R. S.Weinberg. Champaign, IL: Human Kinetics.

Scanlon, T. K., and M. W. Passer. 1978. Factors related to competitive stress among male youth sport participants. *Medicine and Science in Sports* 10: 103–08.

Schmidt, R. A. 1975. A schema theory of discrete motor skill learning. *Psychological Review* 82: 225–60.

Scott, J. P. 1962. Critical periods in behavioral development. *Science* 138: 949–58.

Seefeldt, V. 1980. When are competitive athletics too stressful for children? *Family Forum* (October). Cooperative Extension Service, Michigan State University.

Seefeldt, V. 1982. The concept of readiness applied to motor skill acquisition. In *Children in sport*, 2d ed., ed. R. A. Magill, M. J. Ash, F. L. Smoll. Champaign, IL: Human Kinetics.

Siedentop, D., and G. Ramy. 1977. Extrinsic rewards and intrinsic motivation. *Motor Skills: Theory into Practice* 2: 49–62.

Singer, R. N. 1973. Motor learning as a function of age and sex. In *Physical activity: Human growth and development*, ed. G. L. Rarick. New York: Academic Press.

Singer, R. N. 1980. *Motor learning and human performance*, 3d ed. New York: Macmillan.

Smith, R. E., F. L. Smoll, and B. Curtis. 1977. Coaching roles and relationships. In *Youth sports guide: For coaches and parents*, ed. J. R. Thomas. Reston, VA: AAHPERD Publications.

Thomas, J. R. 1980. Acquisition of motor skills: Information processing differences between children and adults. *Research Quarterly for Exercise and Sport* 51: 158–73.

Thomas, J. R. 1984. Children's motor skill development. In *Motor development during childhood and adolescence*. Minneapolis: Burgess.

Veroff, J. 1969. Social comparison and the development of achievement motivation. In *Achievement-related motives in children*, ed. C. P. Smith. New York: Russell Sage.

Wankel, L. M., and P. S. J. Kreisal. 1985. Factors underlying enjoyment of youth sports: Sport and age group comparisons. *Journal of Sport Psychology* 7: 51–64.

12

The Female Athlete

When coaches and parents are asked to describe the advantages of having a child participate in competitive sport, the common responses are (1) developing personality, (2) learning new skills, (3) setting goals and working toward meeting them, (4) learning how to cope with failure, (5) developing physical fitness, (6) meeting new friends, (7) preparing for the competitive elements in the "real" world, (8) developing a high need to achieve, and (9) enhancing self-image. These advantages hold true for both males and females. However, "are the psychological and physiological effects (of sport participation) different for the female than the male?" asks Dr. Dorothy Harris, sport psychologist from Pennsylvania State University and chairperson of a national research conference on women and sport. Based on all available published information, apparently not. In other words, that females receive the same advantages from sport as males is highly likely. Thus the concern of this chapter is not so much a question of whether a female should compete in sport, but rather how females should be coached to meet their needs and become successful.

After reading this chapter, the student should be able to (1) determine how females become attracted to sport and what struggles they experience as successful participants, (2) compare male and female athletes on factors related to efficient movement and physical conditioning, (3) suggest differences, if any, in the strategies of coaching females and males, and (4) offer guidelines on coaching female athletes.

DESCRIBING THE FEMALE ATHLETE

Effective coaching in sport consists of, among other things, the ability to alter the athletes' attitudes, feelings, and behaviors. Although children are readily influenced, the mature performer is not so easily moved. Each athlete comes to the sport environment with a host of unique personal characteristics — some more desirable than others — for player and team success. Some players are incredibly self-motivated while others need to be consistently supervised and reminded about certain necessary team-related routines and tasks. Male and female athletes do not differ in these respects.

Both male and female athletes are distinct from nonathletes in terms of their willingness to sacrifice time and energy, risk injury, endure pain, and feel the pressures and tensions of competitive sport. But female athletes may be overcoming more barriers than males because they experience relatively lower expectations from parents, teachers, and coaches; and because societal norms —

at least in most Western cultures — place females in roles that fit a "traditional" image of passivity, noncompetitiveness, and relatively low physical activity (Reis and Jelsma 1980). Given all that the female athlete must overcome, what characteristics does she possess? How did she develop her attraction toward sport participation? And perhaps most importantly, how do these characteristics affect the manner in which females should be coached?

Sport Socialization

Socialization is the process by which society communicates to an individual the kind of person that he or she is *expected* to be. Individuals learn to play various social roles to be effective members of society. Over the years, these roles have been rather well defined for males and females in sport. In a recent study (Wittig, Balogh, and Butler 1986), sports were judged to be more important for males than for females *by both sexes*. As the authors explained, females who choose to participate in sport step outside recognized social boundaries and confront a dilemma. It's easy to see the social and emotional limitations placed upon young girls who desire to engage in sport. Moreover, females who do engage in sport, particularly upon reaching puberty and later, are exceptional in terms of over-coming societal barriers. These barriers are less restrictive of leisure activities but do discourage sport competition. How, then, do female athletes and nonath-letes differ in the socialization process?

According to Oglesby (1978), the social learning paradigm is one fruitful way to explain the socialization of women athletes. The paradigm consists of three elements: (1) personal attributes, (2) significant others, and (3) social-ization situations.

Personal attributes. The skills and dispositions that women athletes bring to the sport milieu are a function of abilities and other genetically based physical attributes, and early childhood experiences in which personality, values, and attitudes are learned. Abilities are inherited. Examples of abilities include speed of movement, reaction time, and hand-eye coordination, among others. Abilities, which are different from skills, are also enduring. Skills, on the other hand, are susceptible to short-term conditions such as fatigue, mood, and drugs (e.g., alcohol or tobacco intake). Early childhood experiences include opportunities to engage in motor activities and the environment within which one interacted. Both abilities and one's social environment are important contributors to a person's success as a sport participant.

According to Maccoby and Jacklin in their book *The Psychology of Sex Differences* (1974, p. 69), "The path of development is somehow more fixed by biology for girls than it is for boys." Thus, female athletes may have a genetic disposition to have superior abilities related to successful sport involvement. These abilities may include spatial ability, speed and coordination of gross bodily movements, visual-motor coordination, manual dexterity, and memory.

The fact that women athletes have disproportionately more parents who were former athletes when compared to female nonathletes may also reflect genetic disposition (Greendorfer 1978). Girls tend to select sports identical to those in which their mothers currently or formerly participated. Of course, it's quite possible that the home environment offers the support, incentive, and models for some young girls that makes a sport experience more attractive. In fact, in her review of research, Greendorfer (1980) found that family influence was the best predictor of sport involvement.

Physical activity begins in early childhood when the youngster has the opportunity to explore his or her environment (the use of constraining playpens hampers motor development, according to Harvard psychologist Jerome Bruner). With the encouragement of parents, coaches, teachers, and others, a tendency to remain physically active throughout life develops. The motivation to persist in performing sport skills is a function of the second element in the social learning paradigm: the role of socializing agents.

Socializing agents.   Can you recall any person in particular who had a major impact on your decisions, attitudes, and habits? Did a coach, parent, friend, or professional athlete make a strong impression on you? Have you ever found yourself imitating or following the directions of another person? If you value the opinion or advice of an individual, they are regarded by you as a *significant other*. And if a group of persons has a marked personal influence over you, they are regarded as a *reference group*. Reference groups comprise several individuals who collectively direct or modify a person's attitudes, choices, and behaviors concerning what the person should become. Examples include the nuclear family (mother, father, and siblings), coaches in sport, the peer group, school personnel, the mass media, and neighbors.

According to researchers, female competitors begin their involvement in sport — lessons, extensive training, and competition — *very* early in life (Miller 1974). Parents are the primary source of this early sport exposure. (Who else would escort their child athlete to early-morning and after-school practices?) Miller confirms this extensive parental involvement. In her review of related research, she found that women golf and tennis players tended to be reared in families in which at least one parent was an active participant. When this was not the case, the child athlete was surrounded by siblings, usually older, or other relatives with similar sport-related interests.

Siblings close in age, usually within three years, interact in play groups throughout the socialization years (Leventhal 1968). Leventhal's *sibling-similarity hypothesis* suggests that secondborn children model much of their behavior from the male or female firstborn sibling. Thus, girls with older brothers would tend to identify more strongly with, and practice, activities in which boys typically engage. Several studies support this premise.

But does this mean that coaches should ignore female sport participants who have older sisters? Not according to the *social system balance theory* of Parsons and Bales (1955). The reasoning of this theory is that persons with opposite-sex siblings can identify more with the like-sex parent. With same-sex siblings, the opposite-sex parent is a more powerful model. Thus, females with sisters will tend to identify more strongly with their fathers and be overrepresented in sport. But contrary to the sibling-similarity hypothesis, females with male siblings will have a greater tendency to emulate their mothers. Research findings are less than conclusive in support of these hypotheses.

The important points to remember about the role of significant others and reference groups for participation of girls and women in sport include the following:

- Female sport performers are more likely to come from families that are active in or support participation in sport for both males and females.
- The interest in developing sport skills and maintaining athletic participation begins in childhood, but participation should not be restricted to one sport. Specializing in a particular sport need not occur until the adolescent years.
- Females are more likely to persist at sport involvement if they are surrounded by proper models with whom young girls can identify or receive reinforcement. Brothers and fathers in particular should encourage continued play and skill improvement.
- When examining the factors that contribute to an athlete's desire to compete in sport, researchers find no differences between males and females. Both sexes experience similar socialization in the development of attitudes and feelings about becoming and being an athlete.

Finally, girls want and need an opportunity to play competitive sport, a factor addressed in the third element of social learning in sport, socialization through situations.

Socialization situations. Women who have received extensive exposure to sport situations during their growth and development are more inclined to have a positive attitude toward athletic participation than women who have been relatively isolated from such experiences. Specifically, the home, neighborhood, school, role models, peers, and exposure to the mass media are influential agents of sport socialization. The importance of each agent and situation varies for different age groups and sports, and for different societies. Eastern Europeans, for instance, have more exposure to soccer than softball — both as athletes and spectators. Therefore, one would expect young females from Eastern Europe to be more attracted to soccer participation as an athlete than to softball participation. A higher percentage of Japanese females engage in volleyball than do females in the United States; and Swedish women tend to become more involved in distance running than do women in most other societies. During my visit to Sweden in 1974, I learned that exercise to music — or aerobic dance, as the Americans and Canadians call it — had been practiced in Scandinavian countries for decades before it became popular in North America. Thus, the degree to which a female engages often and successfully in a certain sport is frequently a function of her society's norms and expectations.

Apparently, a combination of forces best explains if and how much a female engages in sport. Situations and significant others interact. It is imperative that the opportunity to play sports is accompanied by the presence of others who act as reinforcers, teammates, or opponents. A young girl would be unlikely to experience gymnastics lessons and to maintain her interest if she did not receive the approval and reward (through positive feedback, successful performance, or both) from a parent, peer, or instructor. But another factor apparently has significant impact on a female's participation in sport — the person's age.

We develop attitudes and preferences toward certain activities beginning in childhood. At that time, we are most susceptible to the perceptions of our parents about the appropriateness of certain habits and feelings. Consequently, if parents perceive a particular activity as more appropriate for a female, and others as more restricted to males, the young female will tend to develop attitudes about which sports she may choose to learn. This is referred to as *sex typing*. Mothers and fathers may worry about their son's attraction toward ballet or their daughter's willingness to play touch football. But it isn't usually the mothers who decide which sports are appropriate for their children.

Researchers Lewko and Greendorfer (1977) found that fathers are the most "important others" in making these judgments and that girls are more negatively affected than boys. Thus, when a female desires to participate in a sport deemed more appropriate for males, she receives more negative feedback — especially from dad — than if she were male and played a sport that was perceived as feminine.

What *are* "feminine" and "masculine" sports? Respondents to questionnaires in several studies indicated that sports such as swimming, tennis, and gymnastics are generally sanctioned sports for girls even though they involve competition. Track and field, basketball, and softball are much less acceptable. Apparently, running, jumping, and throwing activities were considered by some to be "unladylike." Sheriff (1969) found in one study that sports least desired for females by parents and peers included field hockey, soccer, basketball, and softball. Of course, *desirability* is a highly subjective term depending on the cultural background of the parent and the context in which the sport is being played. It may be fine for a female to play soccer in a physical education class but less so in a competitive soccer league.

The reader might note the publication date of the Sheriff study (1969) and wonder whether attitudes haven't changed — at least moderately — since the late 1960s. The answer is yes and no. Recent studies show that female athletes are feeling less guilty and more comfortable about being competitive sport participants (Silva 1982). Holding onto traditional or conservative views of a woman's role in society, referred to as "apologetics," is decreasing among female participants. Positive attitudes are now being carried into the more traditionally male sports of softball, basketball, golf, and field hockey. Track and field, however, still has not received similar recognition (Greendorfer 1980).

Another apparent change in the female athlete's attitude concerns the fear of success in sport. It has been reported in literature reviews by Ogilvie (1979) and Harris (1979) that women in sport may be inhibited by an above normal fear of success. This might be due to a learned disposition resulting from social rejection and loss of femininity when successful behavior involves aggression or competition against males (more about the personality of women athletes is included later in this chapter). Reis and Jelsma (1980, p. 284) assert that a fear of success among women "still remains a valid concept to describe a pattern of taking the blame for failure (lack of ability) and denying credit for success (luck, easy task). Since sport is an opposite sex-linked task for females . . . we might see more 'fear of athletic success' among female athletes than males." More recent research (Blucker and Hershberger 1983; Silva 1982) does not support the contention that women are intimidated as athletes. In fact, females in sport (as well as in academic and professional pursuits) are becoming more and more comfortable with setting high goals and working hard to achieve them. And they are doing just that with less guilt. The sex-role conflict appears to be fading — but not completely.

Although women athletes appear to be winning the battle of sexism in sport, social norms die hard. Sport models such as Mary Lou Retton (gymnastics) and Chris Evert (tennis) help women to feel more comfortable with both participating competitively and winning in sport. However, what is "acceptable" sport participation remains essentially unchanged. Retton and Evert participate in sports that are viewed as acceptable for women. However, the female athlete must battle sex-role stereotypes that channel her into competing in certain sports that emphasize low-key, graceful, less intense activity, such as gymnastics, tennis, skiing, dance, swimming, or bowling. Sports such as track and field, softball, basketball, and soccer have not been recognized as appropriate for females. Consequently, girls do not receive similar recognition, acceptance, or reinforcement for their participation in these vigorous sports.

Apparently female sport participants must possess certain favorable characteristics in order to overcome societal values and sex-role stereotyping and to achieve sport success:

- *Socioeconomic background.* Miller (1974, p. 20) concluded that "female individual sports participants come from medium-sized cities, from middle-class and high economic and high educational levels, and that they develop their skills in locations other than public school facilities under the direction of specialists (e.g., country club professionals) in the sport."

- *Reinforcement by significant others.* The continued presence and reinforcement of parents, coaches, private tutors, and friends who support competitive play are imperative if females are to develop a favorable attitude toward sport participation. This reinforcement may help them to overcome societal roles, expectations, and what might be called "hang-ups"; that is, personal prejudices about what people believe to be the roles of males and females in society.

- *The right attitude.* Female performers have the personal attributes (e.g., motivation, persistence, and the ability to overcome failure) to handle themselves in situations that nurture the desire to play competitive sport. Most have been raised since childhood to feel good about physical activity. Like her male counterpart, the female athlete has a desire to feel competent on the court or field as well as in the classroom. In overcoming the few or many obstacles that members of society place in her path, the female athlete is likely to be as mature and motivated a competitor as her male counterpart, if not more so. Such a person must possess unique personality traits, the topic to which we now turn.

PERSONALITY CHARACTERISTICS OF ELITE FEMALE ATHLETES

Traditionally, research results have not been particularly complimentary about the personality traits of female sport competitors, especially when compared to male athletes. Studies from the 1960s and 1970s, as referenced earlier in chapter 2, have shown that female participants in competitive sport:

1. Show more evidence of the fear of success than do men, particularly when competing against college-age males.
2. Fear behavior that is inappropriate to their sex role, thus avoiding activities such as wrestling and football but feeling comfortable playing tennis or volleyball.
3. Display lower self-confidence.
4. Prefer that their performance not be compared to others.
5. Have relatively high trait (personality-based) anxiety and tension.
6. Are categorized as field-dependent (as opposed to independent), which means that they are less accurate about their body positions and are more misled than males by the surrounding visual field (a distracting background will inhibit performance more for women than men).

7. Are more emotionally sensitive (in sport, this can be more positive than negative).
8. Are less dominant as opposed to males but relatively more dominant when compared to norms of the general female population.
9. Are more conservative in their attitudes and behaviors (i.e., they tend to follow rules).
10. Have an external locus of control, which means that they tend to attribute their success to luck or to low task difficulty rather than to their own ability or effort.

Research findings on the female athlete's personality can be very complimentary. Women who participated in the 1959 Pan-American Games scored relatively higher in achievement, autonomy (independence), and affiliation (enjoying friendships and interacting with peers) than did nonathletes. And in a study by Peterson et al. (1967), women players tended to be more serious than average women and to express themselves less freely. Miller's (1974) literature review indicated that collegiate female athletes were more intelligent, tough-minded, assertive, stable, conscientious, persevering, and happy-go-lucky than their college peers.

In a more recent study, Kane (1982, p. 293) found that female sport participants in a junior college emphasized skill over victory as the most important outcome derived from game playing. Based on the female's relatively noncompetitive attitude toward sport and play, Kane suggests that "women should resist an overemphasis on winning and should not adopt an overly competitive attitude toward play and sport."

Are the personality characteristics of women athletes similar today to what they were ten to twenty years ago? Some changes are evident. Female performers have been more communicative in more recent years, especially when talking to female coaches (Officer and Rosenfeld 1985). In my own experience as a consulting sport psychologist with collegiate volleyball and basketball players, I have found female athletes to be increasingly comfortable in disclosing personal feelings (both positive and negative) about the surrounding sport environment as compared to the more inhibited male athletes. Females are more apt to share concerns about their coach, teammates, and especially themselves than male players. And they become more upset than males if communication channels are blocked.

As a consultant to the women's volleyball team at a university, I had the opportunity to meet individually with each athlete. By far the most important concern of the players was their relatively infrequent communication with the head coach. The second most important issue centered on discussing feelings with teammates, especially with respect to player performance and game strategies (e.g., "Why don't I receive more passes at the net?"). Male athletes, on the other hand, tend to be less emotionally affected by the absence of communication than their female counterparts despite similar needs to communicate feelings.

Another characteristic that is changing, albeit slowly, is taking credit for positive performance outcomes (locus of control). Whereas females have traditionally attributed success to external agents such as luck or task simplicity, women are now more comfortable in feeling responsible for favorable outcomes. They now tend to feel more in control of a sport situation and to attribute winning to their skill rather than because they played against an easy opponent (see chapter 4 on attributions).

Williams (1980) reviewed personality research on female athletes who completed one of two paper-and-pencil tests: the Cattell 16 PF Questionnaire or the Edwards' Personal Preference Schedule. She found certain desirable characteristics for women judged as "highly skilled" who participated in fencing, ice hockey, track, swimming, lacrosse, and race-car driving. The athletes were found to be more assertive, dominant, self-sufficient, independent, aggressive, intelligent, reserved, achievement-oriented, and to have average-to-low emotionality as compared with nonathletes.

The contention that sex-role stereotyping has vanished from the contemporary North American scene would not be accurate. Taboos, traditions, sex roles, and perceptions are sturdy components of our culture. Although you now read about the occasional female wrestler or about participants in fast-pitch baseball, soccer, and even football, young girls receive far more exposure to dance, gymnastics, tennis, bowling, and golf.

One study (Garari and Scheinfeld 1970) reflected the depth of sex-role stereotyping in our society. It found that the perceived needs of men and women varied significantly. The needs of women were identified as the need to be safety-oriented, passive, defensive, submissive, and sedentary (feminists would disagree, I presume). Men's needs, on the other hand, were found to be vigorous physical exertion, aggression, achievement, motor activity, independence, and dominance. The tendency to characterize males and females differently is reinforced by the traditional use of separate norms in personality tests for men and women, in which a difference between the ideal or even the average male from his female counterpart is presupposed. However, in more recent research, sex-role stereotyping appears to be diminishing.

In a report entitled "Moms, Dads, Daughters and Sports," sponsored jointly by the Women's Sports Foundation and Wilson Sporting Goods, attitudes toward females in sport are now more positive than ever before. Based on fifteen hundred interviews with girls aged seven to eighteen years, researchers found that (1) 82 percent of the girls participated in sport at some level while 89 percent planned to make sport a part of their adult lives, (2) 79 percent of the girls were encouraged by their parents to participate, (3) 97 percent of parents were "happy" with their daughters' participation in sport or preferred that they be even more involved, and

(4) 63 percent of parents whose daughters quit sports would have preferred that they continue. But the study, reported in *USA Today* (8 June 1988), also showed a marked drop-off in sport involvement during the puberty years, an issue that some researchers call a *puberty barrier*. Researchers aren't certain if dropping out is due to fewer sports programs for adolescents or because of role conflicts. But apparently, according to sport psychologist Dr. Dorothy Harris, research director of the Women's Sports Foundation and professor at Pennsylvania State University, "The word *tomboy* is going to become obsolete."

Perhaps one of the most noticeable changes in the acceptance of physical activity for women has been the recent popularity in aerobic exercise. Whereas women in the post–World War II era viewed most forms of vigorous exercise as "unfeminine," in recent years a tremendous surge in the physical fitness industry has occurred. "Sweat is in" for women. In fact, coed exercise classes are now accepted in most schools, clubs, and organizations. Certainly the inclusion of music to exercise was an important factor that made exercising more enjoyable than with the preceding militaristic, more monotonous style of calisthenics.

Another direction of contemporary change in the female societal disposition comes from studies in the world of business and management. Researchers conclude that women are becoming more secure in management positions, being more assertive in their areas of expertise, and displaying a need to achieve closer to that of males than was the case in the mid-1970s. The tendency of women to feel less threatened by men has been reinforced in a recent sport-related study.

Results from research presented in the Women's Sports Foundation Report (1985), based on a survey of 1,682 randomly selected members of the Foundation, showed:

- Young girls who have boys as playmates tend to (1) have a lifelong interest in sports, (2) grow up to be leaders, (3) play school sports, and (4) work with males to improve their skills.
- A generation gap in attitudes and behaviors among female athletes. When trying to improve their skills, 53 percent of those aged twenty-five years and younger choose male partners versus only 35 percent among those over age thirty-eight.
- A preference to play to improve health and reduce stress (68 percent) rather than to compete (only 8 percent).
- Higher self-esteem among women who were sport participants in childhood.
- That women no longer regard sport participation as threatening to their femininity (94 percent), although 57 percent agree society still forces a choice between femininity and athletics.
- That 73 percent feel that women should be allowed to play contact sports such as football, although 69 percent said that women's sports should remain separate from men's sports (ostensibly due to a desire

to develop their own skills, a goal more difficult to reach if men
consume playing and practice opportunities).

- Finally, the respondents had both male and female sport role models
  as children.

The authors of the research concluded that stereotypes still exist, but only
in the minds of males. Apparently women participate in athletics for self-
gratification and not to prove something to someone else. This view is supported
by research in the area of intrinsic motivation.

Intrinsic motivation, performing a task because it is enjoyable and fun rather
than to earn an external reward, is prevalent among women athletes. In a
comparison of male and female college athletes who had been awarded athletic
scholarships, females were found to be more intrinsically motivated (Ryan
1980). The males were more extrinsically motivated—more emotionally dependent on the scholarship award than for the fun of it. In a more recent study
(Brennan 1986), collegiate female athletes on scholarship enjoyed practice more
than their male counterparts. Further, scholarship male athletes in team sports
found their sport to be less enjoyable now than in high school as compared to
female athletes in team sports.

Based on his review of the literature, Cratty (1983, p. 179) concluded that
"there is little data that the motivational orientations of high level female athletes
differ very much, if at all, from those of their male companions in sport." He
recognized that any special psychological strategies, personal needs, and defens-
es are of equal importance to both male and female skilled competitors. The
important point is that female sport competitors take their roles as athletes
seriously, perhaps even more than male performers. And women seem to enjoy
their sport experiences as much or more than men; they derive great satisfaction
from their sport involvement.

In summary, women athletes still tend to be far more achievement-oriented,
aggressive, and emotionally stable when compared to female nonathletes and
the norms of paper-and-pencil tests. Because, as indicated earlier, different
norms often exist between males and females, comparisons between the sexes
are sometimes difficult. In addition, research on personality in sport for both
males and females has greatly decreased in recent years. Numerous criticisms
of personality research in sport for both males and females have surfaced (see
chapter 2), which partly explains less contemporary interest in this area.

Cratty (1983, p. 171) asserts that women in sport "may hold back in exposing
their 'true' selves when being confronted with personality assessments and
personal interviews. . . . That women taking personality tests may answer in
preconceived ways regarding aggressive tendencies is not unexpected, given
their early child-rearing experiences, their knowledge of what is expected of
them when taking such tests," and how the female athlete is perceived by others.
He concludes that the "negative judgments" made of them by persons threatened
by an achieving, successful female "may extract an 'emotional price.'"

Even the manner in which researchers design an experiment can lead to faulty conclusions. For example, Birrell (1978), in reviewing related literature, found that males displayed a higher need to achieve than females. However, she concluded that faulty research design helped lead researchers to this conclusion. When researchers attempted to arouse higher achievement needs with an emphasis on intellectual and leadership qualities, the achievement motive decreased in females and increased in males. But under relaxed, nonaroused, noncompetitive conditions, women had achievement motives equal to or greater than men. Thus, the situation within which a person's achievement is measured can bias the results.

Women have been found to have different motives as sport competitors than men. The incentives for achievement rise in female athletes in response to a need for affiliation, whereas males strive for task mastery as an achievement motive (Reis and Jelsma 1980). Thus, if motor skills are tested in a competitive situation, female competitors will feel less inclined to excel and to perform optimally compared to male athletes. However, if the focus of an athlete's performance is to determine whether she would be part of a group—trying out for a team or proving to herself that she deserves membership in an elite group, for example—her need to excel will more likely be equal or greater to that of a male.

Female athletes might be more assertive and have other traits traditionally attributed to male athletes as compared to female nonathletes in any given sport (Miller 1974). Both male and female athletes may exhibit one set of behaviors as sport performers but behave very differently in nonsport situations. To categorize female athletes in a certain personality mold (or any other athlete for that matter) may be inaccurate. For women particularly, there may be a strong desire *not* to be perceived as "unfeminine," and therefore, responses may be designed to meet the expectations of others in personality assessments.

Another limitation in personality research comparing the sexes is the use of different norms, or standards, for males and females. A person might be labeled high, low, or moderate in certain traits when compared to standards obtained through a large sample of individuals possessing similar characteristics. Based on the preconceived notions of "masculine" and "feminine" traits of the test's author, categories of the norms against which a person's scores are compared might be invalid.

For example, Landers (1970) conducted a study on the psychological femininity of prospective physical educators using the MMPI and the Gough Scale of Psychological Femininity. He reported that college physical education majors were less "feminine" than general education majors. Closer inspection of the data showed that only two of the eleven item categories accounted for these differences. Further, the traits "restraint/caution" and "religious beliefs," defined as "feminine" in the study, were higher for education majors when compared to PE students. The use of such labels would not meet with widespread agreement.

What is masculinity or femininity? Psychologist George Kelly in *The Psychology of Personal Constructs* (1955) suggests that they are nothing more than hypothetical constructs, abstract perceptions based on our need to seek definitions of sexuality. Not only are such definitions unknown, they are irrelevant (Oglesby 1978, p. 76). Oglesby concludes, "We must immediately disavow the idea that traditional masculinity-femininity, as measured by social science methods, is dependent upon biological sex." In other words, personality tests that attempt to discriminate between the sexes based on a person's behavior or attitude are not valid because they are tainted by cultural stereotypes and expectations. Paul Rosenkrantz and his colleagues (1968) published a list of valued male and female traits. Very few of these could be restricted to only one sex. For example, the listed male traits of "logical," "ambitious," "aggressive," "adventurous," and "self-confident" easily fit into the desirable female traits of today. And what male would not prefer to possess the following valued female traits: "neat in habits," "gentle," "interested in own appearance," and "religious"?

In summary, personality tests have not been shown to be the panacea of predicting a successful female sport performer. Their use to separate the elite from nonelite performer has been questionable at best. Comparing male and female performers has not produced a model or set of traits unique to success in sport. Finally, faulty research designs and interpretations of test results have been widely criticized by specialists.

What this all means about the development and training of women athletes from a coach's perspective is that:

1.   Women athletes should not be judged solely on the basis of personality tests, which have not been shown to predict athletic success or to demonstrate clear, unequivocal trends in the *accurate* identification of desirable traits.

2.   Females who "appear" and "behave" in a so-called feminine manner may be as skilled and successful a sport competitor as the female athlete who does not possess similar "feminine" traits.

3.   According to researchers, female athletes see themselves as instrumental (i.e., expressing leadership, dominance, and competitiveness) during sport situations, but also view their behaviors as typically feminine (expressing traits such as understanding, sympathy, affection, and so on) in social situations (Oglesby 1978).

4.   Female athletes should be viewed as possessing desirable character traits for competition; after all, they have had to maintain their interest and desire to play despite the social obstacles of sex stereotyping placed in their paths.

5.   Women players most likely began the involvement in sport at an early age surrounded by positive and influential others such as peers, family, and coaches or teachers who supported their desire to participate.

Female athletes are highly motivated, achievement-oriented, and "coachable."

6. However, women athletes need the same understanding, compassion, sensitivity, and communication from their coach as their male counterparts. The so-called "expressive" traits are highly desirable for *all* athletes for the promotion of the coach's credibility (the athlete's belief and trust in the coach's actions, philosophies, and knowledge) and loyalty.

Not all authors agree about male-female athlete similarities. When sex differences *are* found in research, underlying environmental factors may be the causes of such differences. Miller (1974) concludes that "the significance of these reports is simply that, for whatever reasons, cultural or otherwise, women are different from men, and the same generalizations regarding the psychology of coaching cannot be applied to both."

For the female athlete, what this means is that it's OK to feel feminine and still be a sport participant, and that research on personality, especially the athlete's own scores, should not inhibit further involvement in athletics. Such tests should be ignored. The bottom line is, What are these scores telling us? Not much, apparently. In fact, studies on adjustment in marriage, personal growth, and a healthy lifestyle condone active sport participation.

Should male and female athletes be coached similarly? Should coaches expect female and male athletes to use different performance techniques? In the next section, the processes that underlie sex differences in sport performance will be explored.

SEX DIFFERENCES IN PHYSICAL MATURATION

Growth

During the first ten years of life, girls grow and develop muscular strength and speed faster than boys. In addition, girls are twelve to eighteen months ahead of boys of the same age in the maturation of bone tissue. Between ages 10.5 and 13 years, girls begin their adolescent growth spurt. It terminates at the onset of menstruation, at which time skeletal growth virtually stops. No significant differences in size between boys and girls are apparent, however, until testosterone is produced in significant amounts in males at about age twelve or thirteen years.

The growth spurt of boys occurs between the ages of 12.5 and 15 years. These extra years of physical growth account for the greater size of young males. Males generally become 10 percent taller and heavier than females when growth ends. The muscle mass of boys is twice that of girls at maturity. Growth generally ends at age sixteen years for girls and eighteen years for boys.

Body Composition

Body weight comprises primarily two components — lean weight (muscle) and fat. At about age nine years, boys become leaner than girls. Before menarche, girls usually have less body fat than boys. But soon after the menarche (between ages twelve and fourteen years), percent body fat in females increases and surpasses that of males. Starting at preadolescence, boys and men are generally leaner than girls and women.

The percent of fat in the female is an important factor in coaching, teaching, and implementing conditioning programs. Relatively more fat means less muscle per unit volume (Astrand 1977). Thus, the work capacity, endurance, and athletic performance of women and girls are affected by this high fat-to-muscle ratio. Coaches of female performers should have different standards and expectations of physical performance in female athletes and should avoid comparisons to male competitors, particularly at the beginning stages of puberty.

After puberty, females have a higher percentage of body fat (25 percent on the average) than males (about 15 percent). This is partially due to a slower basal metabolism rate for women than men, which facilitates fat storage. Although body composition of relatively higher fat percentages might reduce sport performance speed, no differences between the sexes exist in neuromuscular efficiency in skilled, low-intense work. However, if we were to compare men and women for *maximal* performance, including both strength and aerobic endurance, performance scores would average better for males (Astrand 1977).

Strength

The peak growth in strength for females occurs at the age of 12.5 years and is optimal the year before menarche. The strength spurt in the female is related to maturational factors such as maximum growth in height, sex maturation, and bone age rather than to chronological age. By age seventeen years, men are two to four times (30 percent to 40 percent) stronger than women due to the males' greater muscle mass. Strength differences are particularly obvious for the upper body. Two factors contribute to these differences: (1) the effect of male sex hormones, primarily testosterone, and (2) the greater ratio of muscle to fat in males.

Increases in bone and muscle tissues should be reflected in similar increases in strength. Eckert (1973) reports that girls register their greatest gain in mean isometric strength between the ages of nine and ten years, while the greatest gain in mean strength for boys is between eleven and twelve years. Unquestionably, the adolescent growth spurt reflects a pronounced increase in strength in boys but much less so for girls.

The strength capacity and muscle mass for females is about one-half that of males. This is due to a difference of thirty to forty pounds of body weight (at maturity), which is associated with more muscle mass and strength for males. The decision in recent years to allow women basketball players to use a smaller, lighter ball than that used by the men is a recognition of these strength differences.

Physical Performance

Boys and girls perform similarly up to the time of menarche. After this time, females generally do not improve — and may even slightly decline — in their ability to perform motor skills. They also decline rapidly in maximum endurance, usually starting at about age fourteen years, and have a slower response to physical training. Women seem to require more time and work to increase strength, although not all researchers agree. Possibly social and cultural norms and habits lead girls to become less active in competitive sport and to reduce physical activity in general during the preadolescent and adolescent years, which contributes to the slowing of the female's response to training (Eckert 1973).

Eckert reviewed studies in which Bulgarian and American mean performance scores for girls were compared. She found, for example, that scores for the distance throw and dash indicated a leveling off for American girls at age fifteen and thirteen years for the respective skills. The Bulgarian girls, however, continued to improve through ages sixteen and eighteen years, respectively. She concluded that improvements in performance are "similar for Bulgarian and American boys whereas the performance of Bulgarian girls does not show the marked adolescent lag of American girls. It would appear, therefore, that differences in cultural attitudes toward strenuous physical activity for girls may account to some extent for performance differences" (p. 173).

Nevertheless, exercise physiologists report research from their observations in the laboratory; they are not sociologists. Therefore, whether the reasons for inferior performance are partly cultural or have strictly a physiological basis is still an open question in North America.

Height

What is less questionable, however, is that the average male at maturity is five inches taller than the average female. Combined with the aforementioned differences in body weight, muscle mass, and strength, the average male has an obvious advantage over the average female in certain sports in which performance is directly related to height (e.g., basketball or volleyball) or body mass (e.g., putting the shot).

Amenorrhea

Menstruation usually is delayed until later in life for physically active females. The condition, *athletic amenorrhea,* is characterized by the absence of menstruation in an athlete who has experienced menarche. Most amenorrheic athletes are infertile because the ovary does not release an ovum. This is advantageous to younger female competitors because menarche is accompanied by significant increases in body fat and poorer physical performance. At this time, or soon after, differences between the sexes become more evident. Amenorrhea is reversible, however. It dissipates as a person's exercise load decreases.

What do the physical differences between males and females tell the coach about working with female athletes? Before puberty, girls are similar and in many instances superior to boys anatomically and physiologically. Thus, at or before this time, coaches, teachers, and parents should feel comfortable in encouraging coed sport competition in which boys and girls can engage jointly, with the exclusion of contact sports in which *no* child should engage before puberty (Astrand 1977; Eckert 1973), and in coaching girls and boys in a similar manner. No evidence supports the use of a double standard in which girls are automatically assigned substitute roles or asked to play positions of less importance, or worse, not given the same opportunities as boys to learn and improve their sport skills.

Although female athletes have psychological attributes similar to those of male performers, clear physiological differences emerge at puberty. Some of these differences lead directly to superior performance for males in many competitive sports.

Coaches should realize that even mature female athletes have physiological limitations. This is not to say that training and conditioning are of less importance or should be less vigorous for females. But anatomical characteristics unique to women should result in different *expectations* for training.

Women have a higher percentage of body fat than men. So coaches should not mandate that female athletes reach a total body weight or fat percentage at dangerously low levels. I've observed a collegiate volleyball coach make such a demand. This strategy is dangerous to good health. Physical training often adds weight to any person owing to an increase in muscle tissue. At the same time, body fat may decrease because more calories are being burned in exercise than are ingested on a day-to-day basis. The overall effect is a possible increase in body weight but a decrease in body fat. This is highly desirable and is much healthier than excessive dieting.

Women typically have lower increments in muscular strength with weight training because they have fewer muscle fibers and less muscle mass than men. This means that there are limitations as to the additional strength and size of the female physique that can be achieved with weight training.

The average female cannot compete with males of equal ability after puberty. Nevertheless, it is mentally and physiologically healthy for men and women to remain physically active, even jointly where possible. Promote sport involvement for females, *particularly at relatively young ages* when women are less conscious of culturally based sex-role stereotyping and engage in sport because it's fun. This is when they possess sport skills similar or superior to those of boys. Attitudes about sport involvement later on are developed and nurtured early in life.

In general, comparisons between males and females should be avoided by coaches. There are skilled as well as unskilled female sport performers just as there are different skill levels among males. Despite scientific evidence of superior physiological performance in males when compared to females, there's little doubt that the development of skills and relatively limited participation in sport by women is a cultural, rather than a genetic, outcome. Coaches, educators, and parents have an obligation to develop healthy attitudes, mental well-being, and physical stature for both sexes. It makes good sense to give both men and women, boys and girls, the opportunities to reach these objectives. To do so makes winners of all sport participants.

BIOMECHANICAL COMPARISONS OF MALES AND FEMALES

Our purpose in comparing males and females is not to point out inferior qualities of female performers, but to indicate that females — athletes and nonathletes — are capable of attaining proper form when performing sport skills. The perceptions of many individuals, even researchers, that males perform sport skills more efficiently than females and use better form in doing so are based on averages. That is, *most* females tend to use certain motor habits when performing sport skills that do not contribute to efficient performance outcomes. However, the use of averages is often misleading. The production of sex hormones, the element that governs sex differences, varies greatly within each gender. These hormones are partly responsible for a person's technique because they cause differences in strength and bone skeletal structure. Males and females commonly possess characteristics similar to the opposite sex.

Have you ever heard someone say to someone else, "You throw like a girl"? When we hear this statement, what comes to mind is the tendency to throw with a leading elbow, with the arm held close to the body. Similarly, some girls run in an awkward manner with a noticeable side-to-side movement as knees seem to come closer together. This form is inefficient. And because of it, these girls move slower than runners who move with better mechanics. Why is that, and what can be done about it?

Average male, as compared to female, competitors have more efficient movement mechanics and, as a result, sustain fewer injuries and have better performance scores. This is primarily due to sex differences in (1) bone mass and strength (males have more of both), (2) muscle mass and strength (again, males rank higher), (3) the shape of the pelvis (typically narrower for males), and (4) the size of the body in general. The average male has greater muscle force acting on longer bones that have a larger bone mass than the average female. Thus, it is not so much that males automatically perform motor skills more efficiently than females. Each individual, regardless of gender, is capable of possessing the appropriate skills and movement mechanics. According to Adrian (1973, p. 391), "Sex is of lesser importance to how the skill will be executed than are individual differences or individual attributes."

Males and females do not necessarily differ on a number of motor activities. Running patterns, for example, should be similar. The primary factor for faster running is changing the rate and length of each stride and the angle of leg lift as speed increases. No sex differences in form have ever been found in the high jump, the dolphin butterfly swim stroke, the long jump, and swimming kicks. Any existing differences in favor of males are not due to form, but to the speed of movement. Sometimes, however, body structure limits movement efficiency.

Women are often identified with a round, relatively wide pelvis. Males, on the other hand, are characterized with a wedge-shaped, narrower pelvic structure. However, both pelvic shapes occur in males and females with similar frequency.

Other examples of traits that vary widely within each sex include strength, muscle size, and the size and density of bones (Wells and Luttgens 1976). Perhaps one of the most important traits that separate the sexes on how well both perform sport skills is speed of movement.

Speed of Movement

Males can generally run both faster and farther than females. Why? One primary cause is the distribution of weight in the various body segments. In studies that compare weight distribution between men and women, females tend to have more weight in the pelvis, abdomen, shanks, and thighs with less weight in the torso than men have. The combination of heavier thighs and less muscle mass in females means more resistance to rotary movement than in males, given the same muscular force. The end result is slower movement speed with females. Musculature and strength, the foundation of sex differences in physical performance, also help to explain varied outcomes in ball throwing.

Throwing

Skilled males are able to project a ball one hundred to two hundred feet per second, while skilled women achieve only seventy to eighty feet per second. Again, the differences are due to form. Males are found to have greater angular velocities of wrist flexion and shoulder rotation. Females maintain more spinal rotation. When researchers break down the contributions of wrist flexion and spinal and hip rotation in ball-throwing velocity, the men perform more efficiently. They achieve 73 percent contribution from the wrist, whereas the women offer nearly equal effort to each of the three dimensions. It makes sense to teach all athletes proper ball-throwing technique, given the importance of angular velocity for throwing speed. In fact, using more efficient movement patterns will also help to reduce injuries.

Injuries

Women athletes are injured significantly more often than male performers. If an individual lacks musculature strength surrounding joints, which prevents the abnormal positioning of ligaments, tendons, and muscles, injuries are more likely. A joint may be injured if it is forced beyond its normal range of motion. Alignment of the body parts should be maintained to preserve the strongest anatomic position. This is particularly important when quick changes of direction are made. For example, the toes should be in alignment with the knee and with the direction of movement to avoid vulnerable angle positioning of the knee. Further, during play, the knees should be slightly bent, tensing slightly the thigh and leg muscles. This stabilizes the knee joint.

The importance of strength training becomes obvious for injury prevention. Injuries usually occur when the total force generated by motion is concentrated on a small area. Therefore, it is important that the shock of direct trauma, direct contact with an opponent, for instance, be absorbed through the muscles rather than in the joints. A sufficiently strong musculature is necessary under this condition. Relatively smaller muscles offer the joints less stability; thus, they are less efficient at the task of shock absorption.

To avoid injury, women athletes should:

1. *Avoid contact sports*. Football, wrestling, rugby, and lacrosse come to mind.

2. *Avoid contact drills*. Coaches should not require female athletes to engage in any practice drill that might lead to an accidental injury. Examples include basketball players diving after a rolling ball, softball athletes diving for a catch, or volleyball players diving for the ball in an uncontrolled manner and without proper padding. Cautious approaches to game preparation help to prevent injuries and lead to a more motivated and healthy athlete at game time.

3. *Use a progressive strength training program during the off season and during the season*. It's essential that the female athlete develop muscular strength that will help her to withstand the stresses of sport competition that come with all-out effort. It's the coach's responsibility to control reckless diving and jumping in volleyball and basketball drills. It's also necessary to ensure the protection of athletes who encounter various levels of continued physical stress in other sports. Tennis players need to protect legs and shoulders (and to avoid tennis elbow), golfers should strengthen upper limbs, bowlers should protect wrists, and athletes who continuously run and jump should avoid shin splints.

IMPLICATIONS FOR COACHING THE FEMALE ATHLETE

I asked the women's basketball and volleyball head coaches and assistants at New Mexico State University how coaching female athletes differed from coaching males. They all agreed that, to a large extent, it didn't. The same components are used to prepare athletes of both sexes: physical conditioning, skill teaching, motivational techniques, effective communication, mental preparation, and so on are inherent in athletic competition. These coaches believed that the techniques used to affect the sport performance of men and women are similar. However, they did not suggest that males and females are the same athletes. Inherited traits related to physical stature are clearly responsible for the stronger, faster male athlete compared to his female counterpart. But should we be comparing the sexes in sport? Yes and no.

Perhaps the only time when cross-sex comparisons of sport performance are valid is when considering coed athletic programs: the joint participation of boys and girls in sport. According to researchers, prepubescent children should be able to engage in competition together. Neither sex has an advantage over the other. After puberty, however, the situation changes. "Where sports success is greatly related or dependent upon strength and power, the average woman cannot hope to achieve, much less surpass, the man's performance. Furthermore, the woman is more apt to be hurt physically from this imbalance of force situation" (Adrian 1973, p. 393). Comparisons between the sexes are important when deciding on joint sport involvement. Otherwise, there is no reason to perceive and respond to female athletes much differently than to males in sport situations.

Nevertheless, some coaches do interact differently with female athletes. For example, coaches are less inclined to demonstrate anger and verbal hostility toward female participants as compared to males. Perhaps this is good. The women I interviewed for this book indicated that they respond to reprimands with various intensities of stress. Not a single player indicated a favorable attitude nor improved performance after receiving verbal abuse.

There are four possible reasons why women do not respond productively to a coach's anger:

1. Relatively few women receive scholarship funding, and thus, they do not feel obligated to take abusive treatment from the coach. They are not dependent on college funding for living expenses as are most athletes on scholarship (Ryan et al. 1980).
2. Women have been shown to be more intrinsically motivated than men (Brennan 1986). Their primary reason to participate in sport is for enjoyment — to have fun. Verbal abuse is very contradictory to this objective.
3. A primary need of women sport competitors is affiliation (Reis and Jelsma 1980). Anger and hostility are anathema to creating an atmosphere that fosters this need.
4. Females are less inclined to take credit for favorable performance outcomes and, instead, tend to take more than their share of the blame for negative outcomes (Rejeski 1980). Continued negative feedback may lead the female to feel helpless toward making greater effort for performance improvement.

Coaches who express hostility toward female athletes are behaving in a manner contrary to their needs. Female sport participants do not claim to want, nor do they need, to be treated in this manner. Male athletes do not enjoy such treatment either, but they apparently respond to such stress with somewhat less unpleasant psychological consequences (Cratty 1983).

However, another side to the argument of coaching females differently than male competitors exists. It should be remembered that women competitors are a select group. They are individuals who have many desirable characteristics including a commitment toward competence. They have had to overcome sex-role stereotyping throughout their athletic careers and have had role models for many years. These women view sweating, physical activity, and competing as natural, healthy, and ongoing, although they are comfortable appearing and feeling more feminine in other areas of their lives. Perhaps, then, they aren't any less capable of coping with the competitive situation than male athletes. In fact, women may be better stress-reducers than men in sport.

In their literature review, Neal and Tutko (1975) conclude that women use emotions more effectively and productively than men both in and out of sport. They are not afraid to exhibit emotions; therefore, game-related stress inhibits their sport performance to a lesser degree than men. Women also have a healthier perspective on sport; women want to win, but the world doesn't come to an end if they don't. Their total self-image is not reflected by athletic success or failure. The female athlete has had a good deal of experience in overcoming obstacles simply to become a female athlete.

WHAT FEMALE ATHLETES HAVE TO SAY

I interviewed women collegiate athletes from golf, tennis, volleyball, basketball, and track for this chapter to determine their unique needs and how they differed from male performers. I also wanted to hear their perceptions of their own coach as well as coaches of women athletes in general. It is known from the literature that male athletes have more negative feelings toward female coaches than toward male coaches (Officer and Rosenfeld 1985). On the other hand, women tend to favor disclosing feelings to other females rather than to males. Women also have a greater need than men to perceive the coach as trustworthy, sincere, and to be accepted by their coach *before* communicating openly. Interviews with college coaches confirm the need of female participants to have a female leader with whom to relate.

This is why, according to fifteen coaches and athletic directors canvassed for this book, most male head coaches of female competitors tend to have a female assistant coach. Female head coaches often have a male assistant. I have often wondered if such an arrangement is really necessary. Perhaps the need for an assistant of the opposite sex serves the purpose of offering personal and social skills that the head coach does not possess. For example, a male coach may be less comfortable and may communicate his discomfort to female athletes when discussing menstruation. He may be less tolerant and sensitive than a female coach in understanding the player's discomfort and inability to practice due to stomach cramps and other occasional manifestations of her condition. He may be intolerant of tears shown by the athletes, especially in response to verbal hostility.

Some female head coaches may need a male assistant who is less threatening — perhaps fatherly — to offset a more demanding female head coach. Officer and Rosenfeld's (1985) review of the literature reveals that male coaches are often an extended father figure for female competitors. It appears that a coach of either gender could be equally effective in communicating with and leading female athletes, given an ability to show empathy, warmth, a sense of humor, and mutual respect. That was one widespread message from the women interviewed for this book.

The interviewees were candid about themselves and the common shortcomings of their male coaches (none had a female head coach). The following were some of their observations.

About Emotions

"Women are as emotional as men athletes but simply express it more openly. We keep less pain inside, that's why we cry. But we feel better when we do, and that's one reason competing is fun for us."

"Joking around is important for me. Competing has its pressures, so I need to unwind and have fun sometimes. Coaches should always have a sense of humor."

"The menstrual cycle of women definitely affects their emotions. I have my ups and downs. My coach needs to understand that."

"Menstruation changes my attitude. Sometimes I feel depressed and this affects my ability to play my best. Also my weight goes up, which upsets my coach. He needs to understand a woman's chemistry."

"Girls need to develop mental toughness and overcome the affects of menstruation. To do this, the coach should show he cares about her — that he cares about the individual. She'll respond better to him."

"To be mentally tough, you need confidence. My coach doesn't understand that criticizing me decreases my self-confidence. I feel less able to cope with failure. I'm not his idea of a tough player, but that's one reason."

"When I have less self-confidence, the coach's negative comments are more difficult to deal with. It's like kicking me when I'm down."

"Women are very sensitive. They react strongly to minor comments from the coach. It seems we need more positive strokes than the guys."

"To be emotionally up for the game, I need a low-key pregame approach, which I get. I'm glad my coach doesn't rant and rave before the game; it would destroy my concentration."

"My coach is very very patient with me, and that's just what I need."

"The worst thing a coach can do to motivate me is yell and scream. I absolutely 'freak out.' I need to be respected. Straightforward, honest talk is all I ask."

"Men shouldn't think that a woman athlete's tears are a sign of weakness. Tears help me express how I feel. It's OK to feel — and appear — upset. Tears are my way of dealing with feeling down, but they don't say I'm out."

"I've never heard my coach make a sexist remark, which I respect. If he did, the team would stop going all out."

On Leadership Qualities

"I respect my coach because he shows respect for me. I like the adult-type of relationship even though I know he's still the coach."

"My coach shows favorites. That's bad."

"A strong coach should not take everything so personally. If we lose, his feelings are hurt. He's insulted. I'm uncomfortable with that."

"Female coaches seem to have greater insight into the feelings of players than male coaches. I think the word is empathy."

"Females (athletes) need more encouragement than males."

"I respond the same to a male coach as to a female."

"Women athletes are not too receptive to aggressive commands from coaches. My coach demands that I charge the net when I'm more comfortable playing the baseline. His assertiveness reduces my concentration and self-confidence."

"A female athlete is more responsive to the coach if the credibility is there."

Attributions: Taking Responsibility for Performance

"If my opponent is too easy, I don't feel very satisfied after winning."

"Sometimes I wish I received more criticism from my coach. I feel responsible for how I perform, so being criticized will help me. Don't go soft on me."

"If I succeed, I feel it was due to my skills which I worked so hard to perfect. I don't feel my victory was due to a poor opponent — not at this level."

On Being a Woman Sport Competitor

"Before he left the school, my coach tended to flirt with his favorite players. That wasn't right."

"Women athletes have a high need for self-expression and one-on-one contact with the coach."

"Some women have a stronger need to compete than others. It's important to me to beat a certain school and especially beat a higher-ranked opponent."

"The more aggressive women seem to have more affiliation with other male athletes and male coaches."

"I love being an athlete. My teammates are great friends, and even the guys seem to respect me for my skills."

Based on the comments of these athletes, it appears that the needs and feelings of female participants are strikingly similar to those of male performers. The players need respect, communication, physical activity, competition, and close relationships with teammates. So do male athletes, although perhaps a bit less so in some of these areas. The women also enjoy winning—and they become upset when they lose, just as males tend to do. In general, their comments conflict with the findings of Reis and Jelsma (1980) that males and females compete in sport for different reasons: Men considered winning and status most important in sport, whereas women referred to successful participation and affiliation with teammates as most important. The women interviewed here were equally concerned with winning, playing well, and enjoying their involvement as were male competitors.

What this says to the coach of the mature, skilled female participant is that it's wrong to assume that women do not need or do not want to win. They'll make the same commitment—perhaps even more so—to play their best and be a successful athlete.

This chapter ends by asking the same question posed near its beginning. How unique and different are female athletes, especially in comparison to their male counterparts at the elite level? Pemberton and Petlichkoff (1988) reported that the research evidence is, indeed, scant to answer this question reliably. Certainly the sexes are not identical in terms of their experiences in competitive sport. Research evidence suggests that (1) boys and girls are socialized into sport differently, (2) gender differences exist in sport regarding types of achievement goal orientations and attributions for their success and failure experiences, but that (3) males and females are affected similarly by psychological outcomes that lead to "retiring" from competitive sport. Nevertheless, the authors call for far more research on the female athlete to determine if the available research in sport psychology, most of which has examined male performers, is valid for women participants.

As the late syndicated columnist Sydney Harris wrote, "Ninety percent of what we call 'feminine' or 'masculine' characteristics have been culturally conditioned, not biologically determined; and these social fabrications obscure both the basic differences and the more pervasive similarities."

SUMMARY

Girls are not socialized in most societies to be sport participants. The traditional approach to child rearing holds that physical activity, especially of a competitive nature, is a masculine trait. Consequently, little attempt has been made over the years to promote sport for females. The paucity of research on female athletes in the sport psychology literature lends support to this point. Recently, however, researchers have found attitudinal changes toward the benefits of physical activity, even competition, for females. Nevertheless, puberty is still the time at which girls tend to drop out of sport disproportionately more than boys do.

The girls who do remain active in competitive sport or physically active in noncompetitive endeavors have similar needs and personalities as male athletes. This may be because they have needed to overcome the stereotypes and expectations of others throughout their lives — and their femininity has "survived." Despite inherent physical differences between the sexes that separate the level of male and female sport performance, effective coaching techniques prevail for all athletes.

REVIEW QUESTIONS

1. What effect does a society's culture and process of socialization have on female participation in sport? How does a female's home environment influence present and future sport involvement?
2. How are the personality traits of male and female athletes similar? How are they different?
3. What problems exist in measuring personality in general? What special problems exist in personality measurement of female athletes?
4. Males tend to be stronger than females. This is a primary factor that allows men to perform sport skills at higher levels than women. How do differences in strength lead to better performance?
5. What special considerations should be considered in coaching female athletes? Should the coach have different expectations of female performers as opposed to males in terms of conditioning and sport performance? If so, what would they be?

REFERENCES

Adrian, M. 1973. Sex differences in biomechanics. In *Women and sport: A national research conference*, ed. D. V. Harris, pp. 389–400. University Park, PA: Pennsylvania State University Press.

Astrand, P. O. 1977. *Textbook of work physiology*. New York: McGraw-Hill.

Birrell, S. 1978. Achievement related motives and the woman athlete. In *Women and sport: From myth to reality*, ed. C. A. Oglesby. Philadelphia: Lea and Febiger.

Blucker, J. A., and E. Hershberger. 1983. Causal attribution theory and the female athlete: What conclusions can we draw? *Journal of Sport Psychology* 5: 353–60.

Brennan, S. J. 1986. Intrinsic motivation of intercollegiate male-female athletes in team and individual sport groups. Paper presented at a national conference of the North American Society of Psychology of Sport and Physical Activity, June, at Scottsdale, Arizona.

Cratty, B. J. 1983. *Psychology in contemporary sport*. Englewood Cliffs, NJ: Prentice-Hall.

Eckert, H. M. 1973. Age changes in motor skills. In *Human growth and development*, ed. G. L. Rarick, pp. 155–75. New York: Academic Press.

Garari, J. E., and A. Scheinfeld. 1970. Sex differences in mental and behavioral traits. *Genetic Psychological Monographs* 81: 123–42.

Greendorfer, S. L. 1978. Socialization into sport. In *Women and sport: From myth to reality*, ed. C. A. Oglesby. Philadelphia: Lea and Febiger.

Greendorfer, S. L. 1980. Gender differences in physical activity. *Motor Skills: Theory into Practice* 4: 83–90.

Harris, D. V. 1979. Female sport today: Psychological considerations. *International Journal of Sport Psychology* 10: 168–72.

Horsfall, J. S., A.C. Fisher, and H. H. Morris. 1980. Sport personality assessment: A methodological re-examination. In *Psychology in sports: Methods and applications*, ed. R. M. Suinn. Minneapolis: Burgess.

Kane, M. J. 1982. The influence of level of sport participation and sex-role orientation on female professionalization of attitudes toward play. *Journal of Sport Psychology* 4: 290–94.

Kelly, G. 1955. *The psychology of personal constructs*. New York: Norton.

Landers, D. M. 1970. Psychological femininity and the prospective physical educator. *Research Quarterly* 4: 164–70.

Leventhal, G. S. 1968. Sex of sibling as a predictor of personality characteristics. *American Psychologist* 20: 783.

Lewko, J. H., and S. L. Greendorfer. 1977. Family influences and sex differences in children's socialization into sport: A review. In *Psychology of motor behavior and sport*, ed. D. M. Landers and R. W. Christina. Champaign, IL: Human Kinetics.

Maccoby, E. E., and C. N. Jacklin. 1974. *The psychology of sex differences*. Stanford, CA: Stanford University Press.

Miller, D. M. 1974. *Coaching the female athlete*. Philadelphia: Lea and Febiger.

Neal, P. E., and T. A. Tutko. 1975. *Coaching girls and women: Psychological perspectives*. Boston: Allyn and Bacon.

Officer, S. A., and L. B. Rosenfeld. 1985. Self-disclosure to male and female coaches by female high school athletes. *Journal of Sport Psychology* 7: 360–70.

Ogilvie, B. C. 1979. The personality of women who have dared to succeed in sport. In *Sports, games and play*, ed. J. Goldstein. Hillsdale, NJ: Halsted.

Oglesby, C. A. 1978. *Women and sport: From myth to reality*. Philadelphia: Lea and Febiger.

Parsons, T., and R. F. Bales. 1955. *Family, socialization, and the interaction process*. Glencoe, IL: Free Press.

Pemberton, C. L., and L. Petlichkoff. 1988. Sport psychology and the female Olympic athlete. *Journal of Physical Education, Recreation and Dance* 59 (March): 55–58.

Peterson, S. L., J. C. Weber, and W. W. Trousdale. 1967. Personality traits of women in team sports vs. women in individual sports. *Research Quarterly* 38: 686–89.

Reis, H. T., and B. Jelsma. 1980. A social psychology of sex differences in sport. In *Sport psychology: An analysis of athlete behavior*, ed. W. F. Straub, pp. 276–86. Ithaca, NY: Mouvement.

Rejeski, W. J. 1980. Causal attribution: An aid to understanding and motivating athletes. *Motor Skills: Theory Into Practice* 4: 32–36.

Rosenkrantz, P. S., S. R. Vogel, H. Bee, J. Broverman, and D. Broverman. 1968. Sex-role stereotypes and self-concepts in college students. *Journal of Consulting and Clinical Psychology* 32: 287–95.

Ryan, E. D. 1980. Attribution, intrinsic motivation, and athletics. In *Psychology of sport and motor behavior*, ed. C. Nadeau. Champaign, IL: Human Kinetics.

Sheriff, C. W. 1969. The social context of competition. In *Social problems in athletics*, ed. D. M. Landers, pp. 18–36. Philadelphia: Lea and Febiger.

Silva, J. M. 1982. An evaluation of fear of success in female and male athletes and nonathletes. *Journal of Sport Psychology* 4: 92–96.

Vanek, M. and B. J. Cratty. 1970. *Psychology and the superior athlete*. NY: Macmillan

Wells, K. F., and K. Luttgens. 1976. *Kinesiology: Scientific basis of human motion*. 6th ed. Philadelphia: Lea and Febiger.

Williams, J. M. 1980. Personality characteristics of successful female athletes. In *Sport psychology: An analysis of athletic behavior*, ed. W. F. Straub, pp. 353–59. Ithaca, NY: Mouvement.

Wittig, A. F., D. W. Balogh, and F. Butler. 1986. *Importance of sports for young women: A social dilemma*. Paper presented at a national conference of the North American Society for Psychology of Sport and Physical Activity, June, Scottsdale, Arizona.

13

Athletes Speak for Themselves

In the final analysis, it is the athletes who play the games, score the points, and serve as the primary sources of victory or defeat, not the coach. Perhaps the often-heard phrase "winning coaches" should be replaced with "coaches of winning teams." The athletes' feelings, attitudes, and performances dictate the extent of individual and team success. The focus of this book has been on acknowledging the importance of the "mental game" on performance outcomes. Certainly, using X's and O's, planning game strategy, and engaging in physical conditioning are inherent aspects of game preparation and success. But, as the Peggy Lee song from the 1960s goes, "Is that all there is?"

As a consulting sport psychologist, I've had the opportunity to talk with hundreds of athletes in different countries of various ages and skill levels. Other sport psychologists and journalists have also published their observations. From these personal and documented conversations, one thing appears to be clear: *The athlete is a powerful, but often untapped, source of information to the coach for the team's benefit.* Powerful because of the information's validity. This is not just any spectator or fan who is giving the respected and experienced coach advice. This particular informant is a team member, the target of the coach's behaviors, the person whose performance and attitudes lead directly to the contest's outcome. But this rich source of information is left untapped; his or her views, perceptions, experiences, and dreams are—as they say in the movie

393

industry — left on the cutting room floor. What the athletes have to say is simply not often taken into account. Let's look at just a few examples of input from a player that might be valuable.

Football coaches do a superb job of observing, critiquing, analyzing, and strategizing. Based on their observations, sometimes from optimal vantage points, assistants forward recommendations to the head coach, who, in turn, directs changes in the team or player performance strategy. But wait. Is there something the athlete knows based, after all, on his own experiences on the field that would offer new insight to the coach? Is an opponent doing something that is making a certain skill difficult to carry out? Is the opponent showing certain tendencies that coaches may not have picked up or that was not practiced as part of the game preparation? And perhaps most risky, is the athlete free to articulate his uncertainties about the opponent's strategies or skills? Does the defensive back lack the receiver's speed, making him susceptible to the long pass? If so, should a double coverage defensive strategy be planned and used more often?

The baseball coach orders the pitcher to intentionally walk the batter. But the catcher remembers that this hitter has shown virtually no skill in making contact with the pitcher's curve ball. Given the catcher's insight, is an intentional walk the best strategy?

And what about injuries? Can an athlete feel secure about telling the coach that he or she is injured (before the game) and is, therefore, unable to play at 100 percent effectiveness? Shouldn't the coach condone such total honesty without the athlete's fear of retribution?

The purpose of this chapter is to hear what the athlete has to say concerning his or her perceptions of the coach and the effect of this image on performance. The reader may get a slightly different perspective about effective coaching; about what works, and what doesn't. What do athletes need, and how can these needs be met? Just as important is understanding the degree to which coaches and athletes observe the same situations differently. Statements of athletes will reinforce the crucial importance of communication between coach and athlete.

The content of this chapter is based almost exclusively on personal interviews with athletes of different ages and skill levels and on my own empirical observations and informal discussions with players and coaches. Other information was obtained from the media and from the applied sport psychology literature. Athletes of all ages and skill levels seem to have similar needs — including the professionals, as indicated by a major league baseball coach.

Athletes have personal needs, and the coach has the responsibility of determining and, if possible, meeting these needs. The following sections deal with the feelings and attitudes of athletes that affect their motivation, commitment, energy, and ultimately, their game performance. The players' comments also reflect certain coaching behaviors that either enhanced or detracted from their mental readiness. Their opinions are grouped into five time periods during which coaching behaviors in some way affected the athlete's feelings, attitudes, or performance: practice, pregame, game, postgame, and off the field or court.

ABOUT PRACTICE

Performers and coaches agree that the primary purposes of practice are to learn and improve upon skills and to perform game strategies that simulate game conditions. Many of the athletes, high school and collegiate, felt that both objectives were either unclear or unmet. Many of the comments centered on the manner in which coaches and players interacted:

- "I'm afraid of my coach. He's very critical. The more he yells at me, the more nervous I get and I make more mistakes. I need compliments once in a while."
- "My coach is always hollering. Sometimes I get tired of listening to him."
- "It seems the only reason we do wind sprints is after losing. It would be nice to know why we do certain things during practice."
- "I give my coach credit for trying to teach us things. But he talks very fast, and I don't always understand and remember everything he says. So I mess up and get him mad."
- "The biggest problem I have with practice is that it's boring. Why can't it be more fun? If it was, I bet the team would try harder and we'd be better prepared to play the game."
- "My coach doesn't say much to me. He's really quiet, and I don't know what he's thinking."
- "I know I'm better than the guy starting ahead of me, but the coach won't tell my why he's starting and I'm not. I wonder sometimes if this is all worth it."
- "My coach is a great guy. The only concern I have is that he expects us to hurt our opponents. I have trouble with that."
- "I'm just not psyched when we're practicing during the off season. The coach works us just as hard, but with no game coming up, I'm not as motivated. I think he expects us to go at 100 percent every minute all year, but that's impossible for most of us. And he gets real mad if we don't."
- "The one word that describes practice to me is 'boredom.' We do the same thing all the time. I'd love to try some new and different things or even have some time off to study once in a while."
- "I wish I knew the basis on which the coaches evaluate me in practice. I'm told I'm an average player, but no one tells me what that means."

- "We sure do a lot of sitting around."
- "I get real uptight when the coach yells at me after I make a mistake. I know I made the error. What I need is encouragement, not put-downs."

What these players are saying is that they have needs that are not being met, which is detracting from their motivation to persist, learn, improve, and help the team succeed. Players are saying, "Hey, Coach, be honest with me. Tell me what I need to do to be successful. What are my limitations? What am I doing well? Be patient with me while I learn new skills and improve; this takes time. Treat me with the same respect that you expect from me, and I'll give you all I've got. I can't play my best after I've been insulted or embarrassed in front of the team. Do you think we can have some fun occasionally and still win?"

Practice is the time for learning, improving, taking risks, and yes, making mistakes. At this time, attitudes of self-confidence, self-image, positive player relationships, trust between coach and athlete, and motivation are developed. It's the time for coaches to establish rapport, communicate openly, and use strategies that enable performers to be mentally and physically prepared.

Based on the players' views, a coach who is interested in meeting as many of the athletes' needs as possible would do the following:

1. *Honesty*. Be discreetly honest with the players. The coach can be candid about the player's weakness in a constructive manner in the hope that improvement in future performance is possible, even likely. Statements such as "There's no way you'll ever be a starter with your slow speed" are destructive, unmotivating, and unnecessary.

2. *Make practice exciting*. Repetition breeds boredom. Change practice procedures and content on occasion. In fact, follow the strategy of a few teams in the National Hockey League and take a few days off in the middle of the season to get away from the sport. This means *no practice*. Maybe an affordable trip can be planned that will entertain or relax the athletes. This will help to prevent burnout.

3. *Player roles*. Be sure that all team members have a significant role in every practice period. This is the time to teach skills, attempt new strategies, and fail. Coaches sometimes say that it is impossible to work with all the athletes equally. One coach indicated a split of 80 percent with starters and 20 percent with nonstarters. This approach alienates a large number of team members who feel excluded from the coach's attention and instruction. Further, substitutes are only one injury away from starting or playing. It makes good sense to work with them as much as possible for better team morale and more skilled athletes.

4. *Athletes can't go all out all the time*. Coaches do not want to maintain the same level of intensity in all team-related situations. Sometimes it is a good idea to use a relaxed, low-key approach, especially in practice

or during the off season. In this way, players will respond more enthusiastically when conditions warrant it.

5.   *Separate anger from instruction.* Athletes do not integrate information when they are tense and anxious. But these are exactly their feelings when the coach reprimands an athlete in offering instruction or feedback on performance. Nothing sinks in. The suggestion for coaches is simple: Don't teach and be angry at the same time, especially during practice when instruction is most appropriate.

An often-quoted adage in sport is that players play in the game as they practice. An athlete who has worked hard and performed optimally in preparation for the game is predicted to play better than if practice sessions were uninformative, unstimulating, and poorly planned. The best way to prepare a person to play at optimal levels under game conditions is to *practice* under game conditions; simulate the competitive situation. Game-simulation techniques

need to be instituted during practice. Coaches should try to imitate game conditions as closely as possible so that athletes are better prepared to make appropriate responses during the game.

For example, take the quarterback aside and tell him what play to call. The quarterback then calls out the play in the huddle. After the ball is snapped (assuming that all players are dressed for contact), have everyone perform at full speed. Research clearly indicates that artificially slow movement does not prepare participants to meet the demands of actual game conditions.

In baseball, simulate game conditions when a runner is on first base contemplating "stealing" second base. The batter tries to bunt when the pitch is in the strike zone. Infielders must decide where to go: either ensure against the stolen base or field the bunt. Team members should act the role of spectators using both positive and negative (i.e., realistic) verbal messages to the batter in an intrasquad game. Thus, hitters can practice filtering out potentially obtrusive noise as they would need to during an actual game. This suggestion should *not* be used during the first few weeks of practice, until players are conditioned and have mastered fundamental skills. The batter is required to guess the type of pitch to hit, a curve or fast ball, as he or she would during a game. Pitches are thrown at game-like velocity.

In gymnastics, some practices should occur in a noiseless environment, similar to a gymnastics meet. Gymnasts are given the opportunity to perform their complete routine without interruption — errors included — then receive assessments by "judges."

The focus of practice behaviors is game preparation. The closer an athlete is able to mimic a game condition during practice, the closer he or she will replicate successful practice performance during the contest. The coach's job is to provide these opportunities. Another aspect of coaching that helps to prepare the athlete for competition — and an area about which athletes had much to say — is related to behaviors and strategies before the game.

PREGAME ISSUES

The day of a sport contest is usually filled with a preplanned routine devised by the coach. How does the coach determine this schedule? From interviews with thirty-five high school and college coaches and one major league baseball coach, I concluded that coaches carry out their pregame strategies based on one or all of the following: (1) techniques used by their coach when they were athletes, (2) discussions with colleagues at different programs, (3) readings in coaching publications, or (4) "tradition." Not one coach indicated that the needs of, or input from, his or her players were a factor in deciding pregame strategies. Nor was it indicated that consulting a sport psychologist or reading related literature influenced pregame protocol. Here is what the players had to say:

- "I prefer not to eat meat at the pregame meal. It's too heavy for me and makes me feel sluggish. The coach feels a pregame steak is necessary."
- "The day of a night game is usually boring. But one thing my coach makes us do is spend time with him or an assistant coach during the day. Usually we just relax and watch T.V. but I'd rather be alone or study."
- "When my coach tells me to relax and don't be nervous, I get *more* uptight. I'd rather no one would say anything to me."
- "I'd prefer to prepare for the game alone rather than being with the team the whole time. I value my private time."
- "I don't enjoy hearing a lot of false chatter — stuff that coaches and players say that is supposed to motivate me. I need honesty. Coaches should talk from the heart."
- "My coach is a good guy, but he says the same thing all the time. It (his message) doesn't affect me anymore."
- "I'm uncomfortable when my coach loses control before the game. It gets me nervous because if anyone has to remain cool, he does."
- "Sometimes I want to hear other players and team captains talk to the team rather than the coach. I like hearing what my teammates are thinking."
- "I'm glad the coach has banned music in the locker room before the game. It drove me nuts. Now, players have a choice of using headsets if they want music."
- "I don't want to hear how important this game is to us. I already know that. We all want to win. I don't need to be reminded. My advice is (to have the coach) say nothing to us or just review a few things."
- "I saw the movie *Bear* about Bear Bryant (the legendary University of Alabama football coach). He reminded his players that mom and dad were watching, so have a good game. I'd rather not hear that. I'm nervous enough without thinking about who's watching me."
- (Football player): "I'm not in favor of the pregame warm-up ritual. We spend too much time going through the motions and using up energy, especially when it's hot outside. I also think we warm up too early before the game. By the time the game gets going, we're not as psyched. It takes us awhile to get the adrenalin going again."

These athletes are saying things that go against the traditional practices of coaching in sport. The pregame meal is an example. Although many coaches think that the value of food intake on game day is in the player's minds, researchers are not so sure. True, the "placebo effect" is alive and well in sport. Players who *think* they'll do better if they eat steak just might perform less effectively if denied a pregame meat meal. On the other hand, meat has been found to take significantly longer to be digested and used for energy as compared to complex carbohydrates. Many college teams, for instance, eat pancakes or spaghetti four to six hours before game time, as indicated by sports medicine literature.

Other examples of a disparity between tradition in pregame coaching procedures and player preferences include (1) having all team members stay together as though team unity and morale will be negatively affected if the athletes go their separate ways hours before game time, (2) following an exhaustive pregame warm-up procedure despite air temperature and research that contraindicates the need for prolonged warm-up, (3) in the pregame talk, reminding players about the importance of winning the game and who's watching them from the stands (an attempt to motivate that usually results in more tension), and excessive hollering, (4) using captains or other team leaders to communicate information or deliver messages to heighten incentive instead of relying on only the coach for pregame verbal communication, and (5) respecting individual differences among athletes. Some performers enjoy and even need intensive group affiliation, while others are less gregarious and prefer more solitude, particularly on game day.

It is virtually impossible for coaches to please every member of the team. Sometimes athletes need to adjust to situations that are not to their liking. Further, some situations warrant a certain protocol. Golfers and basketball players would not prepare for their respective contests in the same manner, for instance. But if coaches were to follow many of the suggestions offered by athletes in my interviews, here are some procedures that should seriously be considered.

1.   Try to give the athlete a choice as to the type of pregame meal that he or she would prefer. Or read in the scientific literature and discuss with the players your rationale for choosing a particular team meal. If they believe you, performance will likely increase — the placebo effect or self-fulfilling prophecy.

2.   Treat all players alike. Avoid giving starters more time and attention on game day than other participants. The use of a double standard when interacting with players backfires. It plays a divisive role in that the support that substitutes offer starters is minimal and insincere.

3.   Ask the players about their feelings toward game day procedures. Would they rather be left alone than go to the coach's house to relax? Do they need more study time? Are they more comfortable in their own home or room than somewhere else? Some structuring of the day's events is necessary, but how much is too much?

4.   In general, players seem to prefer a more subdued approach to the game than a boisterous, highly vocal style. The low-key locker room allows athletes to save their energy, think about their playing assignments and team strategies, and communicate voluntarily instead of

feeling compelled to "make noise." Of course, certain games and situations may warrant a highly aroused response from players. It's the coach's job to set the tone and to know which direction — from highly intense to low-key — will enhance performance.

5.   Perhaps one of the most discussed and overrated coaching strategies in sport is the pregame talk. Hugh Campbell, the highly successful Canadian football coach, is depicted as having a low-key approach before game time. According to a story in *Sports Illustrated* (1984), Campbell has been known to give such "riveting" pregame talks as, "Well, men, the other team showed up, so I guess we better go out there," or "Don't trip going out the door." This comes from a coach who finished with a win-loss record of eighty-one and twenty-two with five ties in only six seasons. Chapter 5 discusses more about effective versus ineffective content and styles of the pregame talk.

6.   Finally, try not to fatigue your players prematurely during the pregame warm-up period. Valid reasons exist for following a certain warm-up procedure, particularly physiological reasons such as raising internal body temperature and providing more flexibility and range of motion. But in warm temperatures, the length of warm-up time should be reduced. Moreover, the mental advantages of the warm-up, which include increasing arousal and lowering anxiety, have a threshold beyond which arousal becomes too low. The incentive to play at optimal levels is reduced.

DURING THE GAME

Well, sports fans, the time to separate the teams according to talent, preparation, and readiness is here. It's game time. Players interviewed for this book had much to say about the strengths and weaknesses of their coach's behaviors during the game. I was not surprised to learn that certain coaching behaviors led directly to less effective performance — and yet sometimes they didn't. The most salient and typical player complaint was based on the coach's use of anger and other negative communication during the game. Often, this had a devastating impact on the athlete's tendency to take risks, relax, attend to proper cues, follow the coach's directions, and play in a highly motivated state. Here are some of the more typical comments from players:

- "Don't yell at me to motivate me. It makes me nervous and ruins my concentration."

- "I don't like to be criticized. It makes me nervous. I mean, I get blamed for something I couldn't help. It wasn't my fault."

- "Every quarterback has to learn to accept criticism . . . the one thing that has to be within your personality is that you don't let criticism affect you or it will affect you all year."

- "I think my coach is an honest guy, but when he says I'm going to play and I don't, I stop believing him. This may be wrong to say, but whether we win or lose, I won't be happy if I was promised a chance to get in (the game) and don't."

- "Our team has two co-captains, but they never say anything. I don't think they were ever told what to do. Captains should lead, but they don't."

- "I think an effective coach knows how to treat us before the game and at halftime (in football). If we've been lazy, he should give us a tough time about it. But if only a few players are messing up, or the first half wasn't too bad, then I don't think he should get angry at the whole team. If we've been doing our job, it just gets the rest of us down."

- "I wish my coach would ask the players for our input during the game. One time, I was having trouble defending against one of (my opponent's) plays. Instead of asking me to explain the problem I was having, he jumped all over me. In fact, I could have used some instruction at that point."

- "I get uptight when the coach argues with the referee all the time. If he (the coach) is out of control, I start to lose my concentration. The team seems disorganized. I need a coach who remains cool, especially under pressure."

- "My coach is a super bright lady. She really knows the game. The only thing that drives me up the wall is when she threatens us if we mess up. Then we start to choke. And the game isn't fun anymore. I just don't think we play our best when we are afraid to lose. Being threatened with punishment turns me off. The odd part is that even if we win, I feel anger toward the coach who made some pretty terrible statements as her way to motivate us."

- "I learn a lot from my coach. She's made me ten times the player I was last year. My only gripe is her tendency to embarrass individual athletes in front of the team instead of speaking to them privately. I don't want to hear one of my teammates get yelled at and put down. It could be me next time. I'd respect her a lot more if she knew when to go behind closed doors."

- "You know what a double standard is? Well, we have double standards on our team. When an important player (makes a mistake), the coach doesn't get angry. He just tells him to watch it and do better next time. But when a nonstarter messes up, look out. The coach explodes. That isn't fair. If I had one wish on this team, it would be that all players are treated equally — with respect."

- "I notice something interesting about our team. The subs rarely cheer for the starters. That's too bad because we need the support of our teammates. The reason for this lack of support is because nonstarters don't feel they're contributing to the team. They can't identify with the uniform. If they have to get in the game, I don't think they'd know what to do because the coach doesn't include them in many of the drills. They get very little of the coach's attention."

- "The problem with getting too psyched before and during the game is that after we blow it, our mental state falls flat. We get so down, so disappointed, that it's tough to come back."

- "The most upsetting thing my coach ever did to me was complain about my weight right in the middle of the (tennis) match. There I was, down two games to one, and he tells me during the break that I need to lose five pounds. I was frantic. Of course, I lost the match."

A British philosopher named Buckle once commented: "Society prepares the crime; the criminal commits it." A similar situation exists in sport. The coach creates the atmosphere from which players respond accordingly. In doing so, the team leader must ask a very important question: What am I (the coach) doing that is promoting or *inhibiting* the type of attitude and performance skills necessary to have a successful team? The answer to this crucial question will allow the coach to reflect on his or her attitudes and actions that produce player attitudes. What the coach finds might be surprisingly different from what he or she would have predicted.

The coach may want to ask a second very important question: What do my players want and need? In fact, it may be better to ask this question to the players directly (or through an intermediary such as captains, assistants, supportive parents, or the school counselor). Although it is unfair and unrealistic to expect that all of the players' needs will be satisfied, at least the opportunity to communicate feelings to the coach will go a long way toward bringing important issues out into the open where they can be worked on and resolved.

Several coaches I've interviewed on the issue of "open" discussions do not agree that players should have an opportunity to speak their minds. Instead, they feel that athletes must learn to do what they are told and to follow directions. "By creating a free-for-all discussion, you open up a Pandora's Box," one coach told me. My discussions with players of all ages indicate otherwise. A performer with unresolved feelings loses the most important thought processes related to success in sport: inner motivation, persistence, concentration, and loyalty to coach and team alike. The message these players repeatedly offered during my interviews was: "Coach, don't be afraid to ask us what we think. What we have to say can make a difference."

POSTGAME BEHAVIORS

Well, the contest is over. What is there left to say? Should the coach say anything and, if so, how should he or she say it? The events and words that follow the game or match will leave a lasting impression in the minds of all athletes, starters and substitutes. Should players feel guilty after losing a game? Responsible for their victory? Embarrassed for committing an error? Proud to be a member of the team? Clearly, some coaches make more effective and positive postgame impressions than others, as indicated by comments from the players.

- "Often after we lose, my coach cries. I can't blame him for being upset, but he's trying to make us feel guilty with his tears."

- "I like the way our coach handles losing. He just says, 'The game's over and I think we've all learned something from it. We gave it our best shot, so I'd like all of us to feel proud. Let's talk about what we learned from the game before Monday's practice when we're more relaxed, less fatigued, and can reflect on the game less emotionally.'"

- "My coach is at his worst after losing. He's not the same person. He gets so violent it scares me. I stay out of his way."

- "It's funny; I never feel depressed after a game, win or lose. Maybe it's because I've given it my best shot. Or maybe it's because I really have fun playing. But I'll be darned if the coaches on this team don't want the players feeling depressed. I mean, if they see one smile or hear someone utter a single word, they give that player a long glare. We've all learned to keep quiet and stay out of their way."

- "If there's one thing I need after the game, it is to be left alone. I have a hard time talking about the game over and over again. I just wish we could go home and put it behind us. Reviewing the game is depressing."

- "My coach has a split personality. After we win, he's friendly, warm, smiling, and happy. After we lose, he's ready to tear our heads off. It's so predictable that I lose respect for him. I try just as hard after a win as after a loss. If I had my wish, he'd be consistent after all games regardless of outcome."

- "I have a lot of respect for my coach. But he has two habits after we've lost that make me lose that respect. One is swearing. It's unbecoming of the team leader. And besides, he tells us not to swear. The second is doing physical damage to the locker room. Throwing and kicking things won't make us a better team. The game is over. Time to move on."

- "My coach tends to insult us after we lose, especially the players who made an error during the game. The worst time occurs when he singles out players by name and embarrasses them. It's uncalled for."

- "Win or lose, my coach reminds us what we did right during the game. We never leave the locker room feeling defeated as people. He puts sport in perspective. Sport is not life; it's a part of life. We respect him for showing us that."

- "My coach is a nice person, but he thinks the team should be together *after* the game (at home games). Wrong! We need to get away and have some freedom. I like the guys on our team, but all of us can use a break. The worst part is that he (the coach) wants to party with us. Like I said, he's a good guy but I wish he'd simply leave us alone when the game's over."

These players are making very simple requests of their coach when the game is over. "Don't put us down," they seem to be saying. Essentially, that's all they ask. Ignore them if you must. Provide positive verbal or nonverbal feedback if you'd like. Even display emotion if it's necessary. But placing blame, pointing fingers, invoking guilt, and embarrassing team members clearly have deleterious effects on the players' attitudes and future performances. According to the interviews, players respond best to the following postgame coaching strategies:

1. *The use of negative responses.* Players understand anger. Many even feel that it's justified if the team did not play well, although mature players feel more comfortable with the coach's hostility than do child athletes. In general, it is not anger in itself that upsets the athlete. It's

the purpose and content of it that does so much damage. It's one thing for the coach to exclaim: "I'm really upset about how we played today. We could not carry out our plan. . . ." It's quite another thing to say something like the following, especially in the presence of team-mates: "Bill, you blew it. Why didn't you do as you were told? Your fumble cost us the game. If you would have made those free throws, we would have won. Why didn't you catch the darn ball?" Insults breed contempt and disloyalty toward the coach and even the team. Players begin to think twice about the reasons they're participating. "Who needs this?" many begin to think. The result is either physical withdrawal (i.e., quitting) or mental withdrawal (i.e, a lack of effort).

2.   *Consistency*. Players want their coach to react in the same respectful, constructive manner after winning as after losing the game. They do not respond well to a "Jeckyl and Hyde" type of personality who expresses warmth and sensitivity after winning but just the opposite responses after losing.

3.   *Placing the blame*. As indicated in chapter 4, the accurate use of attributions to explain the probable causes for winning or losing leaves a very important impression with the athlete. Athletes are asking their coach to use proper attributions (if they need to be used at all, especially in youth sports): Was it their ability, effort, opponent, or luck that was the primary cause of the game outcome? The accurate *and sensitive* use of attributions will help players to learn from the game — as a reflection of their mistakes as well as from skilled performance and positive outcomes.

The coach is a model for his or her players. As such, there is an image the coach should project if player loyalty and credibility are to survive. In two words, that image is stability and maturity. Someone associated with the team must bring everyone together and maintain a sense of purpose, composure, and direction. That job belongs to the team leader. But even if coaches and athletes agree on this, they do not appear to share the same perceptions about what are appropriate behaviors away from the sport setting.

BEHAVIORS OFF THE FIELD OR COURT

Coaches have told me that sometimes they feel responsible for their players twenty-four hours a day, seven days a week, especially during the season. This feeling reminds me of the writing of clinical psychologist Haim Ginott in his book *Between Parent and Teenager*. It's common knowledge that conflict between parents and their children are most intense during the adolescent years.

This is because, Ginott explains, the primary need of parents is to be needed, to guide behaviors of their children so that growing up is as constructive and as painless as possible. Unfortunately, the number one need of the adolescent is independence. Teenagers are struggling to identify themselves as responsible adults and to escape the control of parents. The inevitable result is conflict. Athletes have similar needs. They yearn to be independent and to enjoy the company of friends — not only because they are expressing normal needs of peer affiliation, but because they need distance from authority.

What this means is that athletes need time away from their coach off the field or court. But there are also times when meeting the coach away from the sport situation to discuss personal concerns is important. Thus, there is a balance as to the coach's availability to the players in a nonsport setting, as indicated by these comments:

- "My coach says he has office hours, but when I try to see him, he's always too busy."
- "My coach shares an office with another coach. The lack of privacy prevents me from being open with him about how I feel."
- "My coach wants to be my drinking buddy. He asks me where I go for entertainment and would I go with him. I sure don't want to."
- "I wish the coach would avoid talking to my parents about me. He could just ask me for the same information he discusses with them. Quite honestly, I love my folks but what I do at school and on the team is between the coach and me."
- "The coach wants to know what we (the players) do on our free time. I don't think it's his business."
- (from a college senior): "I see the coach at the bar every week. For some reason, I'm uncomfortable with his drinking and dancing at the same place the players go."
- "My folks wanted to speak to the coach after the game, and he was nice enough to take the time and do it."
- "This might sound weird, but I view the coach as an authority figure. He's a lot older than me, and I don't feel we should be buddies. He's got his job and I have mine. But I still want to respect him for being a good coach."
- "I really enjoy talking to my coach about things that have nothing to do with football. I mean he actually showers with us and talks politics, history, and other stuff. It shows he respects us as people, not just football players."

Coaching has many roles. It's no easy task playing all of them — and at the right time. Athletes want stability and dependability from their coach. The leader who does not live up to this image will not gain the respect and loyalty necessary to influence the athlete's behaviors, feelings, and attitudes. According to input from the players, coaches should think about doing the following:

1.   Coaches and athletes are not in the same peer group. The coach is invariably older and more mature than the players. Therefore, coaches can never be a true friend of an athlete. Such relationships are uncomfortable at best, and they conflict with roles on the team. Socializing between the two parties should be avoided except at team-related functions. As the baseball pitcher Billy Southward used to say back in the 1950s, "Never fall in love with your ballplayers."

2.   Athletes need and want private time with their coach. It is absolutely necessary for coaches to set aside the opportunity for players to engage in private conversation. If a coach shares an office, one of two strategies should be used: An arrangement could be made to have exclusive use of the office during certain hours of the week, or another facility could be scheduled that would allow private meeting time. The attitude that "My office colleague can be trusted" may be true, but this does not allow the performer to speak openly and without intimidation. Coaches who ask for open communication with their players should show that they mean it.

3.   Do coaches have the right to drink at a bar frequented by their players (or their players' parents)? Yes, they do. But should they? It depends on the type of image a coach wants to project and the effect of this image on the ability to be an effective coach. Athletes do not want to see their coach in any role that will erode the image of a mature, responsible team leader. Bars, with or without entertainment, license certain behaviors that are not compatible with desirable images of a coach. The advice? It's probably better to choose drinking establishments (if you must) *not* located in the local area.

Another disadvantage of associating with the players "after hours" is that it places the burden of feeling responsible for the players' behavior on the coach's shoulders. Coaches realize that there is a time to ignore certain behaviors of their players. This is not to condone these inappropriate actions. However, the coach cannot assume the roles of parent, police, and friend of players in situations unrelated to the team. That would be unfair — both to the player and the coach. Further, the coach is an important model for his or her athletes and, as such, is in a position to influence the behaviors and attitudes of athletes in a positive manner.

4.   This suggestion should be almost unnecessary to mention except that it is imperative that it be followed. Coaches should never become romantically or sexually involved with their athletes. Their respective roles and the image of such involvement would project to others would impede coaching effectiveness. One female athlete disclosed to me that her male coach became inappropriately friendly during a road trip. She felt guilty and confused about rejecting her coach as an intimate companion, yet needing his guidance and friendship as a mature team leader. She was uncomfortable with his flirtation and hoped that her rejection of him would not result in a change in her playing status. This player's concerns illustrate just some of the many reasons why coaches and athletes must

not confuse sensitivity and dependency with excitement and personal relations. Ultimately, no one benefits.

In the final analysis, off-the-field or off-court actions of the coach can either augment or reduce effectiveness in team-related situations. Coaches are correctly concerned with image — their own image and that of the team. What all members of the team — including the coach — do and say away from the sport environment reflects the maturity, stability, and quality of team leadership. Effective coaches ensure that their own positive self-image is compatible with the way they want their players to perceive them; as an intelligent, articulate, knowledgeable, and motivated leader of skilled athletes. But as we'll see in the next section, coaches and their players often see the same thing differently.

DIFFERING PERCEPTIONS BETWEEN COACH AND ATHLETE

Sport psychologists try to understand the perceptions and roles of coaches and athletes. The objective is to help both parties to become increasingly compatible in meeting personal needs and performance and team success. Although both parties want success, they do not always agree on the best ways to achieve it. Even more surprising is often the lack of communication between them; people who desire the same thing should talk to each other, not necessarily to teach skills and game strategies, but to develop trust and loyalty — and to monitor and adjust each person's perceptions about issues that influence attitudes and performance.

For example, one common area of concern for athletes is whether or not the coach likes them. Participants of all ages and expertise feel various degrees of anxiety about the coach's *personal* feelings about them. If the coach is not attending to, or reprimands, the player, the coach is perceived as "not liking me." Often, in the participant's mind, coaching decisions are based on the athlete's personality instead of on his or her sport skills. Yet, coaches say just the opposite. They want to win, of course. So they strongly refute the notion that decisions about who plays or for how long are based on anything but the performer's skills. "I want to field my best players," they often say. But what coaches rarely realize is that the athlete's perceptions must not be ignored. If a player feels unwanted or disliked by the coach, he or she will be less attentive, less loyal, less motivated, and less supportive of the coach and the team.

One purpose of this section is to illustrate just how dissimilar are the views of athletes and their coaches about the same situations in sport, specifically the coach's behaviors. It is partly based on a research study carried out over a three-year period. Because the nature of coach-athlete relationships differ from sport to sport, I restricted my sample to football.

Twenty-two football coaches were interviewed including twelve at the collegiate level and ten from secondary schools. The athletes in the study, randomly chosen starters and nonstarters, consisted of fifty-eight and twenty-three college and high school players, respectively ($N = 81$). The players and their coaches represented schools in the southeast, southwest, and midwestern United States. Thus, because of the selective sources of the data as opposed to totally random procedures, the findings of this study cannot be representative of the total population.

A total of thirty-one undesirable coaching behaviors were depicted by the players and grouped into seven categories. They are ranked from the complaints expressed most commonly (1) to those that were mentioned less often (7), followed by behavioral examples of each:

1. Lack of effective communication between coach and athlete

   a. Athletes are not allowed to express feelings to coach
   b. Lack of praise
   c. Coach makes statements that embarrass athletes in the presence of peers
   d. Lack of sincerity and honesty

2. Not explaining to players rationale for strategies

   a. Reasons for running wind sprints
   b. Rationale for the game plan
   c. Benefits of learning and practicing performance techniques

3. Expression of anger toward athletes

   a. Coach is angry when he gives me feedback
   b. Coach is upset with me when he teaches a skill

4. Not defining the role or status of nonstarters (reported by starters and substitutes alike)

   a. Coach ignores nonstarters
   b. Coaches interact less with nonstarters than starters
   c. Athlete does not know the criteria for starting status or why he or she doesn't start
   d. Athlete feels that coach does not like him or her

5. Inappropriate content in pregame and halftime talk

   a. Coach says the same thing every game
   b. Coach berates us
   c. Coach *requires* us to use imagery minutes before the game

6. Failure to treat players as individuals

a. Whole team admonished or praised regardless of individual performance
b. Coach disregards my pain, injury, frustration, or depression

7. Ineffective use of assistant coaches

a. Assistants are "puppets" for head coach
b. Head coach is always taking over
c. Assistants do not seem to be motivated

The next step was to ask the coaches their opinions about data gathered from the players. Here's what they said:

- Five of twenty-two (22.7 percent) denied affiliation with any of the seven traits.

- Thirteen of twenty-two (59 percent) identified with one of the seven behaviors.

- Four of the twenty-two (18 percent) agreed that they practiced two of the seven traits.

- *None of the twenty-two coaches identified more than two of the traits as their own.*

Which of the behaviors did the coaches admit were theirs? Seventeen admitted to expressing anger toward players, three said that they had not defined the nonstarters' roles, and one acknowledged using assistants ineffectively. Apparently all of the twenty-two coaches felt that they communicated effectively, and only one coach confessed that he didn't meet at least one of the players' needs. The coach's perceptions were in stark contrast to those of their players.

Coaches and athletes differ significantly as to the ways in which they assess coaching effectiveness. The survey revealed that an incredible 87 percent of the players felt that their coach did not communicate effectively. Yet none of the twenty-two coaches agreed with this assessment. Only one of the coaches admitted that he does not provide a rationale to the players as to the reasons for using particular strategies. But a whopping 79 percent of the athletes say otherwise.

In contrast to the coaches' perceptions, the athletes claimed that their coaches express anger (77 percent), that they do not define the team role or status of nonstarters (68 percent), that players are not motivated by their coach's comments at halftime or before the game (47 percent), that coaches do not treat athletes as individuals (42 percent), and that they do not use assistants effectively (36 percent).

From the results of this investigation, two conclusions can be made: First, a tremendous disparity exists between the perceptions of athletes and their coaches on the use of effective techniques in football. Second, the coach and his players view his coaching and personal behaviors very differently. Essentially, the players say, "Coach, you're not doing such and such, and we need that." But he says, "Yes, I am doing such and such, and in fact, I'm quite good at it." What seems to be the problem? Why is it that coaches and players view the same situation — even the identical behaviors — differently?

Mechikoff and Kozar (1983, p. 122), based on their interviews with twenty-two "winning" collegiate coaches in various sports, concluded: "All coaches indicated that athletes needed to be aware of themselves, their abilities, limitations, anxiety levels, wants, needs, etc., yet few had developed a structured system to help the athlete in these areas." In all due respect to many bright, articulate, experienced, and hard-working coaches, I heartily agree. It is one thing to list the qualities of successful coaches and athletes, but quite another to set up situations and carry out the activities that ensure meeting the athletes' needs. Yet this is what athletes say they want when they have the opportunity to speak for themselves.

Psychologists have known for years that our images of our environment are colored by various factors. These include expectations, past experiences, how persons perceive their role in a situation, selective use of feedback from external sources, the influence of others, and even genetic disposition, among others. Possible explanations of apparent misperceptions in sport are that:

1.   Coaches are consumed by many tasks related to skill development and game preparation. As such, they do not actively attend to the area of players' feelings. In other words, coaches might be far more concerned with giving information than they are with receiving it.

2.   Players tend to be too shy to "risk" communicating with their coach openly and honestly. Fear of retribution (e.g., not playing) or intimidation are likely reasons why athletes choose not to approach their leader to disclose feelings.

3.   Coaches are selective about from whom they obtain feedback. Thus, the team captain, certain starters, or coaching assistants become more valuable and credible sources of feedback than other team members. Of course, this limits the reliability of information to which the coach is exposed.

4.   Coaches may not view athletes' feelings as valid. As more than one coach has told me, "What do these athletes know about what it takes to win?" Consequently, team leaders are prepared to risk "turning off" and not meeting the personal needs of their athletes in the anticipation that team success (winning) will justify their behaviors and techniques. In other words, actions will speak for themselves.

5.   Some coaches may not be comfortable with allowing players to offer input. As indicated by several coaches, team leaders would prefer that the players' negative feelings be kept to themselves. That way, meetings do not become "gripe sessions," and team members do not "feed off" of one another's complaints.

6. Coaches typically view themselves as successful, or are imitating the behaviors and techniques of other coaches who are successful. Their philosophy is, "If it worked for so and so, it can work for me."

7. The coach may be, in fact, meeting the needs of selected participants but inaccurately perceiving that all players are receiving the same treatment. For instance, when I've asked coaches to give me examples of explaining to players the reasons for performing certain tasks, invariably they offer two or three individuals with whom they have interacted. And that's it. The rest of the team has not heard his rationale.

8. Coaches may not feel obligated to meet certain needs of players. In fact, many coaches feel that they are using the type of leadership style that athletes want; athletes, especially at higher skill levels, prefer a more authoritative, critical leadership style, a concept supported in the literature (Chelladurai 1984; Sandler 1981).

9. Some coaches simply do not have a personality that is conducive to healthy relationships with athletes. School principals and athletic directors do not observe and evaluate the coach's performance. No personality assessments are made on a coach before he or she is hired. In addition, sport competitors are a captive audience: They participate voluntarily. Consequently, players have the choice of either doing it the coach's way or leaving the team — which, of course, is no choice at all.

SUMMARY

The literature in sport psychology and coaching is primarily concerned with suggested strategies, usually based on research or previous experience in coaching, to optimize sport performance. Researchers tend to gather information about athletes from questionnaires or, in fewer cases, structured interviews, while coaches develop their techniques in response to conversations or materials from other coaches. Rarely do athletes have direct input into the contest strategies or motor skill development that will be executed in practice and competitive situations. Consequently, it is not surprising that coaches and athletes perceive the same situations in sport differently and that the techniques and leadership styles that coaches commonly use are often incompatible with the preferences and needs of their players. This chapter focused on articulating these differences with specific reference to pregame, during-game, and postgame issues. Specific coaching recommendations are offered that encourage coaches to be more sensitive to the value of communicating with athletes about their needs and desires. Every need cannot be met, but coaches can at least become aware of, and sensitive to, them. In this way, athletes would likely become more responsive and loyal to their team leader, and coaches could go about their business with their eyes wide open. This can only happen when athletes have the opportunity to speak for themselves.

REVIEW QUESTIONS

1. Describe two coaching behaviors used prior to, during, and immediately following the sport contest that athletes claim are inappropriate or disturbing. What is the basis for these feelings? Do you agree or disagree with the players, and why?
2. Name five concerns athletes have about coaching behaviors in practice settings. Describe five techniques the coach can use in practice (for any sport) that will meet players' needs and overcome their concerns.
3. Image — how the team leader is perceived by his or her players — is a crucial aspect of effective coaching. Based on the input from athletes as depicted in this chapter, what can a coach do to improve his or her image? What can he or she do to hurt it?
4. In what ways do coaches and athletes differ about how they perceive the coach's actions and attitudes toward the players? What would you tell athletes and coaches to do to narrow this discrepancy?
5. According to player interviews, in what ways are coaches doing their jobs correctly? What do the athletes feel are desirable coaching behaviors?

REFERENCES

Chelladurai, P. 1984. Discrepancy between preferences and perceptions of leadership behavior and satisfaction of athletes in varying sports. *Journal of Sport Psychology* 6: 27–41.

Cratty, B. J. 1984. *Psychological preparation and athletic excellence*. Ithaca, NY: Mouvement.

Mechikoff, R. A., and B. Kozar. 1983. *Sport psychology: The coach's perspective*. Springfield, IL: Thomas.

Sandler, R. L. 1981. Coaching style and the athlete's self-concept. *The Athletic Journal* (May): 46, 66.

14

Conclusions and Future Directions

This book was written for the sport "practitioner" — a coach or athlete — or for persons who plan to make coaching a part of their career. After reading this book, it should be obvious that, for the coach, there is more to sport leadership than telling someone what to do. And for the athlete, playing the game consists of more than putting on a uniform and showing up. What athletes think significantly affects how they perform. Consequently, their thoughts should directly reflect what they want to achieve.

In my research for writing this book, I was surprised by two discoveries. First, relatively few competitive athletes have mastered the art of mental preparation, including the use of positive self-statements, imagery, coping with stress, and others. Second, many sport leaders lack understanding about the factors that affect human behavior in sport. On the first point, athletes are not trusting — at least initially — of psychological techniques such as imagery, progressive relaxation, centering, meditation, cognitive self-control, and others. Participants in competitive sport are often suspicious of anything that they can't feel, physically experience, or observe. This is not a criticism but rather a reflection of an athlete's training and past experiences. Nor are they particularly trusting of the person, usually a sport psychologist, who directs the use of these techniques. The basic philosophy is, "I've been successful up to this point, so why try something new?" Athletes would far prefer to listen to another athlete or coach whom they respect. In his presentation at a conference of the Association for the Advancement of Applied Sport Psychology (AAASP) (October 1986), psychologist Ronald Smith from the University of Washington in Seattle discussed the incredibly strong influence that the great pitcher Nolan Ryan had over the other players in the Houston Astros organization. When he spoke, Smith said, the players were mesmerized by his words. The effect of a great athlete on other participants is far more powerful than that of any scientist, perhaps to the chagrin of many sport psychologists who would give their right arm for such respect.

Second, many coaches, surprisingly, are using the same militaristic tactics and strategies to motivate their athletes as was the case decades ago. Despite the abundant availability of research indicating the advantages of using different approaches to leadership, athletes are still running laps for punishment, being told what to do without explanation, having relatively little input into the development of team strategies or policies, and being motivated through threats and other aversive, unpleasant means. Where is the recognition and use of new approaches in affecting human behavior? With obvious exceptions, advances in the field of sport psychology are going relatively unnoticed, considering the gold mine of information that is available. A library full of information that could help sport participants to become more successful has been ignored more often than not.

What are some of the problems that are preventing sport leaders from "coming in from the cold" and applying (not to mention even reading) the sport psychology literature? Just to put the problem in perspective, I was informed in a letter from the president of the American College Football Association (February 1985) that its policy was not to allow sport psychologists to make presentations at their annual conferences. The coaches obviously felt more comfortable exchanging information with a colleague than integrating information from someone who is not in the coaching field. (I wonder if this is why coaching has been referred to as a "monkey see, monkey do" profession.) Based on numerous conversations with collegiate and high school coaches, I have concluded that these problems are based on at least five factors:

1.   *The lack of credibility and trust of resource personnel outside the profession.* As one coach said, "You folks (sport psychologists) might know your area, but can you coach?" A related problem is that early attempts to use psychological techniques by "experts" proved ineffective at best and, as in the case of a San Diego psychiatrist who was convicted of illegally supplying drugs to professional football players, destructive at worst. Personality tests that purportedly could predict future success in sport were later found to lack statistical validity and reliability. The initial experiences of "sport psychologists" with athletes were usually unsuccessful, invalid, and occasionally even fraudulent. See Ogilvie (1979) for further discussion of this issue.

2. *The need of the coach to take the credit for successful team perfor-mance.* As another coach told me, "We have, and need, a big ego because of the responsibility we feel for succeeding or failing. Coaches have to do it their way, feeling in control the whole time."

3. *The reliance on replicating the tactics of coaches whose teams are chronically successful.* "If so-and-so does it and wins, so should we" is a common response, which doesn't take into account the unique needs of each situation.

4. *The mistrust of using an approach that is unobservable.* "Don't talk to me about mental techniques; I just want solid effort and good performance," I was told.

5. *The absence of applied material to which coaches have easy access and can understand.* "I can't understand the stuff in journals."

Coaches feel comfortable and secure when interacting among themselves. It's a feeling of "We're all in this boat together." However, in recent years as the field of sport psychology has begun to reestablish its credibility with proven techniques based on valid and proven research, and as more professionals in the field have received the proper educational training, the use of applied sport psychology is gaining a foothold among sport leaders. In fact, Alderman (1984, p. 49), among others, believes that "coaches and athletes at all levels of competition seem to be more cognizant of, and more receptive to, psychological consultants than ever before."

Perhaps the best sign of the recent emergence of sport psychology as a recognized contributor to competitive sport is the inclusion of sport psychology services with the United States Olympic Team. (The Eastern and Western Europeans and Canadians have integrated sport psychologists as part of their team training regimens for years.) In August 1982, the United States Olympic Committee (USOC) gathered a group of prominent American sport psychologists to determine the nature of a sport psychology program that would be compatible with the USOC's objectives. The 1984 U.S. Olympic Team for the first time had a consulting sport psychologist assigned for each sport. Another signal indicating that the field is moving in an applied direction is the creation of a new organization, AAASP, whose purpose, according to its constitution, "is to promote the development of psychological theory, research, and intervention strategies in sport psychology." But perhaps the most prestigious endorsement of the sport psychology field is the acceptance of sport psychology as a legitimate field of study and practice by the American Psychological Association.

Where will the field go from here? In his presidential address to the International Society of Sport Psychology at their annual conference in Copenhagen (1985), Professor Robert Singer identified eleven areas that will receive predominant attention in the late 1980s and early 1990s. These include (1) youth sports, (2) the analysis of cognitive processes, (3) longitudinal data on athletes, i.e., the long-term effects of participation, (4) sport-specific psychological tests,

(5) motivation, (6) comprehensive psychological programs for athletes, (7) self-management and coping techniques, (8) a comparison of psychological data of athletes among countries, (9) the development and training of relevant psychological processes, (10) predicting athletic success, and (11) the psychological effects of vigorous physical activity.

Richard B. Alderman (1984), professor and sport psychologist at the University of Alberta (Canada), makes the following predictions about the future of sport psychology in the 1990s:

1. The field will become more applied in the attempt to gain credibility and recognition from the scientific, educational, and sport domains.

2. University faculty who specialize in sport psychology will be required to perform more community service, e.g., direct or advise the governance of youth sport leagues, and publish more and higher quality research.

3. There will be an increase in private consulting and counseling in sport psychology. This tendency will contribute to the orientation of an applied, as opposed to a strictly theoretical, approach to research in the field.

4. Pressure will increase to certify sport psychology consultants and to formulate an acceptable and required code of ethics.

5. Due to the current rise in demand and interest in sport psychologists, especially by coaches of elite athletes (ironically, coaches of less skilled, younger participants are slower to recognize the field's potential), sport psychologists will become more formally involved with professional and elite national sports teams. Eventually, sport psychologists will become accepted as permanent experts working full time with teams.

6. Sport psychologists will become increasingly involved with the parents and families of young athletes and in the advising of community sport agencies in developing sport programs. Through this relationship, child athletes will become acquainted with the techniques that a sport psychologist can offer, a process now reserved for older, skilled competitors.

And what, exactly, can a sport psychologist offer? What functions are they being asked to perform and how prepared are they to meet this demand? Nideffer et al. (1980) have identified six areas of expertise that sport psychologists should master.

1. *Developing performance improvement programs.* The purpose of techniques such as biofeedback, self-hypnosis, progressive relaxation, attention control training, and others is to give the athlete greater control over physiological arousal and concentration.

2. *Using psychological assessment techniques.* Numerous paper-and-pencil inventories, interviews, and behavioral (observational) assessments have been used for the purpose of selecting, screening, and counseling athletes. Attempts have been made to predict the quality of an athlete's performance or the likelihood of becoming successful in sport (see chapter 2 for an evaluation of these techniques).

3. *Improving the communication among participants.* Through the use of personal consultation and behavioral group techniques, sport psychologists are trying to enhance personal interaction among coaches and athletes.

4. *Providing crisis intervention services.* What happens when the stress of sport virtually immobilizes the athlete — or, for that matter, a coach? Team sport psychologists sometimes help the participant to quickly regain control of their emotions so that they can continue to be productive.

5. *Consulting with coaches, trainers, and others who work directly with athletes.* Sometimes team leaders and administrative personnel prefer to work with a sport psychologist rather than to allow direct contact with the athletes. This is less threatening to many coaches who feel that a sport psychologist can disrupt the coach-athlete relationship. At other times, time restraints and the psychologist's professional interests and needs prevent direct contact with athletes. This has its advantages and disadvantages. On the plus side, the sport psychologist may be more helpful to the team when advising coaches on the use of certain techniques. And coaches have already established the necessary credibility and trust with athletes to suggest the use of certain mental strategies. On the minus side, the sport psychologist often needs direct contact with participants to determine individual needs, to suggest alternative approaches in meeting those needs, or to provide a personality style that allows the player to disclose personal information that he or she might otherwise withhold from the coach. In the final analysis, sport psychologists must function in the athlete's world and have "hands-on" experience in working directly with players and coaches if they are to understand the role of sport psychology in competitive athletics.

6. *Functioning as a therapist or clinical psychologist.* A sport psychologist might be asked to provide clinical rather than educational services. Nideffer et al. (1980) warn that only a sport psychologist who has extensive clinical training, essentially a licensed clinical psychologist, should treat severe psychological problems of team personnel. Otherwise, such cases should be referred to a psychiatrist or clinical psychologist who has experience working with athletes.

Let's put sport psychology in perspective. The field certainly is not without its critics. As Mary Ann Roberton, the highly respected researcher in motor development from the University of Wisconsin, remarked in her address to the Tait R. MacKenzie Conference (May 1984) held at the University of Tennessee (Knoxville). "What can sport psychologists *not* do?" Despite the attempt in this book to suggest applied approaches to sport involvement for both leaders and competitors based on established theory and research, the field is still relatively new. Roberton's issue was that sport psychologists should not, indeed cannot, be all things to all people. Much research and trial-and-error experience lies ahead before established, functional techniques are effectively employed. The field must avoid the "Eureka" complex, the need to declare that "the answer" is at hand. It's this rush to make superlative statements and to draw final conclusions based on relatively miniscule evidence that has drawn the ire of scientists and even a few sport practitioners. Based on the advice of some of our most respected and prolific sport scientists, a few recommendations about how the field can grow and mature can be derived:

- *Be supportive of professional colleagues.* Intelligent people can differ as to what constitutes quality research, the validity of using certain techniques in education and sport, and the general direction in which an academic discipline should go. Argument and debate are healthy. Dogmatism is not. Not only should coaches and sport psychologists recognize one another's strengths, limitations, and mutual interests, but so should researchers in the sport sciences. The various interests, challenges, and professional pursuits make the fields of human movement and sport behavior fascinating. Given the vast amount of knowledge that we have *not* as yet acquired, scientists and practitioners can ill afford to diminish the importance of what the other is doing. We have much to learn from each other. And in a free democracy, no one should dictate what form this learning should take.

- *Effective sport psychologists use a multidisciplinary approach.* Attempts to maximize sport performance often go beyond social-psychological factors. Sometimes a performance limitation is a function of improper movement mechanics, poor teaching techniques, inadequate physical conditioning, or a lack of understanding of the needs and limitations of child participants. Sport psychologists need to either work with scientists from the other sport sciences (such as exercise physiology, biomechanics, and motor learning and development) or master the fundamental knowledge base in these areas.

- *Avoid the "quick fix."* The field of sport psychology is still paying a heavy price for the "snake-oil" salespeople of past years. It's one thing to generalize about the effects of certain techniques on meeting a particular objective. But it's quite another to "know the answer" and "sell" the coach on a yet unproven "formula" for success. We need to be cautious and to make promises to no one. An applied sport psychologist should have a menu of alternative treatments and strategies that are warranted in a given situation. No single approach works for every athlete or under all situations. As they used to say on the television police program *Hill Street Blues*, "Be careful out there."

- *Do not take public credit for player or team success.* The Chicago White Sox baseball team employed a sport psychologist during the 1985 and 1986 seasons. When a sportswriter inquired about this person's role with the team, Tony LaRussa, then the team's manager, responded that the team didn't want to publicize the use of any consultants because the players need to feel that they have the skills to succeed. He was on target. Coaches and athletes must take center stage when it comes to their success, and if a sport psychologist had a role in that success, this need not become public knowledge. Any publicity surrounding the "bag of tricks" that sport psychologists bring to the coach or athlete might diminish the discipline's credibility. As the adage says, "actions speak louder than words." The tangible benefits of using psychological strategies is the scientist's best reward.

- *"Research" is not a four-letter word.* Some applied sport psychologists and coaches are turned off by the word *research*. For the practitioner, it represents an area that is unfamiliar, insecure, and disconnected from providing any benefit to the competitive situation. Nothing could be further from the truth *if* (1) more research were conducted that was field-based and applied to sport behavior, as sport scientist Rainer Martens asserted in his address at the first annual conference of AAASP (October 1986) at Jekyll Island, Georgia, and (2) writers of the sport psychology literature translated the findings of credible, sophisticated research for use among practitioners. Providing instruction on how to read esoteric sport research journals is somewhat less practical.

- *"Certification" is a hot topic.* Some professionals contend that as the field continues to grow and become more diverse in its areas of investigation and practice, a measure of quality control is needed. The easy part is to convene a group of sport psychologists and compose a set of guidelines that would dictate the criteria for certification. If a person does not meet the criteria, then he or she is not allowed to practice sport psychology (i.e., the person is not recognized as a sport psychologist). This very complex, inconclusive issue goes well beyond the purpose of this chapter. There are many pros and cons to certification, not the least of which is gaining agreement among educated specialists as to what constitutes a certified sport psychologist. For further discussions on this issue, see Harrison and Feltz (1979) and Dishman (1983).

- *Let's "allow" the practitioner access to sport psychology literature.* When an academic discipline understandably yearns for acceptance from professional colleagues, there is a tendency to demonstrate academic competence through the publication of sophisticated, esoteric research. This often means testing the efficacy of theories and using complex statistical analyses to answer research questions. So far, no problem. Somewhat more problematic is that this struggle for academic identity has resulted in depriving the practitioner, at least to a certain degree, of using the wealth of knowledge that has accumulated in the sport psychology literature. Fortunately, new journals are now being published to help solve this problem. One area of future involvement for sport psychologists is providing more written materials that coaches and athletes find palatable and exciting as a reference for applied sport psychology strategies.

A FINAL WORD

Let's not kid ourselves. The name of the game in sport, quite literally, is W-I-N-N-I-N-G. Perhaps one of the most salient differences between sport psychologists and coaches is the importance that each party places on the contest's outcome and what it takes to get there. Whereas most coaches and athletes are conditioned to perceive physical activity as the primary means of accomplishing goals ("The best way to overcome our problems," one college coach told me, "is to win some games"), the sport psychologist contends that what the performer thinks has a direct link to what he or she can do. No one knows for sure what percentage of success is due to an athlete's ability versus the psychological preparation and effective use of mental skills. But two things remain certain. First, nothing can alter an athlete's genetic disposition in performing sports skills. Abilities, which are stable and permanent characteristics, differ among individuals. In other words, a person's *capacity* to perform sport skills is fixed. Second, the coach's job is to help each athlete to reach his or her capacity.

There are no clear-cut solutions in reaching the objective of performing at optimal capacity. But one factor that separates skilled, effective coaches from mediocre, less effective leaders is understanding the *unobservable* psychological forces that act upon the athlete and markedly influence performance. A second factor is using leadership skills to do something about these forces and to fulfill the athlete's need to feel satisfied as a team participant.

The undeniable fact that unhappy workers are less productive than happy workers is not a recent discovery.

"But isn't it really the athlete's fault if he or she doesn't use the proper techniques to be motivated and mentally prepared to compete?" asked one of my students. Yes and no. Athletes must prepare for competition and ultimately take responsibility for their performance. But to what extent should we expect the participant to have the knowledge base, expertise, and experience in using mental techniques in addition to mastering physical skills and game strategies? Coaches are leaders. With the leadership role comes the responsibility of influencing the behaviors and feelings of subordinates. The techniques to do this successfully are learned through a long-term educational process of observing desirable models and following the guidelines of specialists (through written materials and personal interactions) who have devoted themselves to mastering a different set of skills that are complementary to those of the practitioner (i.e., the coach). The athlete is a recipient of the coach's commands and requests. The extent to which the art and science of sport psychology is a vehicle for sport success is initiated and promoted by the coach.

There's no "right" answer for all athletes or for every situation in sport. And no one has a monopoly on using the "best" techniques. But the recent emergence of new information and cognitive strategies that can possibly improve athletic performance and team success is becoming a very exciting addition to a coach's repertoire of techniques. Here's to giving these techniques every available opportunity to succeed.

REFERENCES

Alderman, R. B. 1984. The future of sport psychology. In *Psychological foundations of sport*, ed. J. M. Silva and R. S. Weinberg, pp. 45–54. Champaign IL: Human Kinetics.

Danish, S. J., and B. D. Hale. 1981. Toward an understanding of the practice of sport psychology. *Journal of Sport Psychology* 3: 90–99.

Dishman, R. K. 1983. Identity crisis in North American sport psychology: Academics in professional issues. *Journal of Sport Psychology* 5: 123–34.

Harrison, R. P., and D. L. Feltz. 1979. The professionalization of sport psychology: Legal considerations. *Journal of Sport Psychology* 1: 182–90.

Heyman, S. R. 1982. A reaction to Danish and Hale: A minority report. *Journal of Sport Psychology* 4: 7–9.

Martens, R. 1979. About smocks and jocks. *Journal of Sport Psychology* 1: 94–99.

Nideffer, R. M., et al. 1980. The future of applied sport psychology. *Journal of Sport Psychology* 2: 170–74.

Nideffer, R. M.; Feltz, D.; and J. Salmela. 1982. A rebuttal to Danish and Hale: A committee report. *Journal of Sport Psychology* 4: 3–6.

Ogilvie, B. C. 1979. The sport psychologist and his professional credibility. In *Coach, athlete, and the sport psychologist*, ed. P. Klavora and J. V. Daniel, pp. 44–55. Champaign, IL: Human Kinetics.

Roberton, M. A. May, 1984. The weaver's loom: A developmental metaphor. Paper presented at the *R. Tait McKenzie Symposium on Sport*, University of Tennessee, Knoxville.

Appendix A

Research and Measurement in Sport Psychology

How would you like to be defended in court by a lawyer who hasn't read his or her professional literature since law school and, therefore, is unaware of the latest legal decisions and laws that could help your case? If you had to have surgery, would you mind being operated on by a surgeon who hadn't read about the latest medical tests and surgical techniques? In sport, how many coaches are using techniques that have been around for decades (no doubt implemented by their own coaches), yet have proven to be ineffective by scientific studies? And how many athletes are not aware of, or refuse to use, mental strategies that have been shown in the literature to improve performance measurably? In many professions, the refusal to continue reading professional literature might result in poor evaluations of performance at best and, at worst, a lawsuit, job termination, or revocation of a license to continue practicing. Individuals who desire to become and remain effective in what they do, be it professional or amateur activities, obtain and maintain one common habit — they read. That's why they have mastered a body of knowledge and have been able to apply it for the good of consumers of their services.

To their credit, coaches in sport are typically avid readers of the literature. Several credible publications such as *Athletic Journal, Scholastic Coach,* Canada's *Coaching Review,* the *Journal of Physical Education, Recreation, and Dance,* and others have served the noble purpose of sharing information among coaches. Most articles have been written by coaches and for coaches in the areas of performance strategies, physical conditioning, and approaches to leadership. On occasion, a sport scientist in biomechanics (movement efficiency), exercise physiology, motor learning, or sport psychology will contribute an article. However, based on my observations of, and discussions with, hundreds of coaches over the years in many different sports, age groups, and sponsorships (schools versus independent leagues, for example), two things are clear about coaches' reading habits. First, despite the enriched knowledge base related to game strategies and rules, coaches have not developed an interest in reading research literature. This is understandable considering the relatively few coaches who have completed an academic course in the sport sciences, particularly sport psychology, which is not typically a required course for undergraduates in physical education. Second, coaches—indeed, most university undergraduates—are not taught how to read, comprehend, and apply research documentation.

Thus, that a voluminous amount of resource material exists in sport psychology journals that is virtually untapped is not surprising. The purpose of the next two sections is to help the student of sport psychology—the athlete or prospective coach—become familiar and comfortable with these untapped resources. Ultimately, the reader should be able to apply the findings of studies to their benefit as successful sport participants. It is also hoped that the basis for using certain approaches to coaching or competing will be scrutinized and either voided or validated by sport scientists. In sport, as in all competitive situations, knowledge is power.

Another important reason to become familiar with the research literature in sport psychology is to know the difference between fact and fiction, myth and reality, and truth versus rumor. Sport psychologists contend that relatively little coaching behavior is based on research. Instead, coaches tend to repeat the actions of other, relatively successful coaches through observations, seminars, discussions, and direct interaction as athletes. When certain actions and beliefs are based on "what everybody is doing" or "that's the way it's always been done," quite often factual information gives way to myth. Here are a few examples of myths in sport that have been dispelled by research.

Myth: Punishment is the best way to discipline, teach, and motivate athletes.

Reality: Athletes frequently become intimidated, disloyal, angry, and demotivated by punishing actions such as running laps (associating exercise with punishment results in a dislike for all forms of exercise), being ridiculed in front of teammates (they'll never forgive a coach for embarrassing them), and increasing the time and intensity of practice (often the players need time off away from the sport arena).

Fiction: Athletes need an arousing pregame talk to prepare them for competition.

Fact: Athletes differ as to their optimal pregame arousal. Some players, particularly in certain positions and in particular sports, want and need to relax before the contest and not get "psyched up."

Rumor: Players who prefer to be alone or not to maintain strong group affiliation are not good "team players." Supposedly, teammates who do not socialize outside of the sport arena or do not like each other on a personal basis cause poor team cohesion and a lack of team success.

Truth: In fact, researchers have found relatively little relationship between team success and team cohesion; a team can win without having teammates like one another or affiliate off the field or court.

Much can be learned from reading sport research. Many often used, typical coaching strategies would go by the wayside if coaches were taught the skills to read research and were exposed to the proper literature. Using a question-and-answer format, let's look more closely at sport research.

Q.   What exactly is research?

A.   In sport, research is a systematic, planned way of solving problems (e.g., Will this mental technique increase self-confidence and sport performance?), testing theories and models (e.g., the validity of Bandura's self-efficacy theory or an individual's conviction that he or she is capable of producing a desired outcome in a given sport or sport situation), and explaining or predicting behavior (e.g., the effect of trait anxiety, a personality predisposition to be anxious, on state anxiety in response to high-anxious situations). Taking the anxiety example further, researchers might determine that participants tend to get uptight under certain circumstances before or during competition. Perhaps through a player's score on a certain paper-and-pencil inventory, a coach can actually predict the player's predisposition (a psychological readiness) to feel anxious under tense conditions. Some players, after all, can cope better under pressure than others.

Q.   How does one go about conducting research?

A.   Researchers need to first find a problem that needs further study, a research question that needs answering.

Q.   Where are such problems found?

A.   Usually in the professional literature. That's why researchers must be avid readers. In case you're wondering, it's also true that in some instances a research idea stems from practical experience. For example, areas such as the "runner's high," the apparent benefits of exercising to music, and the high dropout rate in youth sports received extensive research attention because of everyday experiences. But most of the time, *research actually creates the need for further investigations,* delving deeper into an area or trying to answer an additional question that needs to be examined. Authors of studies almost always suggest exactly what direction these future studies should take. The ideas are located in the journals. That's why it's important for students of sport psychology, including coaches who seek answers to valid questions, to be able to read research articles.

Q.   Are we now ready to conduct a study?

A.   Not quite yet. You need to make testable *hypotheses* that indicate your predictions of the study's results. The hypotheses can be *directional,* e.g., "It was predicted in this study that subjects who were exposed to relaxation procedures would perform better under tense competitive conditions than persons who did not experience this treatment," or *null,* e.g., "No significant difference between the groups was predicted."

Q.   When do you collect performance scores?

A.   Hold on, we're getting there. After making their hypotheses (which are always made prior to a study), researchers must be sure that all relevant terms have been defined so that the results can be generalizable to other studies in which the same problem has been studied. For example, terms such as stress, anxiety (both state and trait), fear, and arousal have been used interchangeably in the literature. This is not such a good idea. Imagine if a researcher concluded that a certain treatment had a particular affect on state anxiety when, in fact, the test used to determine anxiety actually measured arousal? Or what if trait anxiety (a stable, unchanging personality disposition) and state anxiety (a feeling that changes under various conditions) were used interchangeably? And what is the difference between imagery and mental practice? Some scientists recognize no difference, while for others, it's night and day. In fact, mental practice and imagery have been defined and used differently in the literature.

Q.   What happens next?

A.   Before data are collected, two additional steps are necessary: The subjects and instrumentation to measure performance must be selected. *Subjects* are obtained based on the aim of the study. If a researcher is testing high- versus low-skilled basketball players, then obviously subjects must serve the criterion of either having or not having extensive competitive playing experience. But quite often, individuals who have had no experience with the research task are preferred. In this way, no bias exists as to the subject's previous experience, which could mask the effects of the treatment.

With respect to *instrumentation*, it is very important that the materials and equipment in the study meet two standards: (1) they must be calibrated and capable of making accurate measurements (e.g., a bicycle ergometer or treadmill must be tested regularly to ensure accurate and reliable measurement) and (2) they must measure what they are supposed to measure (e.g., a paper-and-pencil test must assess state anxiety rather than trait anxiety or any other mental state).

After subjects and instrumentation are ready to go, the procedures must be planned. Researchers must be sure to standardize the actual data-collection phase so that factors such as noise, lights, instructions, and other procedures faced by all subjects in the study are the same. Often researchers complete what is called a *pilot study* that serves to "iron out the kinks" before data for the actual study are collected.

Q.   What happens after the data are collected?

A.   First of all, researchers must be sure, at least in studies in which behavior or feelings are being measured, that there are plenty of subjects—at least ten per group are commonly recommended, but the more the better. Just a few participants will not be enough for valid (the test or instrument must be measuring what it's supposed to measure) and reliable (consistent) performance measures.

After the data are collected, the appropriate statistics are analyzed to determine whether the treatment under investigation was effective. Were the scores for each group *significantly different*? The types and uses of these statistics differ based on many factors, some of which include (1) the type of data being collected, e.g., accuracy, speed of movement, observations, (2) the best way to answer the research question and each hypothesis (prediction), (3) the number of subjects in each group, (4) whether there are an even versus an odd number of subjects in each group, and others.

After the data have been analyzed, the results are compared to each hypothesis. Hypotheses are either supported or rejected, and the researcher draws conclusions about the effect of the treatment on performance. Why, for instance, were these results different from those in past studies? How does the present data support previous studies? What has been learned from this study that can be applied in future research? Perhaps most important to the coach or athlete, how can the study be applied in coaching or sport performance, if at all? What does the author view as an important direction for future research in this area? All of these questions can be answered in the last section, the discussion, of the research paper.

Q.   Who are researchers?

A.   Typically, persons who conduct research are professors in a university, graduate students who are required to demonstrate research skills as partial fulfillment of a master's or doctorate degree, and sometimes teachers or coaches who want to find the answer to problems they currently face in their jobs. Business and industry also hire scientists to improve a product or create a new one.

Q.   I'm convinced that reading sport psychology research is important, but how difficult is it to understand? I mean, do I have to be a professor to read and interpret what a sport scientist examines? If I were a coach or an athlete, I'd want to be able to use this stuff.

A.   You're touching upon a very important issue that has concerned physical educators, sport psychologists, and coaches. One reason why coaches are not using much of the sport psychology literature in their practice is because they have not been trained to read scientific studies. Further, researchers do not tend to write in a style that is compatible with the nonscientist. Research journals are not magazines. It is the rare person who could understand the research literature unless they have had a university course in research methods. There is little question that a void exists in the professional sport literature for the person who wants to apply scientific sport studies in a competitive environment.

The good news is that new journals that fill this void are here. These include *Sports Coach* (Australia), *The Sport Psychologist*, and the *Journal of Health, Physical Education, Recreation, and Dance*, among others. More research-based publications such as *Research Quarterly for Exercise and Sport*, the *Journal of Sport and Exercise Psychology*, the *Canadian Journal of Sport Science*, and the *Journal of Sport Behavior* can also be applied in sport but with additional understanding of content (ask your librarian for addresses of the publishers of these journals). The purpose of Appendix A is to foster understanding of this important, usually ignored, area of the sport literature.

Any quality research journal is going to include a certain style of writing, use of terms, and a format that is acceptable to the scientific community so that it is viewed as reputable for publication. In fact, to ensure accuracy of its content, such publications are refereed. This means that at least two or three scientists review a paper when it is submitted for publication and judge it as either (1) acceptable for publication (i.e., it's accurate and contributes valid information to the professional literature), (2) acceptable for publication but only after certain changes are made in the manuscript, or (3) rejected for publication in the particular journal to which it was sent for reasons that the editor explains in writing to the author.

READING SPORT PSYCHOLOGY RESEARCH

Congratulations! You've taken the time and effort to obtain (from your library, friendly professor, or through a subscription) a copy of a sport journal. The purpose of this section is to take you through a typical research article in the journal. It's important to know that not all articles are research based. Some include the development of a new psychological inventory or discuss the issues that face sport psychology. Other articles might deal with development of a model that explains or predicts a phenomenon in sport or an intervention technique that can enhance sport performance. Some journals also have reviews of books on related topics, summaries of research from other publications, and other information of interest to the reader.

The Introduction

This section of a journal article (1) makes the topic meaningful to the reader, (2) describes the basis or purpose for which the study was conducted (the point of the study), (3) defines important terms so that the reader is clear about the issues under investigation, (4) briefly reviews previous literature (mostly research-based) that provides the reader with a history of the issue under investigation, and (5) offers predictions (called hypotheses, or hypothesis if only one prediction is made) about the outcome of the study. Let's analyze the content from the introduction of a study that appeared in the *Journal of Sport Psychology* (1982, pp. 354-363), written by Brown, Morrow, and Livingston and entitled "Self-Concept Changes in Women as a Result of Training."

1.   *To attach meaningfulness.* "Although case study and self-report accounts of changes in psychological variables as a result of involvement in physical conditioning programs exist, definitive quantification of these changes is generally lacking."

Translation: Participants of exercise claim to experience changes in one or more psychological factors believed to be the result of the physical activity. However, these changes have rarely been scientifically measured and documented.

2.   *The basis and purpose of the study.* "Self-concept is a personality variable that has begun to receive considerable attention in the literature. These studies illustrate the fact that varied results have been obtained on self-concept changes associated with physical training. . . .The purpose of the present investigation, then, was to determine if self-concept changes in college-age females occur as a result of involvement in a 14-week physical conditioning program."

Translation: The topic of self-concept has recently become relatively popular. But no one knows for sure how or if physical training affects a person's self-concept. However, what is known is that personality characteristics such as self-concept are rarely alterable. If self-concept can, in fact, be changed (i.e., improved) due to an exercise program, this would be a very important finding. So, the reason behind this study was to see if such a change is possible.

3.   *Defining terms.* Although the authors did not define any terms in their introduction, they did define a few factors that they used to measure changes in the subjects' fitness level. For example, "aerobic capacity as measured by the time to complete a 1.5 mile run, and . . . body composition characteristics as determined from skinfold measurements." Also the authors justified the use of the instrument to assess self-concept: "Suinn (1972) reports that the (*Tennessee Self-Concept Scale*) is among the better measures combining group discrimination with self-concept information."

4.   *Brief review of literature.* The authors cite numerous studies and quote researchers to support the validity and need for their study. Why, for example, would they attempt to change a relatively stable personality trait such as self-concept? Because "while Kostrubala (1976) identifies the fact that psychologists are using training programs as therapy for some of their patients, Browman

(1981) suggests that '. . . personality and mood are essentially independent of exercise and fitness alone except in borderline normals. . . '" (p. 355).

Translation: Exercise *can* change some components of personality in the normal population. The authors go on to cite other research articles in which changes in self-concept as a result of physical training were found as well as the use of the Tennessee instrument in past studies.

5.   *Predictions.* Based on the findings of earlier studies, what does the researcher expect to result from the experiment? A hypothesis can be one of two types, *directional* (also called a *research hypothesis*) and *null*. The directional or research hypothesis says that there will be a significant difference or relationship between groups or conditions. The null hypothesis predicts no differences, or a very low (nonsignificant) relationship between groups; any observed difference or relationship is due to coincidence or measurement error rather than the treatment.

Brown and her colleagues hypothesized in their study "that the completion of the conditioning program will be a significant event for participants, and that the significance will be related to the physiological changes that occur during the program."

Translation: Exercise participants will consider finishing the fourteen-week program a major accomplishment, and they will both feel better and demonstrate marked improvements on various fitness measures. What about predicted changes in self-concept? The authors come back to say, essentially, that self-concept will improve, but only in the area related to these physiological changes. In other words, because there are different dimensions of self-concept, only the selected dimension most related to the treatment, in this case changes in physiological characteristics, would be favorably affected by the program. Thus, they hypothesize "that significant differences will occur in . . . physical self as a result of completion of the (exercise) program."

The hypotheses of a study are very important because they help to define the research problem. How would researchers know if their treatment was effective if they could not compare their results with a guess as to the likely or predicted outcome? And since hypotheses are often based on the findings of past research, it is important to compare the present results with those of other studies in the long-term attempt to answer or at least better understand the research problem.

The Method

Now that the required background information has been presented, it's time to inform the reader how the present experiment was conducted. The method section should be detailed to the extent that the reader could reproduce the same experiment. The detail also allows readers to determine (1) if the manner in which the study was carried out was valid, which, in turn, may help explain the partial causes of the experiment's results, and (2) to whom the results can be generalized (e.g., only males or females, only with certain types of tasks, restricted to particular situations, and so on). The method section usually, but not always, consists of three sections: a description of the subjects, the equipment or materials used in the study, and the procedures.

Subjects.   Who participated in the study? How many participants were there? How were they selected? Were they athletes? Intramural players or intercollegiate competitors? If a study is to be reproduced at some future time, or if a reader wants to generalize the findings to other populations, the writer must describe in detail the subjects' characteristics and why they were selected for this study.

Equipment and materials.   The objective of this section is to tell the reader about the devices used to record performance. If thoughts, feelings, or emotions were obtained, which inventories were used? On what equipment did the subjects perform? Was the equipment obtained from a commercial establishment? If so, usually only the firm's name and model number are written. Otherwise, the author describes the equipment's dimensions and materials so that a reader could reconstruct the equipment.

Procedures.   As indicated earlier, this section includes a step-by-step description of the subjects' assignment to different groups or treatments and how the data were obtained. In this section, all aspects of the procedures are written out in case the reader would like to attempt a similar experiment.

After the method section, some studies include a section on data analysis or research design or both. Usually this is done to (1) clarify the procedures, (2) transform (preanalyze) data into some other form for further statistical analysis that will eventually answer the research question, or (3) explain the purpose of using various sophisticated statistical procedures.

The Results

After the data were collected (in the procedures section), how were they analyzed? What was found? Did the treatment work? For the person who lacks an enriched background in research, the sections on data analysis and results will be difficult to follow. Quite candidly, the nonresearcher or untrained reader should feel comfortable in ignoring the results section without losing the meaning and application of the study. However, scientists find this section important to interpreting and understanding the treatment's outcome. In fact, occasionally an informed reader will disagree with the type of analysis that was used and replicate the study using a different analysis.

One key issue that needs clarification before leaving the results section is understanding two very important words when reading a research article. The words are "significant difference." If a certain treatment or condition affected the subjects' scores within each group or treatment *consistently*, then group differences should be sufficiently apart to be "significant." In behavioral research, it is believed that *significant findings* mean being able to predict the effect of some treatment or condition at least 95 percent of the time. So, the probability that differences between groups will *not* be due to the treatment or condition and, instead, will be due to chance, cannot occur more often than five times out of one hundred; the effects differences between groups are then said to be reliable. This conclusion is represented in the literature by the symbols "$p < .05$" (representing 95 percent accuracy). The symbol "$p < .05$" means that the probability of an outcome occurring by chance and not due to the treatment will occur *more often* than five times out of 100 (no significant difference).

How does the researcher know whether the group averages are statistically different? First, the proper analysis is computed and reported—such as a t (a comparison between two means) or F value (comparing more than two group means). This value is then compared to a number on a chart called the *critical value*. If the final analysis score—a t, F, or r (correlation) value, for example—is equal to or greater than the critical value, the researcher concludes that group averages were "adequately" apart; the groups were significantly different (t or F) or related (r). (By the way, there is no such thing as "almost" or "a little" significant. Either a statistical test has reached the level of significance, or it has not).

Most of the research articles—in sport psychology and elsewhere—are written for other researchers rather than for the untrained reader (athletes and coaches, for instance). Still, a coach or any untrained reader of research can understand and apply the findings of investigations. One way to be familiar with the scientific literature is to become acquainted with the use of statistics. Here is a brief description of some of the more common statistical terms used in sport psychology research.

Correlations: Relationships Between Factors

1. *Pearson product moment correlation*. This statistic, which uses the symbol r, is used to determine the relationship between two scores on each subject. Relating a score on a paper-and-pencil inventory to a performance score on a sport task is common in sport psychology. For example, I once wanted to examine the extent to which mental arousal, as measured by a questionnaire, was related to physiological arousal, or heart rate (HR). Specifically, are the subjects' feelings of excitation related to more common physiological techniques used to measure arousal? I found that "The correlations were .76 and .88 for the first . . . and second . . . recordings, respectively. The subjects' feelings of arousal and HR were highly related. The psychological and physiological bases for arousal were thus assumed to be similar in this study."

2. *Regression*. Regression is used to predict future performance or some other psychological response. Predictions are based on relationships between factors under investigation. High correlations, .80 for instance, are more accurate

predictors of another factor than relatively low correlations, for example, .30 or below.

3.   *Multiple regression.* This statistic is used to increase the accuracy of prediction. To use it, the researcher must have one set of performance scores (collectively called the *dependent variable*) and two or more sets of *predictor* (or *independent*) *variables.* Actually, coaches conduct an informal form of this evaluation in their minds when the team holds tryouts. Coaches who want to predict basketball playing ability would get a more accurate prediction using various tests of basketball skill than just one test. It would be helpful to collect data on performance and to calculate the probability of future sport success rather than relying on the typical "gut feeling."

For example, Scanlan and Lewthwaite (*Journal of Sport Psychology,* 1984, pp. 208–226) examined factors that best predicted sport enjoyment experienced by male wrestlers, ages nine to fourteen years. They found "the intrapersonal variables, age and perceived wrestling ability, and the significant adult factors, Adult Satisfaction with Season's Performance and Negative Maternal Interactions, emerged as significant predictors of enjoyment " (p. 223). The analysis indicated that younger children, and those who perceived themselves as higher skilled, felt relatively more enjoyment than the others. In addition, greater enjoyment was experienced by boys who thought that their parents and coaches were pleased with their wrestling performance and who felt less pressure from, and had fewer negative interactions with, their mothers.

Experimental Research: Differences Among Groups

1.   *t-tests.* The purpose of this statistic is to determine whether the differences between two group averages (means) are significant. As indicated earlier, the researcher compares the obtained *t* value with the critical value located in a table. If the calculated value is at or above the number in the table, it can be concluded that either the treatment (condition) in the study was effective or that groups differed from each other on some characteristic, before or after the treatment.

There are two types of *t*-tests that are most commonly used in sport psychology, independent and dependent. The *independent test* is a comparison between two separate sets of subjects, whereas the *dependent test* examines differences between the same set of subjects in two different conditions. If a scientist obtains significant differences in any *t*-test, how is it known which group is superior? Simply look at the two group means.

2.   *Analysis of variance.* Frequently depicted by the acronym ANOVA, this is probably the most common statistic found in behavioral research. Whereas the *t*-test was a comparison of the means of two groups, ANOVA is computed to determine differences among three or more group means. Its numerical value is the symbol *F*. As with *t*, the scientist would compare the *F* value with the critical value located in an *F* table. If the computed *F* is equal to or greater than

the critical value, then differences between at least two of the group means are statistically significant. Significant between which of the groups? It isn't known until a *post hoc comparison* is made. The post hoc test (there are several from which a researcher can choose) indicates which of the group means are statistically different from each other.

3.   *Factorial ANOVA*. It's very common to read, "a 2 x 2 x 3 ANOVA was calculated to determine . . . ." Translation: More than one factor (independent variable) is being analyzed simultaneously. An example is in order.

Landers, Min Qi, and Courtet (*Researcy Quarterly for Exercise and Sport,* 1985, pp. 122–130) compared high and low skilled rifle shooters on their ability to perform under different levels of stress. To determine if stress level caused differences in shooting performance as a function of the shooter's ability, the authors computed a 2 (high versus low experience) x 3 (high, medium, and low stress levels) ANOVA with repeated measures on the stress condition. The repeated measures design means that the same subjects at both skill levels experienced *each* of the three stress conditions. Among other results, the authors found no significant differences between the groups nor among the conditions. Although, as expected, higher skilled shooters scored significantly better than their lower skilled counterparts, skill level did not separate the subjects from their ability to perform under stress.

Thus, stress, at least of an auditory nature as was used in this study, doesn't seem to upset even lower skilled shooters. The coach may not have to be very concerned with a quiet environment in which to shoot regardless of the performer's skill level. It's also possible that shooters do not need to use stress-reducing strategies to the same degree as other athletes, perhaps because the nature of this sport (e.g., direct confrontation is absent and the competitor controls the pace of performance) does not solicit the same stressful responses as other types of sport.

4.   *Multivariate ANOVA (MANOVA)*. Multivariate research includes the simultaneous analysis of two or more independent variables (e.g., high versus low skilled performers for two different age groups) and two or more dependent variables (e.g., performance speed, accuracy, and decision time). For example, how does a person determine whether speed or accuracy is more important when performing a motor skill? Do the instructions they receive before attempting the task correspond to the strategy they adopt? That's what researchers Gross and Gill wanted to know. They predicted that when subjects are given instructions that emphasize speed, they are faster but less accurate than when instructions emphasize accuracy. And how would speed and accuracy be affected with both types of instructions? The MANOVA was used so that speed and accuracy, two different sets of scores (two dependent variables) could be simultaneously compared. They found that receiving instruction influenced the subjects' performance priorities. When told to emphasize speed or to emphasize accuracy, the subjects did so while deemphasizing accuracy and speed, respectively.

5.   *Discriminant analysis.* This approach is used to predict one independent variable based on a combination of dependent variables. The researcher is
interested in knowing which factors are most important in predicting the desirable outcome.

For example, in their book *Introduction to Reserach in Health, Physical
Education, Recreation and Dance,* Thomas and Nelson (1985) offer an example
in which eighty-four varsity football players were classified into three groups:
offensive and defensive backs, offensive and defensive linemen, and linebackers
and receivers (twenty-four players per group). The athletes were tested on the
forty-yard dash, twelve-minute run, shuttle run, vertical jump, standing long
jump, bench press, and squat. The objective was to determine the relationship
among these seven test scores. Discriminant analysis was computed to find how
many of the seven dependent variables were important to separate the three
groups of players and predict the players' skill in each group. It was found that
three tests, the bench press, forty-yard dash, and vertical jump, separated the
players by position. The remaining four tests did not significantly contribute.

6.   *Significant interactions.* An interaction is possible only when two or
more independent variables (i.e., two or more main effects) are being compared
simultaneously. Specifically, it means that one of the factors is different from
the rest, i.e., they are statistically significant only in combination with a second
(two-way interaction) or third (three-way interaction) factor. This is almost
always a desirable outcome in behavioral research. It is desirable because most
often researchers predict that a certain treatment will affect performance of
attitude, usually in a positive manner, under at least two conditions, not just one.
The key is meaningfulness of the results.

For instance, it's one thing to say that less skilled competitors suffer a higher
rate of dropping out of sport than higher skilled performers. However, the results
are far more meaningful if a skill level (high and low) x feedback (positive,
negative, and none) interaction was significant. It could be that it's not the level
of skill that causes athletes to drop out, but rather their ability to persevere under
conditions of negative feedback that is the primary reason. Thus, it can be implied
that less-skilled, particularly younger, athletes are less able to tolerate negative
feedback than their higher skilled peers.

A final word about statistics and research results.   Reading and understanding research is a skill. Readers should not approach a scientific journal
with the feeling that information for direct application in sport will drop into
their laps. Further, it may not be possible nor of interest to take an academic
course that explains research. Nevertheless, a person can obtain plenty of useful
material from certain sections of a research article. Primarily the introduction
and discussion sections will offer explanations of the topic and the implications
of the study without requiring knowledge of statistics.

The Discussion

This is perhaps the most important section for the reader who wants an interpretation of a study's findings. The writer tries to answer the following questions: Have the findings agreed with my hypothesis? Why or why not? To what extent do my results support or contradict the results of other studies? What have I contributed to the knowledge base in this area? To what degree have I answered my research question? What conclusions and implications can I draw from my study? What are some of the needs for future research in this area?

The writer can take the liberty of making a few guesses as to what it all means, but he or she had better justify this guesswork with previously published research. Some research articles combine the results and discussion sections. This is usually because of relatively few results to report (making a separate section unnecessary) or simply because the study does not warrant elaborate discussion; it's all relatively straightforward to understand and interpret. In fact, the "readability" of the discussion section contributes greatly to the reader's understanding of the study and the application of its results. The ability to acknowledge recent research findings and new techniques is precisely the reason why coaches should strongly consider becoming better acquainted with the research literature.

Appendix B

Imagery and Progressive Relaxation Sessions

EXAMPLES OF IMAGERY PROGRAMS
Objective: To Learn a New Skill or Strategy

Use your trigger (color or scene) to relax. Now think of yourself slowly learning the new skill. Feel confidence in your ability to learn and perform it with success. You're excited about performing it. It will help you to become a better athlete. Hear the coach give you instructions. At the same time, see yourself perform the skill slowly during practice. First, feel your body go through the motions without any other athletes involved. Just you and the equipment. First in slow motion over several attempts, then, when you get the feel of it, go at full speed. Picture perfect performance and the desired outcome every time. Now include your opponent. Is he or she guarding you in basketball or soccer? Is he or she the pitcher in baseball? Include your opponent in the image and continue feeling confident in your ability. Continue to demonstrate perfect performance and success. Do this for the next few minutes, and repeat two or three times a day.

Objective: Gaining Self-Confidence

Think of that color (scene) to relax. Now, for about half a minute, think about the reasons why you wanted to play this sport: the fun, the chance to compete, and all the other reasons why sport is important to you (short pause). Now think back to a single event in one contest in which you were very successful — something that really stands out in your mind that was a very successful, very rewarding experience. Think of the enjoyment you felt from that event, the feeling of success, the recognition from teammates, the coach, spectators, and friends. Try to remember everything about that event (hitting a home run, scoring a goal, winning a race, etc.). Relive the emotions you felt when the event was over. Think of how much fun it was. For the next few minutes, think of two or three very successful events that occurred during the contest and how confident you felt when it was over.

Objective: Overcoming a Slump

After getting completely relaxed, you should think of your performance problem. Actually go back and see yourself make the same mistakes you've been making for about half a minute. Let's get it out into the open. OK, now say to yourself, the time to turn it around is right now, and here's how you're going to do it. First, recall performing this skill successfully in your past. Picture a perfectly executed skill — the one that's been causing you some problems recently. See yourself go through the motions with perfect form. Recall what it felt like to perform it perfectly. Now, in slow motion, mentally review the skill, keeping in mind all of its parts you practiced when you first learned it. At this point, look through your mind's eye and perform the skill in slow motion. Observe the ball and opponents just as you've seen them during actual performance — just as if there's a camera on your head getting the picture of what it looks like. Now, in slow motion, track the tossed baseball, thrown football, kicked soccer ball, or observe the golf ball sitting on the tee, the target you're aiming at, or your wrestling opponent as he makes his move. See perfect performance. Excellent ball contact, accurate reactions, a perfect response, and a successful result. After a few minutes of slow motion imagery, speed up the action — the same play, the exact skill, a repeat of the slowed version — so that you are now performing perfectly at regular speed. For the next few minutes, review in your mind — perfect performance at regular speed with full confidence of success each time.

PROGRESSIVE RELAXATION

The First Relaxation Session*

1. Select a quiet, dim room and ensure that no distractions or interruptions will occur.
2. Check to see that the athletes are warmly clad and that the clothes that they wear are dry (not damp or sweat laden).
3. Spread the athletes around the room so there is at least one meter between each of them.
4. Explain the principle behind relaxing:
    "Relaxation is important. What we are going to learn will help you to rest and sleep when it is necessary. To get you to relax we are going to do a set of exercises. There is a scientific reason for this because when you contract a muscle and then relax it, it returns to a state that is more relaxed than before the contraction took place. So, to get you to relax you need to do a series of exercises which contract and then relax all the muscles in your body. This first session will take about 30 minutes."
    It should be noted that the verbal instructions given here are for example only. For the coach to give this training session it is best that he or she expresses the content in his or her own way.
5. "Lie on your back with your arms at your side. Check these features:

    (1) the middle of your head is touching the mat so that you are looking straight up,
    (2) your shoulders are exerting equal pressure on the mat,
    (3) your buttocks are exerting equal pressure on the mat,
    (4) your calves are pressing equally on the mat, and
    (5) your heels are pressing equally on the mat.

    You should be lying straight on the mat. Your spine should be straight, your thighs and calves close together touching lightly and your arms extended by your side with your palms facing slightly up. Check for the last time that you are straight, relaxed, and that the pressure of your body parts on the mat is equal on both sides of your body. You most probably will find the exercises easier if you (lightly) close your eyes."
    The coach should then walk among the athletes to see that their position is correct. It is preferable that *no* head pillows be used and that no shoes be worn.

*Reprinted with permission from the National Coaching Certification Program, Level Two, Coaching Association of Canada, Ottawa, Ontario (1979).

6.   "We are now going to do a series of exercises. Each exercise will contain a very hard contraction — hold — and then release sequence. The hold is for a period of four to five seconds. Then relax to the position that you are in now. When you do the exercises, contract only the muscles that are involved in them."

7.   It is good practice to do a preliminary exercise involving the arms. "Slowly move your arms to a position where your hands are together, fingers straight, and palms touching as if you were praying. When I say contract I want you to push your hands together as hard as you can and hold that force for five seconds. Then slowly let your arms sink back to your side as you were before.
Ready! Contract! Only tighten your hands, arms and shoulders — nothing else — three-four-five-relax slowly to your side. Feel your arms relax; they may tingle a little, they may feel heavy, they may feel warm."

8.   It may be necessary to give some pointers to the athletes at this stage. "During that exercise some of you tightened your legs, others your faces. Remember, contract only the part of your body that is being exercised. The exercise we have just done is always the first that you do. Let's do it again for practice. Slowly move your arms to the prayer position. Ready! Contract-two-three-four-five-relax and slide them to your side. Feel your arms heavy, feel them pressing on the mat, relax."

9.   After the preliminary exercise involving the arms (palm press), the exercise routine progresses from the toes to the top of the head. After the following two toe curl exercises there is an introduction to concentrating on breath control. By the time the exercises are completed the emphasis should be on breath control and total heaviness.

10.   "The first exercise is a toe-curl backwards. Moving only your toes and not your ankles curl your toes back to the tops of your feet. Ready, contract-two-three-four-five-relax. Let your toes go to the position that seems the most natural for them."

11.   "The next exercise is the opposite of what you have just done, a toe-curl under. Remember do not move your ankles. Curl your toes under your feet. Ready, contract-two-three-four-five-relax. Let them return to where they feel most natural."

12.   This is the stage where there is an introduction to breathing control. "From now on when you contract do not breathe. When you relax let all the air in your lungs out so that any breathing you do after an exercise is very regular and the very minimum that is necessary. I should be able to hear you all breathe out when I say relax. After each exercise do six breaths where you concentrate on making them even and very slight; six identical, hardly noticeable, breaths.

The next exercise is an ankle bend. Pull your feet back to your shins as much as you can. Ready! Contract-two-three-four-five-relax and breathe out. Breathe it all out, settle into a steady even breathing pattern. Do six identical breaths."

13. "The next exercise is the opposite of the previous one. This is an ankle stretch where you point your feet as much as you can. Ready! Contract-two-three-four-five-breathe out, even breathing.

Feel that your feet are heavy, they may even tingle slightly when compared to the rest of your body. See that there is no tension in your toes or ankles and that your heels are pressing on the mat with exactly the same pressure. Keep your breathing even."

14. "The next exercise is to press your knees together. If your knees are not touching move them slowly together. Press your knees together as hard as you can. Ready! Contract-two-three-four-five-breathe out, steady even breaths. Count your breaths and make them as small as possible."

15. "The next exercise requires you to contract your thighs. Make your thigh muscles as small and as bunched as possible. Ready! Contract-two-three-four-five-breathe out; steady even breathing.

Feel your legs heavy. The pressure on the mat should be equal behind your heels, your ankles and your thighs. Breathe evenly."

16. "The next exercise requires that you make your buttock muscles as small as possible. Make them rock hard and little. Ready! Contract-two-three-four-five-breathe out. Breathe evenly.

That completes your leg exercises. We have reached what is called a *check point*. At this stage go back and check each segment of your legs for the same feeling of heaviness, the same loss of sensation, the same pressure on the mat. If there still is some tension in a muscle group, repeat the exercise for that group.

Check that your toes are loose.

Check that your ankles have no tension — they are hanging in a natural position.

See that your calves are totally loose.

Your thighs should feel heavy and droopy.

Your buttocks should be very soft.

Check that you have the same feeling of heaviness in your feet, your lower legs, the tops of your thighs.

Feel where your legs touch the mat. Make sure they feel super heavy where they touch. There should be the same amount of heaviness in each leg. You should feel that the mat is pressing against your legs.

Concentrate on the heavy, dead feeling. If you wanted to move your legs you could not because they are so heavy.

Do twelve even easy breaths while your legs are totally motionless."

17.   "The next exercises concentrate on your torso and shoulders. As you do these keep your legs totally relaxed. Also after each exercise do eight controlled minimal breaths.
Press your stomach muscles into your abdomen as hard as you can. Do it so that the tips of your spine show through to the front. Ready! Contract-two-three-four-five-breathe out, let out all the tension. Concentrate on your breathing."
(Leave sufficient time to get in more than eight, very even, controlled breaths.)

18.   "The next exercise requires you to contract all the muscles in your back towards your spine. Pull your shoulder blades together and push the points of your shoulders into the mat. Remember only to contract your back muscles, do not rise up off the mat. Ready! Contract-two-three-four-five-breathe out. Let the tension in your back go. Breathe evenly."

19.   "Now we do the opposite exercise. Compress your chest muscles together and round your shoulder points together. Ready! Contract-two-three-four-five-breathe out. Let your shoulders slide back to the most relaxed position.
Breathe shallowly and steadily."

20.   "The next exercise requires that you raise your shoulders up towards your ears; a mighty big shoulder shrug. Keep everything else still, only move your shoulders. Ready! Contract-two-three-four-five-breathe out. Let it go. Feel your body getting very heavy and losing its sensations. Do eight very shallow, hardly noticeable breaths."

21.   "There is one more exercise to do for your body. That requires you to pull your shoulders towards your feet. This is done by pointing as hard as you can with your fingers and reaching down your thighs as far as possible. Ready! Contract-two-three-four-five-breathe out, relax. Concentrate on using as little air as possible when you breathe."

22.   "That completes your body exercises. This is the second check point. Here you check your body and leg segments for the same feeling of heaviness, the same loss of sensation.
Check your shoulder looseness and heaviness.
The middle of your back.
Your chest and stomach should be very relaxed.
Your buttocks very loose.
Your calves, ankles and thighs very loose.
See that the mat is pressing evenly on each side of your body
   — your shoulders
   — your buttocks
   — your thighs
   — your calves

—your heels
Concentrate on feeling heavy.
Count twelve very, very small even breaths."

23. "The last section of your body to relax is your head. There are many muscles in your neck and head so this is very important.
The first exercise requires you not to move anything except to pull your jaw down into your neck. Ready! Contract-two-three-four-five-breathe out. Relax. Count those eight breaths."

24. "Next press your head directly into the mat. Do not arch your neck. Press directly down. Ready! Contract-two-three-four-five-breathe out. Since these exercises use small muscles they require small amounts of energy. Consequently, your breathing should not change much and it should be hardly noticeable."

25. "The next exercise requires that you jut your jaw forward as much as you can. Ready! Stick it out-two-three-four-five-breathe out. Relax your jaw. Breathe."

26. "Next clench your teeth. Bite them together as hard as you can. Ready! Contract-two-three-four-five-breathe. Eight even breaths."

27. "Keeping your teeth lightly together spread your lips apart as much as possible. Ready! Contract-two-three-four-five-relax. Breathe."

28. "Press your tongue against the roof of your mouth as hard as you can. Make your tongue as big as possible. Ready! Contract-two-three-four-five-breathe out. Eight even breaths. Feel heavy *like lead*, all over your body."

29. "Your eyes need to be compressed as much as possible. Pull your cheeks up and your eyebrows down as hard as possible to compress your eyes back into your head. Ready! Contract-two-three-four-five-relax. Let your face go smooth. Smile slightly."

30. "The last exercise requires you to make your forehead as wrinkled as possible while keeping your eyes closed. Ready. Contract-two-three-four-five-relax. Let that tension go right out of your head.
Feel your face as being smooth, drowsy, very, very relaxed. Your jaw should just hang there. Do twelve very small, slow, rhythmical breaths."

31. "Since that is the last exercise check your whole body once again for heaviness.
   —your legs: heels, calves, thighs, buttocks.
   —your body: stomach, chest, lower back, shoulders.
   —your head: neck, jaw, tongue, eyes, forehead.
See that all pressure points on the mat are even and very, very heavy. Do twelve very slow breaths."

32.   At this stage the coach can terminate the first training session. However, it is worthwhile to allow the athletes to remain in this relaxed state for five minutes or so. Some of them may be asleep.

33.   To arouse the athletes be very gentle in your commands.

"After you have relaxed for a while it is important that you do not suddenly jump up. Gradually bring yourself back to normal by doing the following things:

—wiggle your toes
—wiggle your fingers
—move your feet
—move your hands
—open your eyes very slowly
—smile
—move your elbows
—move your knees
—roll over onto your stomach and stretch lazily
—slowly rise to a sitting position
—move to a kneeling position
—stand
—have another good stretch

Subsequent Relaxation Sessions

1.   Subsequent relaxation sessions will be shorter in duration since explanations will rarely be required.

2.   This procedure will usually take at least 15 minutes even when set to a bare minimum of commands.

3.   It is not necessary to follow all the steps in the relaxation sequence all the time. If you find that you are pressed for time, conduct a shortened version by skipping some of the steps.

4.   The athletes should learn the whole process so they can control themselves and relax when needed. It should be emphasized that this procedure is just one of many procedures which exist. The contraction-relaxation action has several advantages for athletes who have been exercising. It affords them the opportunity of gaining control over the relaxation process more quickly.

Learning to relax. The fastest way to learn the relaxation technique described above is to do a number of sessions very close together. A schedule of practices that has proven successful is outlined below. Adapt it as needed to meet your particular situation.

Day 1.   First session under coach control.
          Second session by self as going to sleep.
Day 2.   Third session under coach control.
          Fourth session by self as going to sleep.
Day 3.   Fifth session by self but in presence of coach and other athletes.
          Sixth session by self as going to sleep.
Day 4.   Seventh session under coach control.
          Eighth session by self as going to sleep.
Day 5.   Ninth session by self during day.
          Tenth session by self as going to sleep.
Day 6.   As for day 5.
Day 7.   As for day 4.
Day 8.   As for day 5.
Day 9.   As for day 5.
Day 10.   As for day 4.

The frequent sessions led by the coach are more for motivational purposes than for teaching. They are used to stress the importance of the process and to impress it upon the athletes. The coach should periodically inquire as to how athletes are relaxing and encourage them to practice in various situations (at home, before exams, at practice, at competitions). He or she should also hold "booster" sessions where a coach-directed session is held at varying times.

Index